... uzakta
...meler
...lında b...
... diyebi...
... sen
... e daha
... zaman
... gördüğüm
... yana doğ...
... sonunda
...M geceler
...ki yalından
GÖRDÜĞÜM
BİRDEN BU
BİR KERE D...

Memories of
Distant Mountains

ORHAN PAMUK

Memories of Distant Mountains

ILLUSTRATED NOTEBOOKS
2009–2022

Translated from the Turkish
by Ekin Oklap

faber

To Aslı

First published in the UK in 2024
by Faber & Faber Limited
The Bindery, 51 Hatton Garden
London EC1N 8HN

First published in the United States by Alfred A. Knopf,
a division of Penguin Random House LLC, New York.

Originally published in Turkey as Uzak Dağlar ve Hatıralar
by Yapı Kredi Yayınları, Istanbul, in 2022.

Printed in Slovenia.

All rights reserved
© Orhan Pamuk, 2022
English translation copyright © 2024 by Ekin Oklap

The right of Orhan Pamuk to be identified as author
of this work has been asserted in accordance with Section 77 of the
Copyright, Designs and Patents Act 1988

A CIP record for this book
is available from the British Library

ISBN 978–0–571–38458–7

Printed and bound in the EU on FSC® certified paper in line with our continuing
commitment to ethical business practices, sustainability and the environment.
For further information see faber.co.uk/environmental-policy

Memories of Distant Mountains

Every word

                                  one by one
                            words
        drip
                drop
                                  words   drop

word

each

every

it's raining

on the ocean   one

drop   words

The same dream again woke me up in a fright... Aslı was there to console me in the middle of the night. My darling reminded me about it in the morning, so I described it to her as we lay in bed: Steep mountains, a slope, the nest of a giant bird, a longing for a glimpse of MEANING as it soars toward the heavens, and my own grave, the earth still warm! Aslı listened carefully.
There were also words raining from the sky this time, I told her solemnly.

these are the distant mountains

Aslı was so beautiful and tender

Through the window, Sedef Island grew ever-larger

THE SUN
WAS RISING
FROM WITHIN

Why are you always taking pictures of the ships that sail past?
Why are you always painting these landscapes?
WHAT WE MUST DO NOW IS READ and SEE

A BLACK SUN
the dark sun
of sorrow and melancholy

Words and Images

THE SEA AND
I WAS
AFRAID

if the answers to these questions are always the same . . .

THE LANDSCAPE AS IF IT WERE a DREAM

the place
we return
far away
words
there isn't really one
an even farther one
not in the past
this once more
and maybe never

where I first saw the ant
go along this way
for once . . . finally
THEN AT NIGHT I'M COLD
Perhaps one day perhaps from tomorrow
MOST OF ALL WHEN I FIRST SAW YOU
MY WORDS MAKE YOU THIS TIME
AND ALSO DONE ONCE BEFORE ME
MYSELF FOR SO LONG NIGHT DON'T FALL

olives   olives
         seagulls
i was annoyed about   the airplane looks pink in the light
how dejected I felt.   from the setting sun

the gas bottle ran out just as I was making tomato and eggs but I still cracked an egg
into the tomatoes
We've been picking tomatoes from the garden—like thieves
seagulls—noisy motorboats—how good to swim

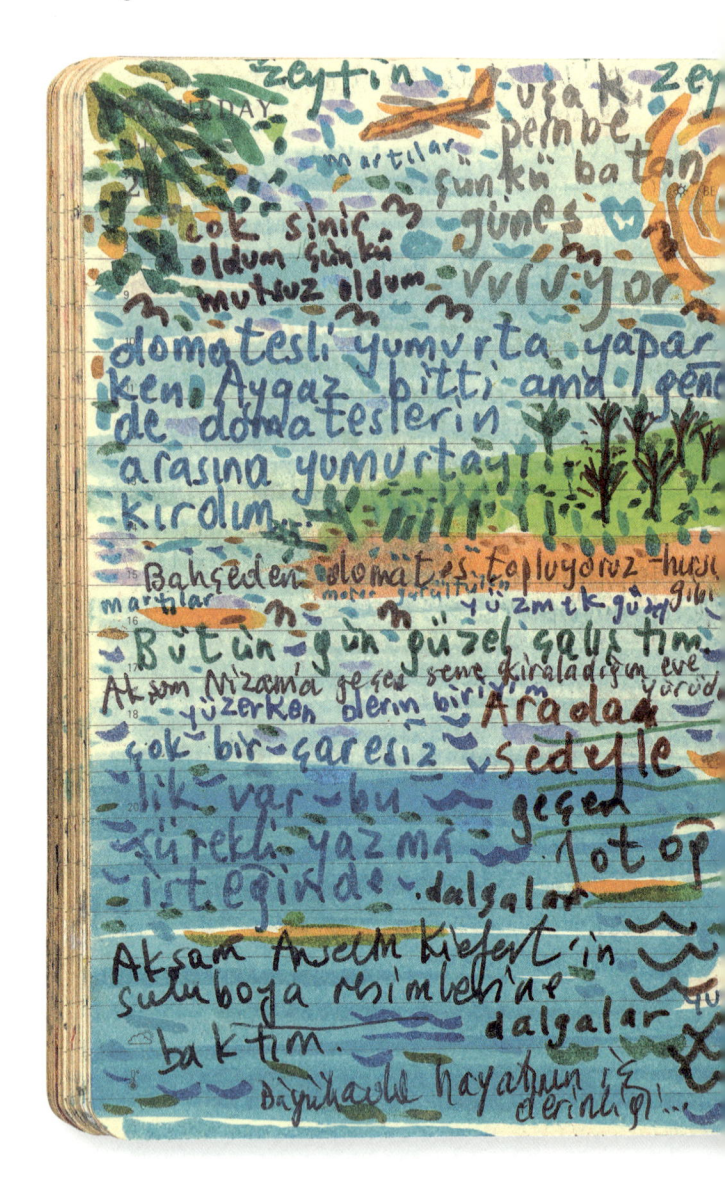

I worked well today.
In the evening I walked to Nizam where I rented that house last year
    I'm a deeper person when I'm swimming
There is a great deal of desperation in this constant urge to write—waves
In the evening I looked at some of Anselm Kiefer's watercolor paintings.
Waves   the dolphins are here
    The inner richness of life on Büyükada

olives

I was at my desk from eight in the morning until eight in the evening, writing and daydreaming. But really I didn't get much work done between 2 and 6, and after that I still couldn't do much because I was annoyed about how little I had managed to do.

    i'm tired of being alone.
    if I could just be alone with my novel, I'd be happy.
    what I'm really doing is punishing myself.
    the director of the Design Museum in London is coming to visit

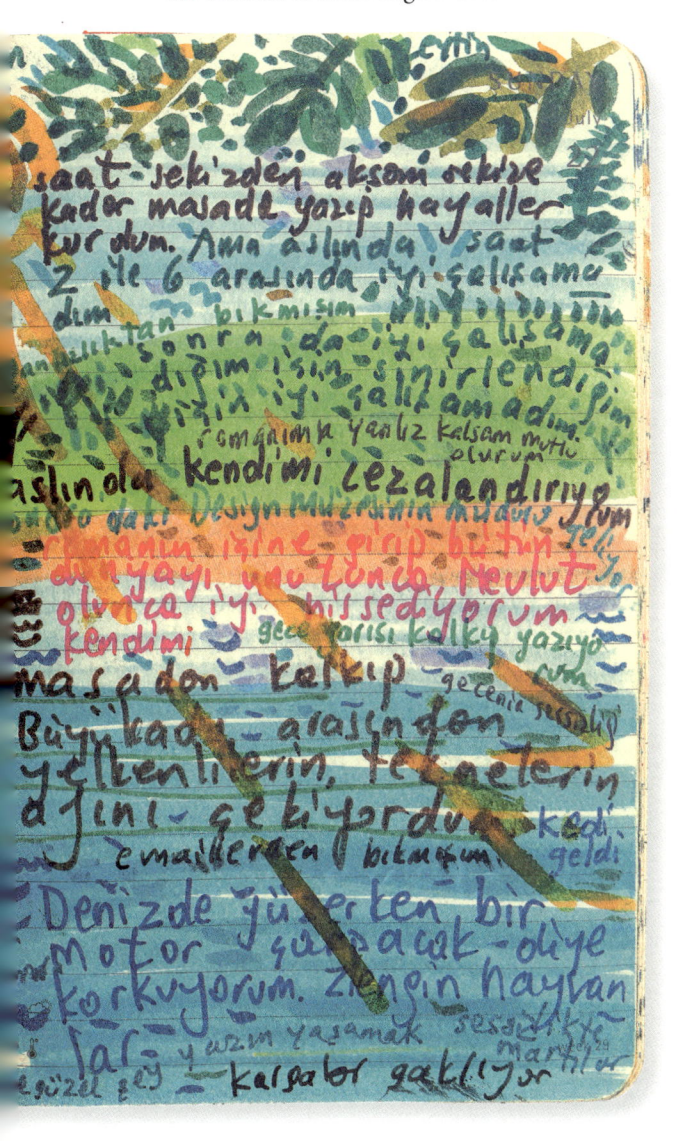

It feels good to step into the novel and forget about the rest of the world, to become Mevlut. I wake up in the middle of the night and write—the silence of nighttime.

Every now and then I get up from my desk and photograph the rowboats and sailboats floating between Sedef Island and Büyükada.

                          i'm tired of emails   the cat's here

I'm worried I'll get hit by a motorboat while swimming in the sea—rich bastards— how glorious to live in summer   seagulls in the silence
                      the crows are cawing

Fried eggs tomatoes and cheese pastry at the Municipal Café by the pier this morning. I like this view of Büyükada Pier, all the people rushing off to work. Met with Yücel from YKY back home in Istanbul and went through the selection Nathalie from Gallimard has made from my journals—from the pages with drawings on them. Roughly 400 double spreads which I must cut down to 150–200. As I work on choosing images and double spreads... Sometimes I can't help but think to myself that this is going to be a beautiful book. But then my gaze falls on one of my diary entries and I begin to wonder whether I am doing the right thing by publishing these things.

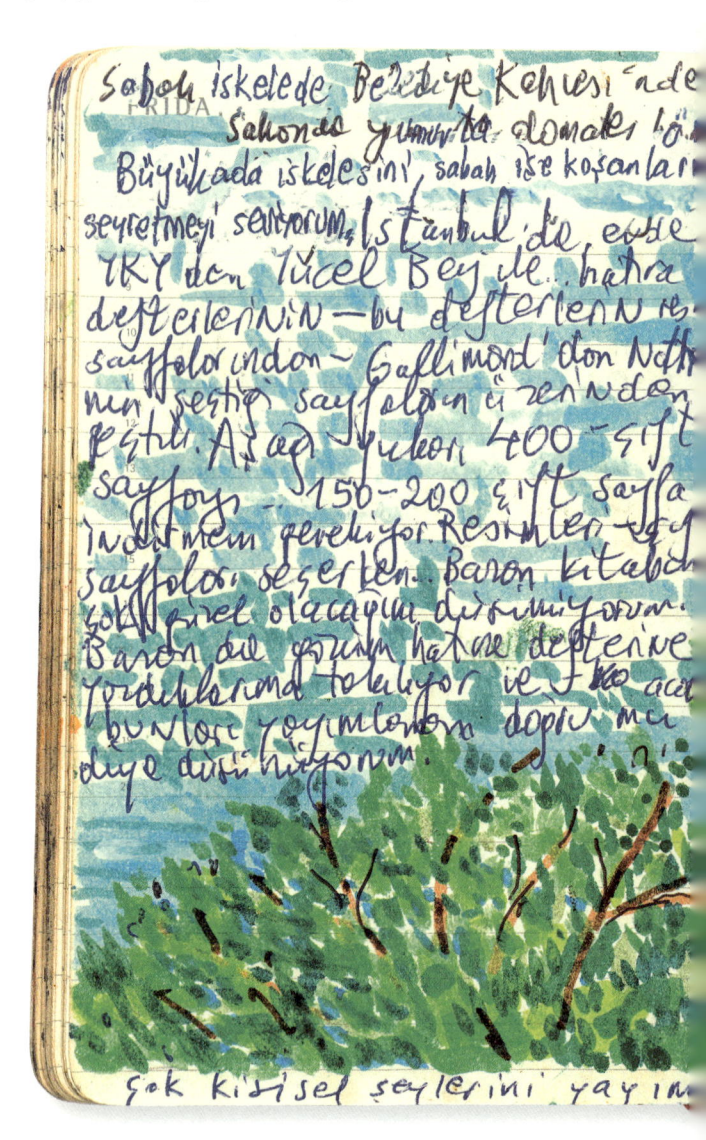

A. says not to publish anything too personal.

Distant mountains

    write about landscape!

Pages from Mingherian History

The secret heroes of *Nights of Plague* are the children hunting green mullet to save the island from starvation.

Across the two pages below, we see Mingherian children hunting for green trout in Kaputaş, at the mouth of the Mingherian river. We are in the YKY library with Yücel, photocopying some of the illustrated pages from my journals to make my work on *Memories of Distant Mountains* easier. I am compiling a book from the diaries I've been keeping for 10 years—from the pages of the Moleskine notebooks that I've drawn on. It's taking a while.

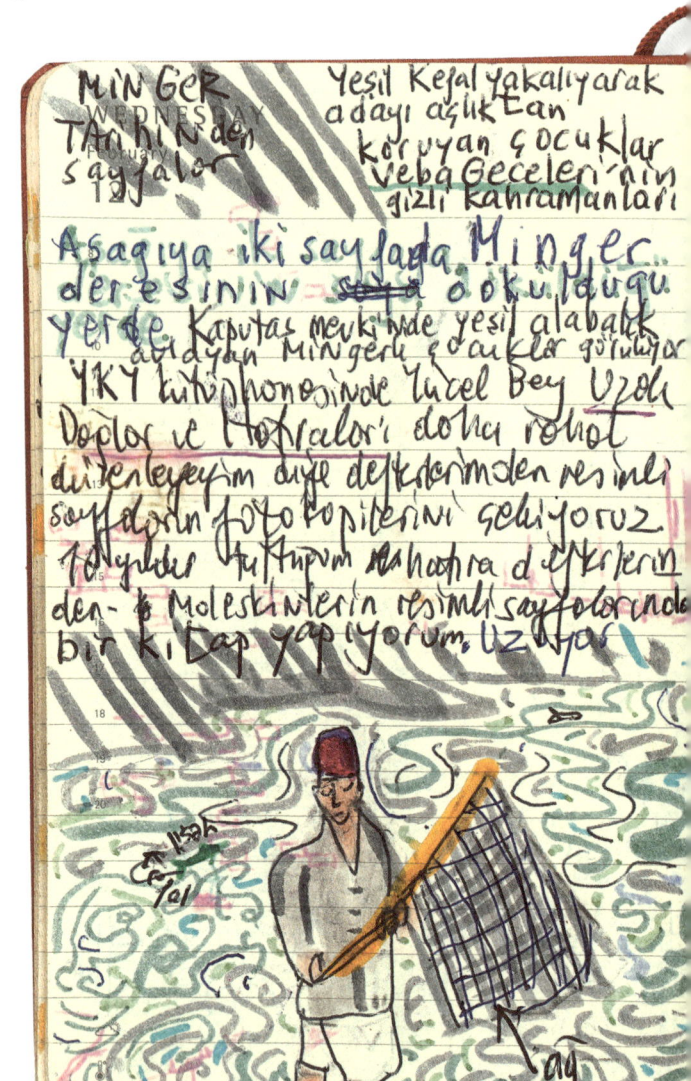

green mullet

net

I wrote 2 more pages of the novel today, very easily. All the leading dervishes from the disbanded sects are being extracted from their lodges and taken away to the dungeons / the Castle's isolation / quarantine zone. Every Thursday for the last two years I've been going to Inci Eviner's studio to paint. I look at photographs taken around 1900 and paint landscapes (horse-drawn carriages, remote Mediterranean ports, train stations, immortal trees, and tired soldiers). I first came across these fishing children in an old photograph. Then I drew them. I drew them again. Drawing them was like placing them—the children—in the midst of my own memories. Finally, I put the fishing children in *Nights of Plague* . . .

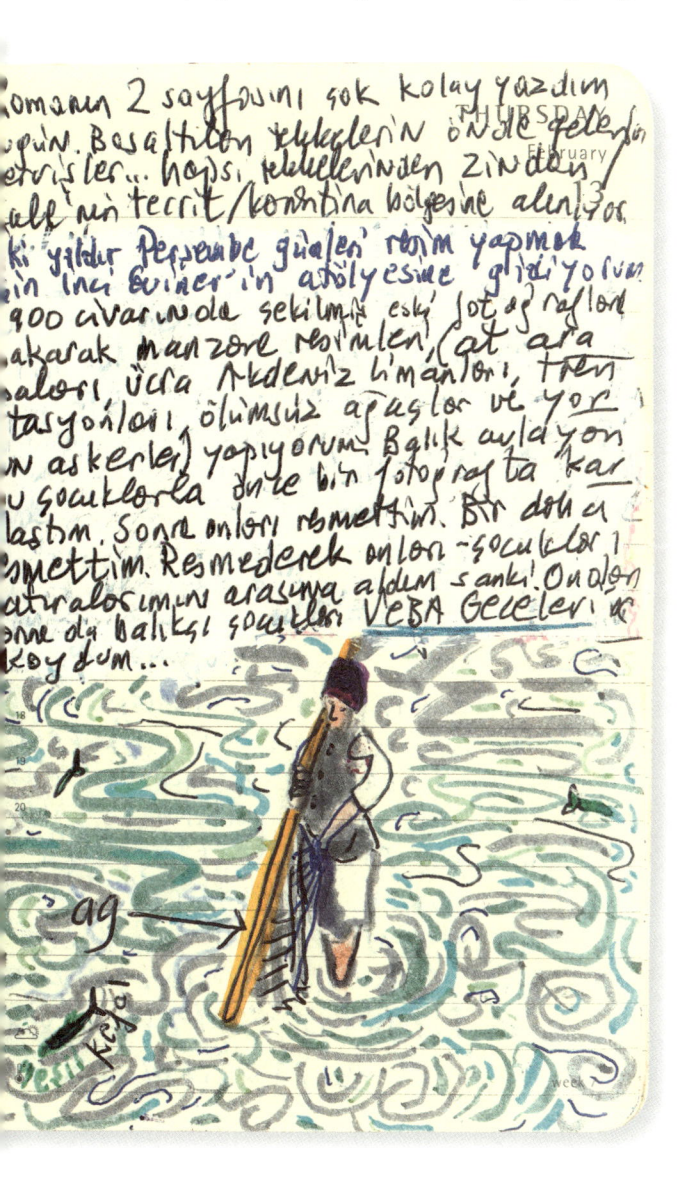

net

green mullet

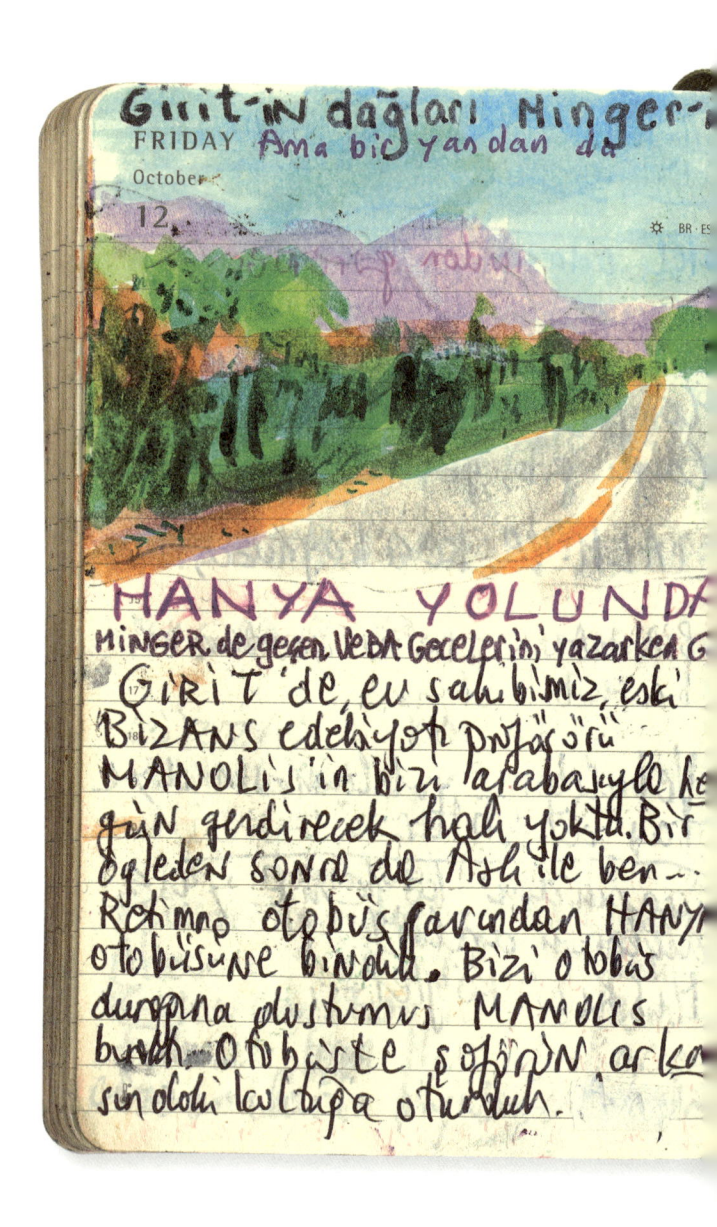

The mountains in Crete are smaller than those in Mingheria
Yet I still feel this place could be Mingheria.

EN ROUTE TO CHANIA
In Crete writing *Nights of Plague,* set in Mingheria
We couldn't really expect MANOLIS—our host in Crete, and a professor of ancient Byzantine literature—to drive us around all day. So one afternoon Aslı and I... went to the Retinmo bus terminal and boarded a bus to CHANIA. Our friend MANOLIS dropped us off at the bus stop. We sat in the seats right behind the driver.

But our seats were a little too high, so I couldn't take any photographs—though I had very much wanted to. Noticing my disappointment, Aslı smiled. "Who needs photographs anyway! You're a painter. Take out your sketchbook and draw what you see." Aslı had a mischievous look on her face. Would I be able to capture what I could see through the windshield as the bus sped toward Chania? I welcomed this old-fashioned skill test. (Of course I set great store by the FRONT SEAT. When

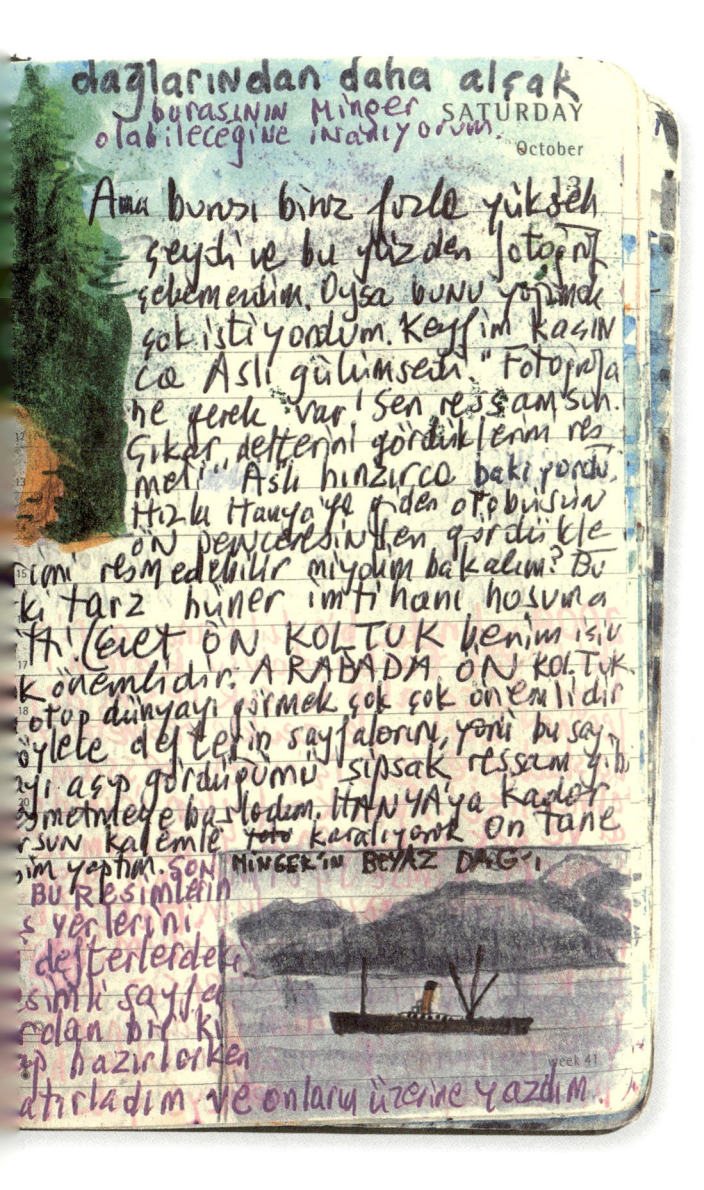

THE WHITE MOUNTAIN
OF MINGHERIA

traveling in a CAR, it is imperative to sit in the FRONT PASSENGER SEAT and look out at the world.) So I opened up my notebook, to this page in fact, and started drawing what I saw, like a street artist would. By the time we reached CHANIA, I had sketched out ten pencil drawings. Later, when I began to work on a book composed of a selection of these illustrated journals, I remembered the empty spaces I had left on these pages, and wrote all over them.

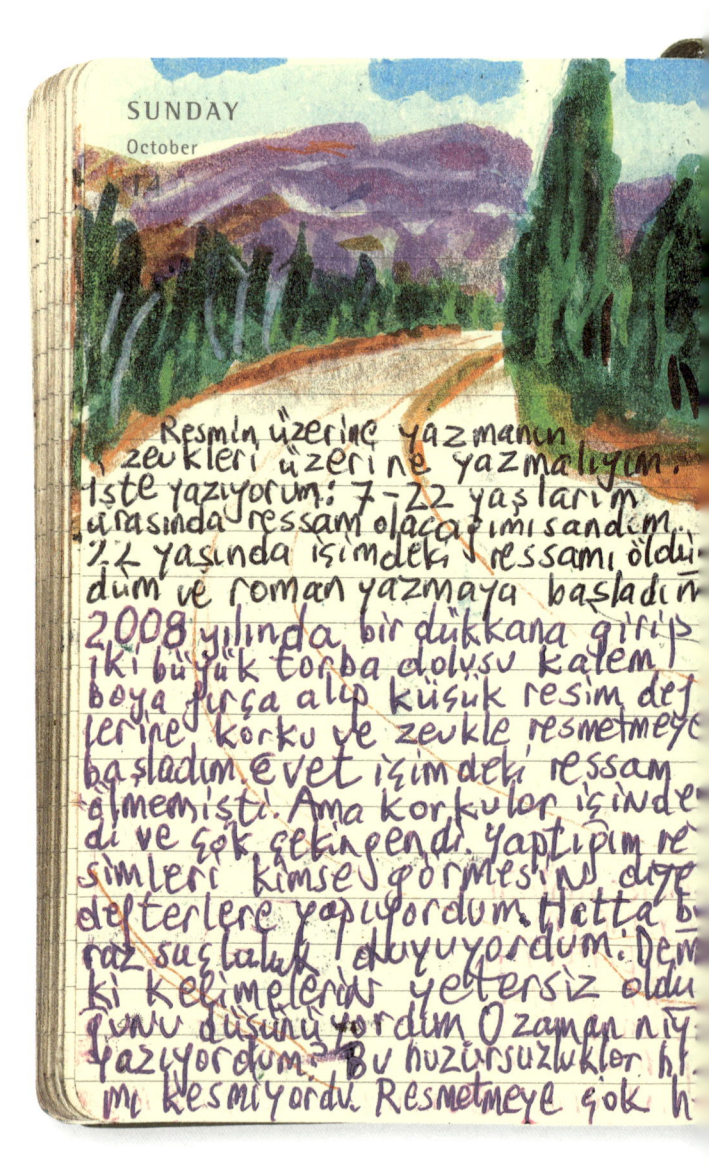

I should really write about the pleasures of inscribing words over paintings. So here I am, writing: Between the ages of 7 and 22, I thought I was going to be a painter. At 22, I killed the painter inside of me and began writing novels. In 2008, I walked into a stationery shop, bought two big bags of pencils, paints, and brushes, and began joyfully and timidly filling little sketchbooks with drawings and colors. The painter inside of me hadn't died after all. But he was full of fears and terribly shy. I made all my drawings inside notebooks so that nobody would see them. I even felt a little guilty: surely this must mean I secretly deemed words insufficient. So why did I bother to write? None of these inhibitions slowed me down. I was eager to keep drawing, and drew wherever I could.

I should create an exhibition—anthology—of paintings inscribed with words ... featuring examples from every culture around the world. of course finding all these examples ... and selecting the best ones will take time.

an eagle's nest
on the mountainside

I started writing in this notebook in 2009. I didn't just write about my day and my thoughts. Sometimes my hand would start drawing of its own accord. There was a page for each day. I would try to keep the writing and drawings small so that they would fit. But some days a single page wasn't enough to contain all the incidents, words, and images I wished to record. From 2012 onward, I began to write and draw even more, filling two notebooks every year.

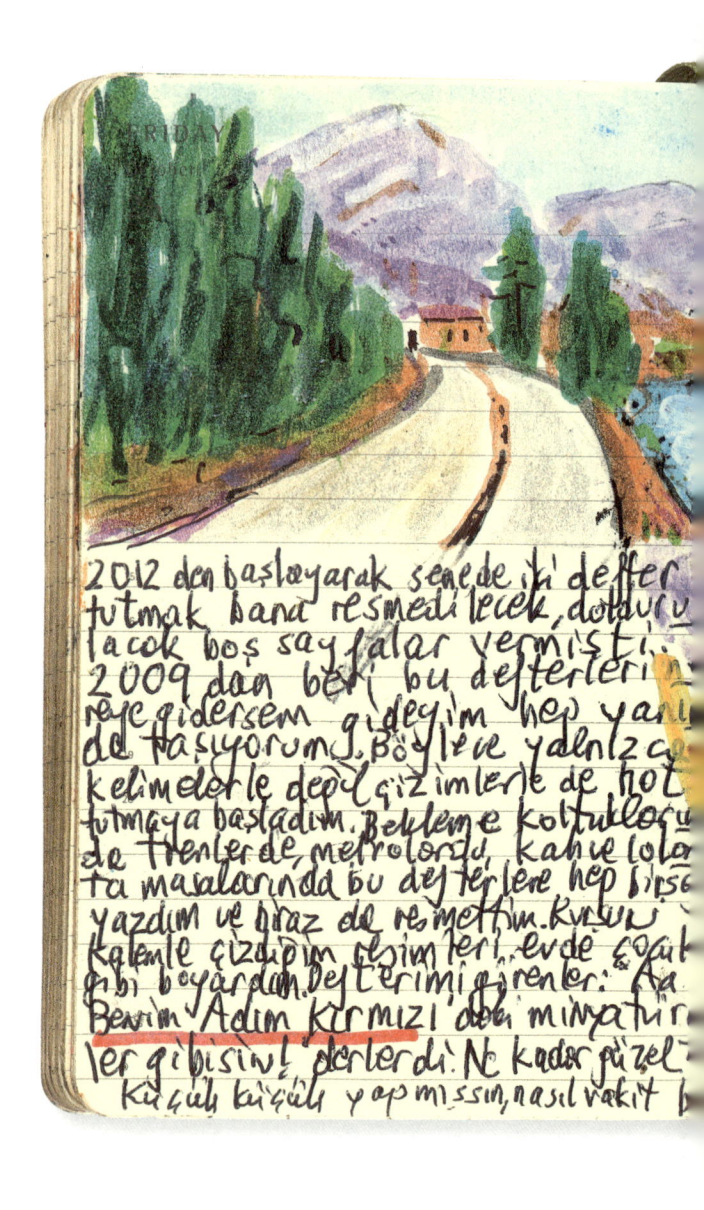

Moving on to two notebooks a year in 2012 gave me many more blank pages to draw on and fill up. Since 2009, I've been carrying these notebooks with me wherever I go. This is how I began taking notes not just with words, but with drawings too. I have been constantly writing things down in these notebooks, and occasionally drawing in them too, in waiting rooms, on trains, in the metro, at cafés and restaurant tables. Back home I would then color in my pencil drawings like a little boy. "You're just like the miniaturists in *My Name Is Red*!" people would say when they saw my notebooks. "All these tiny drawings, how lovely! How do you find the time?"

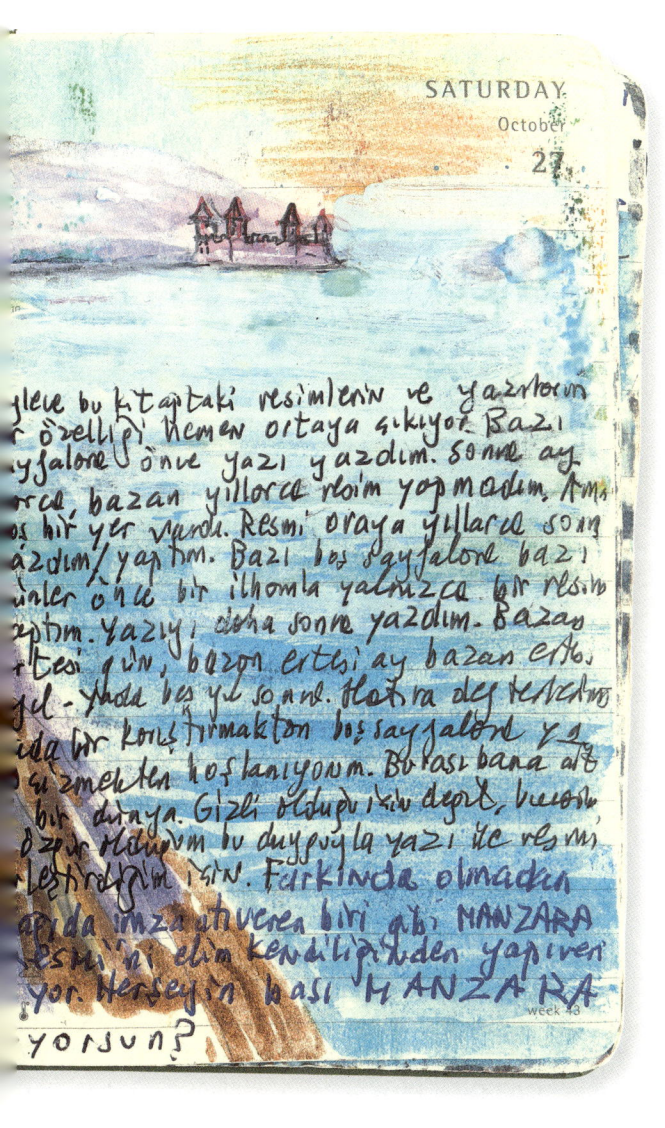

One of the peculiarities of the words and images in this book is thus immediately revealed. On some pages, the text came first, and for months, sometimes years, afterward, I didn't draw anything on them. But I always left an empty space. I made/drew the image there many years later. Some days I would be inspired to make a drawing and nothing else. The text would come later. Sometimes the next day, sometimes the next month, sometimes the next year, or five years later. I like to leaf through my journals every now and then, scribbling and sketching on any empty pages. This world belongs to me. Not because it's secret, but because it is where I am most free, and where I can lean on that feeling as I bring words and images together. My hand draws a LANDSCAPE of its own accord, like someone autographing a page without even realizing they're doing it. Everything begins with LANDSCAPE.

ABOUT THIS LANDSCAPE: I live in Cihangir now, and this is my view. I rarely go to Nişantaşı anymore. With its gruesome new shopping center right across from the Pamuk Apartments, its chain stores, its entertainment venues, bars, restaurants, and crowds, Nişantaşı has sadly ceased to be the familiar, happy place I used to know. The landscape and neighborhood life of Cihangir are more humane. Here you can still find a big colorful greengrocer or a little convenience store just down the road... Slipping into this neighborhood life and feeling its presence from up close reminds me of my childhood, of an extended family, of the vitality, the friendly warmth, the joy of a multitudinous community. But I also realize that I have been cut off from these communities. I have become a lonely man. One who can't walk around the city without a bodyguard...

Gazing at this view allows me to forget all that and instantly transforms me into someone else: when we look at a view like this one, and more generally at any pleasant view, we end up finding our own place in the universe. We yearn to be as open, as calm, as beautiful as the vast landscape before us. More than the landscape itself, this picture I've painted of it becomes something that describes and echoes the world inside of me. But the most important thing about this view is the feeling of security

After a point, complaining about my troubles with the museum and its unscrupulous architects or artists becomes nothing but a waste of time. I'm the one who wanted to build this museum, I brought it upon myself, and now I must of course bear the consequences, but even so, sometimes I feel like I'm drowning; some days I don't even want to get out of bed or do any work. But when I get up in the morning in Cihangir and come face-to-face with this view, the sun rising in the early hours in the midst of that boundless silence, the whole world turns beautiful. Looking out at this view in the early morning silence allows me to forget everything else, all the things that need doing for the museum, the feeling of being so exhausted and overworked that I might pass out, my fear of dying, and my loneliness, reminding me instead that I can handle everything with a smile, and that the world, and Istanbul, and life itself are marvelous indeed. The loveliness of this landscape is a call to respect the world and the whole universe . . .

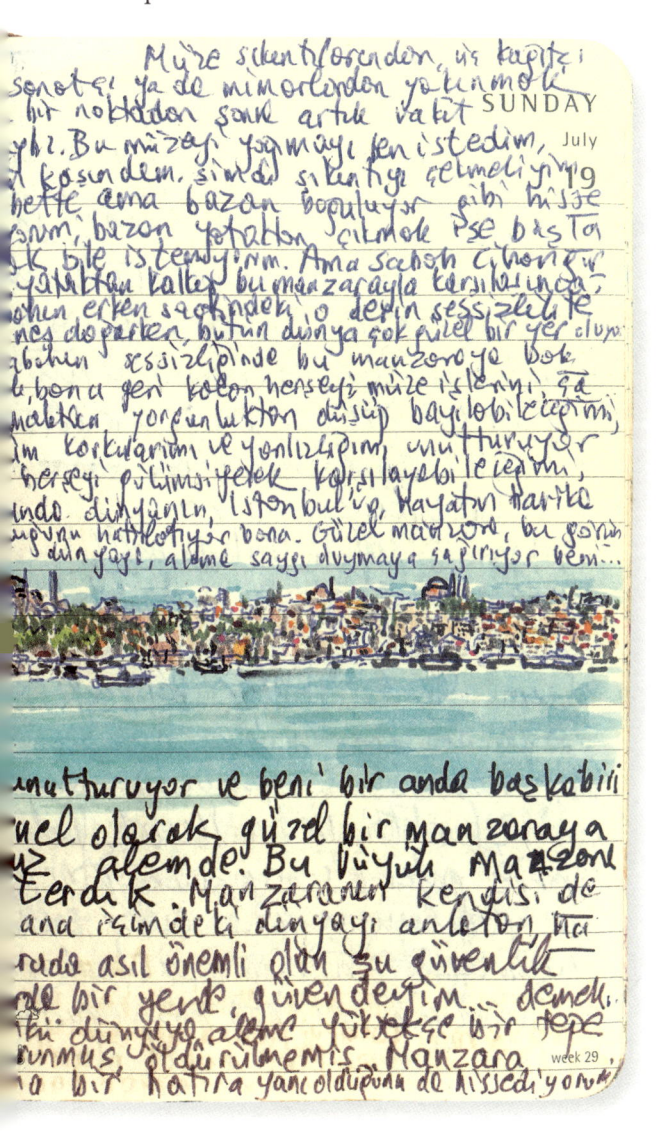

it conveys. It says . . . the road ahead is clear, there is nothing around me, I am somewhere high above, and safe. We love landscapes, we love looking at them, because they gift us with the pleasure of looking at the world, at the whole of creation, from a safe hill which protects us from danger . . . Landscapes fill me with a sense of security. But I can also feel that they contain an element of memory.

This morning I finally finished writing the introduction to the Everyman edition of *Snow*. I should have been done with it a long time ago. It's down to a lack of discipline, to leaving my desk and busying myself with other things, etc. Don't worry and keep writing, Orhan! In parts, the text reads almost like a list of events, lending it a harshness that veers into something intensely political; I do love writing...

In the afternoon we met with Kıymet and Murat in the flat across the landing to work on the museum. The background to Füsun's cigarettes, a cracked yellowish color. Afterward I looked through some old children's magazines to source puzzles and crosswords for one of the displays.

BRILLIANT DISCOVERY: I CAN ALTER AN OLD BLACK-AND-WHITE POSTCARD OF A VIEW OF BERLIN, USING A PAINTBRUSH TO START LITTLE FIRES. PASTELS WORK just as well, and I amuse myself by modifying the GRAYSCALE printed texture of the city. I sign the painted postcard and gift it to Kıymet.

Later, the melancholy before a trip.

I woke up early for the journey to ATHENS, went outside. My bodyguard Nuri and Murat from İletişim were supposed to come, it's 7:40 and they're still not here.

As the plane approaches Athens I tell myself, Be humble, Orhan, don't get into the question of Turkish-Greek relations. For some reason I feel nervous.

I got off the plane early. Nikos, Vassilis... We all hugged each other. I had come here in 1997, exactly 14 years ago, to promote *The Black Book*. We'd gone to Patras, to Thessaloniki. A Turkish fascist (I'm not sure whether he was acting independently, or on government orders) had just fired a gun over the wall of the Patriarchate of Istanbul and killed a priest. There were Greek fascists in Athens demanding an eye for an eye... And I was the Turkish writer who happened to be there. They might try to shoot me.

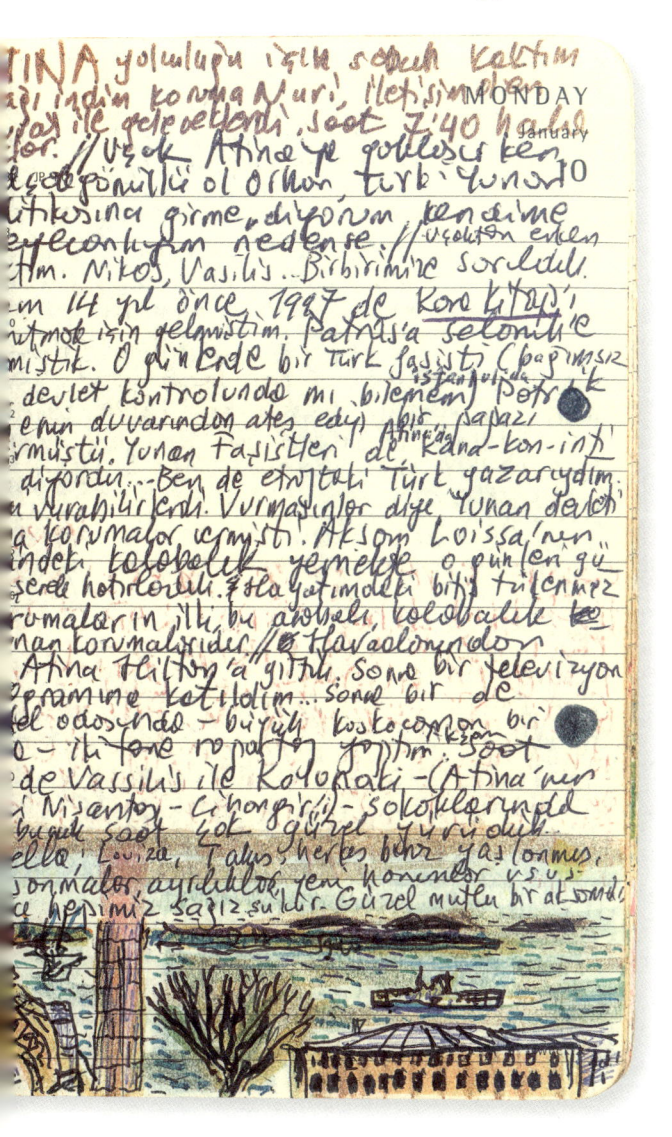

The Greek government had given me bodyguards to prevent that. At the big dinner party at Loissa's house that evening, we laughed as we reminisced about those days. The endless stream of bodyguards in my life began with that first big group of Greek bodyguards who followed me around in their cars.

From the airport we went to the Hilton in Athens. Then I appeared on a TV program... Back at the spacious hotel room, I did two interviews. At 7 I met up with Vassilis and we went on a lovely one-and-a-half-hour walk in Kolonaki (what used to be the Athenian version of Nişantaşı-Cihangir). Stella, Louiza, Takis, everyone looked a little older, there had been divorces and separations, new wives, etc., but thankfully we were all still alive. It was a happy, joyful evening.

23

This morning I worked on the issue of *Milliyet* reporting the assassination of Celâl Salik, basing it in part on the issue of *Milliyet* from when Abdi Ipekçi was murdered. Afterward we did some work with Vahit in the museum office. In the afternoon, nearly 20 German journalists came to visit the museum building. I talked to them for half an hour . . . Everything looks good in the museum, but half finished.

Working with Vahit.

In the evening, long walk toward the Golden Horn. Cihangir-Tophane, Karaköy-Eminönü, Babıâli–Divanyolu Street, Kadırga, the waterfront road. And fish at that restaurant I like.

Checking my emails at the end of the night and seeing that Sarah Chalfant wants to send my introduction to the Everyman edition of *Red* to *The New Yorker* or the *NYR Books*, I went back and read the text George had gone through one more time . . . I was pleased to see how well those memories from the years when I was writing *Red* have come out. Yes, writing really is what I do best. I was about to say that I wish I could be just as good at painting. But that, I realize now, would have made me a different person.

This morning I am writing a column by Celâl Salik for the museum: themes include love, happiness, newspaper columns, etc. . . . Later, the usual phone calls, museum-related tasks, display cabinets. Need to start visualizing these cabinets.

At home in Cihangir at 7 o'clock in the evening, I'm tired from it all, but still sitting at my desk and writing. I wanted to stay in and do some work this evening. Though I suppose I've been home all day anyway . . . I did briefly venture out in Cihangir and bought myself a desk on which to paint. A momentous decision! I set this table up—my drawing desk—a meter away from my writing desk. But I could also tell that this urge to paint was pulling me away from everything else—from the novel I should be writing, whose world I should be entering.

I often find myself feeling these surges of deep, unrelenting tenderness for Aslı. I am always trying to work out what might be going on in her beautiful head. This is especially true when she seems pensive and melancholy. If she is being methodical and diligent over making her morning coffee, that means she's in a happy mood! If she comes home and flings her handbag to one side and that green coat that suits

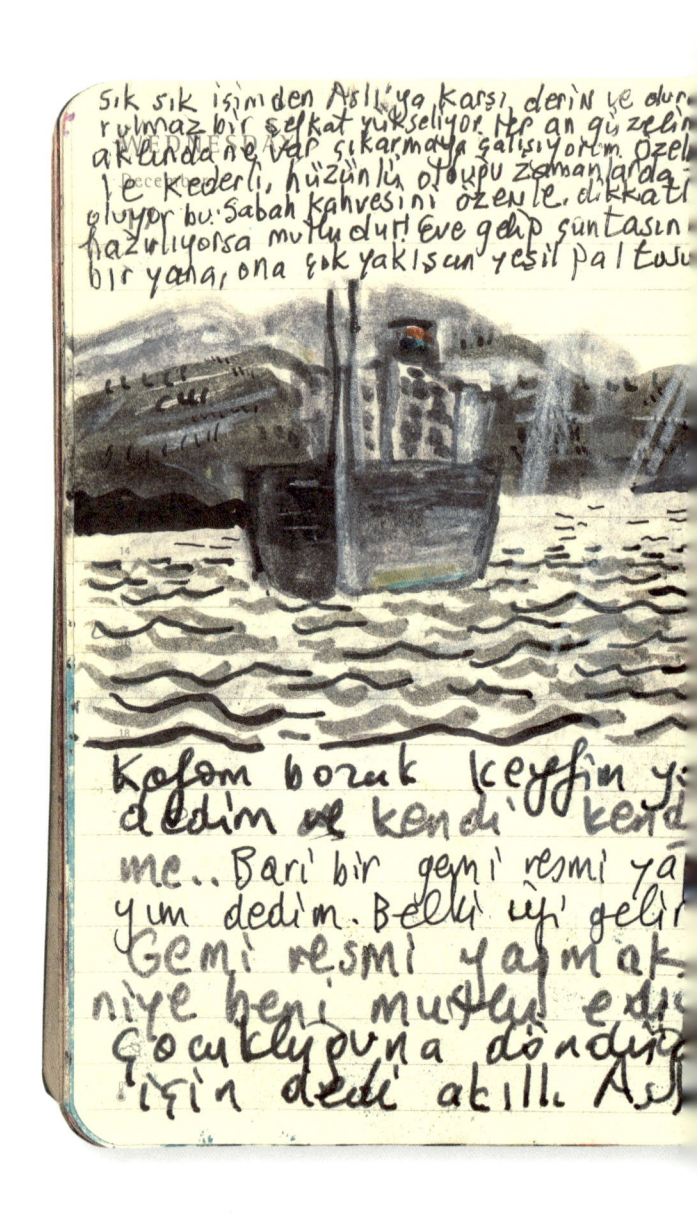

I was thinking to myself, My head's not right today, I'm feeling down... Let me try to draw a boat, at least. Maybe it'll cheer me up. Why does painting boats make me happy? Because it takes you back to your childhood, Aslı observed astutely. But it's not a return to

her so well to the other (onto the sofa), she's tired and angry. If she is watching one of those lousy TV shows, she is tired again, and depressive. If she is reading George Eliot, she is determined, committed, and clever (she has been a much better reader of *Middlemarch* than I have). Sometimes I look at her just like Kemal looked at Füsun, studying her every gesture, her every word, her every movement.

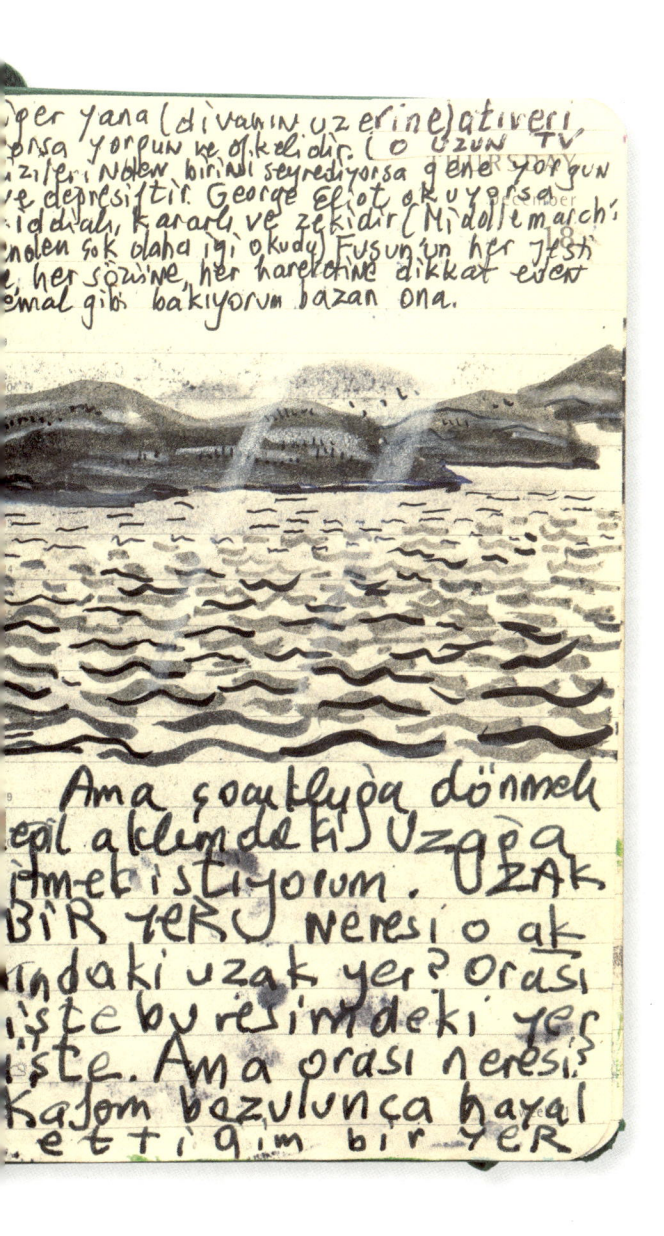

childhood that I have in mind. I want to go far away. SOMEWHERE FAR AWAY. Where is that faraway place you're thinking of? It's over there, see, it's the place in this picture. But where is there? A place I dream of when my head's not right.

At my desk this morning: *Nights of Plague* opens with all the people already living in the Castle of Mingheria joined by passengers arriving on a ship from Istanbul. The delegation sent to quash the Boxer Rebellion . . . ends up staying in Mingheria. I haven't yet managed to settle our young Princess into the city. Should I be reading more memoirs/books? / Should I read more about Abdul Hamid? Meanwhile I'm also thinking and dreaming about the rest of the book, about the novel as a whole. As I construct the island in my imagination, I look outside at the view and at the sea. This will be the last time I write a historical novel . . .

They used to have domes made of lead in the past, too. But not these ones.

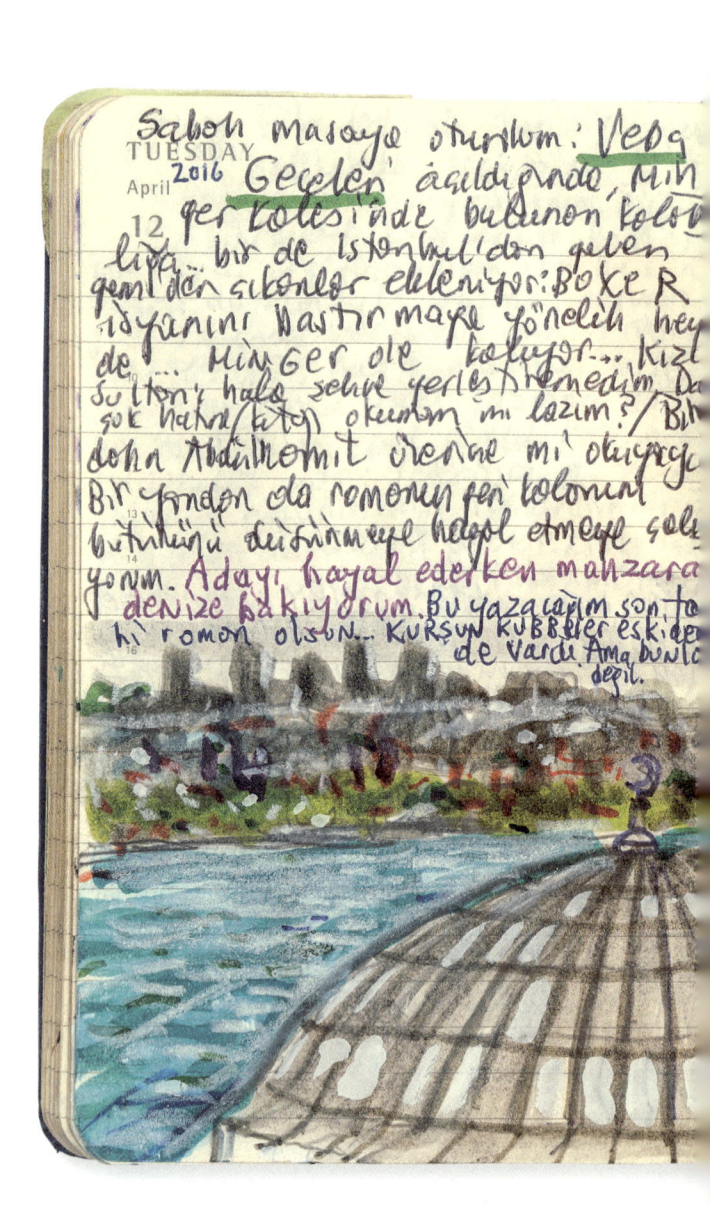

Emre arrived at 9 in the morning: we immediately sat at our desks and started working on our novels. I seem to have become addicted to the silence that suddenly descends upon my desk, my surroundings, and the whole room whenever I sit at my desk and write . . . My imagination won't work unless the silence has set in . . .

I went over the article I wrote for *Magazine Littéraire* about my days in the Cannes jury and sent it off to France . . . Afterward Emre and I went upstairs to number 16 and rearranged my library of English literature. Chatting with Emre about books the whole time—those we've read and those we haven't . . . Putting books and writers in order . . . that's happiness.

We went back downstairs to number 12, where we had some of Sermin's lentil soup. I am writing this as I wait for the car from YKY to pick me up.

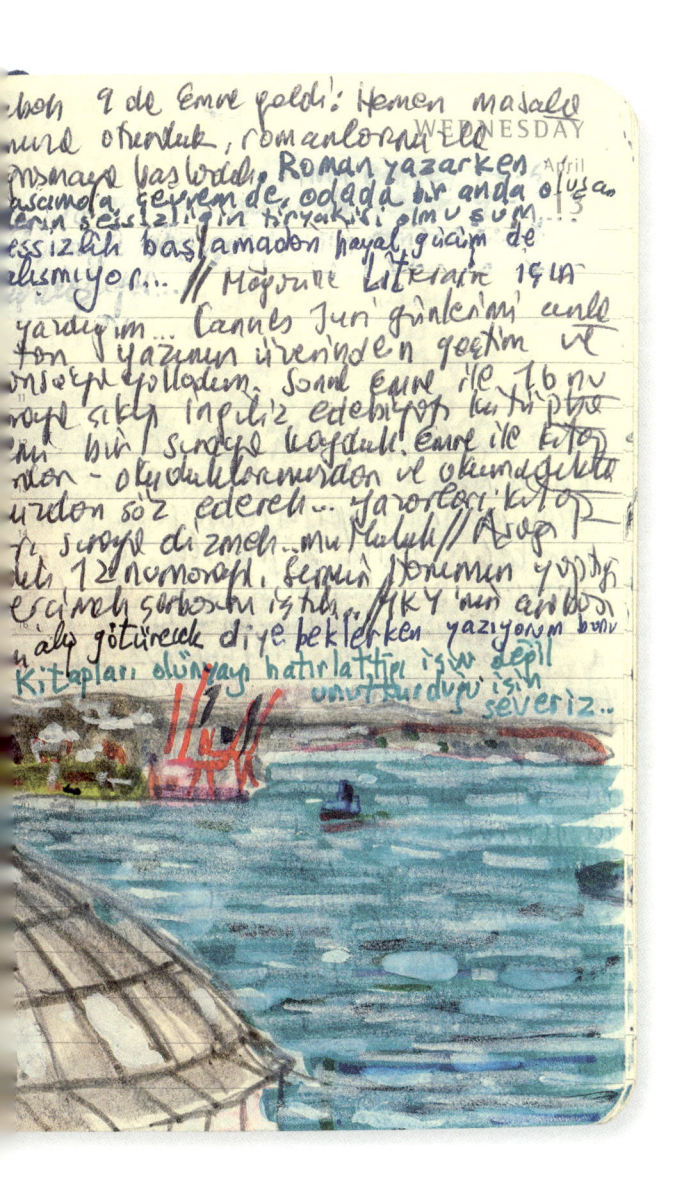

We love books not because they remind us of the world, but because they allow us to forget about it . . .

At the heart of this book there is a dream I had before I ever started writing and drawing in these notebooks. I have managed to make sense of some parts of the dream, but others I still don't understand.

I was watching the dream unfold as if it were the view outside my window when I suddenly woke up, afraid... To help me understand that dreamscape, I have arranged the illustrated pages of this book not in CHRONOLOGICAL but in EMOTIONAL order.

Morning: the city is covered in snow. It's sticking. Even on our balcony, it's thirty–forty centimeters thick. Aslı is sleeping in the other room. I am inside my novel. I have been reading a great deal about Ottoman telegraph offices. I've bought so many books lately! A snowy hush reigns over the house and the city. It's still falling, so visibility is low. And I have to confess: I am so happy. About the house, about the snow, about Aslı sleeping inside, etc. etc. I am hopeful that I won't get into any more trouble, that I will be able to live in Istanbul, and that everything will be wonderful, just like this snow. My interview with *La Repubblica* has been published with the headline "Terrorism Must Not Become an Excuse to Undermine Democracy." Marco sent it to me.

The snow and cold are really striking. That greenish snowy blue... The color of the sea. The snow falling in tiny flakes. My protagonist, the Major, has arrived at the Telegraph Office... Now I'm writing about the history of the telegraph service... It's great fun. But slow going. Aslı keeps going up and down between here and flat 16: in the SNOW, the city is quiet. Thanks to the snow, I have been able to step back, if only for a day, from the dreadful political situation we find ourselves in. In the evening, a walk with Nuri on our tail → out on the icy snowy streets... We had to wade through freezing puddles in Taksim Square. Aslı's feet froze. The streets are cold, no tourists or anyone else around. It's just us, the people of Istanbul. The metro isn't too busy either. We got off at Etiler. Şevket, Yeşim, Zeynep: who is looking for a job as she finishes her PhD at Harvard... Şevket also talking about politics. None of us had anticipated this imperious, foam-at-the-mouth rhetoric, this terrifying Orwellian atmosphere of authoritarianism! We hadn't expected it to happen so soon...

In the MORNING, SNOW again. Falling in huge flakes. As Aslı sleeps and the day only just begins to break, I sit at my desk and write a detailed description of the telegraph coup. I am perfectly content. In fact I can just about admit to myself: the feeling of inwardness brought about by SNOWFALL, that feeling of being left to ourselves, is a kind of comfort. In ISTANBUL, we find comfort in the beauty of snow.

Once in a while I feel like leaving a drawing unfinished. So that years later it can show me or someone else how I came to draw these pictures in the first place. And also because I've suddenly noticed the drawing below looks pretty enough in its unfinished form.

EVENING SUN IN CIHANGIR

Zonaro too would have seen this same light upon the minaret...

But on the other hand, the thought of going back to tweak an unfinished painting is so enticing that I can't stop myself. In fact landscape painting shares a deep affinity with this mood, this feeling of being unable to stop yourself from drawing. Sometimes I will stop in the middle of writing my novel and start a painting of this sort...

For years I have been sitting at this desk and looking at this view. I'm happy here—yes, happy. It's a sunny day. Aslı has gone to see her mother, and I'm back to telling the story of Mevlut and Rayiha. I have been rereading some of the novel's early chapters and realize that: 1. It might be possible to shorten it a little. 2. It's entertaining and great fun to read. 3. It very quickly conveys a lot of information. 4. There is some repetition that could be cut.

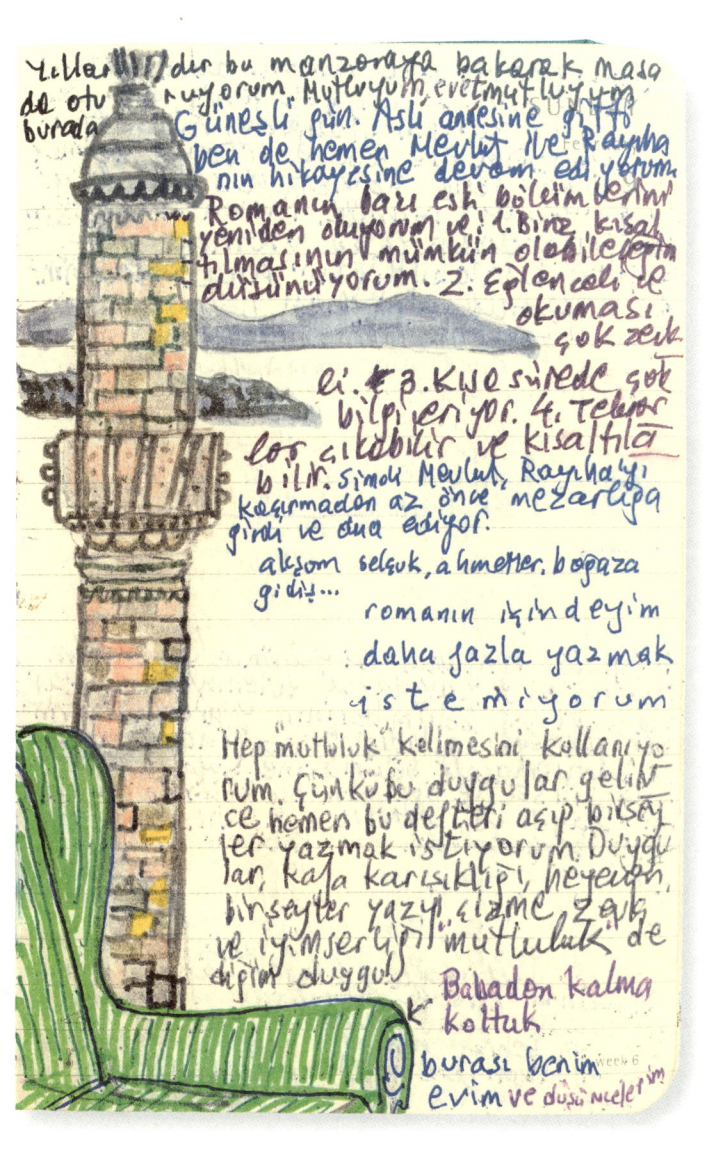

← Armchair inherited from father

this is my home and these are my thoughts.

Mevlut has just gone into the graveyard to pray before eloping with Rayiha.
in the evening, meeting Selçuk, Ahmet and co., down by the Bosphorus . . .
I am right inside the novel
that's enough writing
for now

I keep using the word happiness. It must be because whenever I am in that kind of mood, I feel the urge to open up this notebook and write something down. Emotions, confusion, excitement, the joy and optimism of scribbling away: that is what I mean by "happiness"!

In Cihangir I see DISTANT MOUNTAINS before me. If a person who is looking at a view finds their eyes drawn to mountains in the distance: 1. They may have visited those distant mountains before, or may even have once lived in the village behind the range. That's how I feel when I look out at the Princes' Islands from Istanbul, remembering my happy days there. 2. Or perhaps the distant mountains may be part of a landscape we have never traveled to. We are always dreaming and wondering about what we might find there...

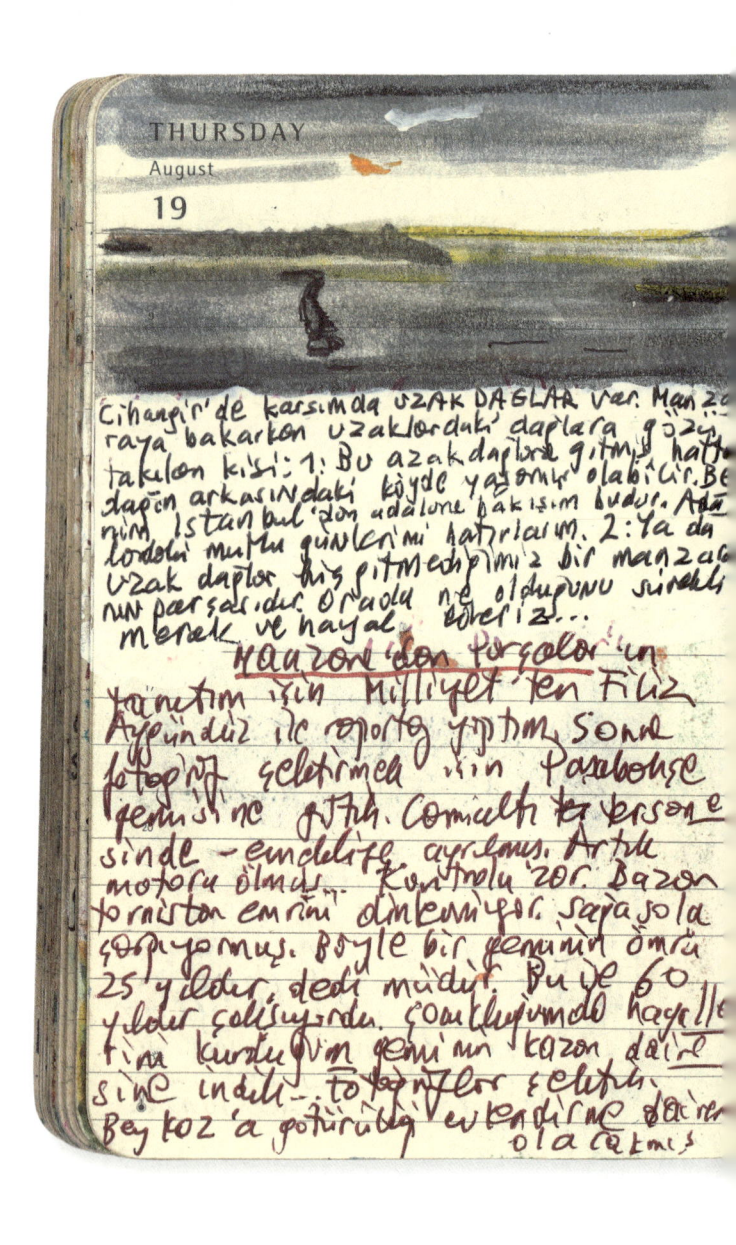

I did an interview with Filiz Aygündüz from *Milliyet* for the publication of *Fragments from the Landscape*. Afterward we went on board the *Paşabahçe* for a photo shoot. It's docked at Camialtı shipyard—in retirement. Its engine has died... It's difficult to steer. Sometimes it refuses to reverse, keeps banging into things. The manager told me this kind of vessel is usually built to last for 25 years. This one's been going for 60. We climbed down into the boiler room of this ship I used to dream about when I was a little boy... We took some photographs. They say it'll be towed to Beykoz and used as a wedding venue.

In the afternoon, meeting with Cem at number 9 downstairs. We discuss completing the museum, security measures, etc. The truth is I am worried about the museum being attacked... whether by petty thieves or political hooligans. As much as the ballooning costs, it's this fear too that keeps me awake at night.

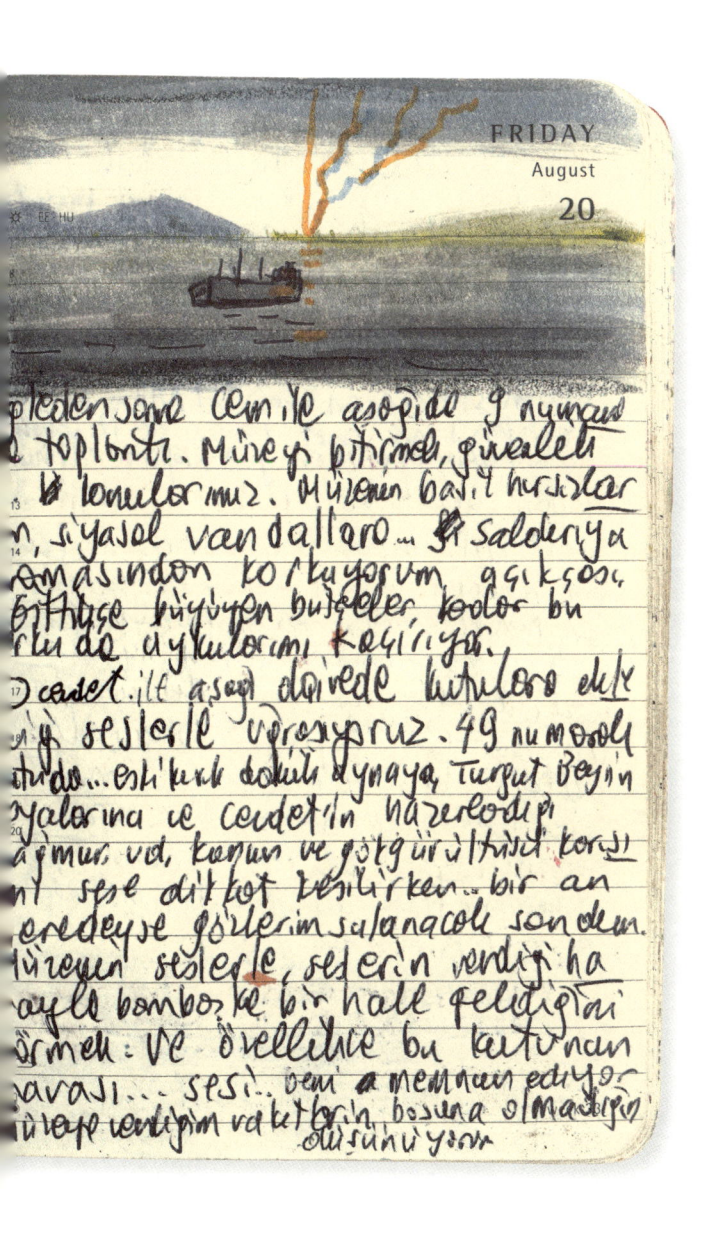

In the flat downstairs with Cevdet, tinkering with the sound effects he has created for the displays. Here's cabinet number 49... as I peered at the shabby old mirror and at Turgut Bey's belongings, and listened carefully to the mingling sounds of rainfall, oud, qanun, and thunderclaps created by Cevdet, I thought, for a moment... that my eyes might well up. Witnessing the museum become transformed by sound, by the atmosphere that sound can create: and the mood... the sound of this box in particular... it's so satisfying. It makes me feel that all the time I have devoted to the museum has not been wasted.

Morning . . . as light begins to dawn . . .

All these hills that are covered in concrete today used to be completely bare.
I gaze at those faraway hills now as if I were staring into my own memories.

Coming back to Cihangir means coming back to this view. As I work on *Nights of Plague* and feel the novel's anguished atmosphere inside of me, I sometimes pause and look out at this view.

this is where the morning begins

I used to memorize poems for Turkish class as the sun rose in the morning. I never liked memorizing poems. I was no good at it ... Too busy scrapping with Şevket, surrounded—at home—by a constant din, I couldn't really concentrate properly. So I would always do it alone in the early hours of the day, and at dawn I would witness these RED-tinted mornings. This was during the final year of primary school and the first year of middle school

Painting starts with the visualization of what you cannot remember. Eventually that same landscape will begin to depict TIME

In the past, whenever cranes and heavy machinery began work on a new construction site in Istanbul, curious onlookers would gather to watch.

I'm one of them . . . I can spend hours watching this crane in action as it lays down the blocks of concrete that have come to hide Tophane's Nusretiye Mosque from sight . . .

My ship, the *Paşabahçe*

Railway tunnel
construction

The *Paşabahçe*
enters the city

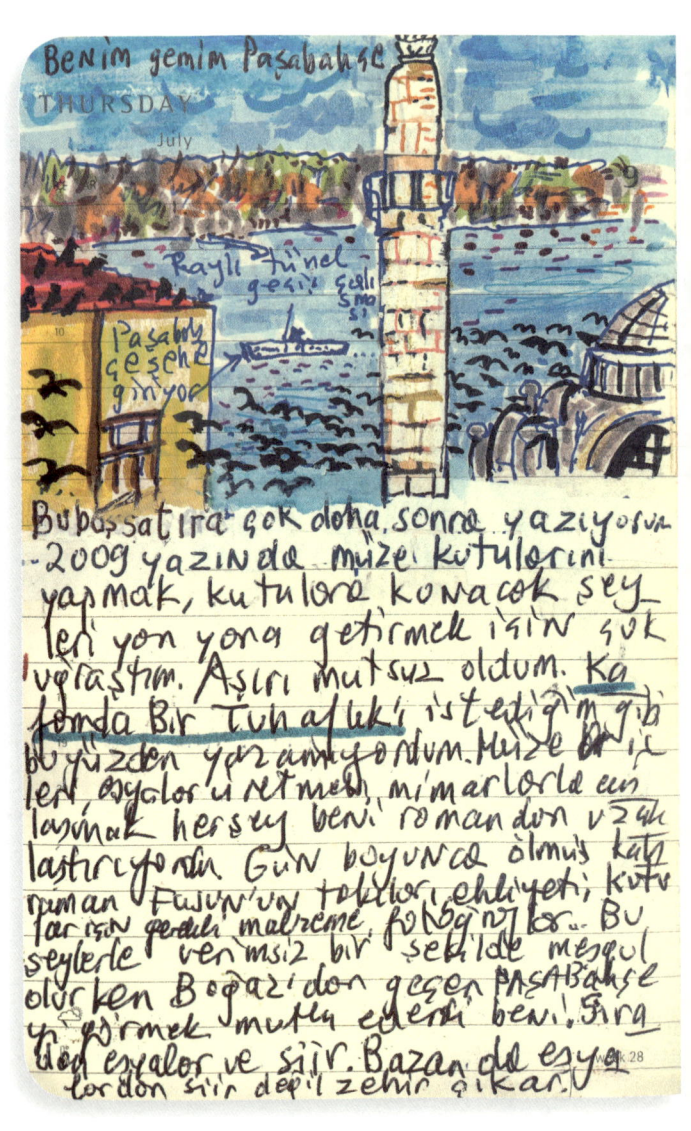

I am filling in these empty lines much later. I spent the summer of 2009 working incessantly on the museum displays and figuring how best to arrange the objects within each vitrine. It was a miserable time. It meant I couldn't concentrate on *A Strangeness in My Mind* as much I would have liked to. Working on the museum, manufacturing the objects for its displays, dealing with the architects and designers, all of it conspired to keep me away from my novel. But even as I spent the day fruitlessly engrossed in the dead heroine Füsun's jewelry and driver's license, in the materials needed for each display, in old photographs, and other similar matters . . . the sight of the *Paşabahçe* crossing the Bosphorus would always cheer me up. Ordinary objects and poetry. Though sometimes it isn't poetry that pours forth from objects, but poison.

Seeing the *Paşabahçe* at the Camialtı shipyard on Thursday afternoon during my interview with *Milliyet* has touched me deeply . . . My ship, the same one I have watched cruising back and forth across the waters of Istanbul, to and from the Princes' Islands, for most of my lifetime, is now retiring. I was going to write about the *Paşabahçe* for *The New Yorker;* in fact we'd already made an agreement with Remnick. Last year, at 17:52 in the afternoon on 21 April 2009, I took some photographs of the *Paşabahçe* as it sailed past me. In the afternoon we met in the museum with Brigitta, the girls, and Cem. It's very hot. But I am pleased with the way the building looks now, and the colors too. Still, that habitual anguish continues to shadow my every thought. Although I enjoy musing over its intricacies, the Museum has diverted me from the novel. But I can still say I have lost only very little of my enthusiasm.

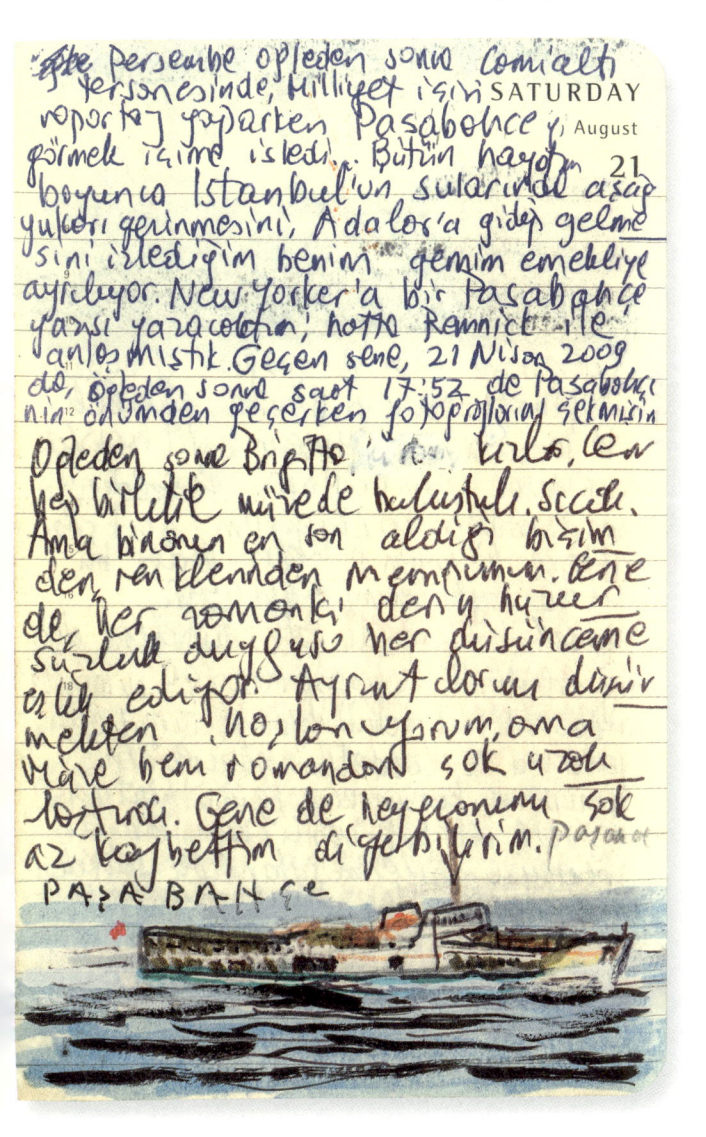

PAŞABAHÇE

I remain under the spell of yesterday's TRIP TO BURSA. They have done an excellent job of preserving the historic center. The GRAND MOSQUE has been skillfully restored. The KOZA Caravansary was equally impressive. You can still feel the presence of that poetry TANPINAR found in the city and the courtyards of its mosques. To be able to see so much at just a short day trip's distance from Istanbul is quite remarkable. I remember coming here at the start of the 1960s, armed with this same sense of HISTORY and of the OTTOMAN past, and visiting all the mausoleums from the early Ottoman period. The OTTOMAN age as embodied in BURSA is no empire yet: it is a finer, more delicate silk cocoon.

In Bursa we also talked about the silk production industry

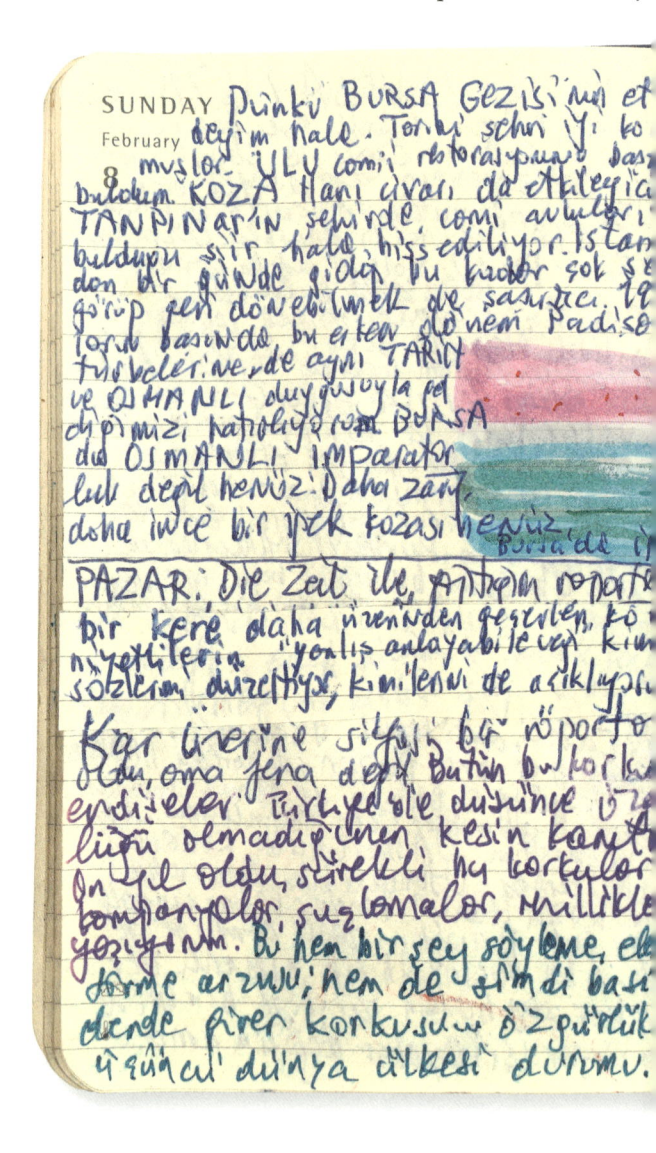

SUNDAY: going over my interview with *Die Zeit* again to revise a few comments that might be willfully "misinterpreted" by more hostile readers, and to clarify some others. It has turned into a political interview about *Snow*, but it's quite good. Ultimately, all these worries and anxieties are proof that in Turkey there is no such thing as freedom of expression. It's been ten years and I am still living with this fear, still dealing with these campaigns and smears and accusations. It is a combination of the urge to speak out, to criticize; and the fear that I might get into trouble—that feeling which is so typical of Third World countries lacking in freedom . . .

When I look out at the view and spot a familiar ship sailing in the distance, it changes the way I see both the ship and the view itself. As I observe the vessel from afar, I can begin to recall what it looks like inside, the seats, how it has carried me across Istanbul before on the way to the Princes' Islands and along the Bosphorus. The ship becomes a pretext for reflecting on landscape and memories.

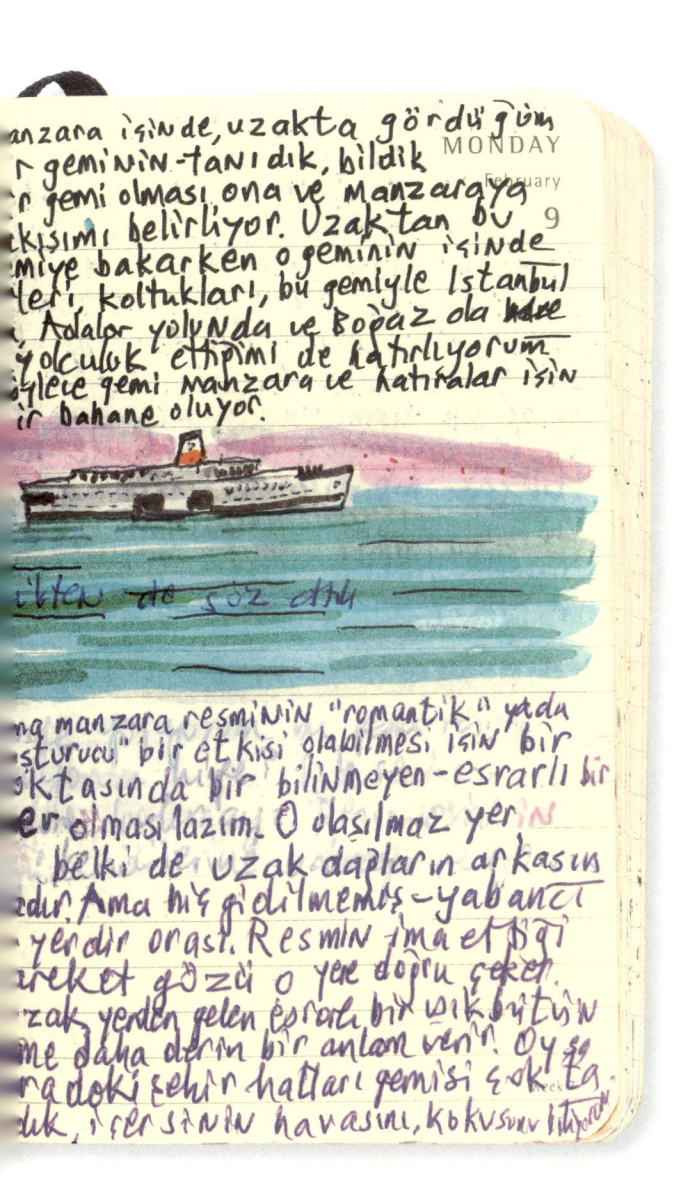

But if landscape painting is to have a "romantic" or "exhilarating" effect, it must make room for the unknown—for somewhere that remains mysterious. Perhaps this place beyond reach lies just behind those distant mountains. It is a place not traveled to—somewhere foreign. The sense of movement conveyed by the painting draws the viewer's eye toward that place, and a mysterious light spreading out from that faraway spot imbues the painting with a deeper significance. But the City Lines ferry drawn here is utterly familiar; I know how it feels, how it smells inside.

inside the tree—far away
please don't look this way
run away as quick as you can—hide it—over here
don't look toward the window

hold on to your ticket don't lose it
run—all of you run away
beyond the edge of the pavement
there's the sea
careful, you might fall
a ship a ship Turgut Uyar
those same men are chasing me again

ONE DAY a SHIP APPEARS IN

It's not your turn yet . . .

Don't look

BECAUSE everyone's gone LIKE IN A DREAM

    I found that ship at the last abandoned pier
    after the plague the fires begin
    BE AFRAID

                                                                   burn, burn!

    you get out, BE AFRAID

                                                                  there's no one there

    the ticket booth is shut   over here   the dog's not there, it's gone
    everyone's gone yes I'm afraid
    there is more I have to say   I haven't yet managed to hide.
    yes I'm afraid
    of the dark brown night.
    it's not for you

MY DREAM . . .

Don't look   the dogs are coming . . .

Mr. Painter's greatest wish was to be able to see the things he always saw in a completely different way. If he could only succeed in this, his ordinary life would be transformed into a New Life. But to be able to do this, he would have to turn into a new person. In painting the same landscape over and over again, Mr. Painter was striving to become a new person. That is why he would have to paint the view he saw every day as if it were an ENIGMA.

I have been rereading the section where Samiha runs away with Ferhat, and I am rather pleased and happy with it. I find it more enjoyable when a novel's protagonist is like Samiha—stubborn, always doing the opposite of what you'd expect, hot tempered, foolhardy. I like showing the darker side of people and of the city . . . I decided yesterday that I've done enough work on the Updike article for now, so I've taken a break from it. But I've already spent so much time today going over older chapters that had already been typed up that I never got around to writing anything new. I swam in the pool at Küçük Çiftlik Park for seventy minutes. In the evening Pollina introduced us to Sabri Gürses, who translates Russian and American literature. We had a friendly, convivial meal at the Karaköy restaurant.

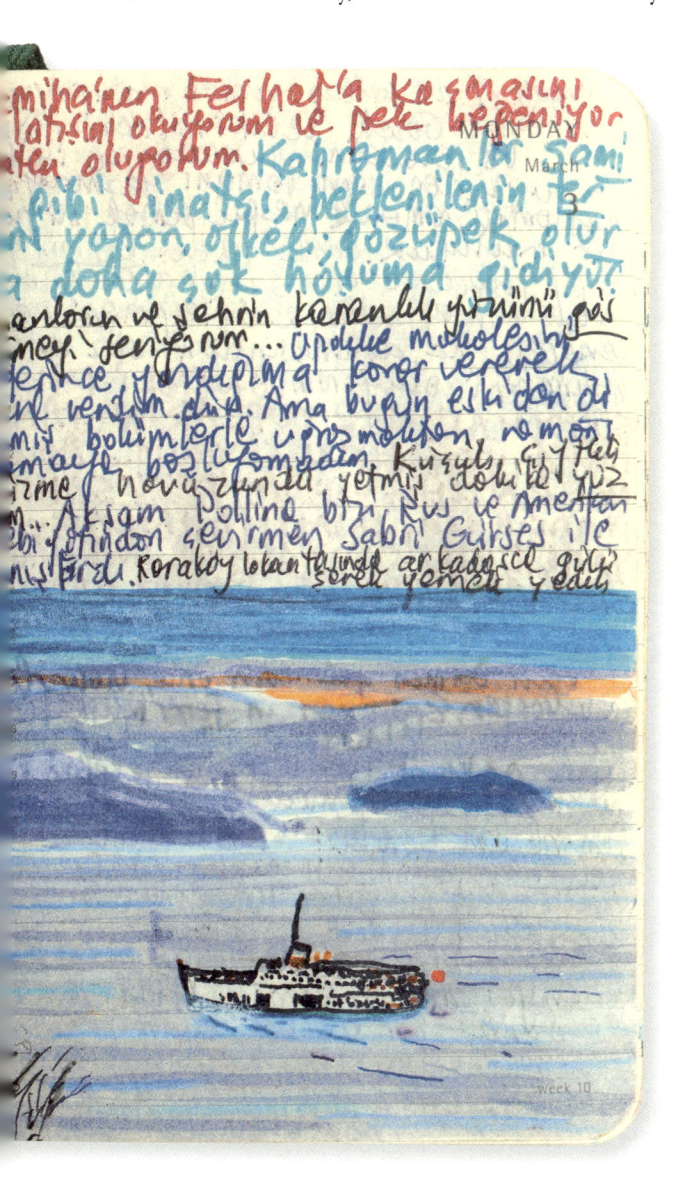

I first read the *Confessions* in one sitting during a 10-hour train journey... and was transformed.

I was thinking of using that line from Rousseau! A son who quarrels with his mother is always wrong... As the epigraph for part III of the novel. It was in the Penguin edition of the CONFESSIONS; I'd marked it out; but I left my copy in NY! In the afternoon, about 2 hours ago, I took some photos of Rüya as she was writing her novel. Then I said: "Now you take some of me. Today is a very special day, I'm about to finish *The Red-Haired Woman*."

At the end of the day, Rüya was ready to leave and I still hadn't finished the novel, but it was in wonderful shape, and I was elated. I read out all the new pages I wrote to Aslı in the morning and Rüya in the afternoon. They both really liked them. What I'm most worried about now that I'm nearing the end of the novel is the Red-Haired Woman's closing MONOLOGUE.

In the middle of the night, I listen to the sound of foghorns and write the final sentences of *The Red-Haired Woman.* To be at home among my books! I don't want to travel anymore. The Joseph Cornell effect. It seems to be transforming my soul, my whole outlook on life. I like winter in Istanbul, its black-and-white feel. I would like to write about Cornell, read all his journals. The pleasures of rekindling my admiration for a WRITER, AN ARTIST I USED TO LOVE twenty years ago.

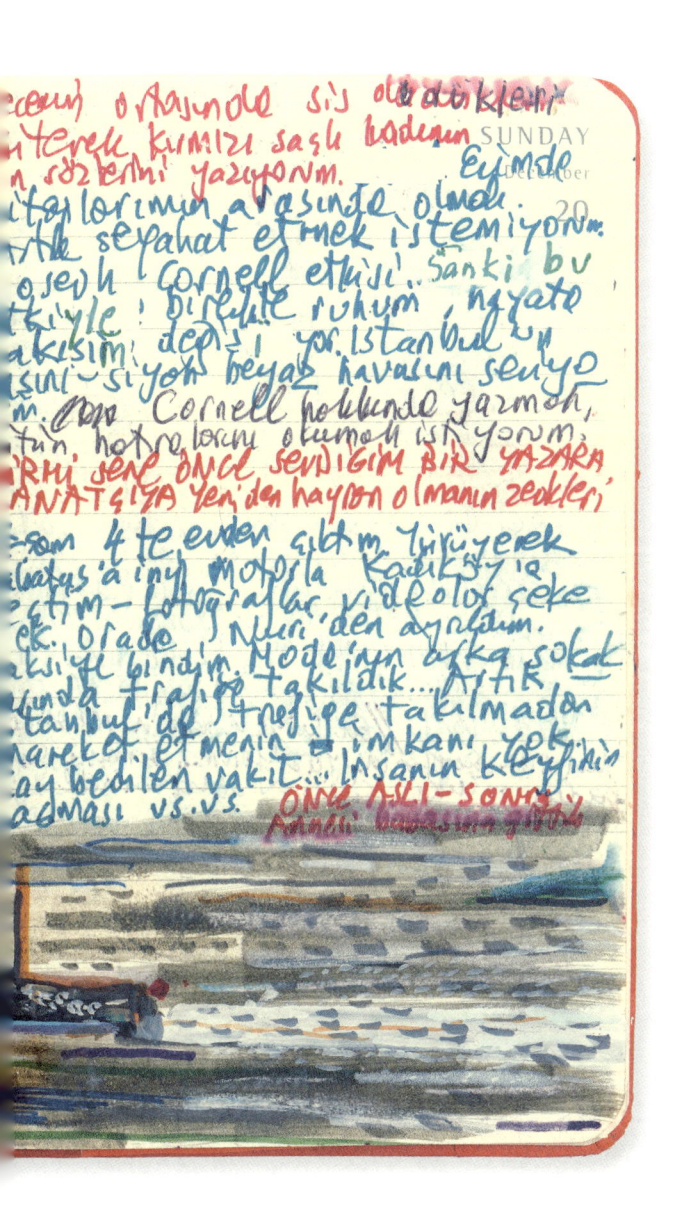

I left the house at 4 in the afternoon. I walked down to Kabataş and crossed over to Kadıköy on a fast ferry—taking photographs and videos along the way. There I parted with Nuri. I got in a taxi. We got stuck in traffic in the backstreets of Moda . . . These days you can't get anywhere in Istanbul without running into traffic . . . Wasted time, frustration, etc. etc.

ASLI first—then on to visit her parents

Woke up early to go through the first few chapters of the Norton book. Feeling both hopeful and jaded. Necessary for these Norton Lectures I'm working on . . . And a neat summary of my life right now: MUSEUMS AND NOVELS. Perhaps I should try explaining what I mean the other way around. I use a series of stories to create a novel. I use a series of objects to create a museum. Both are telling the same tale. The museum is wearing me out and causing me great distress. It's taking away hours I might have otherwise happily spent writing. This whole endeavor could easily have been happier and more enjoyable than it has been. At the very least it shouldn't have been something that made me so miserable; but I haven't managed to avoid that. I've been ground down by the sheer amount of work involved, and by the machinations and grasping calculations of certain so-called "artists." I would have liked to be more philosophical in making my philosophical museum . . .

Some trees and houses
houses here

bird

bird

bird

bird

Gregor, Brigitta, Johanna, our family of architects, arrived at 10 carrying an enormous model, this time on a ¹/₁₀ scale. Impressive and beautiful! I finally believed that the museum will be finished and open someday. Still lots of work to do though! We discussed fire escapes, shutters; Füsun's 4,212 cigarettes in the lobby; how to arrange the attic, etc. Cem Yücel and Murat were also there. At lunch—as usual—we had one of Sermin's salads... How thrilling to study the model and talk about banisters, the placement of the 56 Chevrolet, etc. But by the end of the day I am always tired. I don't even have the strength to answer emails. Afterward we all went out to eat at the Karaköy restaurant...

                                                  bird   bird
                                                    behind
                                       the distant mountains

        bird   hidden
             bird   bird

My hand unconsciously adds these notes while I'm thinking of something else.
One part of my mind is on the ship—the *Paşabahçe*
Another part of my mind is watching the paintbrush doing things of its own accord

Unfortunately it seems the whole world has made a habit of chasing Mr. Painter in his dreams. And Mr. O is always fleeing. As he strides briskly forward he notices how much he has left behind. He has become accustomed to running away from everything and everyone.

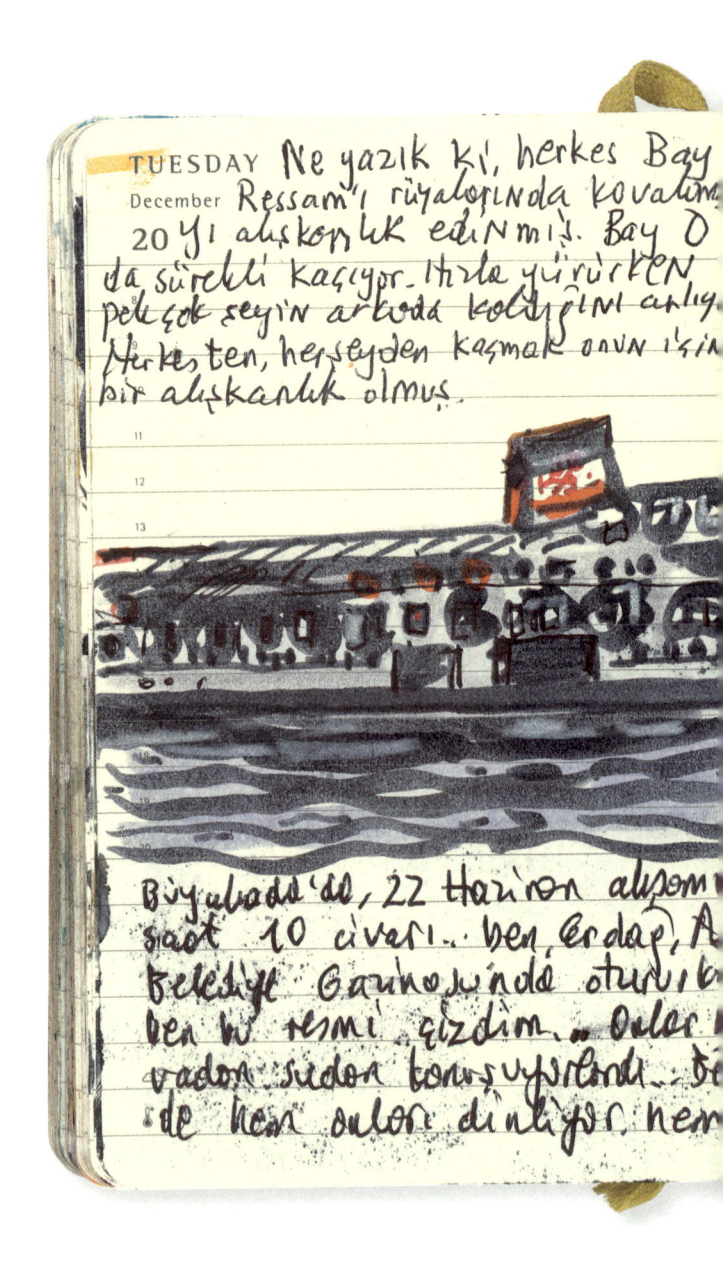

Büyükada, 22 June, approaching 10 in the evening... Erdağ, Aslı, and I were sitting at the Municipal Café when I drew this picture. They were chatting. I was listening to their conversation and drawing in this notebook at the same time. We had moved to Büyükada the day before. The island is empty: local business

So when he approaches the edge of the cliff—the slope—he feels no trace of fear. On the contrary, he knows that he need only climb down to the hawk's nest below to find the answers to all his questions.

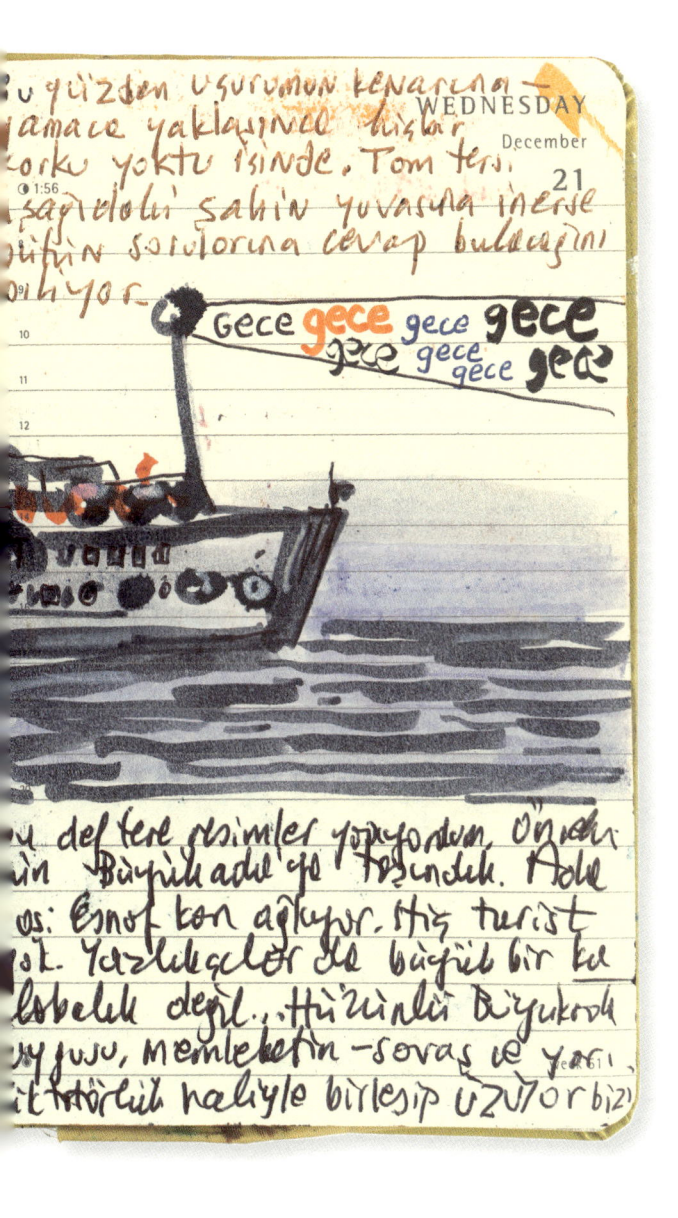

Night night night night night night night night

owners are desperate. There are no tourists. There aren't that many people summering here either . . . This Büyükada melancholy mixes with the nation's warlike, semidictatorial mood—leaving us dejected.

When I saw the film *Trainspotting*, I realized that during all these years I've also been counting ships from my office as they cross the Bosphorus. But my aim is not to while the hours away, quite the opposite: it is AS IF I were trying to convince myself that THE WORLD is as it should be.

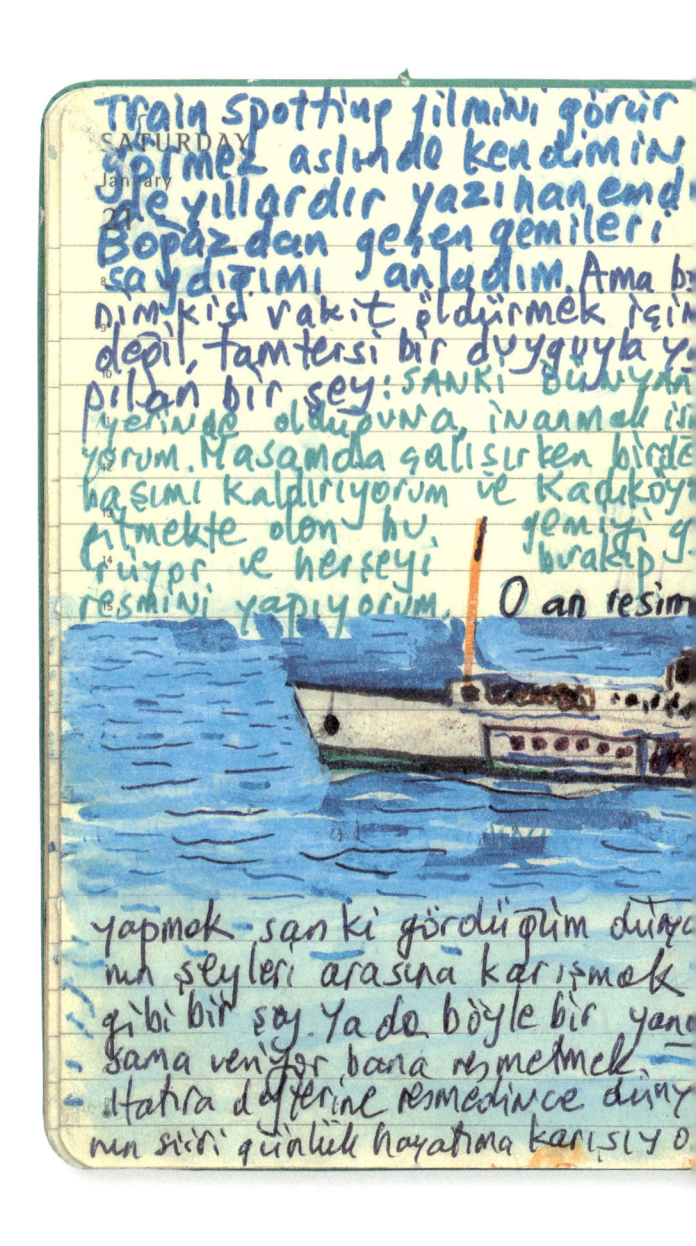

I am working at my desk when I look up to see this ferry making its way to Kadıköy, whereupon I drop everything I'm doing and begin to paint it. In that moment, the act of painting feels like a way of intermingling with all the things that inhabit the world before me. Or at any rate that's the illusion that painting creates in me. When I draw in my journals, the poetry of the world seeps into my day-to-day life.

I like how Joseph Cornell writes in his diaries that it's been a sunny day today. There are some dreams that he keeps having and writing about over and over again. But is the dream we dream the same as the dream we describe in words? Dreams are not ekphrastic. Dreams cannot be described, only felt . . . The only way to transpose the mood of a dream onto paper is to paint it in watercolor.

My literary heroes who were known to keep a diary: TOLSTOY; THOREAU; WOOLF; CORNELL. To be like Thoreau and write everything down. Then to return like a ship to the same diary page

All the distant piers

The sound of waves lapping gently at the shore

I like visiting distant piers at night
let us listen to the sound of our own footsteps

you hear Istanbul's smallest details

and the generator of a ship
folk songs on a radio that's been left on

People
at a coffeehouse

The last Pier

> the captain is watching
> TV in his cabin

Let us look closer at those ships that have docked for the night, washed and cleaned by deckhands who sleep there too

> distant mountains

Sitting at my desk at 8:30 in the morning, trying to finish the Norton volume's section on images, when... I notice the *Paşabahçe* arriving at Kabataş from the Princes' Islands. One hour later I photograph it as it heads back (it's around 9:30). In the afternoon we sit down with Önder and Murat and talk through the museum box by box.

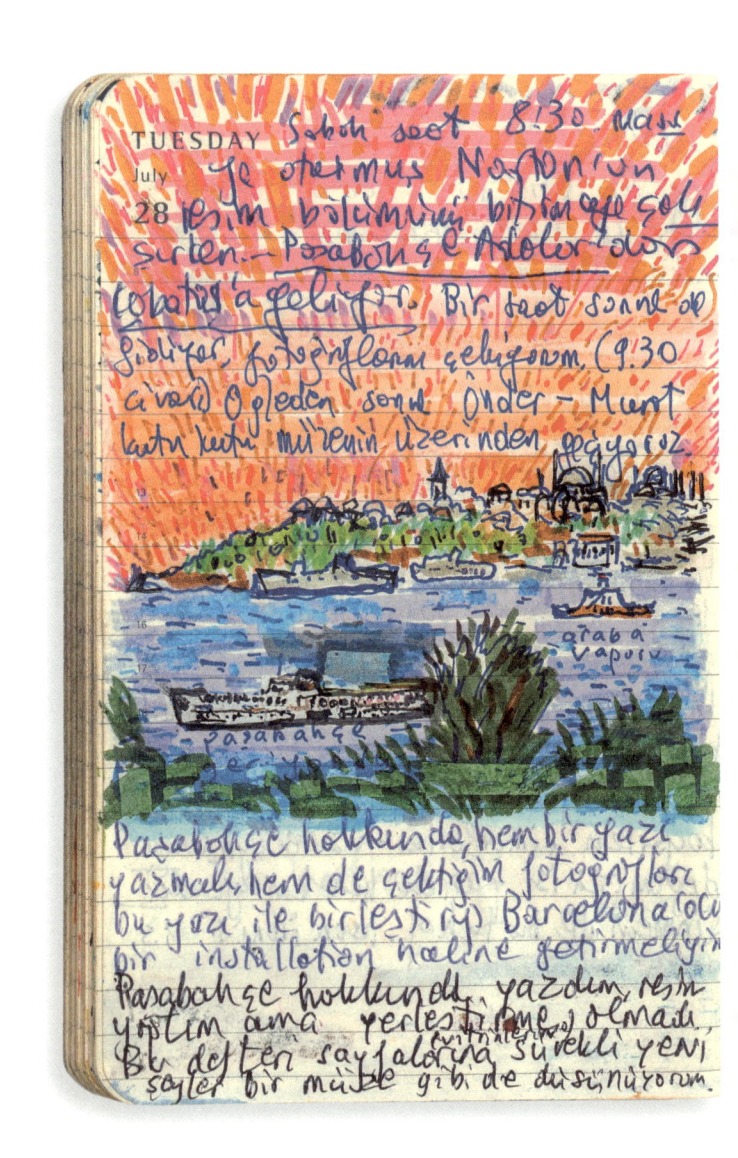

car ferry

the *Paşabahçe*

I should write an essay about the *Paşabahçe*, then combine that text with the photographs I've taken, and make an installation in Barcelona. I've already written about and painted the *Paşabahçe*, but I've never arranged any of those materials in that way. Sometimes I think of this notebook as a museum whose pages (the vitrines) I keep adding new items to.

Rereading the pages where the imam marries Mevlut and Rayiha, and the scenes from their elopement and the early days of their marriage, I'm finding the novel a little too light, a little too humanistic, and I'm beginning to think I should perhaps shorten these sections. I'm already imagining what will happen when Mevlut comes face-to-face with Ferhat returning from military service on his wedding day, and when Ferhat sees Rayiha… Writing a novel is at once to remember and to imagine. As I read through these overly naïve and idealistic passages, I can see that the thing which will make *A Strangeness in My Mind* enjoyable and easy to read is: having EVERYONE'S PERSPECTIVE—A MULTIPLICITY OF NARRATORS—DESCRIBING AND BEING ABLE TO FOLLOW WHAT EVERYONE IS DOING AT THE SAME TIME. Now, time to turn to all the horrors Ferhat witnesses during his military service! Rüya came by. I read her a random sentence from *Anna Karenina*.

Can Öz called just now (the time is 11:10). Says he is starting a new classics series at Can Publishing, and asks if I'd like to be the editor.
Some bad news. Ugh! Ugh. We've had a falling-out with the director of the museum, Esra… I've been annoyed with her since… September, for not having a proper handle on the figures. She's the one who suggested she should resign… The call did not go well! In the evening, I asked Aslı for advice.
    It was my own idea to make this museum. What can I do?

I am sure that somewhere in Gökova there are skies and waves and mountains like these. I'm imagining them now. Then I will become a ship.

I've been thinking the wrong things all day. I must be a ship that thinks the wrong things

It's a mistake to expect every day to have meaning... We experience moments, time passes, and, little by little, the dream we call life begins to fade. A ship sails. Look at the ship and dream of starting from scratch... If I could just be a wave. Yes

I sat at my desk as the landscape to my left carved its way into me like a ray of light. There was lots of time. Time to write and draw.

In the morning, another ship ... blowing its horn long and hard. I'm thinking to myself that if all of these fishing boats have gathered here, there must be a school of bluefish passing through. When I was little, whenever such a large school of fish (bluefish, bonito) appeared, street vendors would be out the next day selling fish from their carts, and school cafeterias would serve baked fish and potatoes. I've seen dolphins swimming in the same spot where the fishing boats are today. They come quite close to the shore. There are some amateurs among the fishermen, too.

Eventually I forget about the world and get lost inside my novel. Much later another big boat sounds its horn as it passes by. But the fishermen won't budge, and the captain loses his temper, blowing his horn again and again. Soon another ship joins in with its own horn. I can see the fishermen in their boats from my desk. There are a couple of boats with only a lone fisherman on board. The ships continue to blow their echoing horns.

Very strange to feel so deep inside the novel. It's like the novel is me. And I'm a landscape. This notebook seems to be protecting me. It might also be hindering me from giving enough of myself to the novel. A nice article, "Orhan Pamuk's Istanbul," out in *The New York Times*. I spent four hours walking around the city with Joshua. I took him to all the places I like, Balat, Fatih, Vefa, the backstreets of Karaköy. I've learned by now how to show other people around Istanbul, and tell them stories about what they're seeing. Sunny day. A lovely morning with Aslı. At 9:30 I sat down to write. Come on, Mevlut. I write nonstop all day. At a gallop. Mevlut is about to elope with Rayiha. I spend the evening alone. Aslı has gone across to the other side to visit her aunt and aunt's husband.

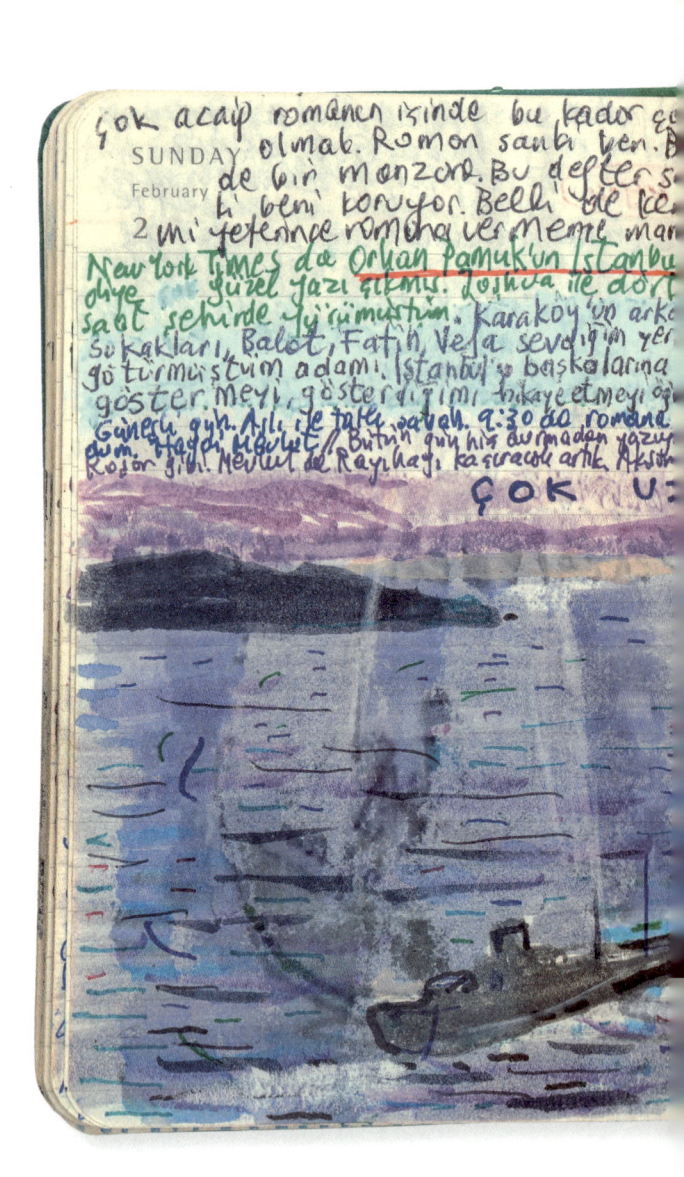

VERY FAR AWAY

Come on, Mevlut. You and Süleyman must run away with Rayiha within the next few pages now. This section definitely needs shortening. I've been writing and writing and Mevlut still hasn't eloped... He's about to do it, but now I'm tired. I was just thinking I'd have a drink to drown my sorrows. Then Aslı arrived... her father's illness is getting worse. She's not in a good mood either. We decided to get out of the house. Thank goodness for the old bookshops in the ASLIHAN ARCADE. We began digging around. We picked up four or five books. I couldn't carry any more, so they'll deliver the rest to the museum. The bookshops did us a world of good... Now we're at the Şehir (City) Tavern. It's a charming little spot right by the street that leads to the Greek consulate and the historical Galatasaray Hamam. Drinking and talking with Aslı. You're doing such a good job with it, well done, she says about the novel. She's doing it to cheer me up.

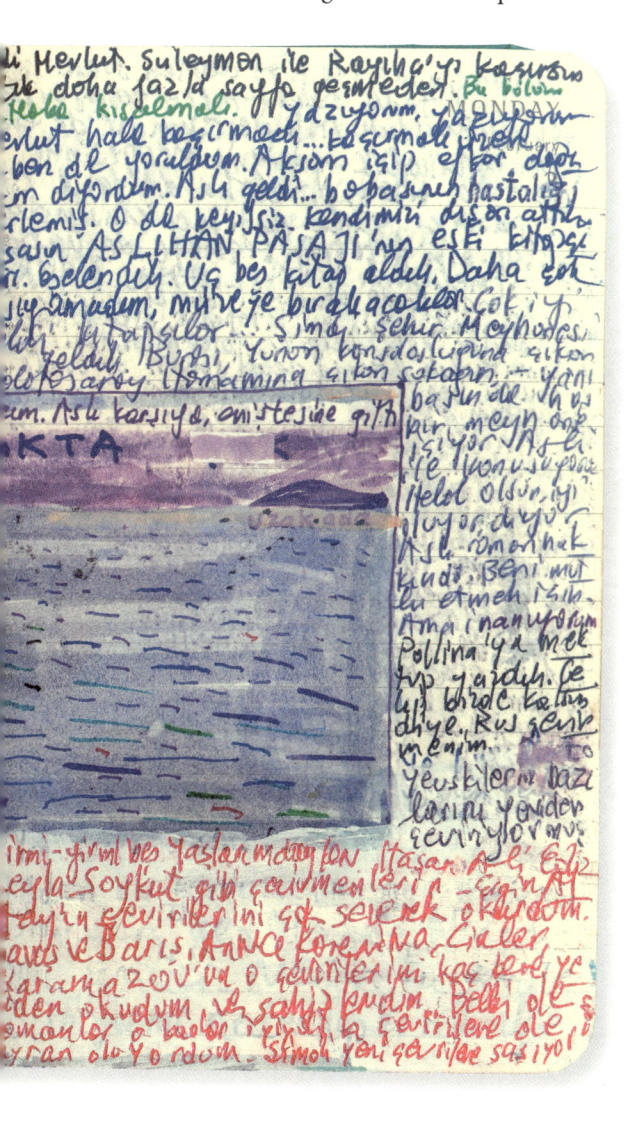

But I believe her. We wrote to Pollina. Invited her to stay with us. She's my Russian translator. I heard they're doing new translations of some Dostoyevskys. In my early to midtwenties I remember reading and loving various translations by Hasan Ali Ediz, Leyla Soykut, Ergin Altay. I read their translations of *War and Peace, Anna Karenina, Demons, Karamazov* over and over again, made them my own. Maybe the original novels were so good that I ended up revering the translations too. Now I'm amazed every time I hear of a new translation.

This is the view Ka saw from the eagle's—or perhaps it was a hawk's—nest. He felt safe there.

But reaching this place did not mean that the MYSTERY was solved . . . He began to feel impatient. An emotion had turned to color, and spread all over.

The world is adorned with beauty where lovers walk;
At your threshold, I gaze at the world mad and intoxicated.
                                                    Bâkî

On 4 May 2019
—we're back in ISTANBUL. Things to do upon return
—Monday: manuscript to YKY for typing
—mid-MAY title meeting // Location, map meeting
I'm roughly 260 pages into the NOVEL
JUNE / Beginning / Up to EID holiday: 30 pages of the book = 50 notebook pages
JUNE: 60 notebook / 40 book = tot. 330 book

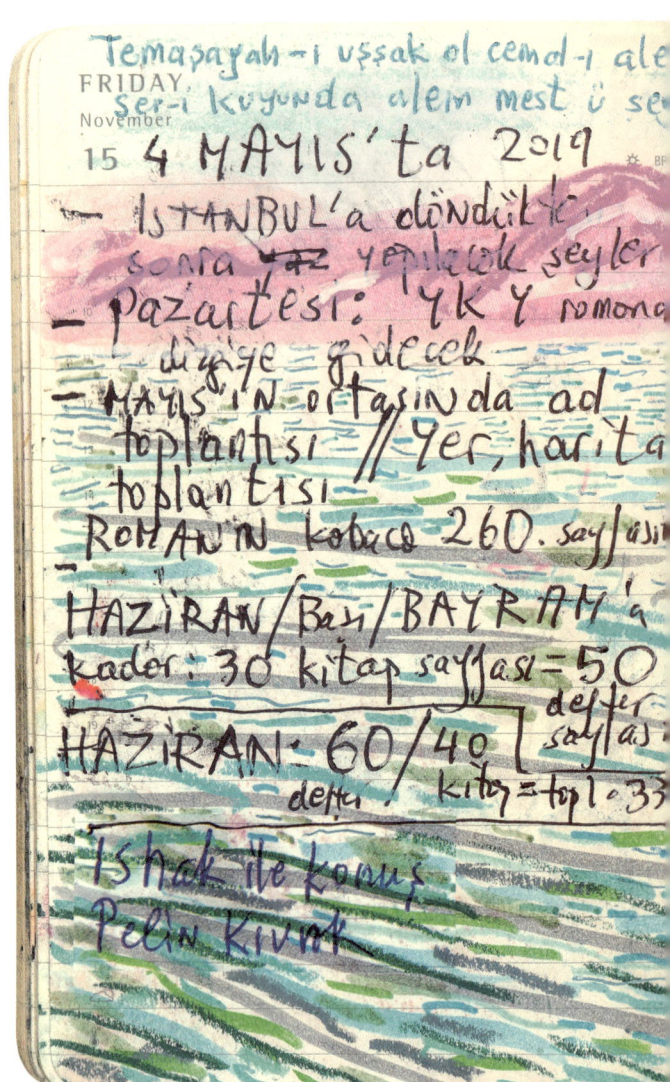

Talk to Ishak
Pelin Kıvrak

I'm on page 260 of the NOVEL

The first Kafka story I ever read,

YOU HAVE ALREADY DONE SO WELL

The dream / movie hero opens his eyes and sees the page you are looking at now. You are looking at the picture. He is in the sea . . .

he lifts his head out of the water

"In the Penal Colony," also takes place on an island.

TO COME THIS FAR.

The sound of the waves, like whispered murmurs, makes the swimmer feel alive as he slowly approaches the island.

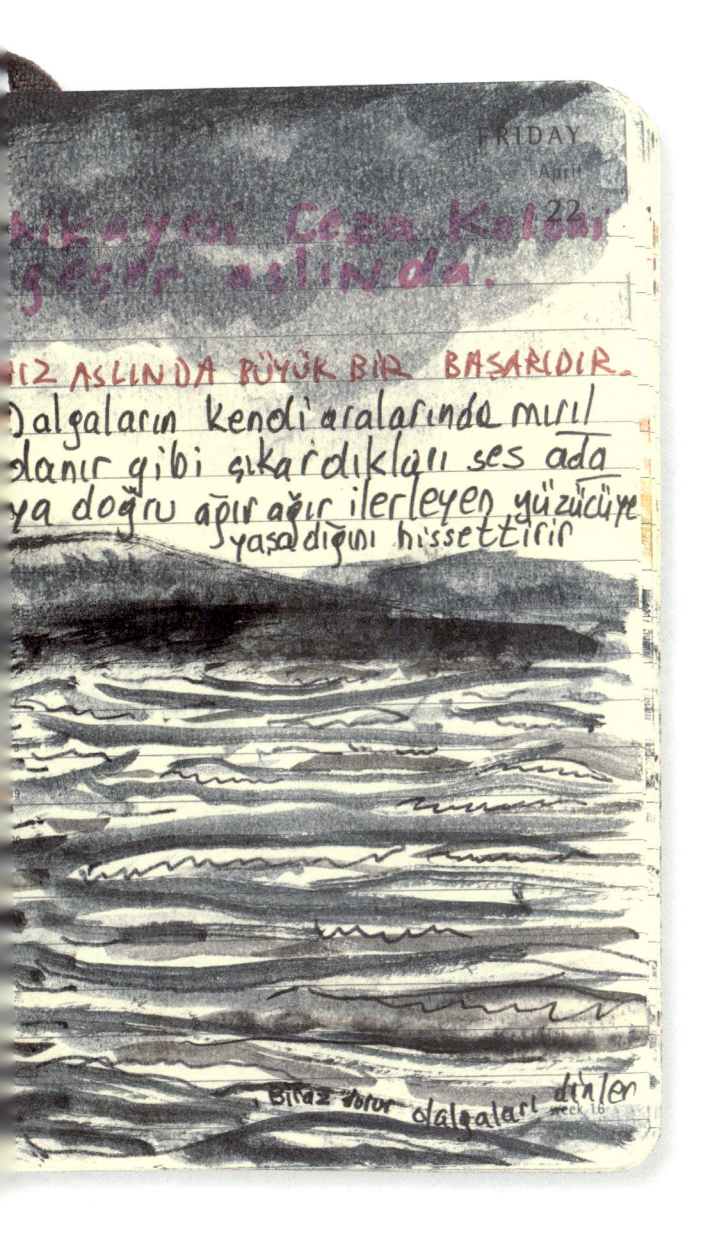

He stops awhile and listens to the waves

THE CURRENT HAD BROUGHT THEM to a place like this.

> TUESDAY AKINTI ONLARI
> April en sonunda böyle bir yere
> 15 getirmişti.

They were amazed and afraid, for they did not recall this view . . .

the urge to draw

A bad day: I couldn't get any work done. A pointless argument with Aslı wrecked my chemistry. I squandered a whole precious day like so much loose change. Alone at home, stewing in my own self-inflicted gloom
When you return to the same page with your (red) pen years later, you can't remember what happened that day, the argument you had, the despair you felt. Back then I was a different person. In truth I am a different person every day.

I like writing over it afterward.

I can tell it looks good

there's a current here

but here the waters run

came suddenly

Rüya came by in the afternoon. We spent the day working on our novels, keeping each other company. She is reading Nadine Gordimer... I'm taking notes from Defoe and Camus on quarantine etc. In the evening, we had some lentil soup etc. at home, then picked a movie from among the CDs on the shelf: a Belgian film; the woman trying to convince her colleagues to refuse the boss's offer of more money is so believable... so humane... These are the moments when we display our humanity!

A GLOOMY DRAWING

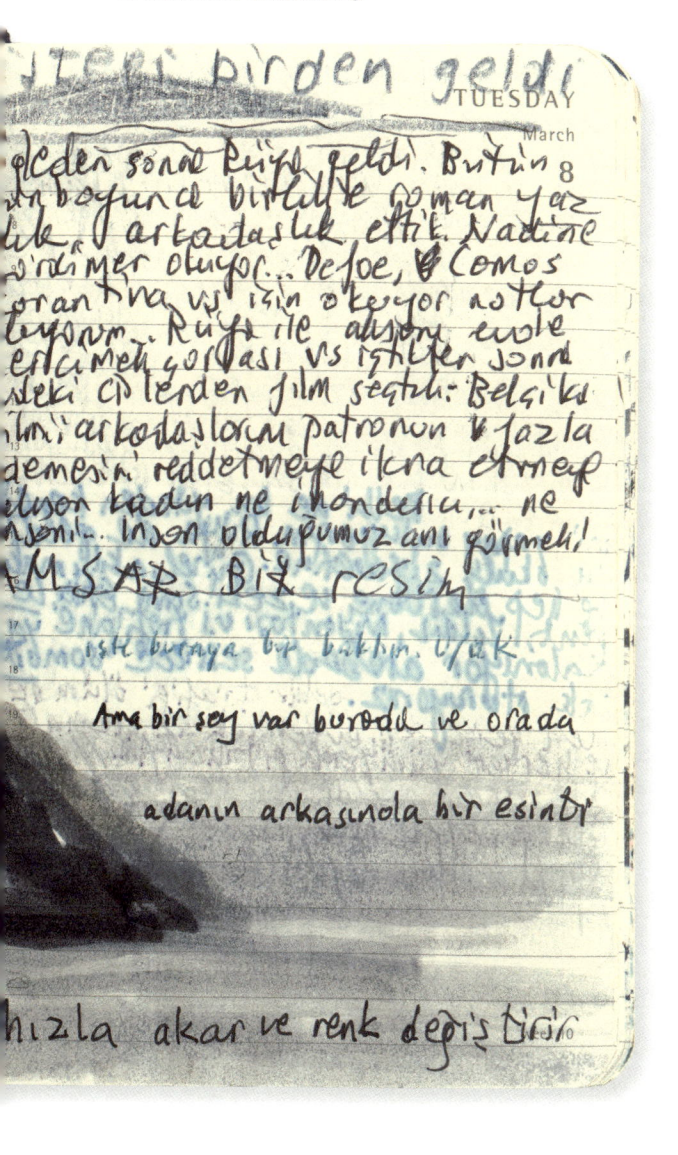

I looked over here.
So small

But there's something here and there

a breeze behind the island

fast and change color

The heat wakes me up soon after midnight. I just want to work on my novels and not see anyone for a few years... I've put writing completely on hold for the past two months. Since... March 15th, in fact... So three months. All I want to do is write, to withdraw into my work. I want to forget about the newspapers (everyone's talking about Deniz Baykal's sex tape scandal), the UK elections (Labour and Gordon Brown have lost), and all the rest, I want to live in a realm of the imagination that is vast, deep, and true... (Midnight, a large ferry's horn echoes across the Bosphorus.) During these three months of not writing anything, I have realized that I'm a novelist through and through. Writing novels means—for me—being able to feel the world in a deeper way than painting can portray...

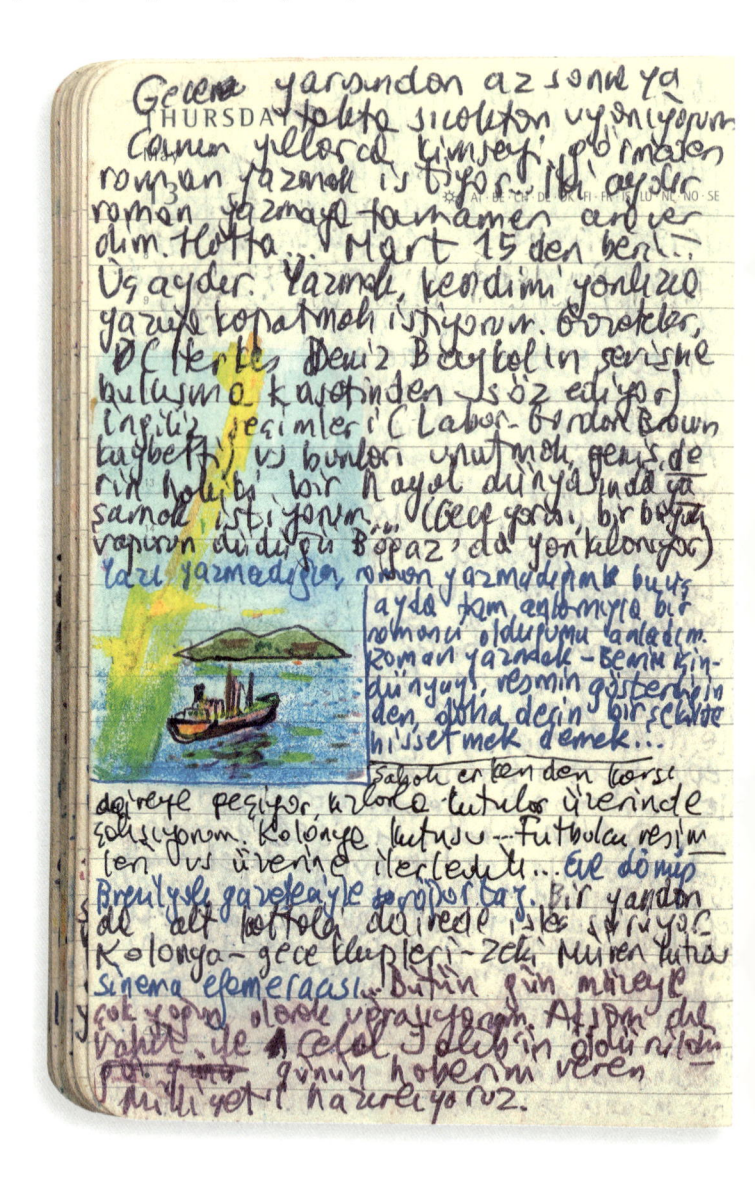

I go over first thing in the morning to the flat opposite to meet with the girls and start working on the displays. The cologne cabinet... Some progress on the footballer cards etc.... Then back home for an interview with a Brazilian journalist. Meanwhile work continues in the flat downstairs. The cologne—nightclubs—Zeki Müren box. Film ephemera... I spend all day working flat out on the museum. Got together with Vahit in the evening to prepare the issue of *Milliyet* reporting the assassination of Celâl Salik.

I have as many personalities as I have moods. With every new mood, I become a new person. When I become a new person, I marvel at my old thoughts, and struggle to recognize them ... How fast the focus of my thoughts seems to shift these days. I am becoming a different person all the time.

The shiver of the sea as we quietly approach the island . . . The smell of damp and limestone exuding from the rocks. Noticing the birds' eerie screeching begin to fade, and knowing that countless sets of eyes are fixed on the approaching boat . . .

We'd said we'd wait until morning to go to the island . . .
It's morning now.

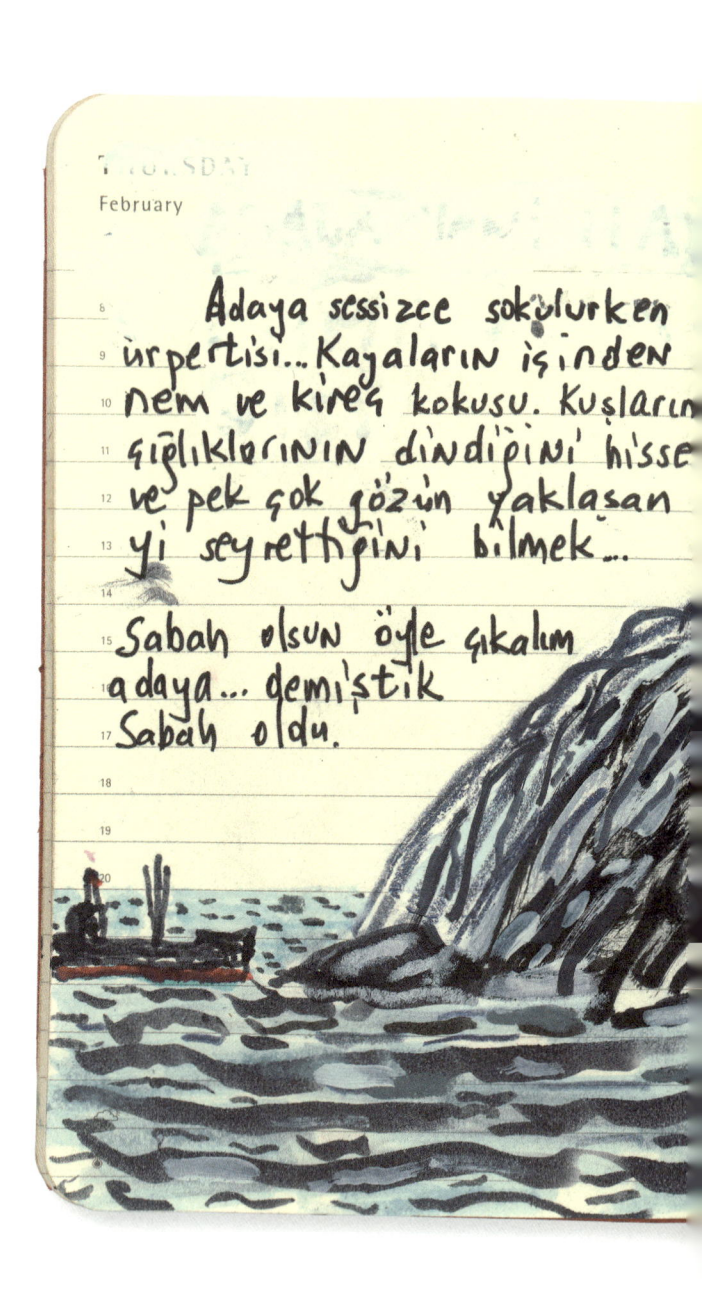

enizin
elen
vhaj
k
mi

An hour and fifteen minutes left until Monday. I've come to Bostancı pier in a taxi from Cihangir. Cihangir is very hot and humid. The smell of dust. Lovely Merve, the IT expert, came by today. We've saved somewhere around 30–40 thousand photographs I've taken over the past two years and transferred them onto a portable hard drive, and in the meantime we've also been going through these archives looking for photos to use for the promotion of *The Naïve and the Sentimental Novelist*. Orhan with Harvard intellectuals, Orhan delivering his Norton Lectures, things like that. I can't stop thinking of how grumpy I was yesterday and worrying that I might have inadvertently upset Bahar, who is so dear to me. There was quite a breeze on the ferry from Bostancı to Büyükada yesterday, I even took my cap off. No one really looks anymore, they don't care, and neither do I. At least not on the way to Büyükada… or on Büyükada itself… Most of my security concerns have abated now.

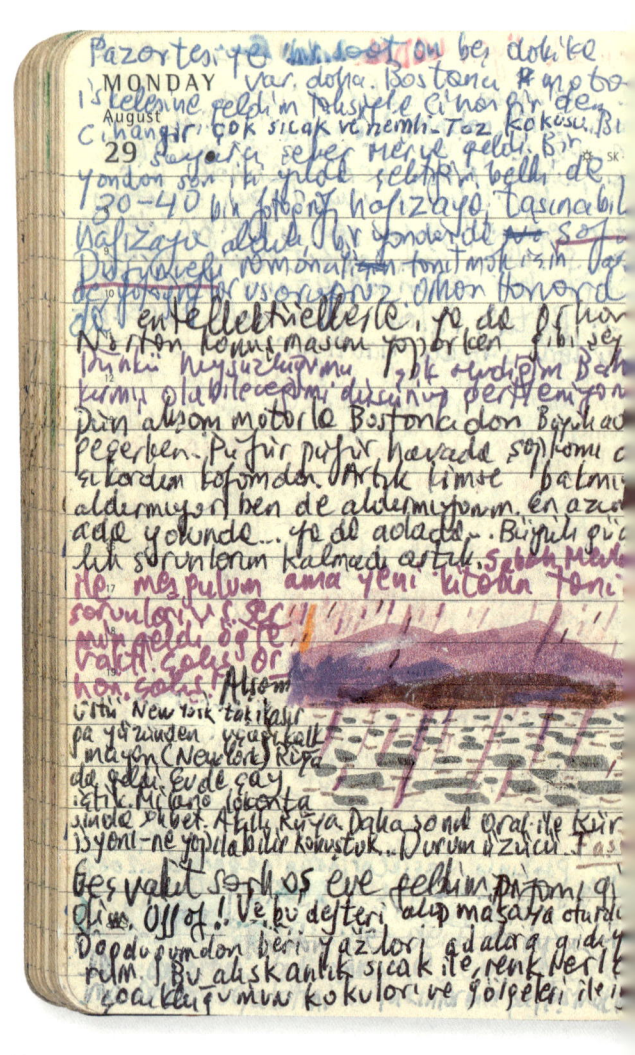

I spend the morning busying myself with Mevlut, but I also need to deal with the promotion of the new book etc. Sermin came around noon. Work, Orhan, work! Rüya, whose flight (to New York) was canceled because of the hurricane in New York, came by in the late afternoon. We had tea at home. Then a chat at the Milano Restaurant. Clever Rüya. Later, talked to Oral about the Kurdish insurgency—and what can be done… An unfortunate situation.

The fascistic Turkish bourgeoisie do not know how to be moderate, and how to treat the Kurds like brothers. And the likelihood that they'll learn is rather slim.

Came home late and drunk, put my pajamas on. Oof! Took out this notebook and sat at my desk. I've been going to the Princes' Islands ever since I was born. It's a habit tied to hot weather, to color, to the smells and shadows of my childhood…

An embarrassment!

Chilly morning! Leaden sky. Had just sat at my desk in my pajamas, making good progress with Mevlut, when I found myself writing in this notebook. Eid al-Fitr tomorrow. Silence. Seagulls. "Calm down, Orhan!" I wrote. That should be the title, the name of this notebook. Should the things I've written here be published someday, that is. There are some passages, certain fears, worries, political frustrations . . . that it may not be possible to publish right away, but perhaps a selection could be made. Still, I'm not thinking about any of that as I write in here. I write in here because it makes me happy to do so. Because I don't want to forget. The day always feels more thoroughly lived, more real, when I fill up a notebook page with a record of all its details. Right now I'm writing about Mevlut and Rayiha making love in the dark when he comes home after selling ice cream.

The house is cool. Busy with holiday visitors. People coming . . . People going. Büyükada is dreadfully crowded. Horse-drawn carts, busybodies peering through the door, giggling youths, hawkers—selling corn on the cob, ice cream, sesame bagels. A man touting flip-flops to beachgoers. There are also people selling sodas and Coca-Cola from plastic tubs. A never-ending stream of children. Lots of people sporting permanent scowls. Kids fighting each other, their mothers and fathers nearby. At ten o'clock, a walk down to the pier where the ferries to Bostancı take off. At night Büyükada is empty again, and inscrutable . . . Strange decor. The world is so rich and complicated that whatever I write in this book is a drop in the ocean compared to what I experience every day, the people, the dreams, and all the rest. I would happily sit and write everything down for hours and days on end . . .

I stood out on the balcony at the house in Cihangir with an English journalist once, and pointed out everything we could see. That's Asia over there, I said, Byzantium, the old city, Hagia Sophia, the Black Sea side, the Maiden's Tower,

Still, windless, tranquil sea. The sky is covered in clouds. It'll get warmer if the clouds clear, and then I'll be able to swim. I'm pleased our Turgenev class at Columbia yesterday went so well. It must be nearly fifty years since I last read *Fathers and Sons*. I enjoyed the novel even more this time around, felt the wealthy provincial family and their country estate deep inside of me.

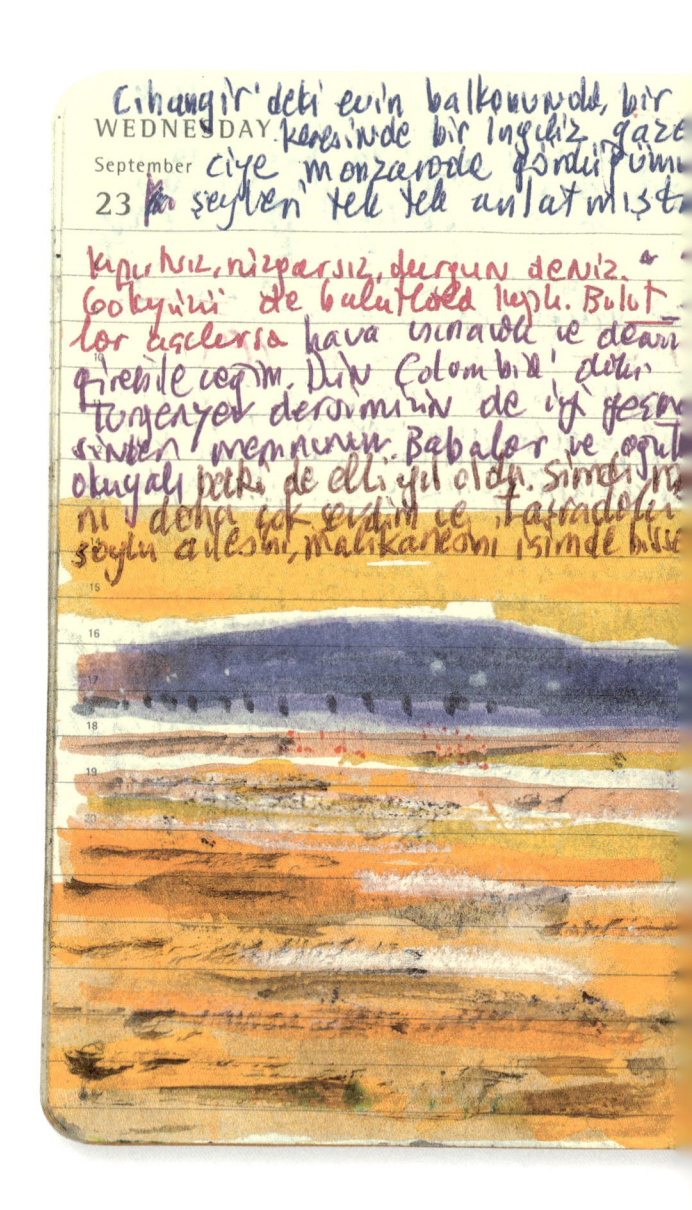

Moda... "What are THOSE DISTANT MOUNTAINS?" he'd asked, indicating the Princes' Islands (the merging silhouettes of Büyükada, Heybeli, Burgaz, and Kınalı).

> I am making a supernatural effort to finish this NOVEL. I keep putting off the need to examine my thoughts/imagination, to interpret what it is that I'm doing here. At sunrise everything is bathed in yellow. As I write this... I can hear Aslı's footsteps pacing about the house, I listen to them, I try to analyze them to see if I can discern her mood. Just like Kemal.

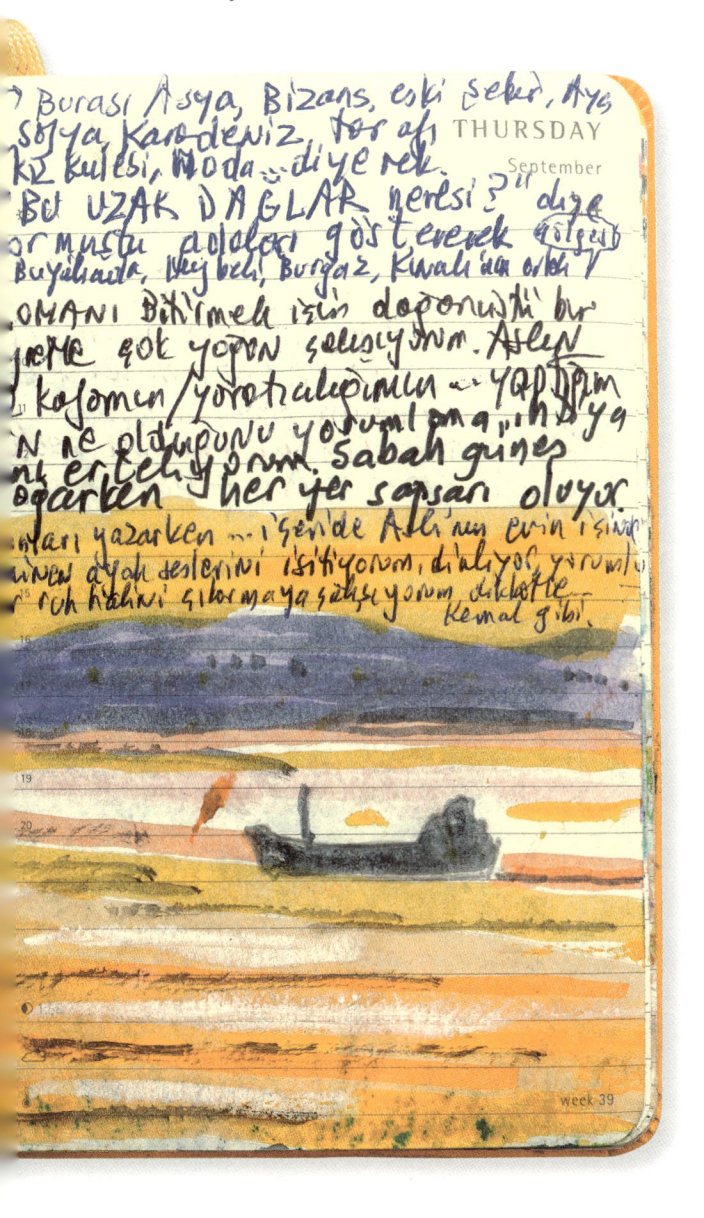

what makes a landscape beautiful is not what it contains, but the emotion it conveys. I love looking out at rusty old ships, forgotten sailboats in distant, secluded seas, boatmen rowing past tiny islands with rocky beaches, the haze forming at the foot of distant mountains, the misty sea, I love letting my gaze run from the top of the view to the bottom, the mountain range before me, and the other mountains behind those

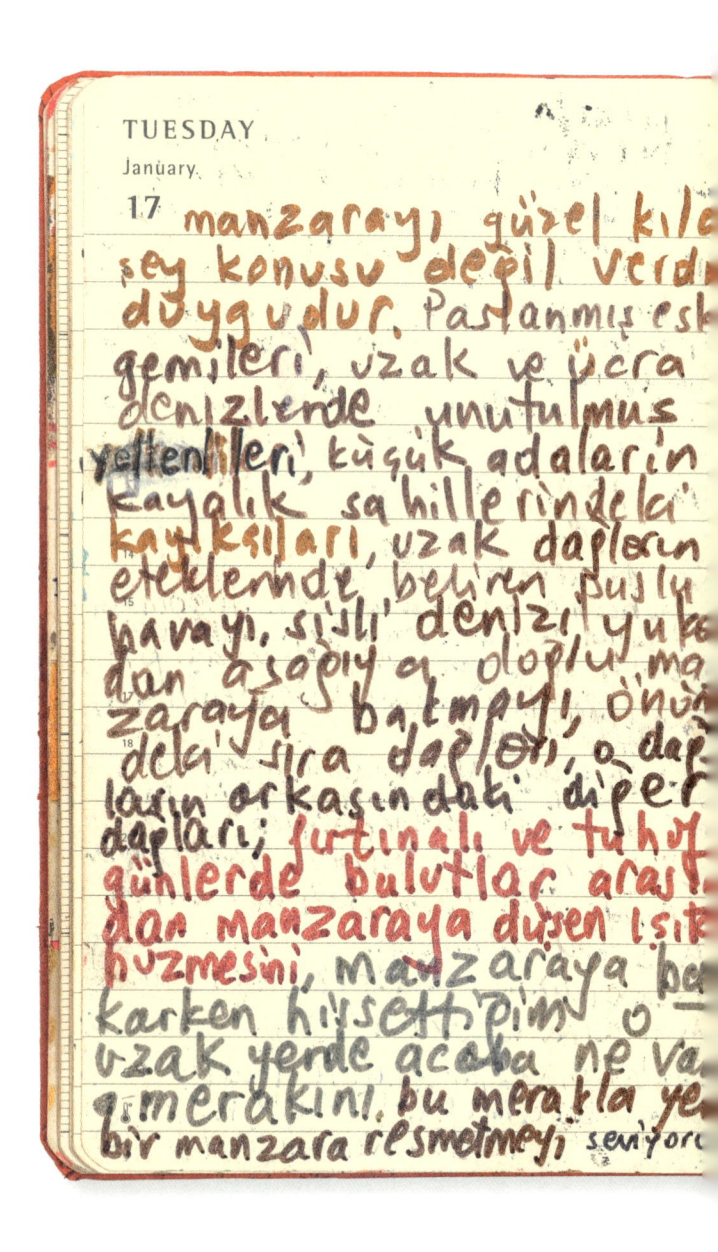

mountains, the beam of light breaking through the clouds and falling upon the landscape on strange stormy days as I ask myself, What's over there in that distant place I can feel when I look at this landscape? and use that curiosity to paint a whole new landscape.

WEDNESDAY
January

2021

In my new novel, the painter K. (the main character) curates exhibitions made up of imaginary paintings by imaginary artists. The *252 Paintings* novel is slowly turning into 252 projects / or dreams . . .

DETAIL FROM BUHARI'S COVER ILLUSTRATION

~~THURSDAY~~
SUNDAY

The exhibition which serves as the basis of the novel will feature K's projects rather than his paintings. One of these will be on the evolution of Ottoman LANDSCAPE PAINTING. Just as I'm doing now, K will pore over the details and the margins of old miniatures held in the Topkapı Palace archives to highlight landscape paintings by Istanbul/Ottoman miniaturists. I first became interested in these paintings when I went looking in the Topkapı Palace for a selection of images—to use in the illustrated edition of *My Name Is Red* and in an exhibition. That is how I first came across this cover illustration by Levni's successor / the WESTERN-influenced Buhari. What is this palace and garden? Is it a real or an invented place? Probably an invented palace inspired by real ones!

As I browse through the many books and catalogs held in the Topkapı Palace—or the Directorate of National Palaces to which it is tied—for materials to use in the ILLUSTRATED MY NAME IS RED, YKY'S exhibition in Galatasaray, and who knows where else, I keep adding more and more volumes to my list. The collector side of me, the dreamer, the part that is constantly fantasizing about new books and museums, is brought to the fore. But then I am disappointed when these dreams do not come true.

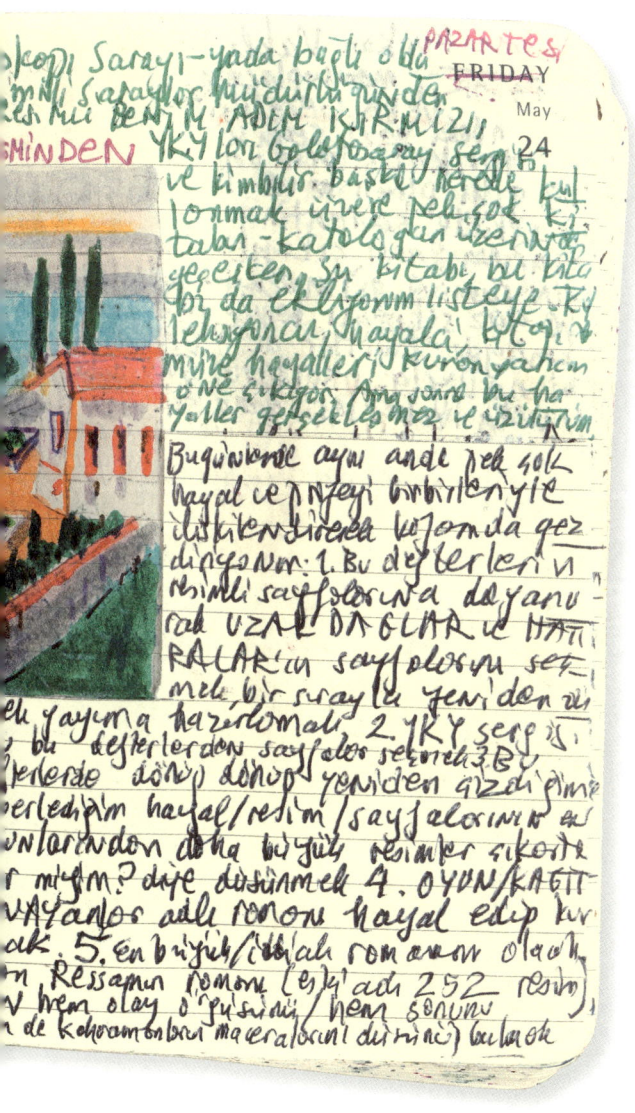

MONDAY
~~FRIDAY~~

These days I am turning many different dreams and projects over in my mind, and drawing connections between them all: 1. Going through the illustrated pages of these journals to select pages for *MEMORIES OF DISTANT MOUNTAINS,* then arranging them in a new sequence and preparing them for publication, 2. Picking a few pages from these notebooks for the YKY exhibition, 3. Wondering whether some of the more dreamlike / illustrated pages I have kept returning to, drawing over them and memorizing them, might be a suitable basis for larger paintings, 4. Planning and picturing the new novel THE CARD GAME / THE CARD PLAYERS, 5. Working out both the plot / and ending and the characters' adventures for what will be my biggest / most ambitious novel yet, *The Painter's Novel* (previously titled *252 Paintings*)

Am I experiencing some kind of intellectual depression? Have I been stupefied by too much work? Yesterday I finally sent DÜNDAR the list of images I hope to receive in digital format from the Topkapı Palace Library. Leafing through a volume on Behzad/Bihzad... I realize there might not be any paintings by Behzad himself in Topkapı. Except perhaps for a handful of indistinct brushstrokes. Genealogies, histories, unusual pages, paintings. This world has me in its peculiar grip.

~~TUESDAY~~
FRIDAY

Notice the shadows of the trees.
Perspective problems

While Aslı is on the phone with Sedef, I'm on the phone with Edhem Eldem, to whom I mention something I've been thinking about for a while: We would do well to publish a dialogue on HISTORY and LITERATURE. On topics like Truth / Fiction / New historicism, etc., with examples from the Ottoman Princes, Murad V, etc.

Things to do / NASA Essay

I am spending my days studying the miniatures in the Topkapı Palace, perusing the pages of the *Shahnama,* and inspecting the wealth of Ottoman art reproduced in this or that volume. I can see myself gradually entering into the realm portrayed by these paintings. And what could be better than getting lost in paintings. I may be the closest person alive to this bygone world.

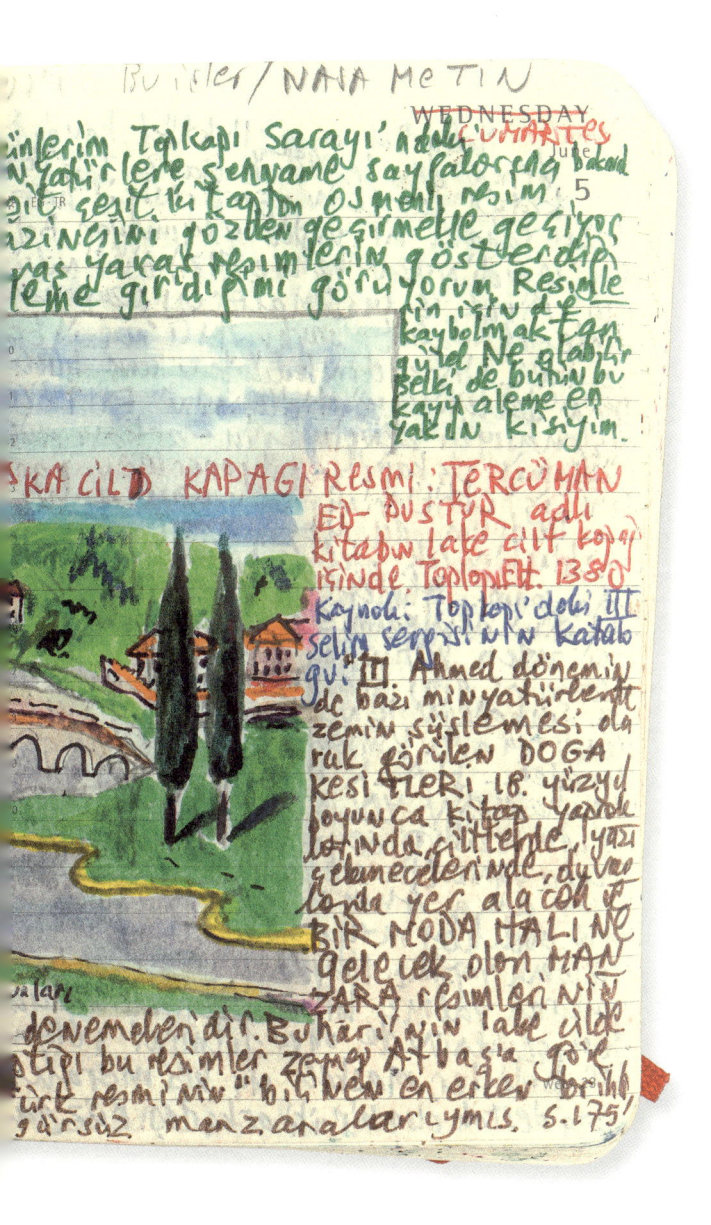

~~WEDNESDAY~~
SATURDAY

ANOTHER BUHARI COVER illustration: part of the lacquered cover of the volume entitled *TERCÜMAN ED-DUSTUR,* item no. 1380 of the Topkapı archives: the catalog of the exhibition on Selim III at the Topkapı Palace: these various SCENES FROM NATURE, which were used as background decoration in some miniatures from the era of Ahmed III, and which began, over the course of the 18th century, to appear on pages, book jackets, walls, and writing desks, soon turning into A KIND OF FASHION, were the earliest attempts at Ottoman LANDSCAPE painting. According to Zeynep Atbaş, Buhari's illustrations on these lacquered book covers are the oldest known examples of unpopulated landscape paintings in "Turkish art," p. 175.

THIS IS HOW *NIGHTS OF PLAGUE* SHOULD BEGIN

painters who paint clouds are actually
        signaling to clouds behind distant mountains
                more roly-poly clouds even farther back

don't know how to finish the picture, keep writing on it instead

water

                every
                drop

The view of a stretch of land from a ship sailing in the waters off an island. Behind the steep rugged mountains is a whole new realm.

                                                  water

                                      water

is a word

        word

When I get out of bed with my mind still in thrall to the lingering fragments of a dream and go down to the shore to dive off the pier and into the sea ... My dreams and the sea seem to mingle.

In the evening, Annie Terrier, who has been running the literature festival in Aix-en-Provence for 35 years, came to Büyükada. Reminiscing about writers like Günter Grass, Philip Roth ... Unfortunately she has no English. I am hoping to get to see Cézanne's studio on 11–13 October. Dark gloomy thoughts in my head. Memories are like sharks prowling my soul

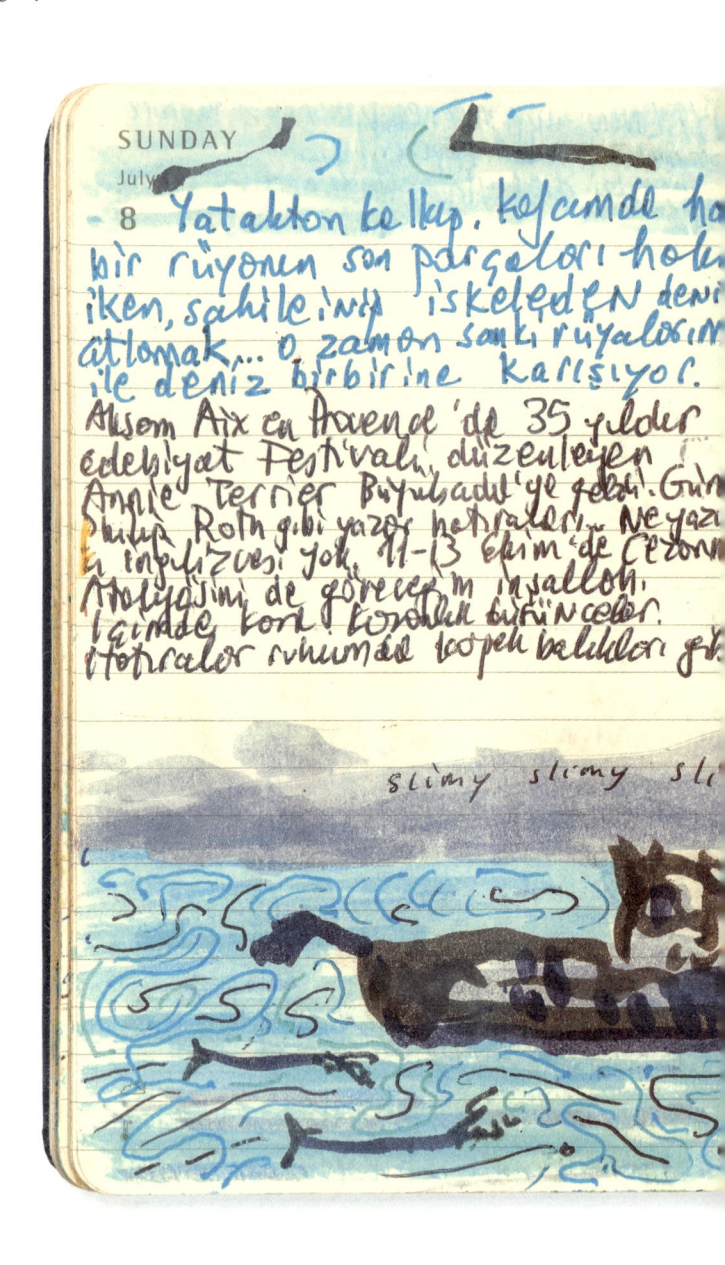

slimy   slimy   slimy

Swimming in the sea. All of a sudden, the feeling that a shark is watching me ... If I could just put it out of my mind, the shark will forget me too. But we can't seem to forget each other. The fearsome sharks lurk as I swim. I can see their tails turning ... When I was a boy, a shark ate a diver in Tuzla, or perhaps: the diver, a very respectable doctor, had sadly taken to dynamite fishing. In his memories, the sea was all sticky ...

Sticky, sticky sea. Viscosity?

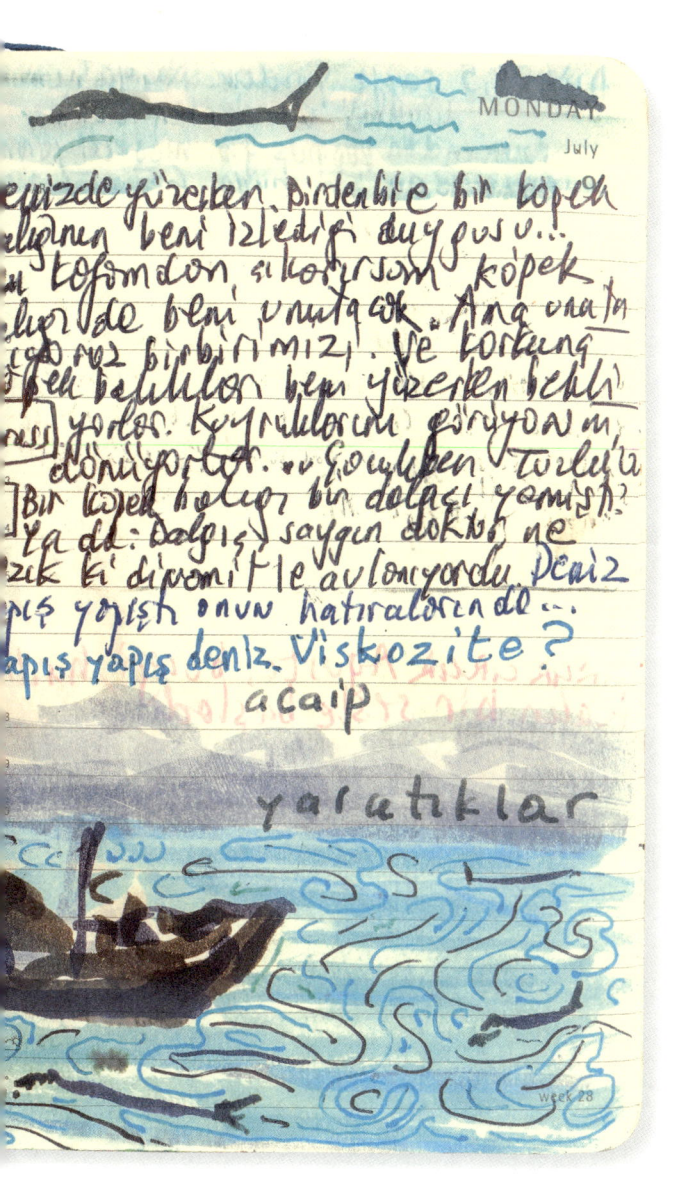

strange

creatures

The desire to paint is just like sexual desire, I can be going about my day as if there were no trace of such a thing in my mind or soul when suddenly it will rise within me, and I'll grab hold of the nearest paint and brush.

The fantasy of a whole other life and realm far from here, the idea of a different existence suggested by remote and feral landscapes, have defined my whole life and always occupied my thoughts.

I am constantly working. It's strange. It's as if I feel the need to prove something. But I like the novels I carry around in my head, and I should write them, yes, it would be good if people could see the world as I would in these books. Afterward, some lentil soup, the kind Sermin always makes, eggplant with chicken, white wine. But it was still very early in the evening. All of a sudden I felt the urge to paint.

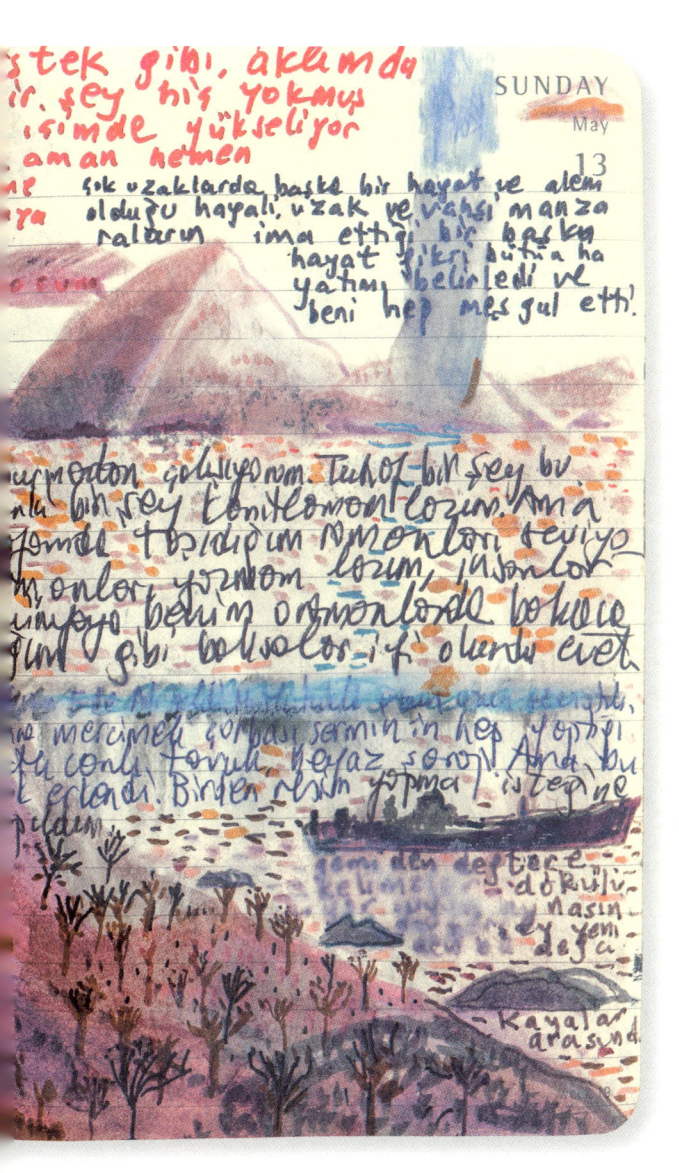

out of the ship and onto the notebook words pour mirrored in the water everything back to this mountain again

among the rocks

The art of portraying a landscape as an enigma relies on

emptiness

eschew spiritual idleness

the roads on the left are neater

sensing the other realm hidden within the world.

the landscape is the storm inside me

windy regions

you are still wind

On my way to get some coffee and start the day, this is the first thing I saw from the terrace: so I immediately gathered my art supplies and began to paint. I very rarely paint in the mornings, so this was an exceptional case. It is possible to memorialize all of time with these kinds of drawings. A picture and a few words for every second of the day. This is the first moment of the day. After this will come the second moment and the second painting. So on and so forth. To live is to see.

this ferry sails past me six times a day

It might have been better if I hadn't told anyone these things

decide the
drawing is done

THE WORLD IS AS PLAIN AS THIS
EVERYTHING REALLY IS THIS PLAIN

A picture for every moment. If we were to put all the pictures in order, they would present us with the illustrated story of a day, a year, a life. Life is the ink from a series of pictures. You find yourself wondering about the next picture. You're curious about the picture after that one, so you don't want to die. When you die, the pretty pictures end and darkness takes over. I think all drawings are beautiful because they make us want to look.

changing something in
a finished drawing
only to spoil it and
regret having done so

distant mountains

the urge to write

15 March: emails // Claudio. // Paris?
Ali Betil // Baricco // Ropac
Signed books to Selçuk Demirel, Gamboni text to Onur, Ropac
—number 9 wages // Christina //
—The Peck *Shahnama* / Simpson

Bülent, Jin, Sophie
Center / Torino / Milano
Erol = This // Filiz
The Secret Face

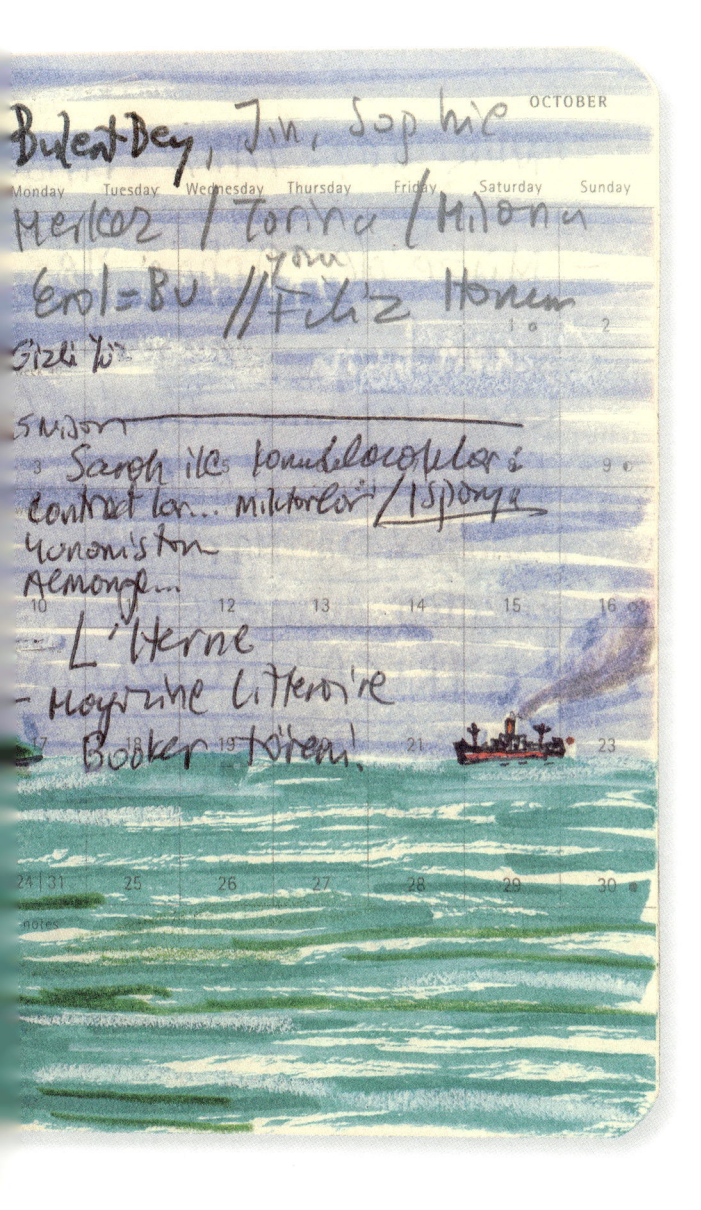

15 April
To discuss with Sarah:
—*Contracts*... amounts / Spain
—Greece
—Germany
—L'Herne
—*Magazine Littéraire*
Booker ceremony.

Seeing his anxious, uncertain childhood self in his dreams would sadden Mr. K. He would also feel guilty. A tenderness and sympathy for the child would awaken inside him.

An imaginary conversation between the painter and the writer within me . . .
I should really introduce readers to the painter Ahmet Işıkçı. In Turkey, the vast majority don't even know his name. One day there will be a volume on his art in the bookshops—yes. Perhaps I'll be the one to write it.

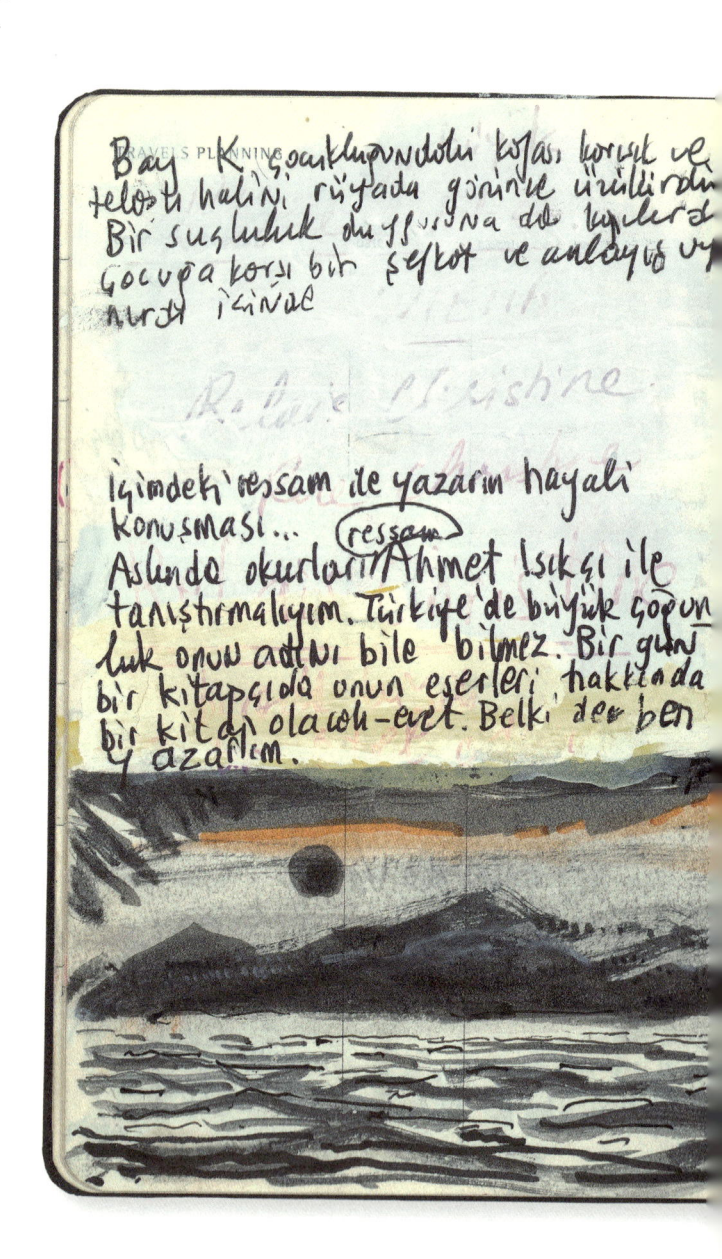

—Mussorgsky: *Night on Bald Mountain*
—Mozart
—Tchaikovsky
—Mahler, on the death of children
—Peppino di Capri
—Old Friends
—Bob Dylan
—Amy Winehouse
my selection for the BBC—music and literature

Choose your favorite songs and talk about them on the BBC!

I was a pointillist in my youth! In high school and at university, influenced by Seurat, I would make paintings out of dots. How exhilarating to create an image solely with dots and fleeting touches of the paintbrush. When it's applying the dots, my hand moves of its own accord. Proper brushstrokes are for braver pointillists. The timid pointillist limits himself to dots. Meanwhile, his mind becomes confused.

His mind becomes confused.

the old masters

poe

A single brushstroke, a single touch, and you start to feel like one of the old masters . . . But you are also always on the verge of thinking that your latest alteration has ruined the painting you were creating. After a long spell applying brushstrokes with unconscious abandon, I take a step back.

                                                           disquiet
the Chinese masters would look here first   the sea is stirring itself
                                                                      maelstrom = Poe

                                                                                       poe

True pointillists disguise
themselves

inbetween

an eye

grass

a shadow

a caterpillar

water
of a little

a bird here

the shadow

don't look

blue mountains, unfamiliar peaks,
distant memories, misty folds,

I passed through here once before, while dreaming up a novel

places I've never been before . . .
But I remember . . .

but it's all over now.
We don't want you anymore.

I've been reading Delacroix's journals. He's serious, hardworking, passionate, erudite. A little authoritarian . . . No sense of humor. But I like how curious he is about everything, how spirited . . .
Aslı leaves early in the mornings. I slowly read through what I've already written. Writing novels with the sound of waste ships, airplanes, and motorboats in the background.

Throughout the day I talk to Aslı and Sermin on the phone. Then I write and write.

It's getting warmer. I went for a swim from 11 to 11:30. Fretting about the fact that once again the novel is getting longer than I would like.
Murat Seçkin has invited us to their place . . . Edhem, Nüket and co., Aslı Çavuşoğlu. I'm happy with these friends. Might be good to talk with Aslı Çavuşoğlu about art . . .

I wrote a scene I've been looking forward to for a while. About our GOVERNOR PASHA's modernizing FANTASIES OF PRISON REFORM. All under the pretext of choosing a location for the quarantine facility. I read somewhere that Abdul Hamid used to appoint retired soldiers—sergeants—as prison superintendents . . .

THE FANTASY OF BUILDING MODERN PRISONS and the creation of MODERN SOCIETY . . . The IMPOSITION of MODERNITY, etc.
A subject I enjoy. In the passage I wrote today . . . Abdul Hamid's Chief Inspector of Prisons carries blueprints for a modern prison with him on his travels . . .

Football's been ruined. I won't watch anymore. There was a match on television this evening. Just a bunch of people endlessly passing the ball around midfield. England could have scored 10 if they'd wanted to. They stopped after the first.

2016 B

                                                                                           bird

                                                               on Büyükada

words

                                                                       bird   wind

                                                    birds

bird   bird   wind

birds   fly

                              a bird

              water/dinner/taxi   3.886
                                   7000
                                   ─────
   and   11.000

                                              it flies

                                              bird

                                              birds

Rüzgarda
ve yaprak
harfler ç

I waited for a long time for words and letters to emerge from among the leaves and branches rustling noisily in the wind.

In the evening I took Elif Batuman and her girlfriend Lindsay on an improvised personal tour of the Metropolitan Museum. I showed them all the paintings I love. I spoke at great length about Panini's ANCIENT ROME and MODERN ROME; the so-called capriccio style; GUARDI and CANALETTO, EL GRECO (and Toledo, which we visited with Aslı), etc. etc. I paused before certain paintings and launched into pompous disquisitions on the history of landscape painting. Sometimes all three of us stopped to study a particular painting, moved only by the pleasure and thrill of looking at art. What's happening in this painting? Which parts of this historical tableau

The boy was being chased by murderers, thieves, villains, and ALL THE BAD MEN. There were so many of them. Mr. KA, who was running so fast his lungs were bursting with the effort, could see that the harder he tried to flee, the more numerous his pursuers became. When he realized that the child he could see in his dream was himself, he felt guilty, and ran even faster.

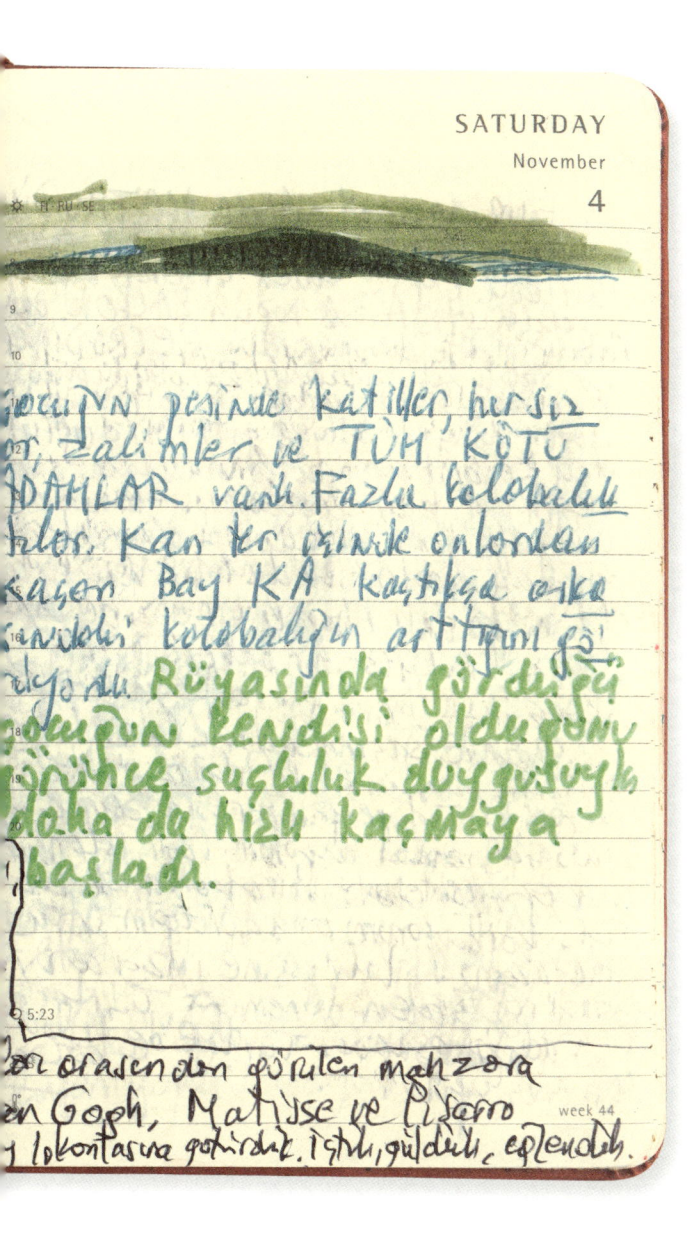

are "real," how much of what we see in this landscape is a figment of the imagination? Eventually I took them to the section on Islam. The *Shahnameh* of Shah Tahmasp, *The Conference of the Birds;* Ottoman edicts, the seal of SÜLEIMAN THE MAGNIFICENT; Mughal/Babur-era art; botanical and animal illustrations commissioned by employees of the India Company, HORSES AND BATS. The landscape glimpsed between the legs of the storks. Of course we spent the last half hour looking at the Cézannes, Van Goghs, Matisses, and Pissarros. Afterward we took the girls to the Orsay for dinner. We drank, we laughed, we had a good time.

The writer most adept at inscribing words over images, at thinking about WORDS and IMAGES simultaneously, is of course William Blake. I'm not sure if I would have liked to be able to write like him. But I would have liked to be the kind of person who, like him, has lived his whole life always seeing and conceiving of words and images on the same page.

Among my contemporaries, the names that come to mind when thinking of painters who visualize text and image at the same time are Raymond Pettibon and Cy Twombly. I do wish I could paint like they do. Actually, no, I would only wish to paint like I do, but I would have wanted, like them, to devote my life to painting. Always envisioning words and images on the same page.

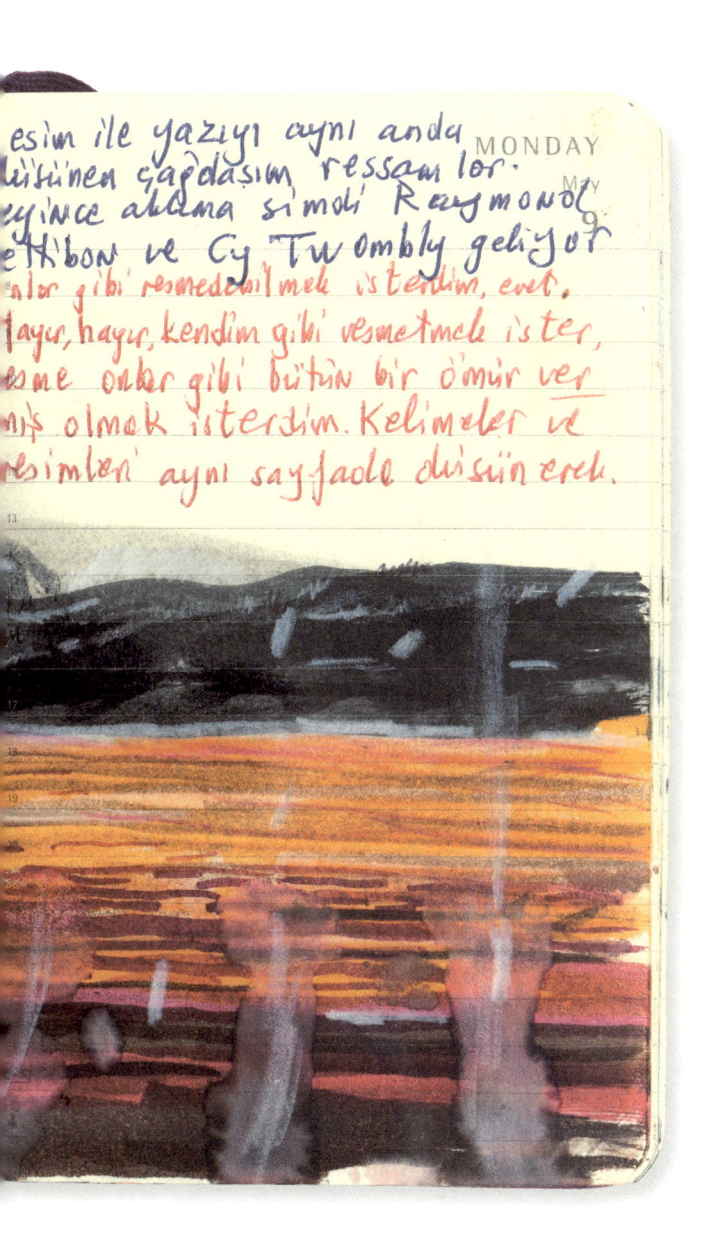

THERE IS ALWAYS AN ISLAND...

You can make your own world there and convince yourself that you are sheltered from all evil. No one ever wants to hear that evil has reached the island. You stop your ears to any bad news.

    indiscriminate   As long as there is an
              smudges   island somewhere on the
                                horizon, far away, all is well.

When I was little, the lodos wind would sometimes blow toward the end of summer. The ferries would stop. While everyone talked about the storm, I would fantasize about the lodos never ending, of being trapped on the island for a long time, and not having to go back to school. One winter's day in 1973, I gave up on becoming an architect, dropped out of Istanbul Technical University, and went to Burgaz Island.

remember.

I wrote most of *My Name Is Red* on Sedef Island.

2017B

ALWAYS ALWAYS

always

The MET   The Met   The
 The Met   The Met   Met
         The

Swedish Inst.

always always

Gerhard Steidl ⟶
(afternoon)

mountains and landscapes

Holiday

My earache is getting worse. I was feeling particularly dispirited this morning. This earache makes everything else I have to deal with feel like a burden. Yesterday we bought some drops from a pharmacy in Spetses and some silicone earplugs to wear when swimming. When I went for a swim in the morning, I plugged my ears with silicone... The swim did me good. Now back to chapter 5 of the novel. I wrote about the girls reading Proust while queuing up to enroll at university. This story is actually about me, but pinning it on Proust works better. I was a little tired in the afternoon. Let's take the car and go somewhere, I said to Kiran, so we drove to Ermioni. I felt euphoric.

ERMIONI

the
road to
Ermioni which
I've drawn here,
the olive trees and
everything else reminded
me of my childhood, of the way
the hills in Bayramoğlu-Gebze used
to look. Crickets, the August heat,
empty roads, sleepy squares, the heat,
dinner at home in the evening.

We go swimming with Kiran around 8 in the morning, quite far out. After that I try to finish chapter 5 of the Norton book, but fail. Last night I translated it into English for Kiran, sentence by sentence. Some passages felt too light, others too personal. I tore two pages up and started again from scratch. At night, I was tormented by the thought of those pages. Torment, torn pages. These things reminded me of my work as a novelist.

Every now and then, while I'm working, I get up from my desk and read a few passages from Calvino (*Six Memos for the Next Millennium*); Borges (*Selected Nonfictions*); and T. S. Eliot (*Selected Prose*).

Working at my desk at 11:35 in the morning when suddenly—BOOM-SPLASH. A soda bottle Kiran was fiddling with, trying to get it out of its plastic wrapping, nearly exploded in her face. I went upstairs to comfort her. A shallow cut on her nose.

We go swimming with plugs in my ears. I still can't finish the chapter. The earache is getting better, but I must see a doctor.

It's ten to 8 in the evening. We are waiting for an ear doctor in the town of Kranidi . . . It turns out there's a virus in my ear. As the doctor is writing my prescription, he asks for my name. He recognizes it, and I tell him about my translator, Stella. Return from Kranidi to Porto Heli. It's just like the return from Gebze to Bayramoğlu. Bought some eardrops and silicone earplugs from Porto Heli. Then some sardines with capers at that nice taverna.

I am so busy with my novel that there's no time left over to write in this notebook and reflect upon life.

The greatest joy is to lose yourself inside a novel. To live with your characters all the time. I am so happy with my novel.

stars

THURSDAY
October
13

karm
Gece kelabah
Gecesi renm

the stream opens up
and flows like a sea
as the dark waters draw near

The night is full. The river is dark
I see the night inside me

IN URBINO I THOUGHT ABOUT *NIGHTS OF PLAGUE*. THERE WERE AROUND 5,000 PEOPLE LIVING IN THE PALACE OF URBINO AT ITS HISTORICAL PRIME. THAT'S THE KIND OF PLACE MY PLAGUE CASTLE SHOULD BE. In my castle, there

Me, once upon a time long ago: fable and history; writing and painting

the IDEAL city

will be Catholics left over from the time of the Crusades; a team of archaeologists; a sheikh, his loyal followers, and the son of a Young Turk; people building railways and the workers laying the tracks. I should begin with the part I am most eager to WRITE . . .

I sensed that this could be
a template—dream for
NIGHTS OF PLAGUE

at night it will become
a completely different place

it's as if it weren't a real place at all
but somewhere I dreamt up for *Nights of* PLAGUE

MANTUA
DUCAL PALACE

the whole world was at peace

everyone   everyone
we sat right here

the square is quiet

Impressions of Amber Fort. I've been thinking that I should set my *Nights of Plague* in a real-fictional castle like this one. Whenever I find myself in a castle like Amber, my "romantic imagination" immediately recasts the setting as part of a story, and that feels exhilarating.

two monkeys

Walking around Amber Fort, I think of *Nights of Plague* and two of my characters, one blind and the other lame. As the blind protagonist advances through the castle's passageways, he will be thinking intently about where he is and his destination, mapping the labyrinth out in his mind for us to see.

BOMBAY: In the morning, breakfast and gentle gossip with Kiran by the pool of the Taj Hotel. Warm weather, colonnades, swimming pool, palm trees, and happiness. Drinking mango juice.

Kiran went upstairs. I'm sitting alone, thinking. THANK GOODNESS I made, I'm making, the museum. I come to the conclusion that I must take it to BARCELONA too. At 10 I start giving interviews in a room inside the old hotel building. 2.5 hours of interviews with the three biggest papers, e.g., the *Hindustan Times* and *The Hindu*. Then went back upstairs, lay in bed, and added another page to the new foreword for *My Name Is Red*. Kiran is sitting in the hotel room, writing her novel. Outside, the hum of Bombay, its smell, its atmosphere. Jerry came to pick us up at 2, and took us to the backstreets, to old neighborhoods, a large cistern, etc. Then we went to an old bookshop. Old Everyman's Library volumes amid the smell of dust and mold. At Hurshid's dinner party in the evening, with no sign of any food coming any time soon, I lose my temper and sulk, just like in Barcelona.

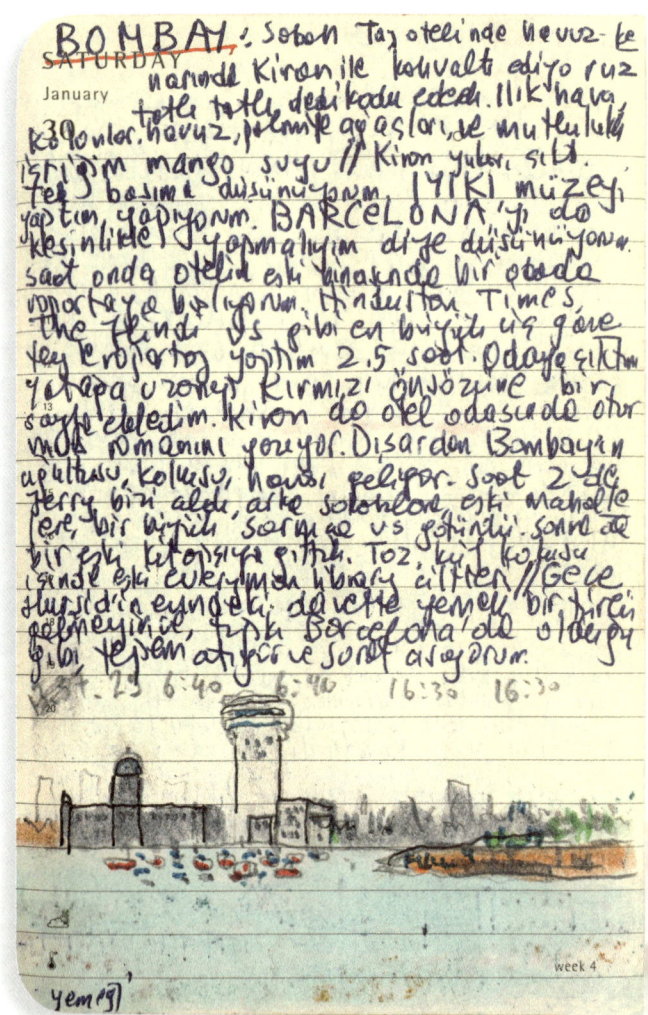

the dinner

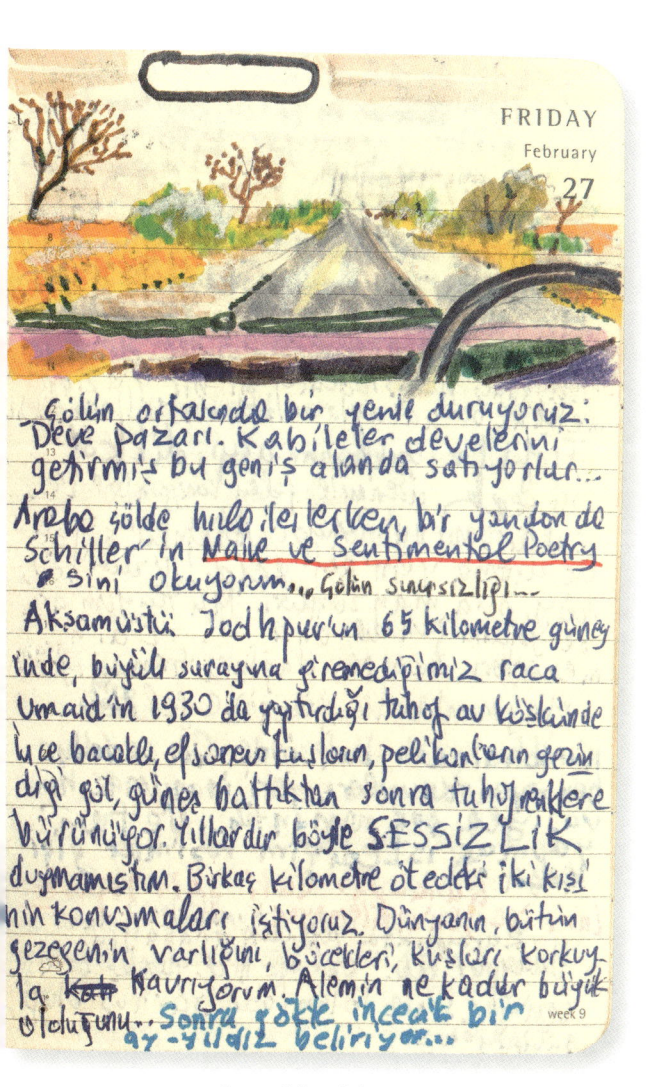

We stop in the middle of the desert: a camel market. The local tribes have brought their camels to sell here in this large field . . .
As the car speeds through the desert, I'm reading Schiller's *Naïve and Sentimental Poetry* . . . The vastness of the desert . . .
In the evening, in the quaint hunting lodge built in 1930 by Raja Umaid (whose main palace we weren't able to visit) 65 kilometers south of Jodhpur, pelicans and mythical slim-legged birds roam a lake whose waters at sunset take on eerie hues. I hadn't experienced this kind of SILENCE in years. We can hear two people talking several kilometers away. The world, the whole planet, every insect and bird, feel terrifyingly present. The enormity of creation. Then a slender star and crescent appear in the sky . . .

Agra. The joys of wandering around the streets... We make detailed plans to evade the city's tenacious guides and hawkers...

I'm at the Taj Mahal now. I thought I'd write a few words about it: Soft light. Grace. Kemal should have spent more time thinking about the Taj Mahal.

The power, the elegance, of the building are impressive... Hazy weather. Mostly local tourists... The love story angle has been amplified in order to distract modern visitors from the madness and megalomania inherent in the structure. Nevertheless, the Taj Mahal is a unique and singular jewel. It brings glory to a whole continent. A feeling of reverence! The pleasures of observation. We walk slowly and respectfully toward it.

octagonal structures are not so common in Ottoman architecture.

Walking around Agra Fort in the afternoon. We can see the Taj Mahal in the distance. A pink-and-orange evening light falls upon it. With its interlacing chambers, its many back rooms, its Harem and its Diwan, how similar the Agra Fort is to Topkapı Palace! One is struck by the incredible might of Akbar and his sons. A display of wealth and power right alongside the poverty and chaos we see on the streets...

Back in the HOTEL ROOM, a thought: Mevlut could be philosophical like Pierre in *War and Peace,* quirky and surreal and symbolic like *Alice*. A few days ago in Jaipur, I said, "My books have been translated into 58 languages, but the hardest part was having my first book published in Turkey." I was referring to the familiar tribulations of the young writer. But in the hands of the lying right-wing press back home, this has been turned to "he's complaining to foreigners that we won't let him publish his books"... I suppose I'm used to this kind of thing by now...

The size, the contradictions, the epic proportions, the cultural richness, the multi-colored variety of India are all helpful to me in thinking through Mevlut's story.

We visited Akbar's tomb, his colossal mausoleum outside of Agra. Immensity, vastness, serenity. Ceramic tiles at the entrance, wall decorations, massive doors reminiscent of Isfahan ... Outside, the endless thrum of motorcycles and the Agra traffic.

We went back on the road, toward Delhi. Right now we're waiting in the car, parked outside a touristic roadside restaurant 100 km from Delhi. Our driver is having a cup of tea.

We reached Delhi at 5 o'clock. Checked into the Taj Mahal Hotel close to where Kiran grew up. We can see the parliament and the towers of the government buildings in the distance. Fog, haze, a lot of pollution. I can't work out if I'm coughing because of the cold.

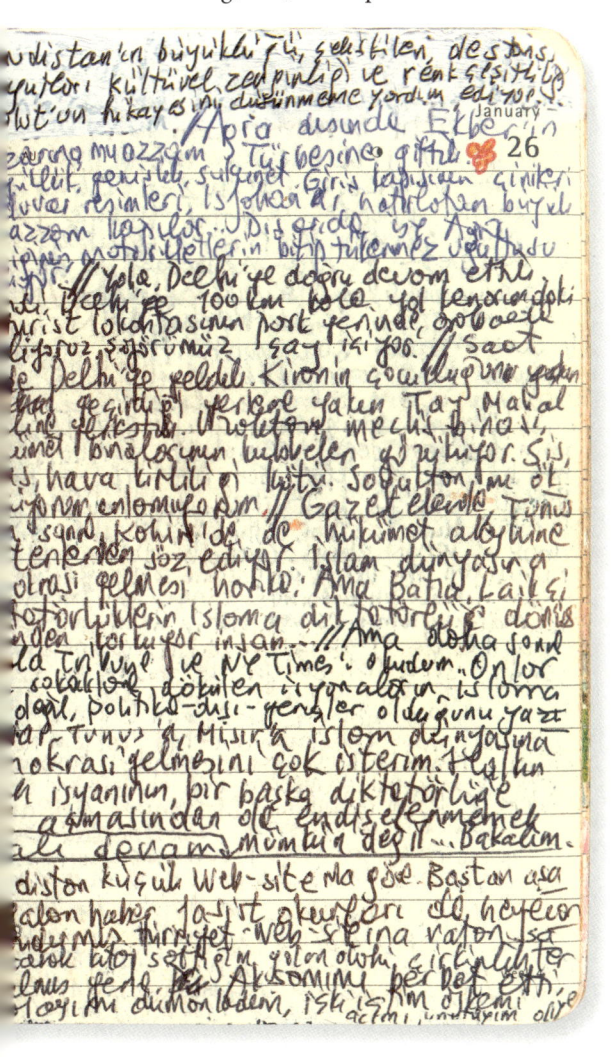

The newspapers are reporting antigovernment protests in Cairo too, after Tunisia. It would be wonderful for democracy to arrive in the Islamic world: though one does worry about westernized, secularist dictatorships giving way to Islamist dictatorships ... But later I read the *Herald Tribune* and *The NY Times*. Even they are saying that the protesters thronging the streets are not Islamists, but apolitical youths. I would really like to see democracy come to Tunisia, to Egypt, to the Muslim world. But it is impossible not to worry that the masses' legitimate revolt might lead to a new kind of dictatorship ... We will see.

Tuesday continued. According to a small website: this completely invented report has galvanized fascist readers. More smears on the *Hürriyet* website suggesting that I would sell my country out if it helped me sell books. My evening was completely ruined, so I decided to get drunk, to douse my anger and my anguish with wine.

Woke up at 9:15. Running late. At the festival tent by 10 o'clock. Opening speeches, politicians. People getting carried away with their orations, others having their books signed as they watch from the sidelines... Columbia's Sheldon Pollock, editor of the Indian classics library. Says that his conception of the classics is not the same as Sainte-Beuve's or T. S. Eliot's; it's different. I'm glad Sheldon is talking about this. "Classics, like dying languages, must of course be preserved; but classics cannot just live in museums, they must be alive out on the streets, too," I said. Sheldon noted that we must protect classics and forgotten texts not because or by virtue of their "universality" (Sainte-Beuve, T. S. Eliot), but for other reasons.

1. The classics remind us that there are different ways of being human (that is the expression he used).

2. For other types, other styles of beauty (he referred specifically to the "Possibility of a new type of beauty"). These utilitarian justifications Sheldon finds for the classics... they are indeed understandable, and represent an improvement on the "universalist" rhetoric of T. S. Eliot and his ilk. But still, "utilitarian"! In my opinion, we read classics not for their utility, but for their poetry, and to experience the feeling that we are the continuation of something older than us. Notes for an essay on why we read the classics... that's what I should call these thoughts.

The 11 o'clock reading and interview went well... The audience was friendly and sincere.

Kiran arrived and I did a TV interview with Sunil Sethi. *The Times of India* put a photo of me and Kiran on their front page.

Various groups protesting against my trip to Sri Lanka... Though we have long since decided not to go. It has even made it to the Turkish newspapers. I've asked both İletişim and Penguin to release a statement. In the afternoon, a visit to the raja's awful palace! Then back to the hotel. I just want to be alone and write my novel.

We were having dinner at the Rambagh Hotel with Kiran last night when we met Coetzee and his wife. In the morning we ran into each other again at breakfast. I like his novels; I told him as much. The newspapers are full of articles about the festival. But I don't feel like discussing festival gossip, nor classics with John Makinson. Kiran has left for a panel. I'm sitting on the hotel balcony, trying to step back inside my novel 40 days after I last worked on it, which was around 12 December. The newspapers are reporting that we haven't gone to Sri Lanka after all. Don't let it bother you, focus on your novel, I tell myself.

Kiran back at 12, a little conversation, then lunch: we've come to an agreement with John Makinson on a Penguin-İletişim classics collaboration. I'll explain it all to Asuman in April . . .

At 3 o'clock, I went to the festival tents at the palace. I watched Kiran's event. Then the "Out of West" panel, which was my idea.

Amber Fort—Diwan

I thought it would be a good opportunity to talk about the position of non-Western or not fully Western writers. It didn't work. The interviewer's manner was too supercilious. A shame. There was a huge audience. Afterward I spent an hour signing books for the never-ending crowd. The astonishingly large crowds, the feverish interest from journalists and readers alike, filled me with an odd sense of guilt . . . I do enjoy seeing these crowds and all this interest, but at the same time I fear the sense of responsibility they bring, and feel guilty. Nice conversation with the Nigerian writer Chimamanda and her husband. Chimamanda is bright, intelligent, fully self-confident. The crowds, the newspapers, the journalists, the noise, the interest, the endless book signings—they might end up killing the novel inside of me. But I love India, and I am so pleased to be loved here . . .

The view from Jaigarh Fort. The mountains that surround Jaipur-Amber, the forts, the view, all stimulate my imagination: it is a landscape I long to be part of.

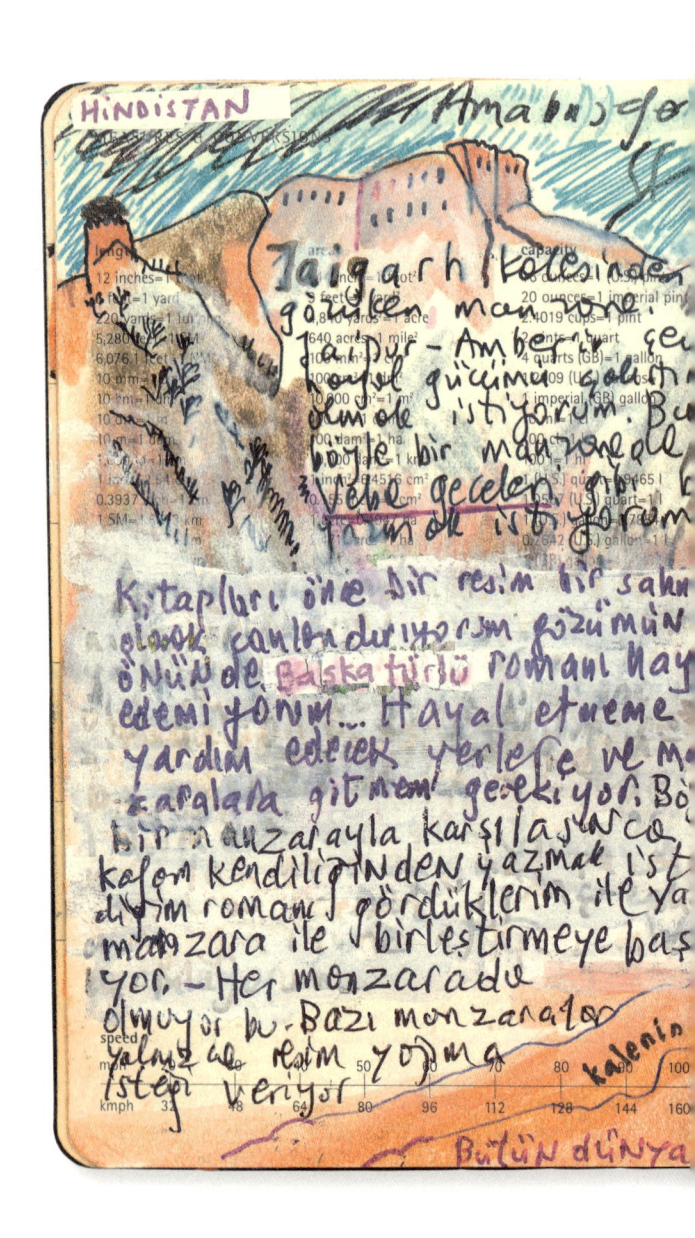

I start by visualizing my books as if they were paintings or scenes. I can't begin to picture a novel any other way . . . I need to visit places and landscapes that will assist my imagination. When I am faced with this kind of landscape, my mind begins of its own accord to merge the novel I want to write with what I see before me—that is to say, with the landscape. This doesn't happen with every landscape. Some views only instigate a desire to paint.

That is why I want to write a novel like *Nights of Plague*, set in a landscape like this one, real or imagined.

I want to write scenes
that take place
in these landscapes

I liked Jaigarh.
Imagining a place
is a way of loving it.

In the labyrinths of the fort

We were late leaving the hotel this morning, and I forgot my camera. We've returned to Amber Fort, which I first visited 8 years ago. The great Diwan halls of Ottoman Persian (Iran) and Mogul civilization; doors embellished with paintings; the inner garden! Just like in the Alhambra, a—small—fountain in the garden, the babble of water.

Why am I so content inside the labyrinths of Amber Fort: if only I knew! Passageways, staircases, rooms, domes, columns, everything seems to awaken some deep memory rooted inside of me. In order to picture every element of a novel like *Nights of Plague*, I will have to imagine a place like Amber Fort, and the evolution of its halls, Diwan, Harem, etc., down to the smallest detail! Which leads me to grumble even more that I wish I hadn't forgotten my camera. Passageways in the back, hidden windows, narrow staircases . . .

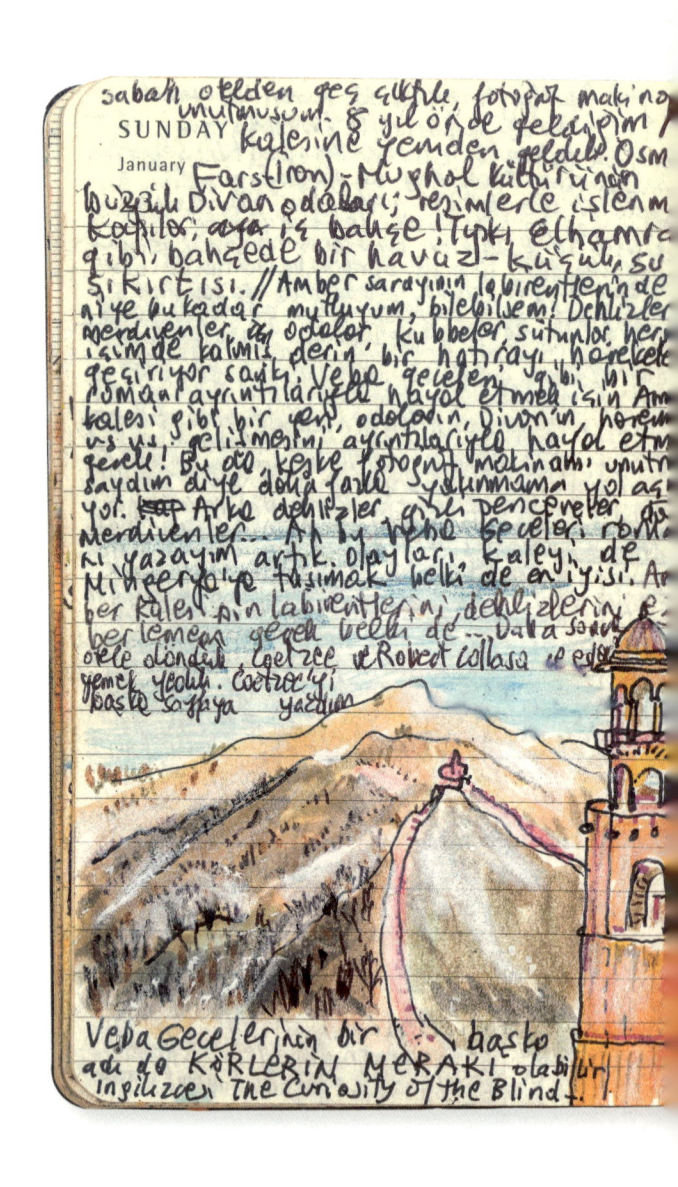

I really should start writing this *Nights of Plague* novel now. Perhaps the best thing to do would be to move the plot, and the castle, on to Mingheria. Perhaps I should memorize the labyrinths and passageways of Amber Fort . . . We returned to the hotel and had dinner with Coetzee, Roberto Calasso, and their partners. I've written about Coetzee on another page.

Another title for *Nights of Plague* could be KÖRLERİN MERAKI. In English, *The Curiosity of the Blind* . . .

I'm at Fatehpur Sikri. It's magnificent. My eyes tear up. I imagine setting *Nights of Plague* here. I take photographs. We entered this ghost town at around 4 in the afternoon (in Jaipur—quarrel with the driver and hawkers; took us 4 hours to get here), and I spent 2 ecstatic hours taking hundreds of photographs. First we strolled around the mosque and its courtyard, so similar to the Jama Masjid in Delhi. Akbar had it all built over the course of 15 years, between 1569 and '85, but then abandoned it, having lived there very little—hardly at all. The reason it was abandoned remains unknown, which is another detail I could transpose to *Nights of Plague.* We roamed around this place—which has been imprinted upon my soul ever since I came here on my first trip to India back in 2003, and which would be an ideal setting for a novel, for *Nights of Plague,* I have in mind—in a state of awe.

Someone in *Nights of Plague* writing the history of a place similar to Fatehpur Sikri, where Akbar played the chesslike game Pachisi. Strange buildings whose purpose and function remain unknown . . .

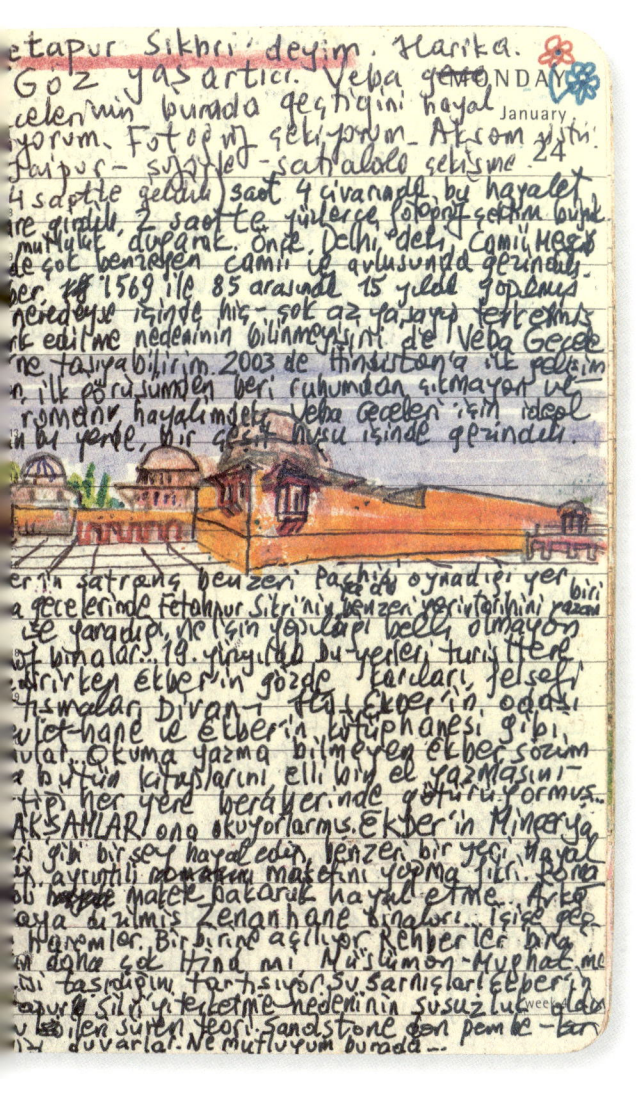

Showing 19th-century tourists around this place, discussing Akbar's favorite wives, philosophical arguments, the Diwan-i Khas, Akbar's chambers, the living quarters, and Akbar's library . . . Apparently the illiterate Akbar took all of his books, fifty thousand manuscripts, with him wherever he went . . . IN THE EVENING, he would have them read out to him. Imagining Akbar's Mingherian campaign, picturing somewhere just like this, thinking I could build a detailed model. Visualizing the novel with an eye on the model . . . The zenana arranged in back-to-back rows . . . Intertwining Harem rooms. One opening into the other. The guides are debating whether there are greater traces of Indian or Muslim-Mughal influence on the architecture. Water cisterns and the theory suggesting that the reason Akbar abandoned Fatehpur Sikri was a lack of water. Pink-red walls made of sandstone. I am so happy here . . .

My Name Is Red! Everyman introduction.
I should begin in the first person singular, or end in it . . . or perhaps both.
Looking at the miniatures in the Prince of Wales Museum now . . . I remember when I first came here in 2004. I was enthralled by the explanatory notes that had been placed next to each miniature . . . It felt like listening to the paintings talk.

In the morning, 6 or 7 major newspaper interviews in the courtyard by the pool of the Taj Mahal Hotel. But my mind was still on the miniatures. It has been more than ten years since I wrote and published *My Name Is Red*. Yet whenever I see Persian Herat and Mughal miniatures—or, rather, paintings—from the 16th century, my imagination stirs back into action. It's as if I were still writing the same novel today.

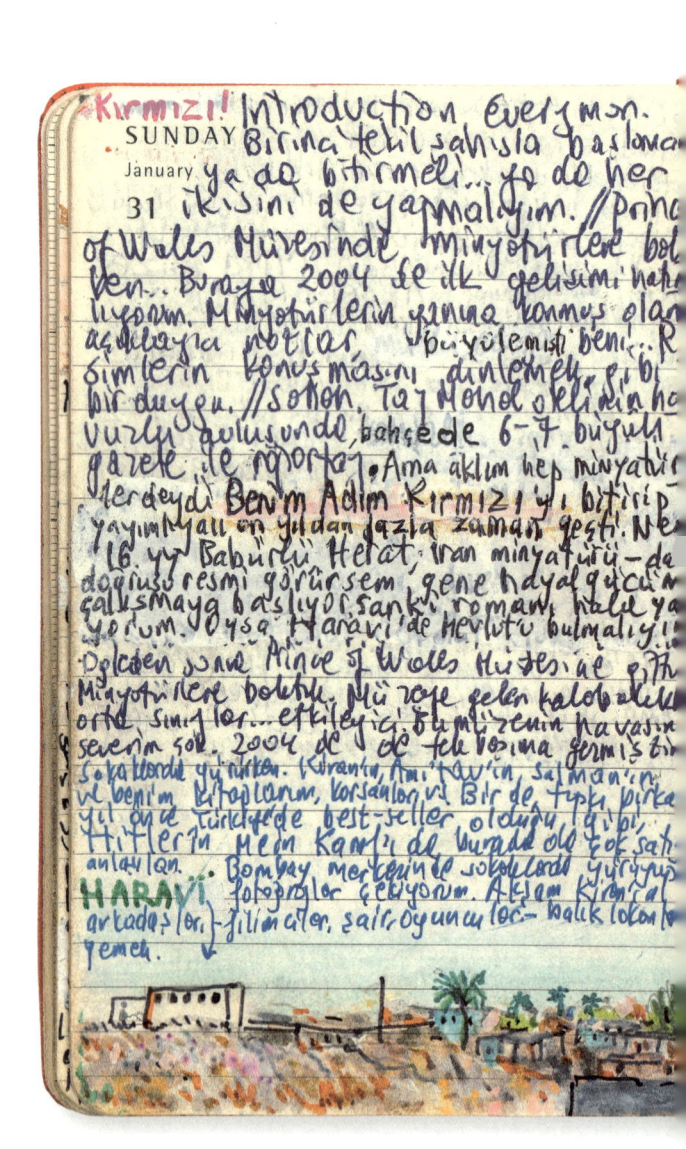

DHARAVI

But I must look for Mevlut in Dharavi. In the afternoon we went to the Prince of Wales Museum. We studied the miniatures. The museum is full of middle-class crowds . . . impressive. I have always enjoyed the atmosphere of this place. I had come here on my own in 2004. Walking around the streets, seeing copies of Kiran's, Amitav's, Salman's, and my own books, pirated editions, etc. It seems Hitler's *Mein Kampf* is very popular here too, just as in Turkey, where it was a bestseller a few years ago . . . I wander around the streets of central Bombay and take photographs. In the evening, dinner at a fish restaurant with Kiran's friends—filmmakers, poets, actors.

Breakfast with Kiran at the poolside courtyard of the Taj Hotel. The newspapers, *The Times of India,* have written about us, but in measured and respectful tones. Meanwhile the Turkish press has been reporting that I canceled a contract with the 2010 foundation and returned the money. (I can tell from the questions the journalists from *Hürriyet* and *Milliyet* have been sending me ... It's a good thing I'm abroad and don't have to deal with these things.) I hope the workmen and architects at the museum don't drop the ball. But I'm delighted to be in India, to have the chance to relax and unwind here in Bombay. Some ideas for my next novels: 1. The boza seller / 2. The commenter (someone writing comments on the internet) / 3. The well / 4. *252 Paintings* and the Painter's life story / 5. The curator / 6. Memoirs of the Blind (a historical and ahistorical novel) / Six big novels! What bliss it would be to write these, to be able to finish them all over the next 10 years and live a contented life.

GOA

On the way to Goa: Things to do there / 1. Everyman—*My Name Is Red* introduction / 2. the Norton introduction / and the afterword to *Cevdet Bey* / must be finished = 20-odd pages in total. It should take me 4 days to do those, then I can immediately make a start on the boza seller, write 100 pages in 5 weeks and get right into it.

We've arrived in Goa. Some shopping from the market in Neptune before settling in. I prepare my desk. A 45-minute swim. I was at my desk by 7. A sense of euphoria. Summer weather. The sea. Silence. Writing. Books ... The other novels I want to write:

7. The well / 8. FEMALE NARRATOR IN THE FIRST PERSON SINGULAR / 9. Old leftists come to raid a village and run into their old classmates / 10. An imaginary country—an illustrated volume in the style of the Knopf guides.

151

2009

In the morning, the shadow of the high-rise Trident Hotel in Bombay falls upon the sea. Hazy sky. Matias, a friend of our Goan acquaintance Rahul, takes us to Dharavi. In Dharavi, a religious community leader called Bau disparages the new modernization plans for the neighborhood. They don't consult us, they see Dharavi as a vote bank, and now people are lining up to get their free house from the state. Whereas here they've got both jobs and homes. Now they are going to have to leave those jobs behind! He's right; we listen. Then we head out into the streets of Dharavi. 5 years ago this place had looked much poorer to me. It has become more prosperous. Though of course Bau is making a point of showing us the success stories and the wealth. The educational initiatives of a selfless Catholic bishop, the streets, all a more slumlike version of Nişantaşı: in the backstreets, textile workshops on the ground floor and homes on the second floor.

Bombay Fish Market

I don't see a huge amount of destitution, but I see people working, and how Dharavi works. A successful shirt manufacturer was very poor when he first came here. The house and neighborhood where Bau was born and raised. Fishermen. A school.

We took a photo in front of the Cathedral and John Connon School, where Kiran used to go. I like walking aimlessly around the streets of Bombay. The hawkers, the traffic, the dirt, the noise, remind me of 1970s Istanbul. I find myself thinking of Mevlut not just in Dharavi, the world's largest and most remarkable slum, but also in the wealthy neighborhood where Kiran spent her childhood. I can't tear myself away from the Bombay train station. The station stands as evidence that this is one of the world's largest cities. The doomsday morning crowds here can sweep you away.

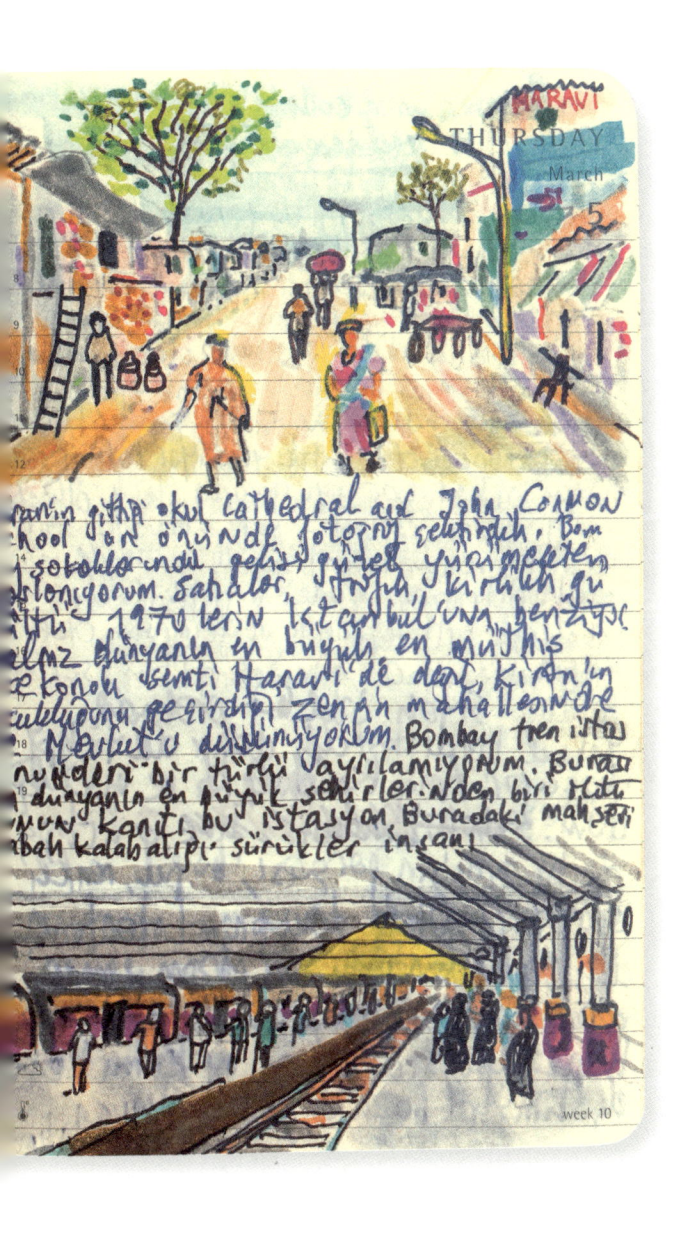

Today flew by like a breeze. We left the house at 12 on Xavier's minibus. Drove around beautiful Goa for hours.

How I love these Goan landscapes. Palms, rice paddies, colonial homes, rivers, marshes, countless little shops, buses, hawkers, bridges, greenery, charred ground, palm trees marking the borders of wide empty plains ... As Xavier drives, I look out of the window, and the people, the flora, everything thrills me. Even the air floating in through the window carries a kind of joy to me. I saw rivers hidden among salt flats, peanut and toasted chickpea sellers, bicycles, green plants, and paddy fields. A dirty creek polluted by a shipyard, workers from the south, tiny ramshackle cafés and diners.

Later we went to a reception for the opening of a new museum in a house that used to belong to a powerful, wealthy Catholic lady from the old Goan landed aristocracy who entered the Portuguese parliament under Salazar's rule.

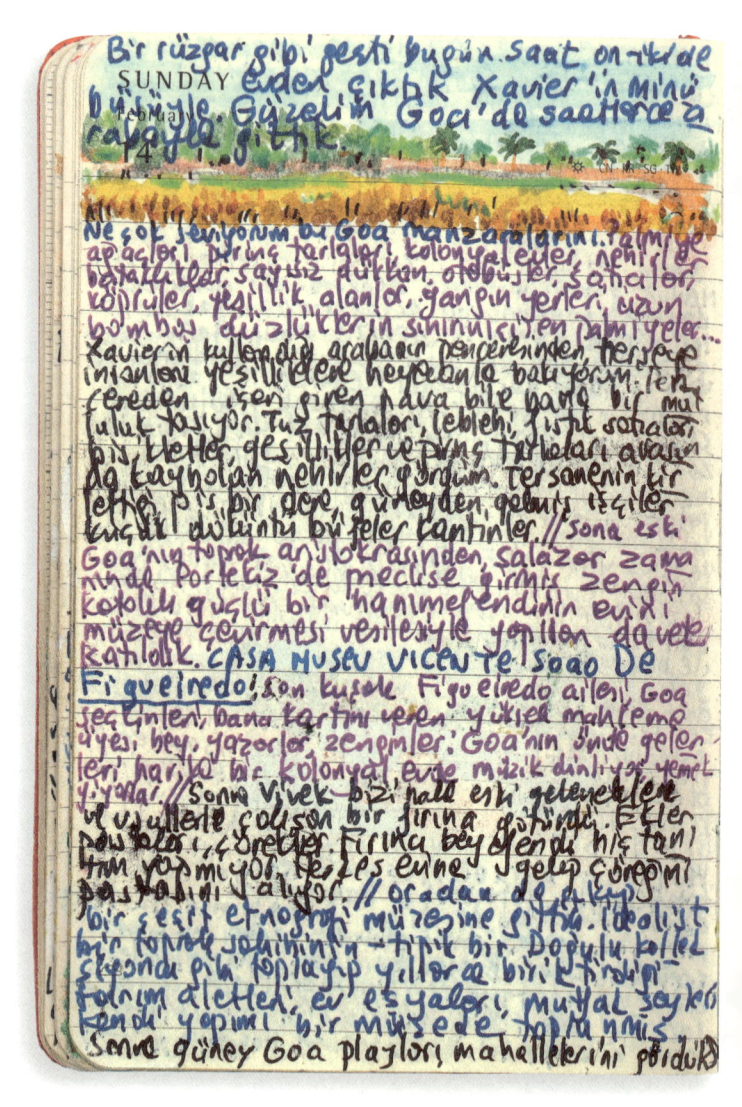

CASA MUSEU VICENTE Joao de Figueiredo. The latest generation of the Figueiredo family, Goan notables, a distinguished high court judge who hands me his card, writers, rich people: Goa's elites eating and listening to music in a magnificent colonial mansion. Afterward Vivek took us to a bakery which still follows the old methods and traditions. Éclairs, savory pastries. The man who runs the bakery makes no attempt at publicity. Everyone just goes to his house for their cakes and pastries.

From there we went on to a sort of ethnographic museum. An idealistic landowner's collection of farm tools, furniture, and kitchenware—amassed, like a typical Eastern collector, over the course of many years—is displayed in a museum of his own making. Later we went to see the beaches and neighborhoods of southern Goa.

Working on the boza seller this morning.

All day I write with this view before me. I lift my head up from my writing and see these colors. Every now and then they burn waste in the gap between the shore and our red wall. A bluish mist forms, then hundreds of squawking crows take flight at once. In the distance, a fishing boat sails through the haze.

Last night in my sleep and just before dawn, I felt as if I'd been snared in a trap made of fear and dread. Our unreliable watchman, reports of robberies, the power outage, all triggered some of my most fundamental anxieties about life. I took a sleeping pill. Kiran makes fun of me when I'm in this state, she laughs about it and won't take it seriously. "Don't make fun of me!" I tell her, just as I used to say to Şevket when we were little. The hostility I face in Turkey—e.g., the museum as a possible target—also triggers my fears. With the sleeping pill I slept until 11. The sea, a swim, shaking the water off, and turning my mind to the foreword for *My Name Is Red* all lifted my mood. I wrote four pages. In the evening I made dinner for Kiran at home: omelette; a salad, etc., and then we watched the film *Gomorrah,* adapted from Roberto Saviano's book of the same name. It's about the Italian-Neapolitan mafia. The first mafia film not to show murder and the mafia in a seductive, alluring light. A peaceful, contented day.

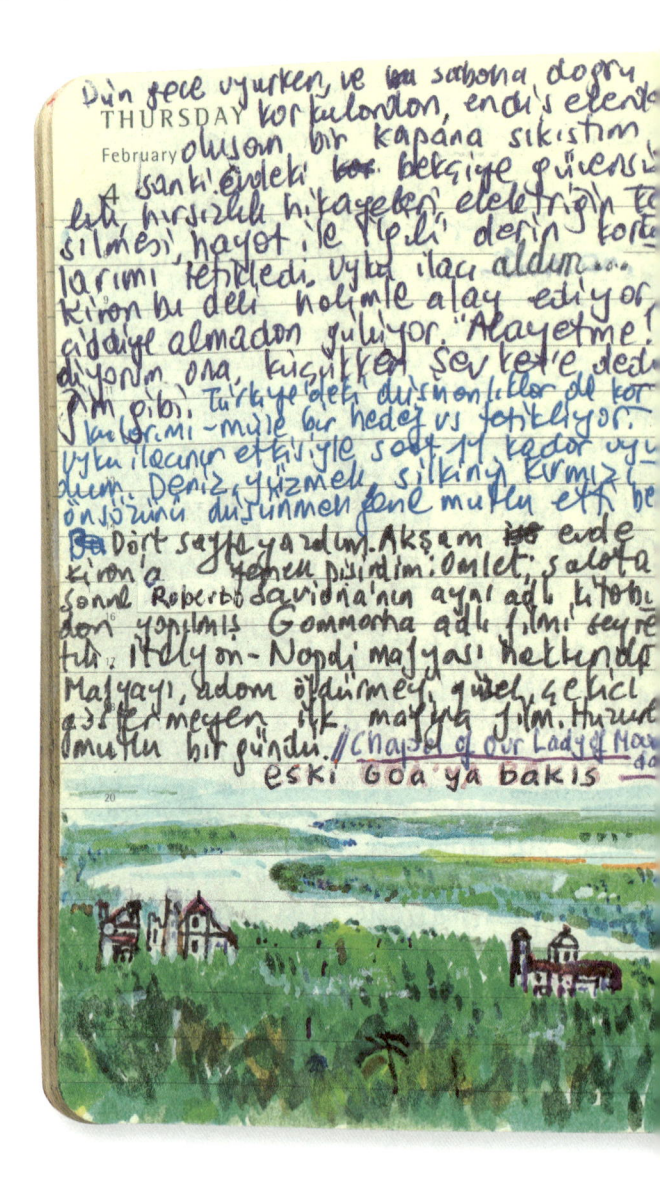

View of Old Goa from the Chapel of Our Lady of the Mount

I drew all of these crows one by one based on a single crow sitting on a branch. The crow was peering curiously down from its perch (it was 7:40 in the morning) at two dogs, Musty and Susty, as they scampered and frolicked merrily across the wooden slats of the boardwalk. Morning bliss in Goa and Candolim . . . Goa has taught me how to pay attention to birds. Sometimes the crows all gather in one place, then suddenly all start screeching—hundreds of them—and take flight. It's almost scary.

In the morning I went for a long swim, nearly an hour. I savored the color of the water, the sandy beach, the murmur of the sea. I felt the urge to paint. I took some photos. It has been a while since I last did any painting, and I feel a strong impulse to do so now. In the evening, some Goan artists who read *My Name Is Red* with Vivek organized an exhibition without even knowing I was in town. After that, a concert inside an old Goan church! A view of this landscape, and dinner with Vivek.

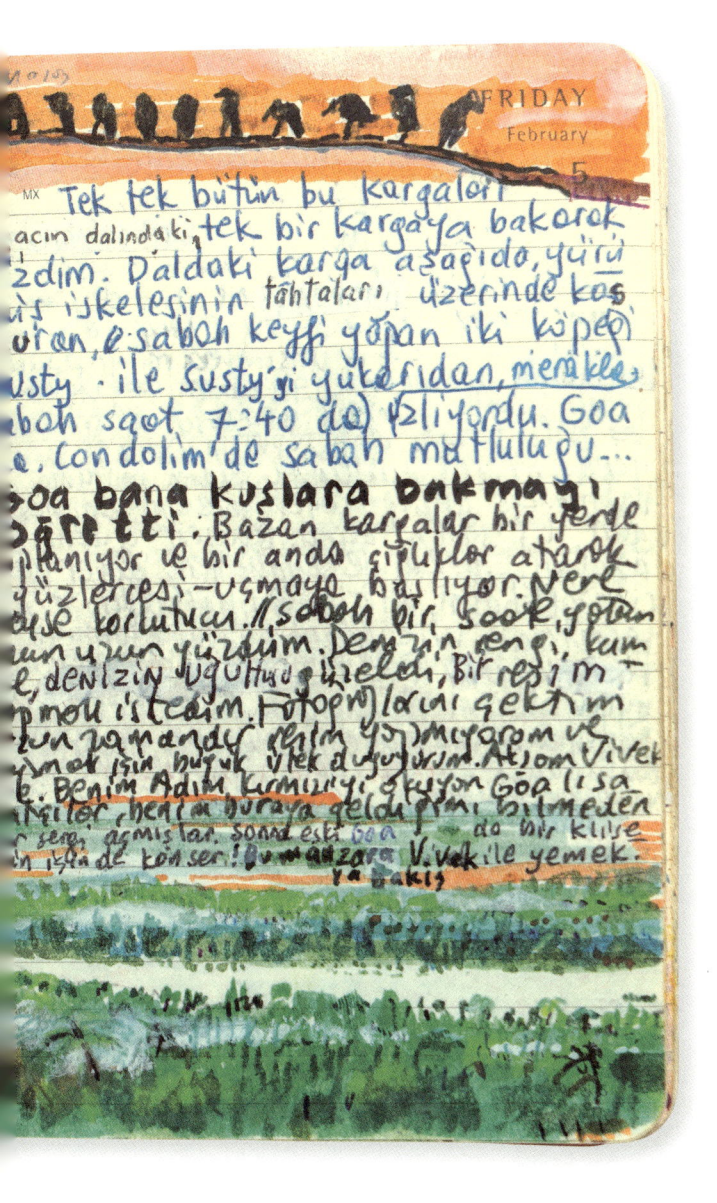

I've finally finished my introduction to the Everyman Classics edition of *Red*. Underneath it proudly bears the date GOA, INDIA 2010. It hasn't been easy. But the urge to write shimmered so bright within me that I lovingly-devotedly kept at it. What's come out in the end is an essay worthy of the novel. I think it should be published everywhere as a postscript in the back of the book.

Later, in the sea, I had an idea: Should I make the title of the book about novels—*Naïve and Sentimental*—different in Turkish, *Naïve and Contemplative*? I thought about the introduction as I swam. In the afternoon, I walked in the heat under the dazzling green trees and over the dusty red earth to the internet shop, to check my mail. 45 minutes! There were times last year when it could take me up to 1.5 hours a day. I must be less busy this year... Maybe because I've reduced the amount of travel and other work I do...

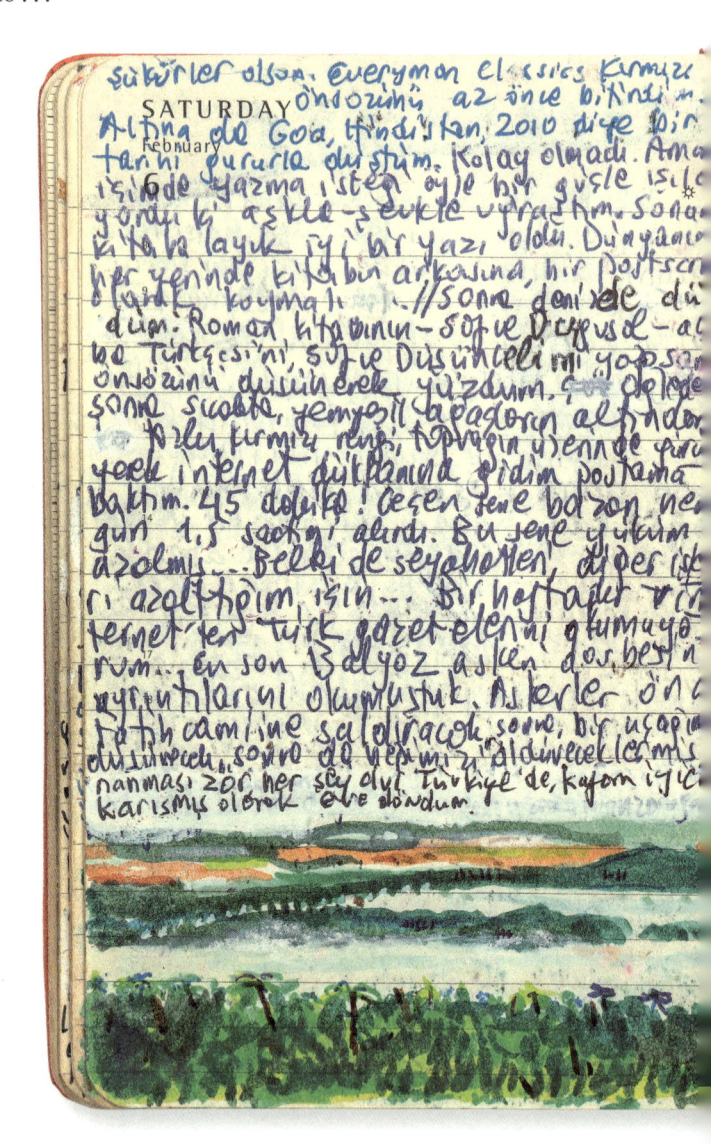

I haven't looked at any Turkish newspapers online during the past week... The last thing we saw were some revelations regarding the planned Sledgehammer military coup. The soldiers were allegedly going to attack the Fatih Mosque first, then bring down one of our own planes, and finally kill us all. It all seems improbable, but anything is possible in Turkey, and I went back home feeling even more confused.

I keep painting views of Goa and the plains. But it's strange: I don't feel I can turn this landscape into a part of my novel. Yesterday evening and this morning I happily drew this view of Goa from above. It reminds me of Frans Post's landscape paintings: I really love those.

He painted landscapes of regions of Brazil that were under Dutch colonial rule in the 17th century... And he observed the "natives" who lived there. The orange soil, the green vegetation. Familiarity with human subjects is not essential to the enjoyment of landscape painting. Caspar David was adept at seeing people. I love seeing Goa. But I could never write a novel set in Goa. Because I don't know Goans. Novels are about people.

I can hear a motorboat in the distance. The sound of this little boat sailing across the sea reminds me of the happy summers of my childhood.

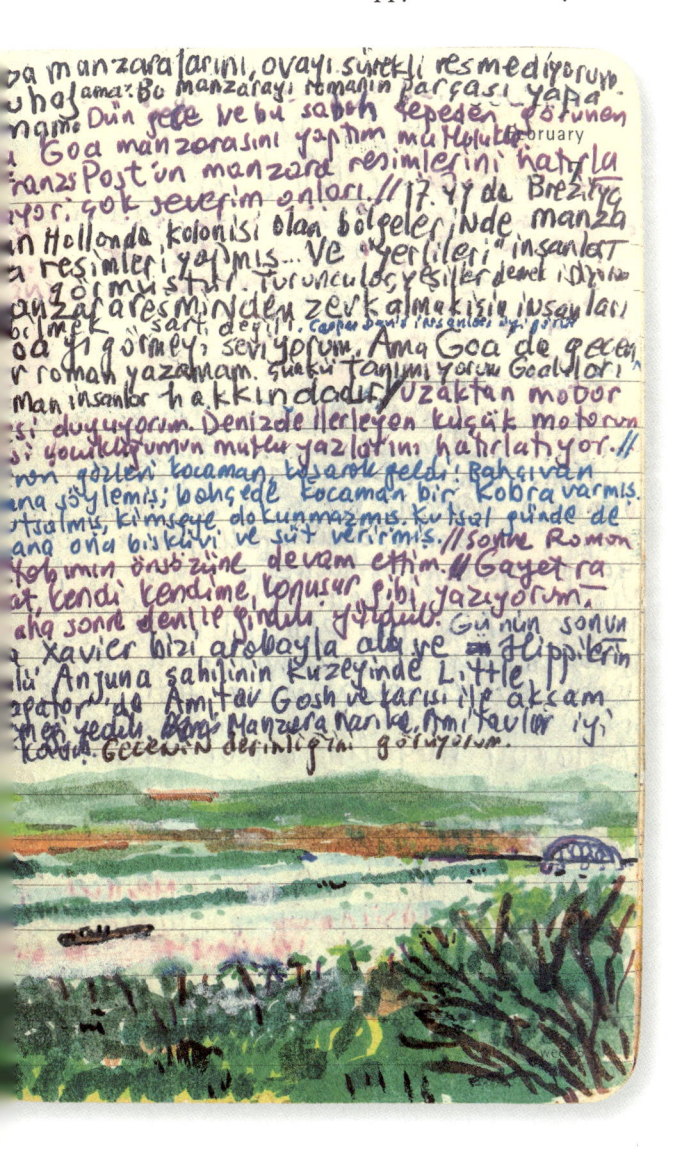

Kiran comes running, wide eyed: Rana the gardener told her there's a huge cobra in the garden. Apparently it's sacred, it won't hurt anyone. When the holy day comes around, Rana will give it a biscuit and some milk.

I went back to the introduction of my Novel book. I find myself writing with great ease, as if I were talking to myself. Later we went for a swim in the sea. At the end of the day, Xavier picked us up in the car and we went for dinner with Amitav Ghosh and his wife in Little Vagator, north of the hippies' famous Anjuna Beach. The view is incredible. Amitav and co. are good company. I can see into the depths of the night.

I'm proud of Mevlut's story and what I've written of it so far, but I can't quite decide how to continue the novel. There are two choices before me:
1. Turn the novel into a Kafkaesque-metaphysical narrative: about identifying with dogs.
2. Make it into a thirty-year history of Mevlut's and fellow street vendors' Beyoğlu—and their illegal *gecekondu* neighborhoods—and a panorama of Istanbul. The second option seems more appealing.
Pondering and working out the PLOT alone at home—Kiran has gone to her aunt Lina's for lunch.

Of course there's quite a lot of the metaphysics-dogs-faith and protection storylines from option 1 that I would like to save and put in the novel.
The main story—plotline—I've come up with is that Mevlut will be attacked by dogs and lose his successful business, after which his main preoccupation will become how to make a living. He lives in a pleasant rented home.

I wake up on the sofa downstairs in the middle of the night, at 2:30. I don't know what time it is. The murmur of the sea. The watchman and the dogs spot me behind the mosquito net . . . a polite noise. I go upstairs and bravely read through Mevlut's adventures. I went back to sleep at 4. Woke up at 7 and made some tea and coffee. Then eagerly threw myself back into Mevlut's story. Mevlut is on the steps leading down from Gümüşsuyu when the muggers sneak up behind him. Afterward I went to the beach with Kiran and swam for half an hour. Came back home. They've blocked Mevlut's path now. I am writing about Mevlut's mugging with an eye on the notes from my interview with Mehmet the boza seller. The writing comes easy. No trouble at all.

I drew the picture on this page to show the fire smoke. The haze from the waste and the weeds they burn in India is always on my mind.

Afternoon with Kiran. It's hot. We are lying on the bed side by side. Chatting aimlessly, gossiping about this and that. Every one of these moments reminds me of the summer afternoons of my childhood. I love Goa also because it reminds me of childhood summers, of laziness, of those days when I would spend hours in the sea.

On the way back from the computer shop garage with Kiran yesterday, they were burning the grass under the banyan tree. We stopped to watch. I'm happy here. In the evening, at the Literati Bookshop, we celebrated the launch of photographer Dayanita's book in Germany. Then back to her place for wine, conversation, silliness. A different world. They want to talk about ghosts. Nighttime. Stars. We went back home. I'm reading through Mevlut's mugging. It's a ghost story!

I seem to have lost my ability to focus and force my way back into a novel. So today I introduced a period of martial law. Never leaving my desk, writing a set amount during a set period of time, all the familiar methods I used to fall back on. There is great satisfaction to be had from looking at the empty page, at your notes, at what you've already done, then will yourself, almost force yourself, to write some more, and finding that it actually works. It means I am still able to use my imagination to escape from this world into the imagined world of my novel. But just before lunch, a conversation with Kiran about whether we're renting this house or another next year, how much it'll cost, etc. . . . and soon I'm distracted again.

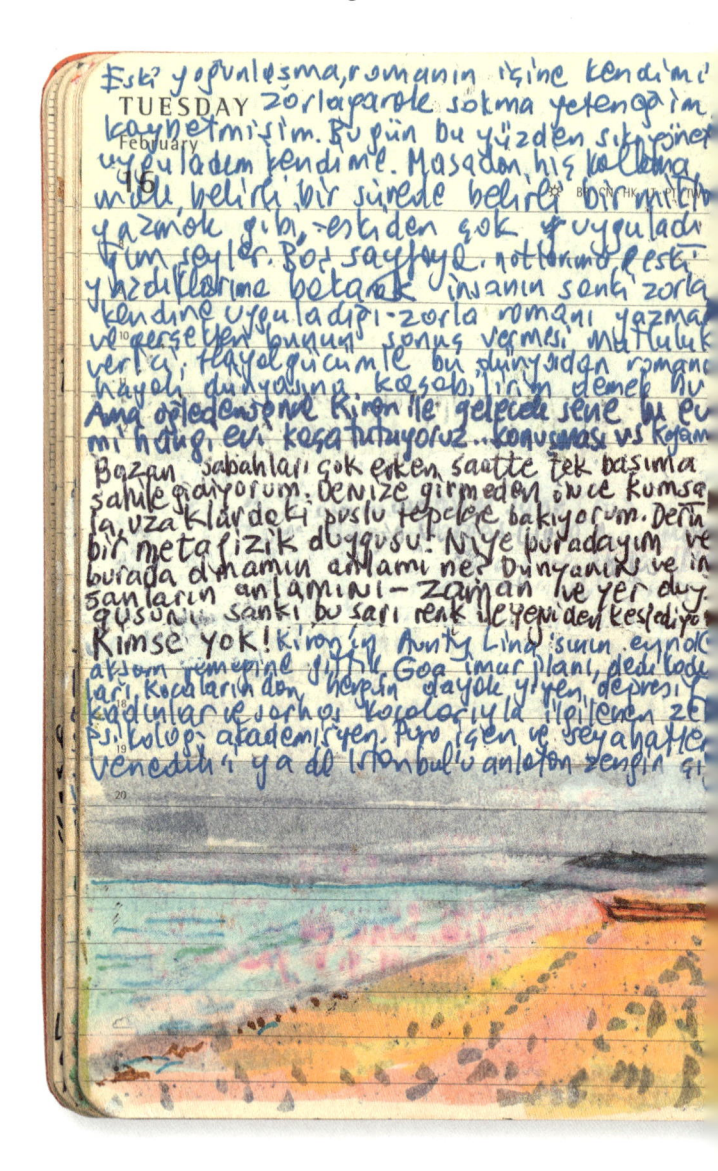

Sometimes I go to the beach by myself really early in the morning. Before stepping into the sea, I gaze at the sand and at the hazy peaks in the distance. A profoundly metaphysical sensation: Why am I here, and what is the meaning of my being here? It's as if I were rediscovering the meaning of the world and of humans—a sense of time and place through this particular shade of yellow. There's no one around! We went for dinner at Kiran's auntie Lina's place. News and rumors of urban redevelopment plans for Goa. Depressive women beaten daily by their husbands, a clever psychologist-academic who treats the drunken husbands. A wealthy cigar-smoking couple who talk about their travels, about Venice and Istanbul.

The hardest part about writing a novel which is set in the past and takes place across many years is dealing with the passage of TIME. This part—this precise moment—could potentially go on for so long that the novel could easily end up taking thousands of pages. Organizing time, arranging every moment: right now I am writing about the evolution of the backstreets of Beyoğlu on the pretext of Mevlut's visit to the Sunshine Club. I wrote 3 pages, then stopped for an afternoon nap, and when I woke up I couldn't quite gather the energy to continue.

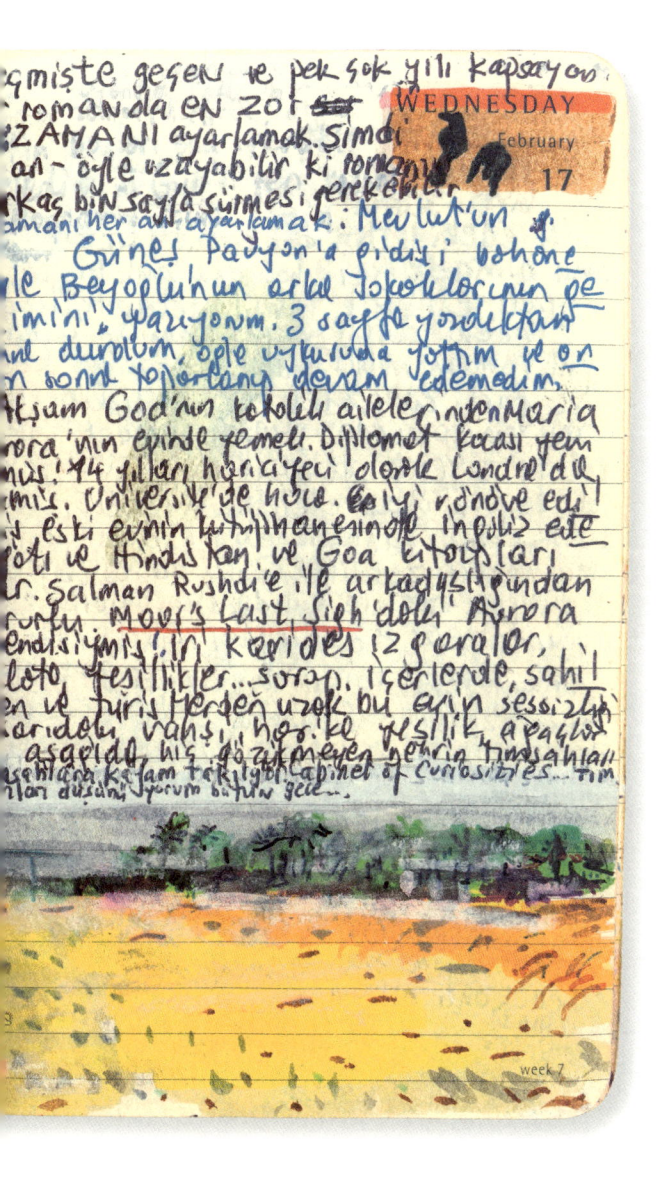

In the evening, dinner at the home of Maria Aurora, from one of Goa's Catholic families. Her diplomat husband has just passed away! They spent 14 years in London when he worked there for the foreign service. She teaches at the university. The library of their old, tastefully renovated home carries volumes of English literature and books on India and Goa. She is proud of her friendship with Salman Rushdie. She is the Aurora from *The Moor's Last Sigh*! Large grilled prawns, salad, green vegetables . . . wine. The quietude of this house in the interior, far from beaches and tourists, the wild, luxuriant trees and vegetation outside, and the river below, out of sight, where crocodiles live. I can't get those crocodiles out of my mind. Cabinets of Curiosities. I think about the crocodiles all night . . .

Dinner with Amitav Ghosh and his wife Debbie at the Burmese restaurant Bomras. As we ate our fried sardines, I thought I'd like to have a more heartfelt conversation with Amitav, maybe talk more about literature, but we never quite got there. Thinking I might as well tell him what I've been doing, I started talking about the section of my new novel where I write about electricity fraud. He interrupted me straightaway. Saying what difference does it make, the money from electricity theft remains within the "local community" anyway… I didn't say that the issue of electricity theft, so widespread in India and Turkey, should actually "trouble" us all, but this does bother me. Because as citizens of the third world and as "intellectuals who have found success in the West," we have this urge to see and to portray the third world as perennial victims.

This is a subject that has interested me for many years, particularly in the context of how the work of Edward Said is read and perceived in the third world…! Amitav does not want to criticize his country, India. Especially not individuals, not the poor… He is right when he says that the real money is being made by those up in Delhi, that that's where the real thievery goes on… But by this logic, you would never be allowed to draw attention to moral corruption within local communities. Reality is much more complex than that. Third world writers who live in the West should criticize, should be able to criticize, their own countries, their people, their everyday culture… But even talking about this subject is difficult. I like Amitav and I wouldn't want to start an argument!

With Kiran all day. I woke up at 7 before the day had fully dawned, but it took me a while to get inside the novel. Evening engagements, other people, other people's pettiness and their quibbles—all of these things have the potential to distract from writing. At two-thirty we walk with Kiran along the backstreets to the internet shop. I like the old colonial homes here, the banyan trees, the walls moldy with monsoon winds and rains, the dog that tails us until we're quite agitated, the little kid on his bike who stops to chat with us. I'm not writing well.

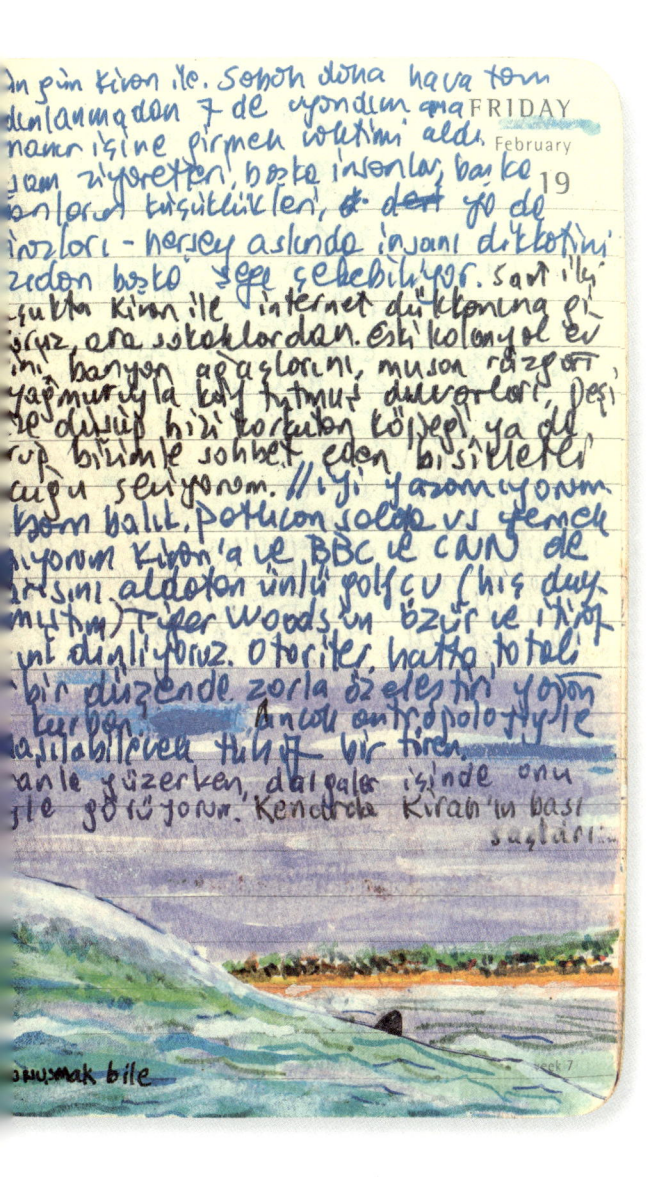

In the evening, I make Kiran fish, aubergine salad, etc. for dinner and we watch on the BBC and CNN as the famous golfer (I'd never heard of him) Tiger Woods confesses to cheating on his wife and makes his apologies. A sacrificial offering forced to perform self-criticism by an authoritarian, perhaps even totalitarian, system! A strange ritual which requires an anthropological approach if we are to comprehend it.

Swimming with Kiran, this is how I see her among the waves.

Kiran's head, her hair, beside me . . .

I took half a sleeping pill and went to sleep at 11 last night, so I woke up nice and early this morning: happy, excited, and full of zeal; I'm eagerly working on Mevlut and his friend's conversation at the kebab shop. A beautiful gleaming morning in Goa. What a thrill to be alive, what a joy to write and to create! After finishing Mevlut's dialogue with his friend around seven in the evening, I wondered if I should perhaps take a break?

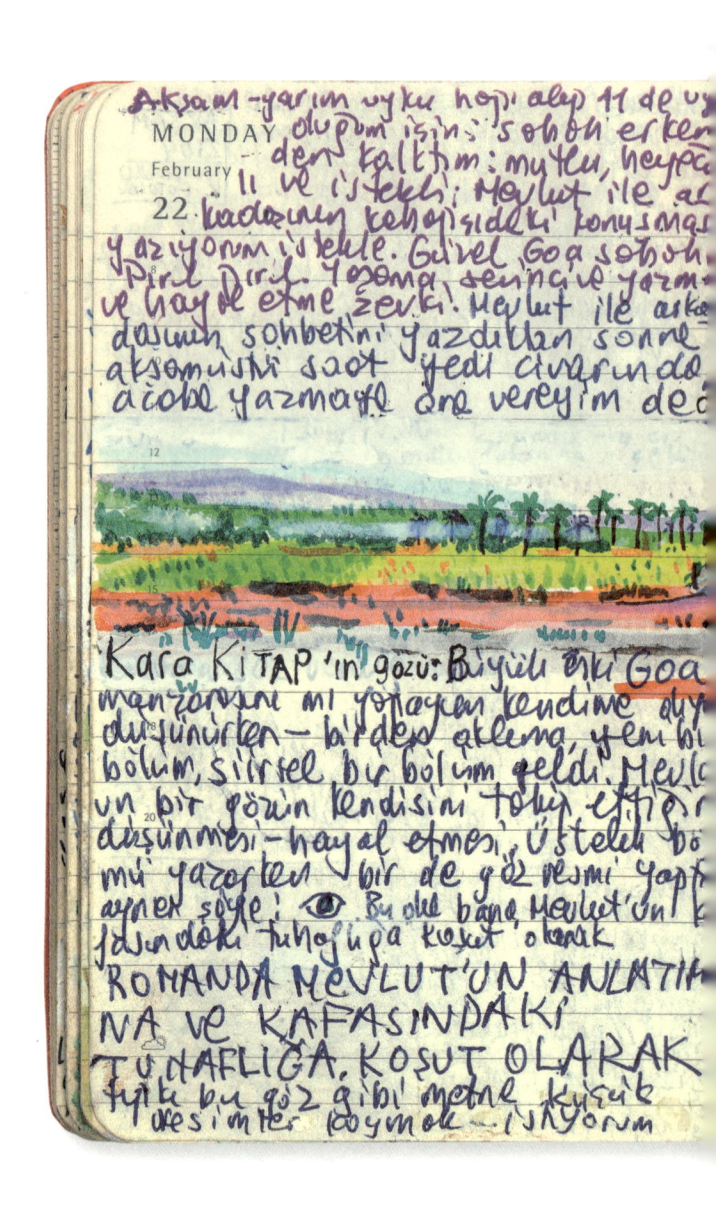

The eye from *The Black Book:* I was wondering whether to do another big landscape of Old Goa—when I had an idea for a new chapter, a more poetic chapter. Mevlut thinking—imagining that there is an eye watching and following him. I even drew a picture of an eye while writing the chapter; just like this: This made me think I could add small illustrations to the text, just like this eye, in parallel with the strangeness in Mevlut's mind, IN PARALLEL WITH MEVLUT'S NARRATIVE AND WITH THE STRANGENESS IN HIS MIND.

To be inside a novel, to experience each day armed with the sense of meaning that the novel gives me . . . That's something I can't do without. When it does not become text, when it does not turn into a sign pointing at what to write . . . the world is a difficult place to live in. My admiration for Rousseau has also been rekindled. Writing, looking at the view, entering the lives of others . . .

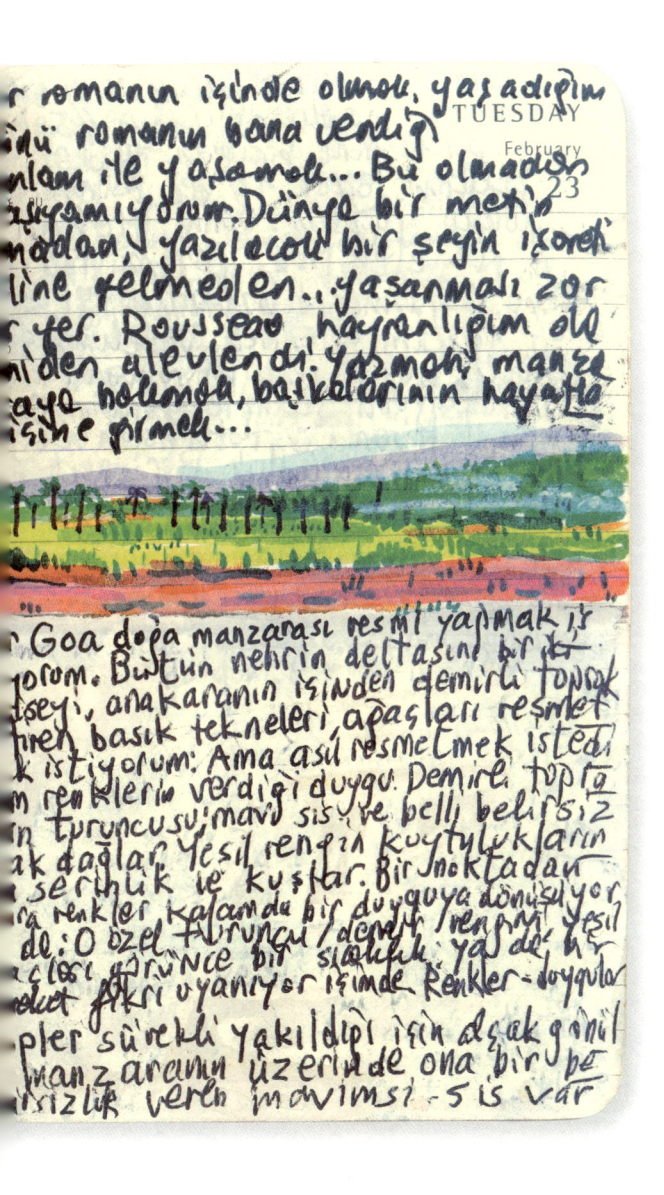

I would like to paint the Goan landscape. I want to show the full river delta, a couple of churches, the squat vessels carrying ferruginous soil from the hinterland, the trees: but what I would most like to capture is the mood conveyed by its colors. The orange of the metal-rich soil; the blue fog and the distant, nebulous mountains. The coolness and the birds hidden in the nooks of the color green. There comes a point when in my mind, colors transform into emotions. Or maybe: the sight of that peculiar orange/metallic glow or of the green trees evokes a kind of warmth or an idea of movement within me. Colors-emotions. As waste is constantly being burned, there is a bluish mist hanging over the humble landscape, imbuing it with a kind of blurriness.

I wonder what the latest political news is from Turkey.

In the morning, beautiful clear skies. I got up at 7. At 10 I went swimming with Kiran for 45 minutes. Then I started working on the first of Mahmut and F's electricity inspection chapters. I wrote well and easily, and I enjoyed myself. And I was ecstatic to realize that I might have the opportunity here to create a big, broad, and enormously entertaining novel. All of a sudden, my encyclopedic imagination kicked in . . . Exciting! In a state akin to inebriation, I started scribbling away notes for the novel's later chapters. The panorama I could write about is so vast.

Hurried out to the internet shop and read about the generals and their would-be coup. Unbelievable! I won't go so far as to say that Turkey will become a democratic country, but perhaps the assassinations on the streets, and the targeting of writers . . . we might have less of all that.

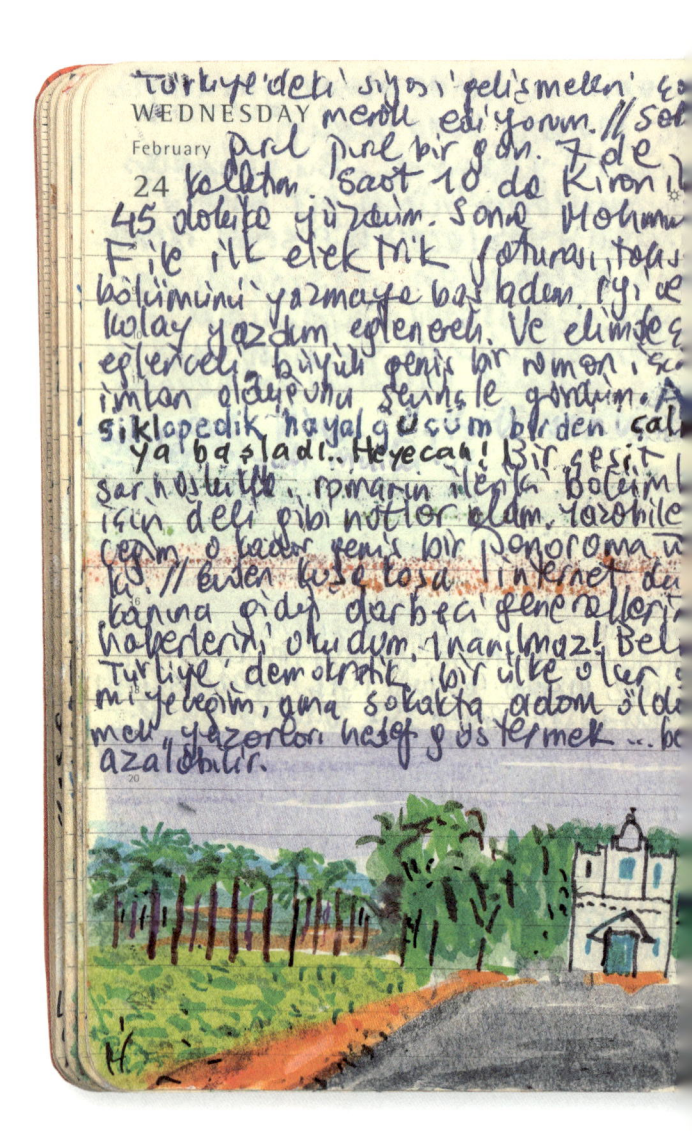

I would be making good and happy progress with the novel if it weren't for everything else I have to do . . . In the mornings I go for a nice long swim, and afterward I'm tired. At the internet shop-garage, it took me 1 hour to scan the Everyman introduction and send it off to Turkey. On the way back home from the shop, I lingered in the backstreets again. Very poor homes, people sleeping on the floor, a dog barking at me, children fighting, then suddenly, suddenly, a dead end, so hot, the European gentleman sleeping in his apartment made of concrete and his wife who loves umbrellas. In the evening, a boat trip in and around Panjim with Vivek, his wife, their family and friends. The view toward Old Goa, steeped in green, is magnificent . . . But all the touristic establishments, the boats brought in from Mississippi, and the casinos have spoiled Panjim. Vivek shows us the lighthouse where the river pours into the Arabian Sea, proudly proclaiming it the first lighthouse in Asia.

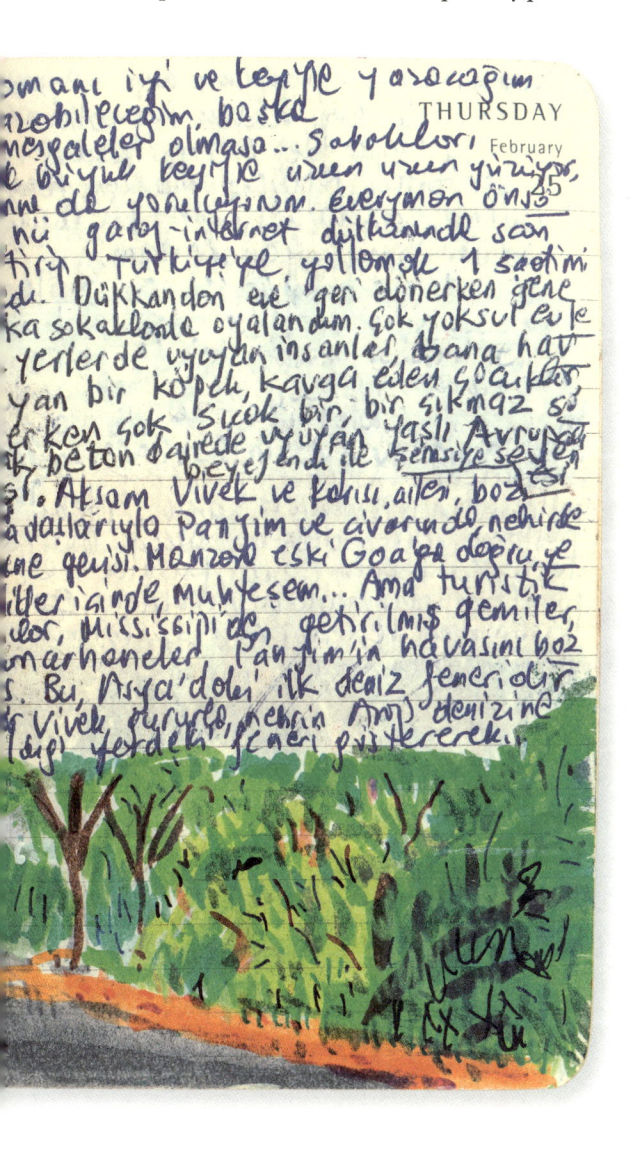

Toward morning I took a quarter of a sleeping pill to try to go back to sleep. Not good. It took me until noon to feel properly awake. It saps me of my energy for thinking, writing, etc. I went swimming and still couldn't wake up.

But I can feel that this new novel has the potential to be really entertaining, and that I could have a wonderful time writing it.

There have also been some . . . snags around sending the Everyman introduction to Hüsnü in Istanbul. Technical snags. I'd sent it yesterday from the internet garage. It seems 5 of the pages didn't go through . . . Checking my other email, reading Turkish newspapers, Tarkan arrested for cocaine; the generals have been let go without being taken into custody. Kiran comes and finds me in the internet shop.

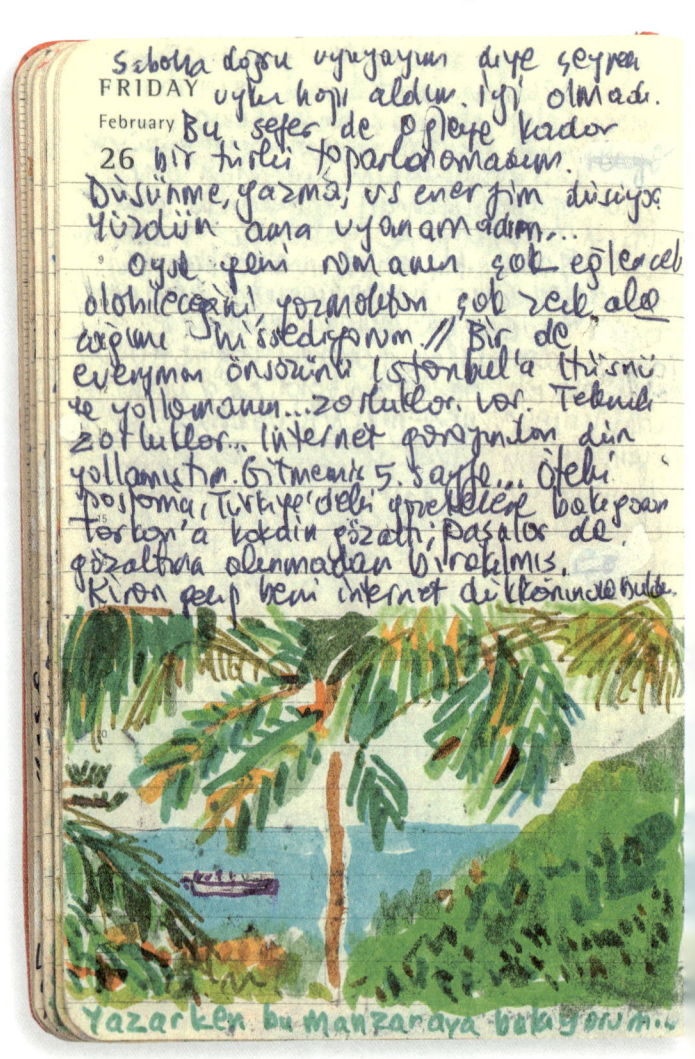

This is my view as I write . . .

Here is what the shore and the beach look like when you're in the sea... But I don't really look at this view when I'm swimming.

I swim on my back. My eyes are mostly closed. I think about what I'm going to write. Mevlut's adventures... Today I started writing about the history of the electricity inspection business in Istanbul. Through my own perspective as much as Mevlut's point of view... I'm thinking I should talk to someone who knows about the electricity business once I'm back in Istanbul so I can use that in my writing, though I'm pleased with what I've done so far.

As the sun set in the evening, I took photographs of the crows in the garden. In my mind the house and garden in Goa and the experience of living and writing here are always going to be associated with these crows. When the sun rises and sets, hundreds of them will come at once like a black umbrella. A great hubbub.

MIDNIGHT THOUGHTS: the CURATOR novel should also include discussions of world politics. Third world artists who prefer to see their countries as being "oppressed," rather than criticizing anything about them... Or ideas like the establishment of a global government—and of course a panoramic sketch of the world. At night, at 5 in the morning, I am reading and liking the latest pages I have written. There is... a vast world, a whole universe here...
1. Mevlut's strangeness, his mind, religion, metaphysics.
2. The city as a chaotic jungle.
3. A history of the other Istanbul.
4. A history of street vendors...

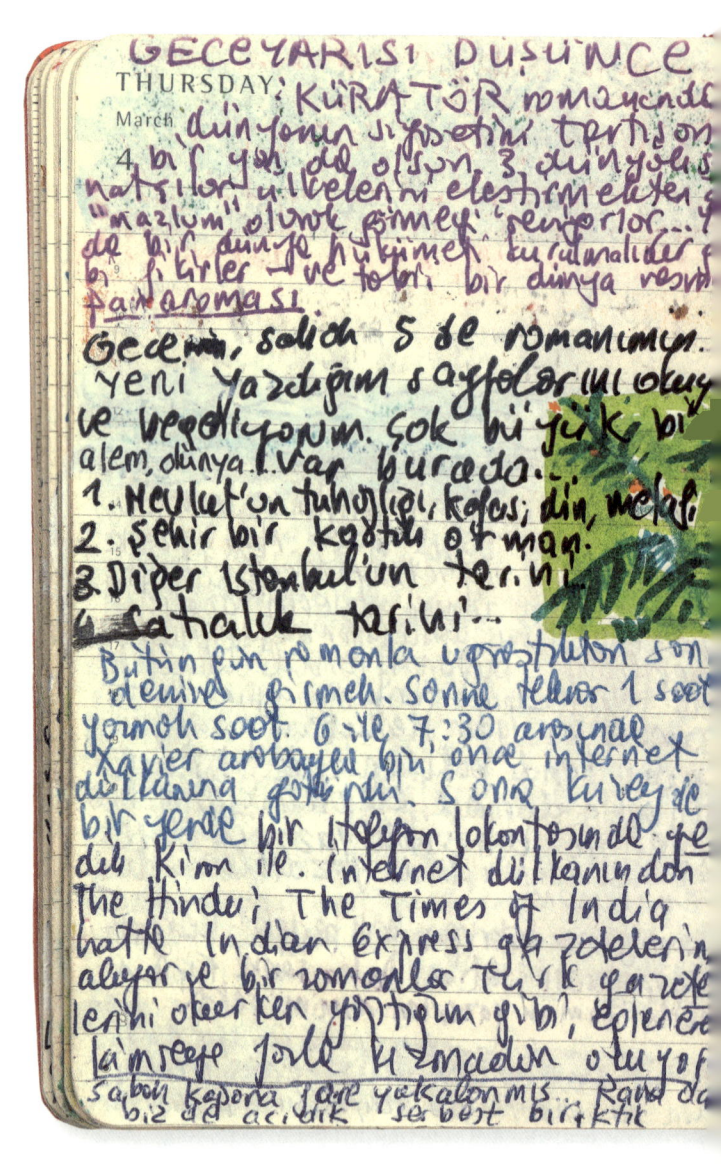

Going for a swim in the sea after working on the novel all day. Then writing for another hour between 6 and 7:30. Xavier drove us to the internet shop first. Then we went for dinner with Kiran to an Italian restaurant in the north. I buy newspapers, *The Hindu*, *The Times of India*, and even *The Indian Express*, from the internet shop, and read merrily through them all without getting too annoyed at anyone, just as I used to be able to do with Turkish newspapers. A mouse got caught in one of the traps this morning... Rana felt sorry for it, as did we, so we set it free.

I wake up in the middle of the night and start thinking about my new novel and Mevlut's story. I'M PLEASED WITH MY NEW NOVEL. A STORY NO ONE HAS TOLD BEFORE OF AN ENORMOUS CITY OF 10 MILLION PEOPLE...

Migrants new to the city, hawkers, *gecekondu* neighborhoods; electricity fraud, *gecekondu* wars, etc. etc.

Our last few days in Goa, but I'm not feeling too dispirited. The best part of these 5 weeks here is that: entirely unexpectedly, I've been able to step back into my novel, into the story of Mevlut. I am right inside the novel now. Sure, dealing with the museum back in Istanbul is going to be taxing and draining, but at least I have been reunited with my novel. And it feels like a glorious and truly original creation.

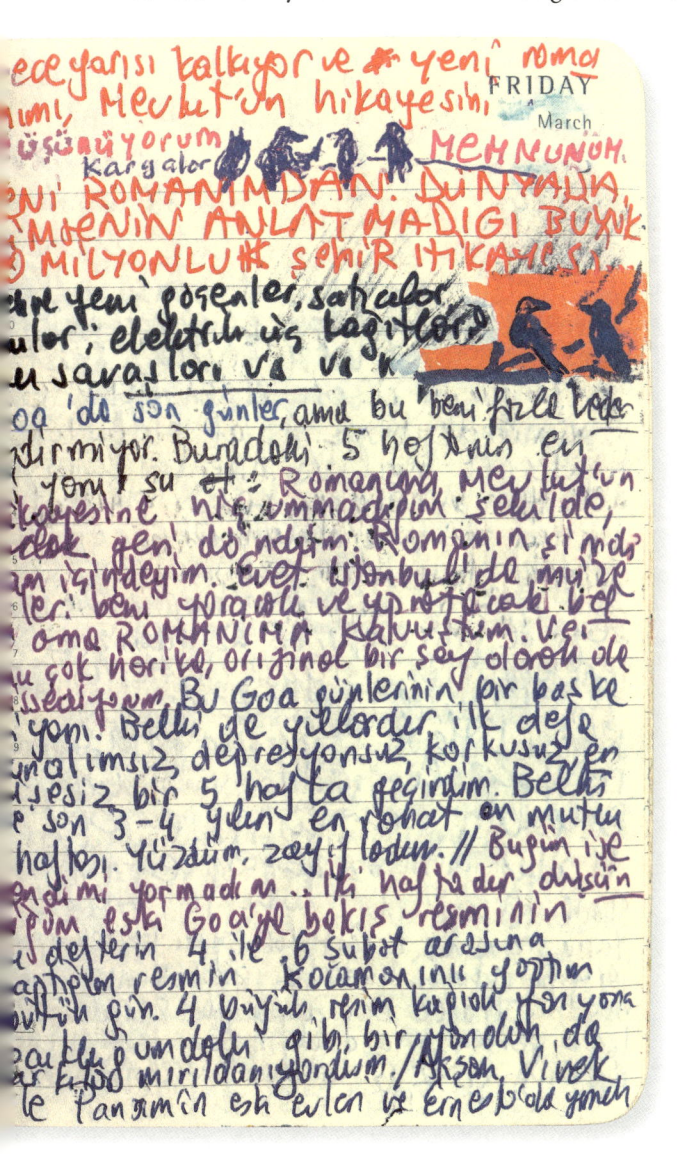

Here's another positive aspect of these Goan days. It may be the first time in years that I have spent 5 weeks without feeling despondent, depressed, afraid, or anxious. These might be the happiest 5 weeks I've had in 3 or 4 years. I've swum, I've lost weight.

I didn't work myself too hard today... I spent all day painting the view of Old Goa I've been thinking about for two weeks, a much larger version of the drawing I made on the pages for 4 to 6 February of this notebook. 4 large pieces of drawing paper side by side. I kept humming songs while working, just as I would do when I was a boy.

In the evening, a tour of Panjim's old homes with Vivek, and dinner at Ernesto's.

More thoughts on the novel last night. In brief: Mevlut should be directly involved in the construction of the *gecekondu* house, starting from his school days… The construction and demolition of *gecekondu* neighborhoods needs to be a story Mevlut personally lives and battles through. It can't just be an old story his father happens to tell him.

So during my first day in Goa I wasn't quite able to step back into the novel. I will need to rethink and revise the chronology and plot of the first 250 pages. DOLPHINS! AT LAST I've managed to catch a dolphin leaping out of the water and take a photo of it (10:15)

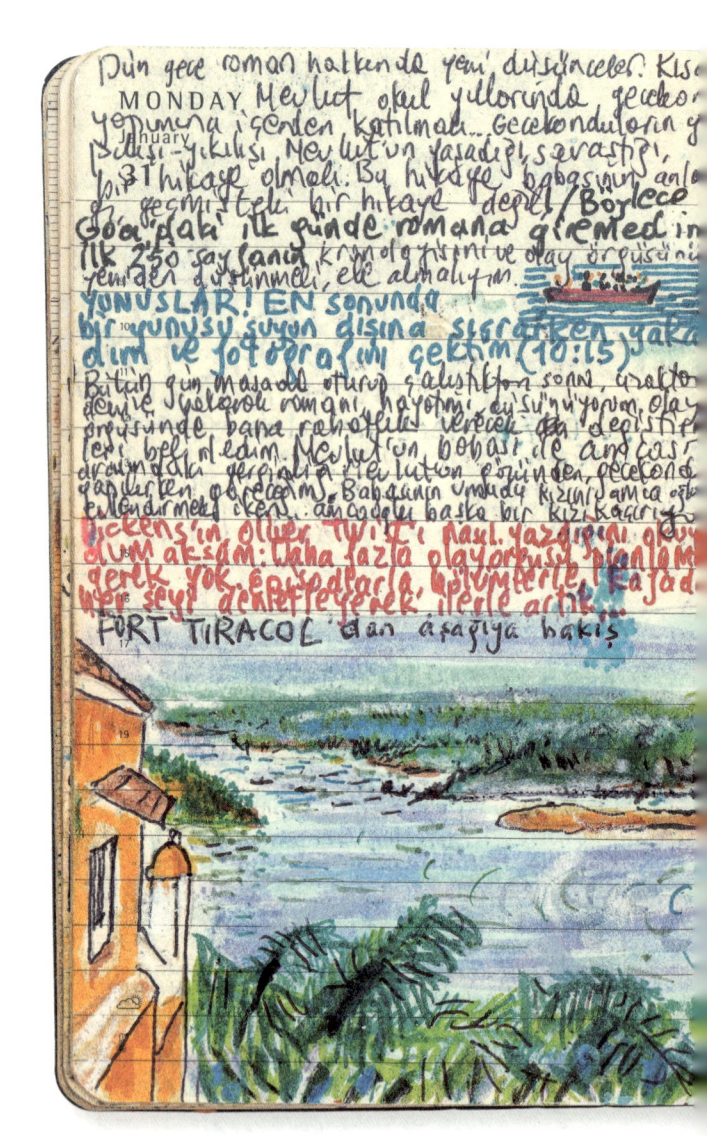

The view down from FORT TIRACOL

After spending all day writing at my desk, I look out at the sea in the distance and think of the novel and of my life. I've identified where to make the changes that will reassure me about the plot. I will portray the tension between Mevlut's father and his uncle through Mevlut's eyes during the construction of the *gecekondu* house. The father's hope is to marry his daughter off to a cousin, only for the cousin to run away with some other girl. In the evenings I'm reading about how Dickens wrote *Oliver Twist:* there is no need to spend any more time on plotting the novel. Time to advance by episode and by chapter now, improvising and checking as you go along…

I wake up at 7 and look out at the fishing boats in the distance and the fog wafting up from the forest as I picture Mevlut's school days. I worked from 3 to 5 in the morning. Asleep in bed and in every other moment I'm thinking of Mevlut and of his school.

But I haven't been able to write about it yet. I'm still making corrections.

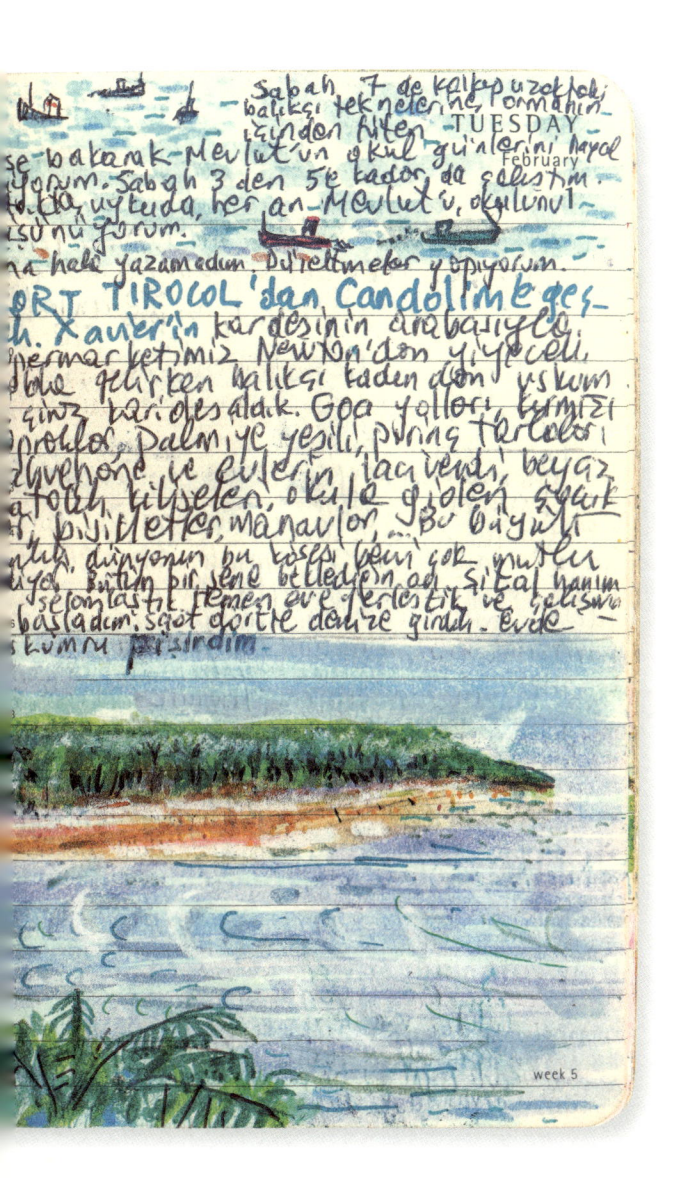

We moved on from FORT TIRACOL to Candolin. Went in Xavier's brother's car to buy food from our supermarket, Newton, then on the way back got some fresh and dried mackerel and prawns from a fisherwoman. The streets of Goa, the red soil, the palm tree green, the rice paddies, the coffee shops and the dark blue houses, the white Catholic churches, the children going to school, the bicycles, the greengrocers . . . This cheerful bustle, this corner of the world, bring me so much joy. The moment you've been waiting for all year . . . We exchanged greetings with Ms. Shital. Then we quickly settled into the house and I started working. At four we went for a swim. I made mackerel at home.

Courage, Orhan. Have more faith in the strangeness of the story and in Mevlut's dreams. Be more yourself, Orhan. Go on, dream harder; spread your wings, take flight! Oh, Mevlut. I need to think only of Mevlut's world and forget about any other.

Happiness is getting up and going downstairs in the morning, opening all the doors and petting the dogs, walking around the garden and along the wooden pier in the cool morning air and listening to the crows and the chirping of all the other birds as you wait for the water for your tea to boil in the kitchen. Then I sit at my desk and go back through what I wrote the day before. I'm enjoying writing about Mevlut's exile to the back of the classroom, his eagerness to sit at the front, all the mischief going on in the back row, etc. What fun it is to savor, to enjoy being Mevlut!

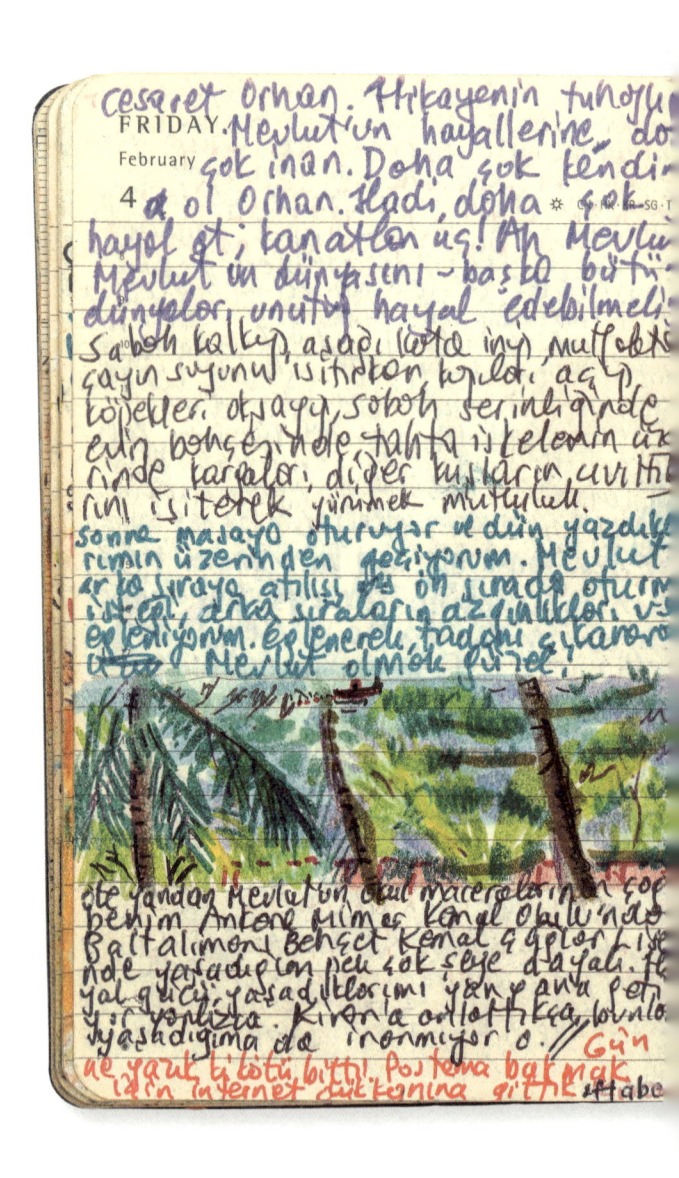

Yet most of Mevlut's adventures in school are based on incidents I experienced at the Architect Kemal School in Ankara and at the Behçet Kemal Çağlar High School in Baltalimanı. All that my imagination does is gather my experiences into a sequence. When I tell Kiran that all of these things once happened to me, she doesn't believe me.

Sadly the day ended badly. We went to the internet shop so I could check my mail. The news.

The news from back home is always bad, so it's best not to look at it. There's either someone threatening you, or someone else telling you some harrowing tale until you feel ashamed.

I slept ten hours last night and woke up at 8. Come on, Orhan, time to write about Mevlut, it's a beautiful morning, you're strong, you're wide awake, so come on then, write . . . I went for a swim in the beautiful sea. The water is blue. Clean. Deep. Sunshine. As I swam, I came up with a list of paragraphs—pages about Mevlut's school days showing how much he actually loved going to school. I'll write it all down today. If I manage to do it right, they might turn out to be some of Turkish literature's strangest-ever passages written about school.

I'm working on the list now. But it's not good to be too ambitious. I love writing. In truth, I am Mevlut.

I just wrote now about how much Mevlut enjoyed history class. Then I slowed down. Damn it. Sometimes the details are so clear that I end up missing the whole.

The sea

Today I sat at my desk and wrote for 9–10 hours. Dinner at Bomras. Just before bed, feeling tipsy, I picked up *The Black Book*—I have a copy of the İletişim edition with me—and said to Kiran there's Delhi and Firuz Shah in this book! and found them on p. 151 in the chapter "We're All Waiting for Him." What a chapter it is! Astonishing! Well done me . . .

I brought a copy of *The Black Book* with me, this novel I published twenty-two years ago, to read and be inspired by. What was Galip thinking as he walked around the streets of Istanbul at night? The moss and the writing on tombstones and walls. My job is to turn the city into text, and the text into a city. I am doing this here, surrounded by nature.

2011

Woke up late. Swam for forty minutes, feeling the lavish beauty of the sea on my skin . . . Meanwhile I was also thinking about what I'll write today. It's 11:40 now and I feel a kind of joy-euphoria. I have just finished writing the scene from Mevlut's account of his school years, with the librarian Aysel's speech on how to read books. Great fun. The chapters on Mevlut's school years are so entertaining, so colorful, and even I keep bursting into laughter when I go back and read through them. If I can take this cheerful, vibrant, faintly cynical voice and mix in the tenderness Mevlut deserves, as well as all his demons and his metaphysical universe . . . I know that *A Strangeness in My Mind* will be a glorious novel. I am tempted to just write and write, but I keep thinking I must not go past the 400-page mark. It shouldn't be longer than *The Black Book,* and I have a copy of that here on my desk—it's 430 pages.

I also have Borges on my desk: *El Aleph.* In keeping with the spirit of *The Black Book,* I seek to enter into Mevlut's metaphysical universe, and armed with the enthusiasm of feeling good about my novel, I start thinking about the other novels I must make sure to write over the next ten years: 1. A STRANGENESS IN MY MIND. 2. NIGHTS OF PLAGUE. 3. THE STRANGE TALE OF THE DOG THAT FED ON EUROPEANS. 4. THE WALL. 5. 252 PAINTINGS. These are all big, unsettling novels; they have the potential to be. I would like to finish these 5 books in the next ten years. I would like to open the museum, to dip my toes into the art world with paintings, prints, and replicas of the museum cabinets, to enjoy myself, to be experimental and happy. It's a lot of work, but it is also happy work. I left the house at 2 to check my mail and the rest of the day was ruined . . . All over the merest of trifles . . . There is no end to villains!

Near the house there is a huge and striking BANYAN tree. I respectfully acknowledge its presence every time I walk past, as if it were an elderly sage. The same kind of reverential awe I might feel upon seeing a colossal old fig tree in Turkey. But the BANYAN is not a fine and regal tree. It's an angry, withdrawn, troubled, but ultimately fascinating old man. A hidden nook on the dusty road . . .

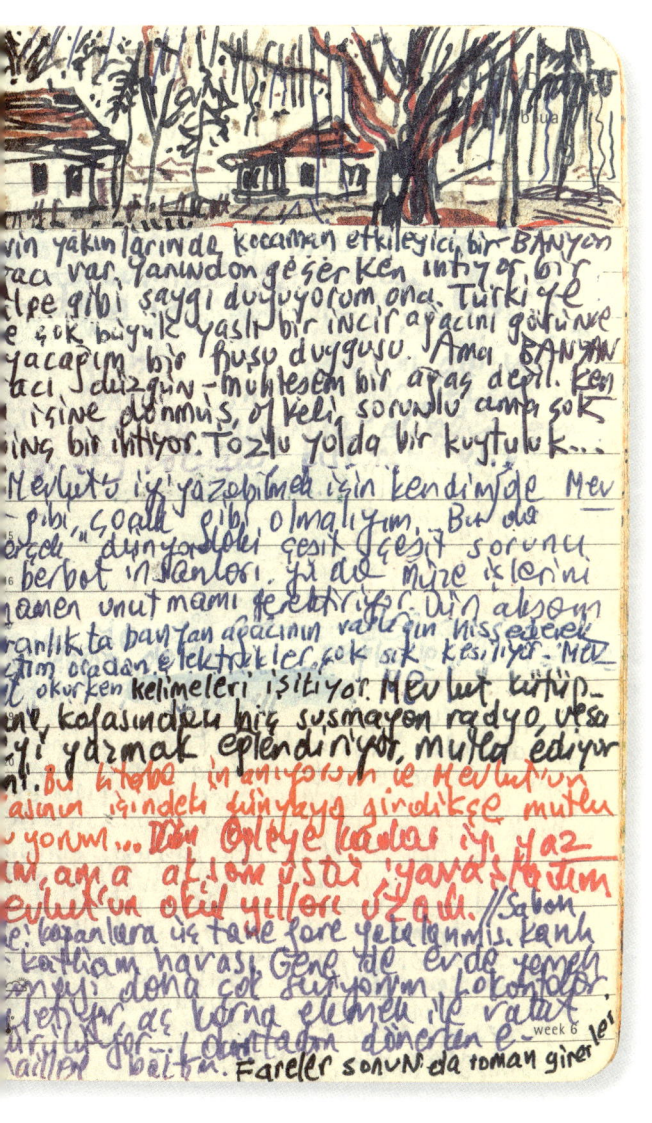

To write about Mevlut properly, I need to be like Mevlut, be a child again . . . This requires me to put all kinds of "real world" problems, dreadful people, and museum-related tasks out of my mind. Last night I walked past the banyan tree feeling its presence in the dark. We keep having power cuts. Mevlut hears words aloud in his head when he reads. It entertains and gladdens me to write about Mevlut, about the school library, about the radio always playing in his mind. I believe in this book, and the more I immerse myself in the world inside Mevlut's mind, the happier I feel . . . Yesterday I wrote quite well in the morning but slowed down in the afternoon. Mevlut's school days are taking a while.

At home in the morning: three rats caught in the traps. An atmosphere of bloody slaughter. I still prefer to eat at home, though. Restaurants always keep you waiting, they while away the time by feeding you bread on an empty stomach . . . On the way back from the restaurant I checked my emails. The rats will make it into the novel eventually.

Finding joy in small things and working all day without seeing anyone. There is no greater happiness than that. As I write, some part of my mind is also occupied with the sounds that drift all the way up to my desk, the chirping birds, the barking dogs. I savor the green, orange, yellow light, the color of the sea I can glimpse in the distance, feeling its presence there. It's been three or four days now and I still have Kars, the photographs, those lies weighing on my mind. Mevlut "sees" the math equation on the blackboard and solves it. The legend of Mevlut is born. I'd like to be able to dive into scenes faster, to write this chapter more quickly and lavishly than this. Sometimes I survey this wealth of detail and wonder if I will ever finish the Adventures of Mevlut. I'm advancing very slowly. It's a little like swimming across an ocean! I LOVE MEVLUT... I MUST PROTECT HIM AND MAKE HIM INTO SOMEONE EVERYBODY LOVES.

AFTERNOON IN INDIA

I didn't even leave the house today. Good old Mevlut, I'd do anything for you. I'm enjoying spending time at home this year. I'm swimming more, and being more disciplined about it. In the evenings I make grilled fish for dinner—kingfish. And some salad... We've been following the popular uprisings in Egypt on CNN and the BBC. How popular are they really? *The Wall Street Journal* has asked if I'll write a piece... Those who've been claiming all these years that you can't have Islam and democracy at the same time!... are now wondering would Israel be upset if democracy were to come. You do feel elated, exhilarated at the thought of democracy arriving in Muslim countries. But I know that if I do end up writing the piece, I won't be able to devote my time to Mevlut... *The Spy Who Came in from the Cold*—Richard Burton's performance is exceptional. The BBC—on Caravaggio. In the evenings, after dinner, we sit at home and watch DVDs with Kiran.

We get back home from the Italian restaurant where we've just had dinner, determined to go to bed early: I switch the television on and I am overjoyed to see that there has been a REVOLUTION in Egypt, and that Hosni Mubarak has fled Cairo. What crowds! Power is currently in the hands of the army. You can never trust the army, they can turn their backs on the enraged masses at any time and cling to power . . . But for now there is only joy, and I too am full of great joy, of happiness and excitement. CNN and the BBC are showing the crowds in Cairo's Tahrir Square . . . The interviewees are conscious of the euphoric mood and say that the people of Egypt have achieved a great revolution without any recourse to violence. We spend a long time watching the jubilation, the joyful dancing, the scenes of happiness among the multitudes gathered in the square. Young women in headscarves, soldiers lifted up on people's shoulders, and the indescribable low roar coming from the gleeful crowd. The roar of joy and exultation.

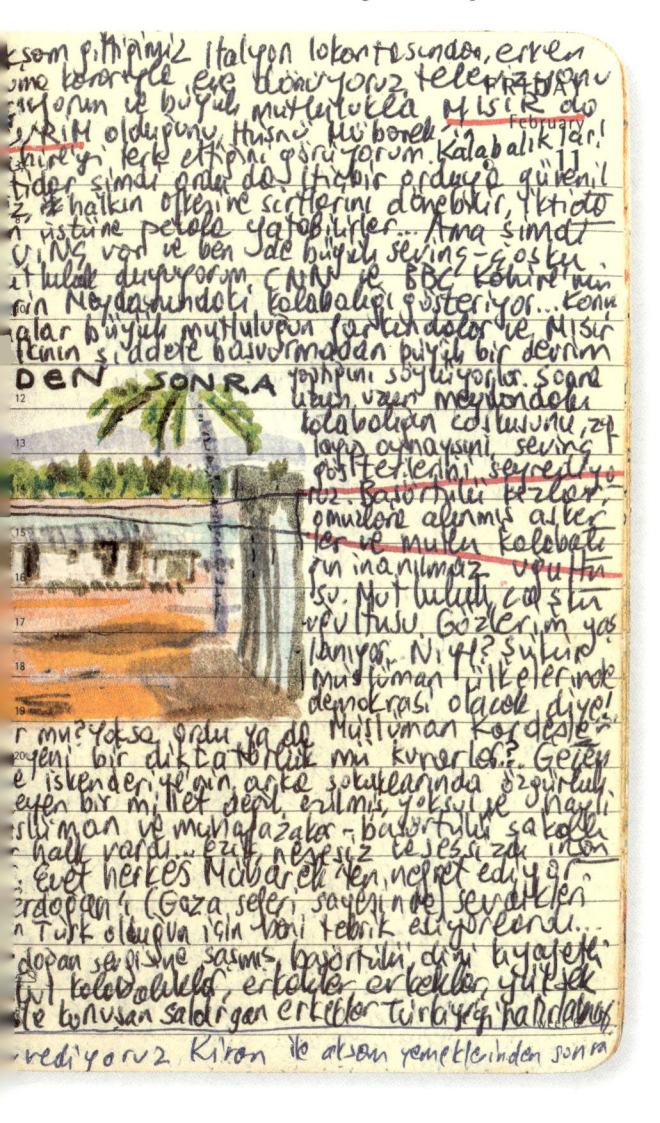

My eyes fill with tears. Why? Because Muslim countries will finally experience democracy! But will they? Or will the army or the Muslim Brotherhood establish a new dictatorship? I saw no great yearning for freedom on the backstreets of Alexandria last year, only an oppressed, destitute, pious, and conservative—bearded and headscarf-wearing—populace . . . Everyone seemed quiet, joyless, downtrodden. Yes, they all hated Mubarak, and since they loved Erdoğan (thanks to his Gaza expedition) and knew that I was Turkish, they kept congratulating me . . . I was surprised to discover their love of Erdoğan. The impoverished throngs in headscarves and religious garb; the men, the men, the loud aggressive men reminded me of Turkey.

181

In the morning I set my usual swimming schedule etc. aside and decided to devote the whole day to writing about Mevlut's adventures, without wasting time on anything else. By 11:30 I was still on the first page. The story of wretched Talip, who complains to Mevlut about how he is always being beaten up by a high school thug. Then the story of Hamdi, student number 1573, who—like Mevlut—has a crush on the English teacher, Eda, and also the story of little Ahmet, who prefers playing with the girls rather than the boys. Then on to two brothers stealing copies of *Mind and Matter* from the library… All of these details and episodes, such as the brothers stealing books from the library; or pupils coming to the library and being given a random issue of some old magazine—including, of course, *Mind and Matter*—are drawn in some way from my own life. That's what they used to do at the Architect Kemal Primary School in 1960–62. Same with the powdered milk from UNICEF, and the fish oil. Or even the vice principal Skeleton and Blind Muhtar from the Terakki Foundation School in Şişli.

Many of the incidents from Mevlut's school days are actually modified versions of my own experiences. But the chapter and all these details have gone on for too long… I would have preferred to round the chapter off in a simpler fashion… Nevertheless, I'm relieved to have written three pages today.

In the evening Kiran and I watched the movie *City of God* at home. I saw it for the first time with Elif in New York, then one more time on DVD with Rüya. A vast and shocking *gecekondu*-slum-favela story. With criminal-mafia-drug gangs mixed in. It was a little too gory. But I admire its depiction of police violence, and its uncovering of life in the favelas. Of course I brought the DVD to Goa because I thought it might help me write my novel. An epic tale set among the poor and in *gecekondu* neighborhoods. Though in this case the violence and bloodshed overshadow the particulars of building and running cities, etc.

I wake up in the morning and lie in bed, thinking. I'm writing at great length about Mevlut's school days. Just as I had hoped, there is both a documentary side to Mevlut's story, and a rather strange side . . . But is it a little too long? Think about *A Bend in the River* . . .

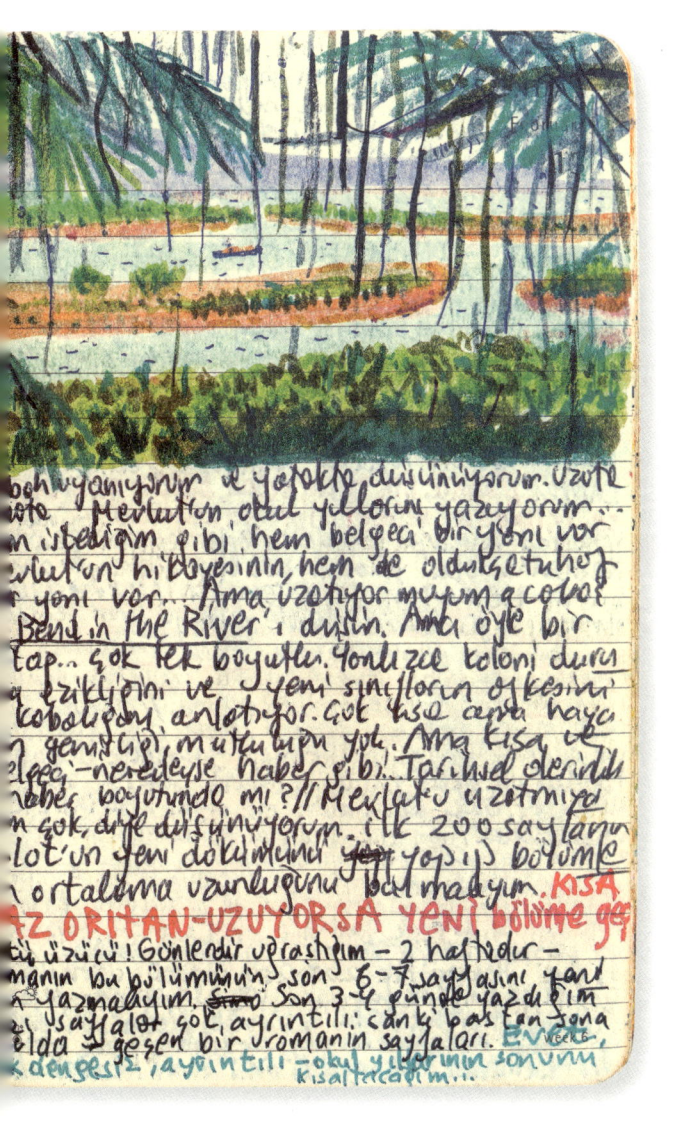

But that kind of book is too . . . one-dimensional. It concentrates only on the oppression of the colonized and the rage and callousness of the emerging classes. It's very short, but it contains none of the joy and expansiveness of life. It is brief and documentary—almost like a news report . . . Does historical depth belong in that journalistic dimension?

I keep thinking I mustn't let Mevlut's story drag on. I need to make a new plan for the first 200 pages and for the Plot, and find the right average length for each chapter. KEEP IT SHORT, ORHAN—AND IF IT GETS TOO LONG, move on to the next chapter.

Bad, depressing news! I will need to rewrite the last 6–7 pages of this section in this chapter I've been toiling over for days now—for the past 2 weeks. Some of the pages I've written in the last 3–4 days are far too detailed: they read like the pages of a novel set entirely in a school. Yes, they are unbalanced and too detailed—I will need to trim the end of this school section . . .

distant mountains...

In GOA, on Freud and the impossibility of describing dreams in words

Last night I had that familiar bad dream again. In the end I woke up in fear, though it wasn't exactly a nightmare. I was alone in the room where I write. I wasn't sure how much I had screamed. The dream was the same as always—but there were differences too... The scary part was not so much the "subject" of the dream, but the dark, black-and-white, dramatic mountain landscape. I was afraid of the landscape but at the same time I wanted to keep looking at it. There was that same sheer cliff again—then a slope, the meaning of life, and that tall soaring thing I could never quite see. But it wasn't even that important! I have no idea how to interpret this dream.

The summer when I was nineteen, I read Freud's INTERPRETATION OF DREAMS and his other book on slips of the tongue. These are beautiful, literary books, and for the rest of my life I have believed everything I learned from them. But I did not find Freud's general system equally impressive or convincing. I would have liked for Freud to tell me the MEANING of my dream, but in order for that to happen, I would first have to tell him Everything. The problem: using words to describe your dreams to someone else is... a futile task. Dreams cannot be distilled into words. (Is it possible to describe the *Mona Lisa*—or one of Caspar David's paintings in words?) Dreams are made to be seen.

Before I go to sleep at night, and in the middle of the night (waking up like my father used to do), I always get lost in my thoughts and take a long time to fall asleep again. Words and images coming to me of their own accord: I love my notebook. I like flipping it open and reading what it says, I like drawing in it, and I like flipping it open again to look at my drawings. The notebook allows me to write all the time, to experience—if I want to—the pleasure of writing down, of having the opportunity to write down, everything I'm feeling.

I woke up at 8 this morning. The whole world is perfectly calm. I put on my swimsuit and walked to the beach. It's still cool outside. The sea is dead calm. There's hardly anyone on the beach. Some staff placing cushions on the loungers and sweeping rubbish. I swam without tiring myself out too much. Basking in the full splendor of the sea, the world, the morning. Now I'm sitting at my desk. I'm eating fruit, drinking tea, and thinking with immoderate optimism of how glorious it is to be a novelist.

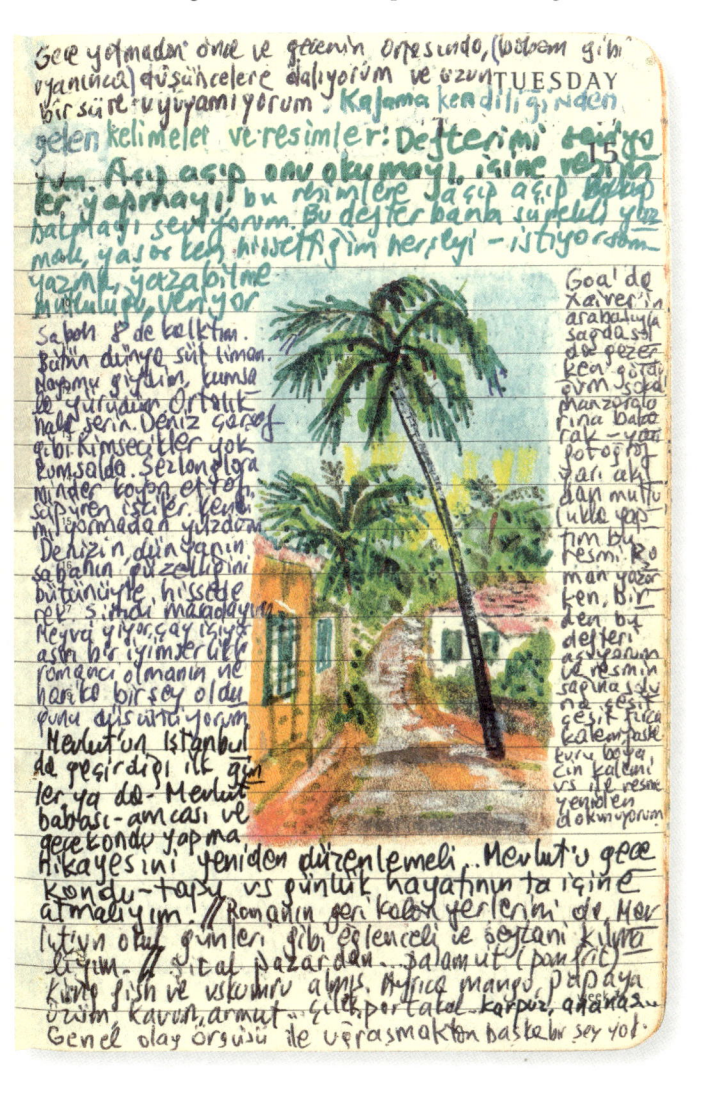

I enjoyed drawing this image, which is based—partly from photographs and partly from memory—on the streets I have seen when roaming around Goa in Xavier's car. When I'm writing, I sometimes flip this notebook open, pick up a paintbrush, a pencil, pastels, colored pencils, Chinese ink, etc., and add a few more touches to the drawing.

Mevlut's first few days in Istanbul or the story of Mevlut and his father and uncle building the *gecekondu* will need to be revised. I must throw Mevlut into the thick of things, of *gecekondu* construction and title deeds.

As for the rest of the novel, I need to make it as fun and devilishly mischievous as the chapters on Mevlut's school days.

Shital has bought . . . pomfret, kingfish, and mackerel from the market. Plus mangoes, papaya, grapes, melon, pears, strawberries, oranges, watermelon, pineapple . . . No choice but to keep working on the overall plot.

I didn't write a single word yesterday either. It's because I've been revising the overall plot of the novel instead. Which essentially means rewriting most of the first 40–50 pages of the book. These pages have already been revised before. It isn't the first time I've thought about rewriting various chapters, or indeed the whole thing, from scratch. And eventually I do rewrite them. I wouldn't say I've never changed my mind about the start of a novel this often. I wrote the beginnings of *The Black Book* and *My Name Is Red* many times over. But I'm getting tired now of having to work on these first few chapters again and again . . .

I was weirdly tired yesterday. I slept for 10 hours. Now, after a swim in the sea, I'm sorting out the order of events—the timeline for when Mevlut's father and his uncle (Uncle Mehmet) arrive in Istanbul for the first time in the 1960s.

I don't want to plan the novel, I want to write it, to be Mevlut.

View of the shore to the left from the front of the house

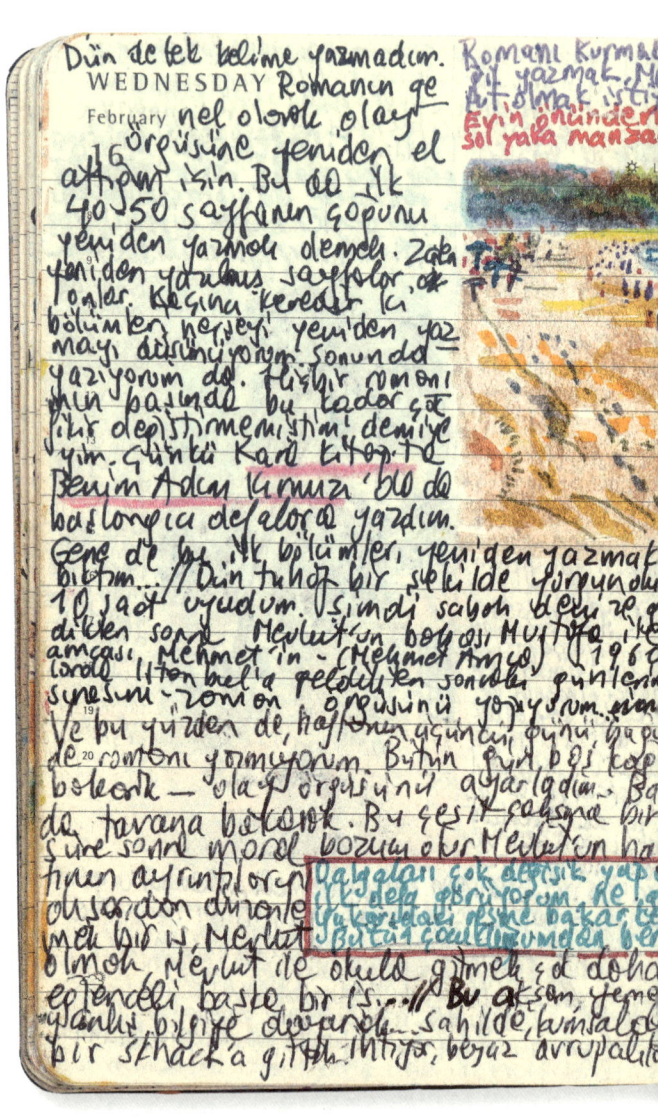

So even today, the third day of the week, I still haven't written anything. I've spent the whole day staring at a blank piece of paper—working on the plot. Or sometimes staring at the ceiling. After a while, this kind of work can be demoralizing. It's one thing to arrange the details of Mevlut's life from the outside, and quite another, and much more entertaining, to be Mevlut, to go to school with Mevlut . . .

The way you draw waves is so unusual. No one draws waves like that. I'd never seen them before, they look wonderful, says Kiran, study-

We followed some poor advice tonight and ended up having dinner . . . at a seaside shack on the beach. Elderly white Europeans sitting on the veranda, looking out at the sea and

Today, after a great deal of agony and self-reproach over another day in which I haven't written anything new, I returned to my novel at 6:30 in the evening... by making additions and edits to some of the older chapters. I feel like a bad person when I'm not able to write.

An idea for *Nights of Plague*. The Western delegation arriving at the castle is there to dismantle the building (or a significant structure within it, such as a temple, say) stone by stone and carry it, with Sultan Hamid's permission, back to the West. The group therefore includes architects and experts with knowledge of the castle's artistic history... Halfway through *Nights of Plague,* anyone who is not a Muslim—or is not religious—any Christians, Westerners, etc., have been removed, killed, driven out, or forced to convert to Islam. The very few who remain are nowhere to be seen!...

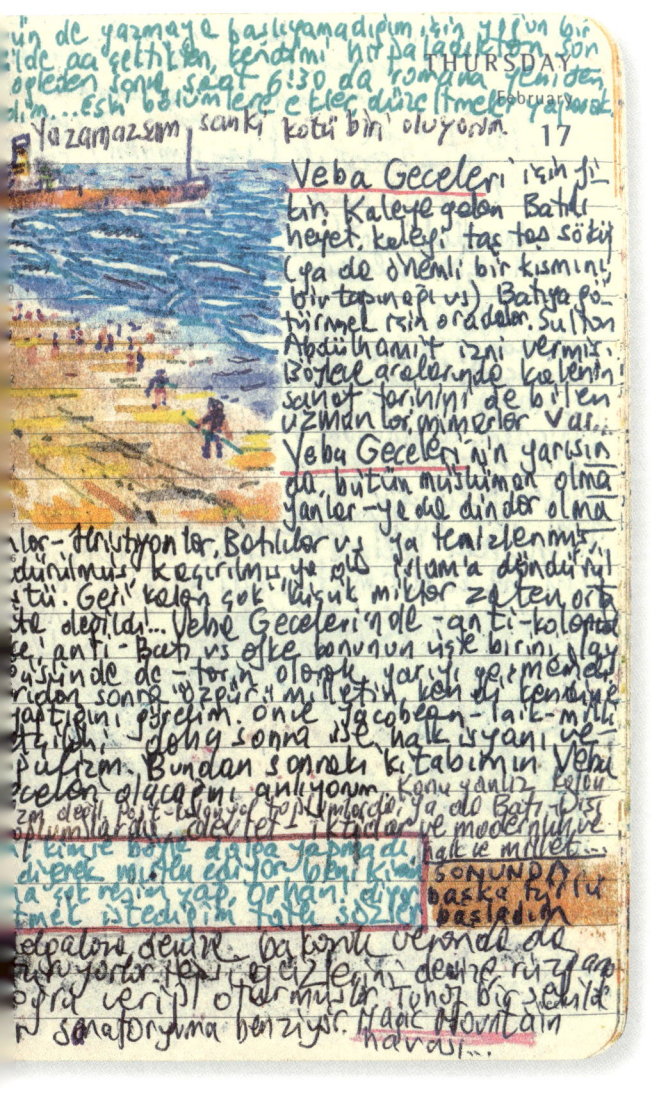

Anticolonial rage in *Nights of Plague*, anti-Western rage, etc., must not take up more than a third of the novel's subject matter, and within the development of the plot itself—along the timeline, it must not go past the halfway mark. Once the first half is over, let us see what the liberated populace will achieve on its own. First a Jacobin—secularist—nationalism—followed by a revolt of the masses and populism. I can see now that the next book I write will be *Nights of Plague*. The subject is not just colonialism, but also modernity, peoples and nations, and the nature of the state and government in postcolonial or non-Western societies...

---

ing the picture above and making me very happy. You should paint more, Orhan! she says. Kind words I've yearned to hear ever since I was a child.

IN THE END I began in a different way

---

the waves. They're all sitting with their faces turned toward the water and the breeze. Weirdly, it feels like a sanatorium. Like something out of *The Magic Mountain*...

The book: some indecision around Mevlut's adventures. On the one hand I want to tell a wholesome realist tale in the style of Dickens, or even Hamsun and Steinbeck... On the other, I also keep thinking of a more entertaining story, one that makes more room for imagination, for plot and drama... But I do enjoy being Mevlut. Phoned Rüya in New York. Told her I'm writing this novel for the fun of being Mevlut, for the pleasure of writing just for the sake of writing, without thinking about anything else. I said I'm writing a Dickensian story about a poor but lovable child. "Wonderful, keep going!" replied clever Rüya. Mevlut is going to turn out great. In the afternoon, I fell asleep. Then I happily wrote some more. After that I went for a swim, still thinking of Mevlut. Then I wrote again. In the evening I put the oven on to bake some fish while picturing Mevlut's first visit to his uncle's home in Istanbul.

The Libyan revolt on TV, and cruel Ghaddafi. While the West is reacting appropriately to these uprisings, China and Russia immediately take Ghaddafi's side. Non-Western states dislike democracy. I called Asuman to discuss the Penguin-İletişim classics collaboration.

After midnight I wake up toward 5 o'clock as I do every morning, but unfortunately I can't go back to sleep... Yet all I want to do is fall asleep again so I can wake up strong and well rested, and think of my dear Mevlut, write about him, bring him to life. Last night, after turning off the lights and getting into bed, I had this strange thought: I forced myself to get up, and here is the thought as I wrote it down in my notebook. I should spend one or two chapters writing about Mevlut's ascent to heaven, his journey to the realm of the angels, his experiences and emotions up there in the skies.

In the morning... we swam with Kiran in the calm unruffled sea. At 8 I went and sat down with Mevlut. It's 1:30 now... I haven't burrowed so deep into a novel for years. Happiness. Mevlut is at his uncle's house, there has just been a power cut, etc. I am completely inside the novel. For the last two hours I've been making up and writing a story about a man who returns one snowy night, drunk and alone, after his daughter runs away in the snow. It's been a very happy day. I've written 4 pages. We watched Visconti's *Death in Venice.* Come on, Mevlut!

The HOUSE AND DAILY LIFE in GOA

This is the room I've been steadily working in for the past three years, where I sometimes take naps in the afternoon, and where I occasionally go to sleep after midnight.

In 2009 we would sit on these chairs on the balcony in the evenings

The bedroom

fan

desk

swimsuit
towel

The TV where we watched DVDs and followed the Arab uprisings on the BBC and CNN in the evenings is in here

Musti

Lazy Susti

The crows are terribly noisy and steal our fruit

I wrote these words and drew this picture to amuse myself as I sat in this room thinking of Mevlut and writing about his adventures... Coming to this room upstairs to concentrate on Mevlut is the greatest happiness there can be. In the evening Vivek took us to some ridiculous discotheque–rock music establishment that young people go to on Anjuna Beach (from the word Hanjuman—Arab horse merchants). People sitting on the floor, eyeing each other as they fiddle with their mobile phones. Should've stayed at home and read Tolstoy...

Sometimes I'll get stuck on some inane detail until I can't go on with the story in my head. Like now, for example: I want Mevlut and his cousin to wander around Duttepe for a little while, but try as I might, I can't seem to get them out into the darkening night. These moments of impasse are the most draining and time-consuming aspects of writing a novel. Anyway, I've managed to get the boys out now—Mevlut and Ali. But I never got the chance to go on . . . because we took the car and went to Panjim pier. We met up with Wendell and Gerome and got on their motorboat to sail around the Mandovi River, the streams and canals where the branches of the mangrove trees reach across the water, and all around the bird sanctuary. I took some photographs. Inland along the river, they are slicing a colossal mountain up as if it were a wheel of cheese and sending iron ore to China and the rest of the world in trucks and rafts.

KIRAN's towel and blue bikini

KIRAN writing her novel on her computer

Behind her, the kitchen and dinner table

A poisoned mousetrap

And that's me. I'm waving at you. I'm rather pleased to be here in Goa, thinking about Mevlut, and to appear in this drawing.

This image here conveys Goan bliss! This coconut green, the garden, the dogs, the yellow sand, the trees, the joy of writing together in this enormous house, the fruit we eat in the morning, the sun, writing, swimming, and the happiness all of these things kindle within me! Optimism! The strength of this drawing is that it portrays our life both in a documentary style (by showing what we do at home), and through colors and emotions . . .

Alhambra: after the press conference etc. this morning, I finally managed to visit this extraordinary place. My mind has been steeped in architecture for the past two weeks, so the Alhambra was utterly engrossing. It's not the history I am interested in, but the architectural details, the patterns, the *muqarnas*. I study everything with an eye to how I might transpose some of the details here to ... the Museum of Innocence. Tranquility, profundity, refinement. There is much to relish here if you can just avoid thinking about the brutality of history. Half of my mind is on the museum in Istanbul, the other is on the emotions elicited by this wonder I am seeing here. How to bring together classical Islamic architecture with the Museum of Innocence? I wander around the Alhambra in something of a daze, without a guidebook, trying to feast my eyes on everything I see ... And thinking to myself, I will be back ...

Outside, at 3:30, a meal at a restaurant and a glass of wine. I slept in the hotel room. Internet: mail: museum business ... Photos of the house at Harvard, journalists in the lobby wanting to do interviews. Had a sandwich on the hotel's terracelike balcony with Vikram Seth and Juan (a Colombian novelist). I had some wine and left for my evening event at the Festival. It was raining, so it was held at night at the theater in the city. It went well. Just a niggle in my throat. It's been a long day. I'm tired.

Morning: Before going down for breakfast on the hotel balcony ... A feeling of optimism. Sunshine. Kiran is having a shower. I peer through the bathroom window that opens onto the balcony, and startle her. I'm in Granada, at the Alhambra, but the back of my mind is on the museum, in Istanbul ... Breakfast: we are guests on a radio program. The newspapers talk about us, but respectfully, not in the language of the paparazzi. In the morning a conversation with the architect Bereket. He's a good man, but slow. Then I went to the Alhambra, and there a *shadirvan* and the sound of splashing water reminding me again of Tanpınar's poem "Time in Bursa" ... Cypress trees. An atmosphere that reminds me of Bursa, where we went on a family trip back in 1962, its Green Mosque, and early Ottoman mosques. The cypress trees, the splash of water, I see my childhood again ...

I find the most humane, the prettiest, most geometric, and mightiest side of Islamic architecture. Self-confidence. Serenity, calm.

There is a beauty in the Alhambra that can make you forget all the savagery of history. I went back to the hotel, Rüya called, I wished Şeküre a happy "mother's day." Then we went into the city for the first time ... We ate fish at a pizzeria in Granada. We walked around for a while. We sat in a coffee shop where I wrote in this notebook. I wrote on empty and half-filled pages too: I don't want to forget my days here. I find forgetting painful ... What sticks to my mind from these two days is: the elegance of thuluth calligraphy, the *muqarnas,* white lacelike thuluth script, plaster, timber, water: all of it so full of dignity and grace ... The dreamlike beauty of Andalusian architecture ...

In the painting *The Adoration of the Magi,* hanging in the Uffizi Gallery, the painter Botticelli looks at us from the bottom right of his painting. Perhaps I or others could do the same in Füsun's bird paintings.

A 2nd important thought while visiting the Uffizi: To decorate the vitrine covers, the walls, the ceilings, and any empty spaces with paintings. To make sure the glazed wood coverings are not too plain. And as there is no way I will be able to finish doing all that within 1 year . . . to open the museum anyway but continue over the years to embellish it with more paintings. 3. To put a video recording on the ground floor explaining that the museum is not yet finished, and that it may never be finished even if I were to keep working on it for the rest of my life. In other words, an 8-to-10-minute video of me methodically talking the visitor through the museum and its meaning. All while pointing from the screen at the museum itself, at this or that detail, and at the world . . .

There should be a rainbow in one of Füsun's paintings. Slender and dainty.

In the morning we went to the Palazzo Vecchio first with our gracious guide Emanuela. The *studiolo,* a tiny room covered in paintings, had made just as deep an impression on me when I had first come here with Rüya 4 years ago. It's like a Cabinet of Curiosities. The display cupboard doors, the ceilings, everything is a painting. The Innocence should be the same. Then on to the Uffizi. Botticelli must have had a Scandinavian model. I took a long time studying Caravaggio's *Sacrifice of Isaac.* We spent a total of 5 hours in the Uffizi and its bookshop. Back in the hotel room, emails. Dinner at a restaurant, wine.

Sleepless night. Bad dreams, but when they wake me up I can't even work out what it is that's scaring me. I slept 6 hours. Stared at the ceiling for 1.5. The emptiness of life. A deep-seated dread. It's as if I were in space. Woke up early with Kiran. Breakfast. Walk to the station . . . It feels good to be in the world, but there's a feeling of unease in my soul, in my blood. Sleeplessness!

At the Laurentian Library, an idea: in the Museum of I, the books tied to chains, hanging from the ceiling, etc., must all be very special editions, not ordinary ones. And they must be available for purchase in the museum. A deck of cards made from the most exceptional items displayed in the museum. To be sold in the library or museum gift shop.

Ahmet Öğüt, who depicts TV celebrities as if they were greengrocers, say, could do one of me too: he's joining us for dinner this evening.

We drank so much at the restaurant, so so much. It was wonderful! The fascists in Turkey keep making trouble. So Kiran and I drank and made merry. In Florence—nighttime.

We spent another two hours this morning wrestling with the novel. I realized that the tombola chapter is a little tedious and wearisome, so I make some parts shorter. I wrote this chapter in bits and pieces in New York, in autumn 2007, while promoting *Other Colors*. The reason it is a little weaker and looser than the others is because I did not write it in one go . . . Around midday we left the house and went down to San Marco in the vaporetto . . . Crossing and touring Venice in a vaporetto is the best thing there is:

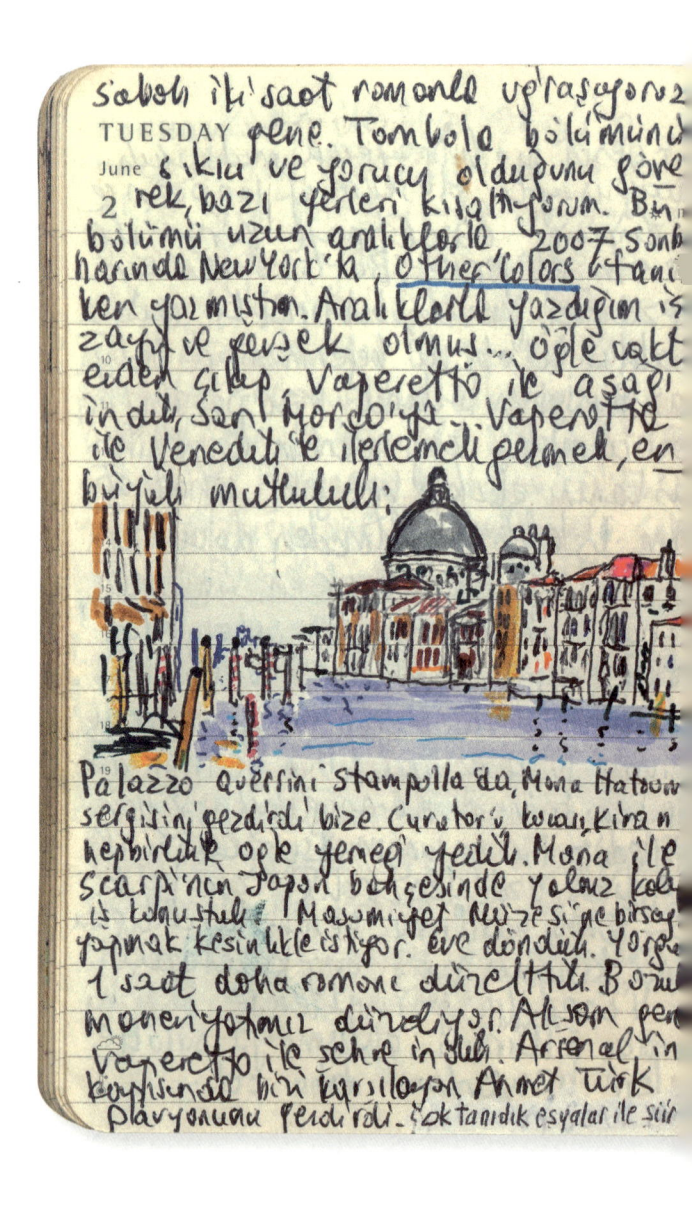

Mona Hatoum showed us around her exhibition at the Palazzo Querini Stampalia. We all had lunch together, with her curator, her husband, and Kiran. Later Mona and I were alone in Scarpi's Japanese garden, and talked about work. She definitely wants to do something for the Museum of Innocence. We went back home. Tired. We spent 1 more hour fixing the novel. Our spirits are beginning to lift. In the evening, we took a vaporetto to the city again. Ahmet met us in front of the Arsenal and took us on a tour of the Turkish pavilion. It's difficult to find poetry in such familiar objects!

THIS IS WHERE WE STAYED

Museo Grassi   Campo di San Samuele   Palazzo Cappello Malipiero

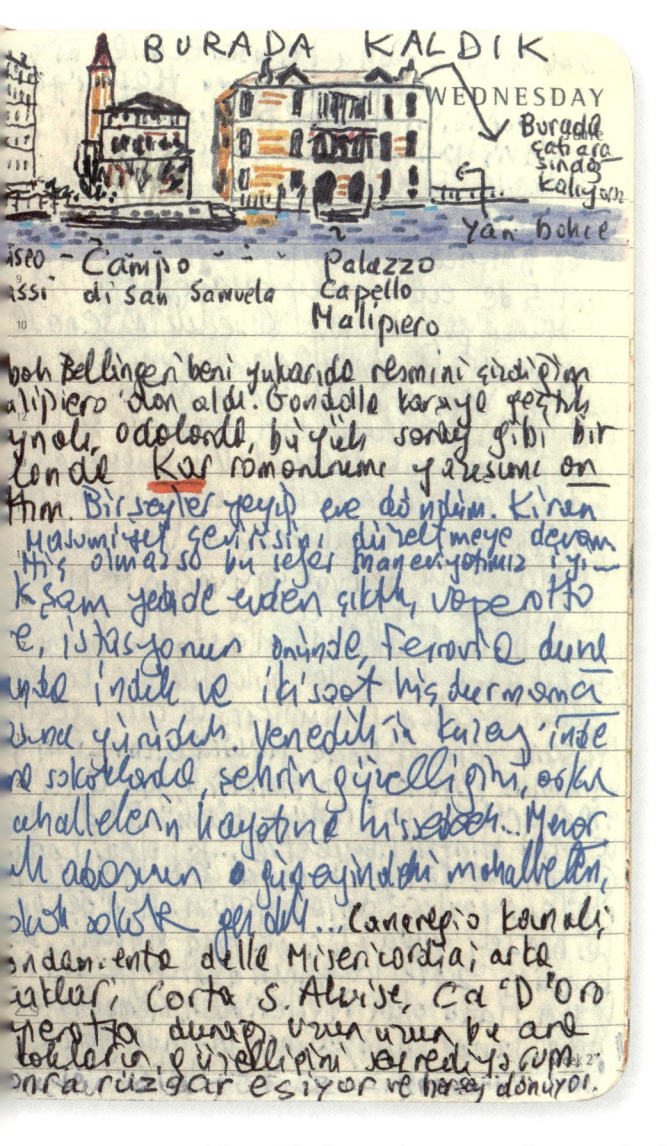

We are staying in an attic room here

side garden

Bellingeri picked me up in the morning from the Malipiero, which I've drawn above. We went across in a gondola. In mirrored rooms and in a large palatial hall, I talked about how I wrote my novel *Snow*. I had something to eat, then went back home. We continue correcting the translation of *Innocence* with Kiran. At least this time our morale is high . . . We left the house at seven in the evening, got off the vaporetto at the Ferrovia stop by the station, and walked nonstop for two hours. In these northern backstreets of Venice, we could feel the beauty of the city, the life of its more peripheral neighborhoods . . . We walked up and down every street in the neighborhoods just south of the cemetery island. The Cannaregio Canal, the Fondamenta della Misericordia; back alleys, Corta S. Alvise, the Ca' D'Oro vaporetto stop. I spend a long time contemplating the splendor of these backstreets. Then the wind begins to blow and everything changes.

A long day. Morning: I get up at 8, work on the translation, respond to the last few queries. Then back to the university with Giampiero, Mario, Yasemin—the whole team. I give a long speech, remembering the Norton Lectures too. We had a coffee all together in Campo Santa Margherita. Then I went home.

We went to the Biennale for a second time. This time I lay on the floor at the end of a long corridor in the Arsenal, in the darkness of an Italian artist's . . . installation designed to evoke deep space, infinity, etc., and had a good nap. After 6:30 we took the vaporetto to Calle D'Oro and wandered around the backstreets there for ages, taking photographs. Dinner at a lovely restaurant. Then we went home. By now we've stopped getting drunk and lost on the way back.

I spend the morning writing my 4th Venice piece, on the Biennale. We leave the house around noon and visit the New Zealand pavilion, etc. The palazzi are more interesting... The Singapore pavilion; the young man who has collected cinema tickets and lobby cards could well be Turkish... They've reshot famous scenes from classic Singaporean melodramas: or at least they've pretended to. Scenes reflected in mirrors; or reshoots and replays from *In the Mood for Love:* it was all very striking, and congruous with the atmosphere in the Museum of Innocence.

Film memorabilia, posters, tickets, and an insight into the culture of melodrama outside of the West. The modern middle-class non-Western "individual" interested in collecting will always start off with film paraphernalia.

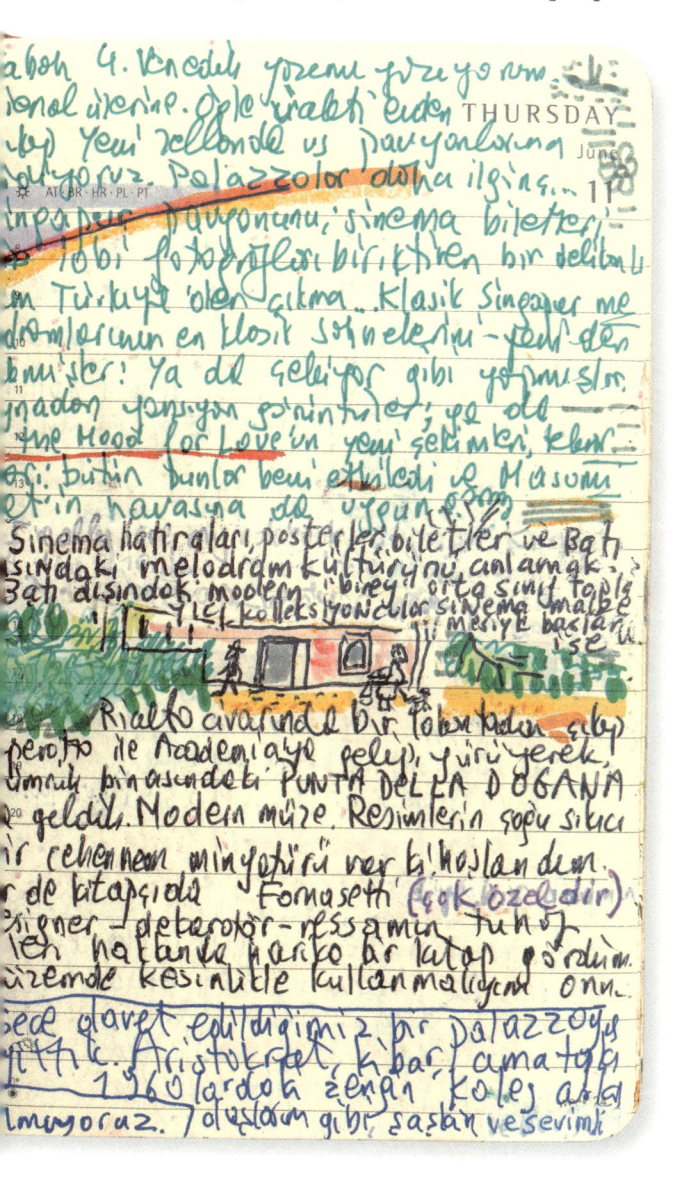

We left a restaurant in the Rialto area, took a vaporetto to Accademia, and walked to the PUNTA DELLA DOGANA in the customs building. A modern museum. Most of the art is boring. A miniature painting of hell! which I loved. And I saw in a bookshop a wonderful volume on the designer–interiors expert–painter Fornasetti (a remarkable figure) and his curious projects. I must use it in my museum.

In the evening we were invited to a palazzo. Our wealthy host, a courteous aristocrat who seemed to be stuck in the 1960s, had the same wide-eyed charm as my private school classmates.

199

Morning in Asolo. We devoted the day to *Palladio*'s oeuvre. We went to nearby Villa Barbaro ... A cream palette and pastel-hued landscapes on the walls. A whole trompe l'oeil culture ... I would have liked to be the Turkish Palladio. He transposed the classical Greco-Roman architectural style into the Renaissance villa, but not without domesticating it first ... Villa culture. The soft light of the interiors, the gardens, it is all magnificent. The spaciousness, the geometry of the rooms.

We've sat down for lunch in Bassano. This after a nice lazy stroll out on the streets. The splendid old wooden bridge that connects the two halves of the city was designed by Palladio. It collapsed and was rebuilt. Now we're waiting for the elaborate meal we ordered.

The Rotonda

VILLA BARBARO

D'Annunzio's plane

Then we went to Vicenza. First, the Villa Rotonda outside the city. Very elegant. The beauty of old gardens. The fact that it is still standing 500 years on. The astonishing simplicity and geometry of the design, how it nestles among the trees, the symmetry, are all a feast for the eyes. The most luminous of Palladio's designs. The staircases, the columns; then we went around the streets of Vicenza to find and visit every other Palladio. It is all so stark and geometric that you almost can't believe what you're seeing. Villa Valmarana, Palazzo Thiene ... I would like to learn more about PALLADIO and to be the Turkish Palladio.

We left Asolo at 11 and went all the way to Lake Garda without stopping anywhere. We spent a full four hours going around every room in the Vittoriale, a personal-narcissistic museum, almost like a temple, that Gabriele D'Annunzio built himself behind Lake Garda during the last twenty years of his life, and financed in part by Mussolini. I was very happy, as happy as I always am in museums, personal museums, writers' museums. The feel of the rooms, of the scenic archive spreading vertically over several levels connected by a spiral staircase, and in particular of the archive boxes, is glorious. D'Annunzio's house, filled to the brim with bric-a-brac, knickknacks, statues, paintings, plaster busts, Latin aphorisms, and countless books, is extravagantly baroque and overflowing.

His office, the spot where he would write, his desk and its surroundings, are spacious and impressive. The rooms, sealed off from the radiant light outside and kept dark by heavy fabrics, are at once suffocating and alluring. Then on to our semifascist writer's military museum, his plane, his warship, and his opulent mausoleum overlooking Lake Garda. Garda's cypress-decked romantic landscape, the mountains, the lake, a paradise! In the evening, dinner at the farmhouse hotel on the peak, and heavy rain. To dream up imaginary homes and buildings with a computer and photoshop so that they might bring together Ottoman-Turkish elements with a sense of Palladian symmetry, to create cities and models incorporating all of these elements, and then to write novels that are set in these places.

I woke up feeling content after eight hours of uninterrupted sleep. I used to do this in the troubled nights of my childhood too, jumping straight into bed without changing out of my normal clothes. This was usually after having been beaten up by Şevket. I am so exhausted. For the past few days in Istanbul, I've been making do with 5–6 hours of sleep every night.

Another sign and cause of distress . . . are these red boils that have been appearing on my chest and abdomen. I showed them to Sermin and to Rüya. They blame unhappiness and too much work. I showed them to Kiran too. I often wish I could die, to find a way out of this slog. Or perhaps I should say I used to wish that.

POROS

POROS

View from
our room
in Poros

I'm happy here, as we travel from Poros—somewhere on the tip of the Peloponnesian peninsula—to Porto Cheli. Stella greeted us there. We rented a car and drove 5–6 kilometers from Porto Cheli, where we settled into a house which reminded me a little of Bayramoğlu and a little of Sedef Island.

This is the view as I write in the summer holiday home we have rented (for 10 days) here 4.5 km from PORTO CHELI.

A strange drowsiness today. Though I was relieved to be rid of the boils on my belly and the aching in my ears. I thought I might even finish chapter 5, but then . . . Perhaps because the chapter seemed to keep getting longer and longer . . . or maybe because it is difficult to write about politics, I just got stuck again. Does anyone remember anything about 1970s Istanbul and politics these days?

Afterward, I slept for two hours. An interminable afternoon nap, legacy of my childhood . . . Since I'd got stuck with the Norton book . . . I started working instead on one of the texts for the museum, Celâl Salik's essay on Love and op-eds, but then set it aside. In the evening we went to Stella's house first. Up on a hill a 10-minute drive from Porto Cheli, a beautiful view, evening merriment, and a silence outside that I hadn't experienced in a very long time. Then dinner in Porto Cheli at a well-kept restaurant established in the 1950s, where Stella told us tales about all the rich people and the famous swindling politicians who came to eat there.

I go to my desk at 7 in the morning and return to the last chapter of the Norton book.

Do not commission artists to work on the museum! Every day, part of my mind is consumed for a time with museum matters. Vahit! The best thing to do would be to buy his work and *forget about him.*

New Jersey

the HUDSON

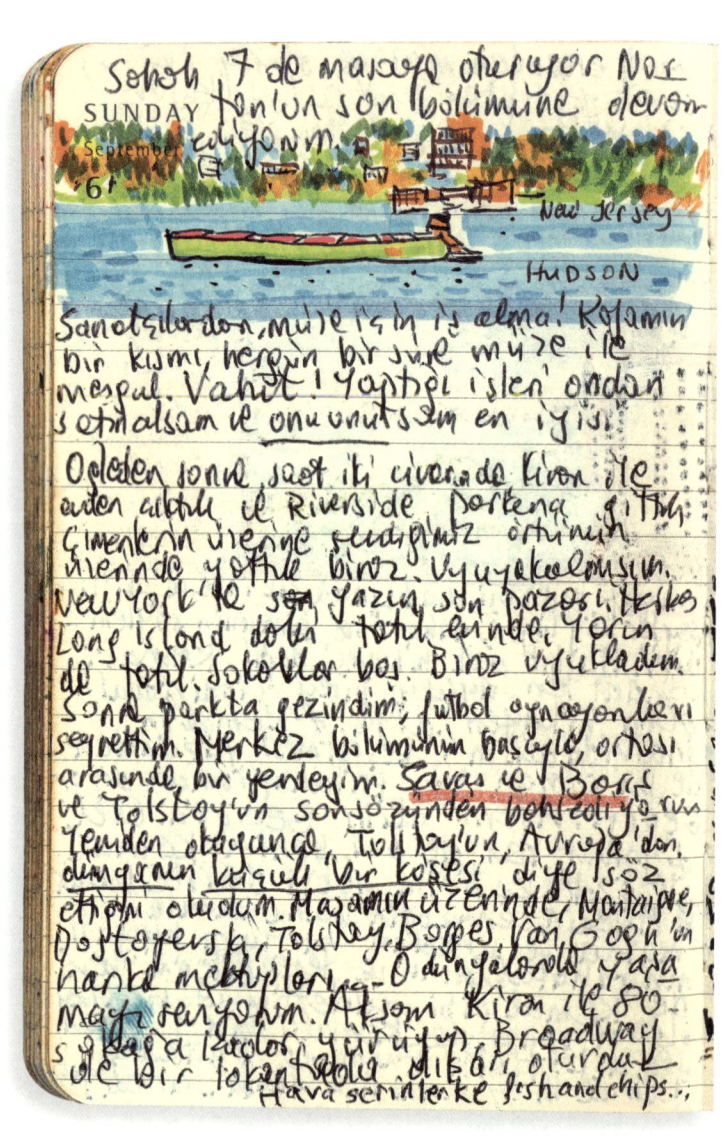

At around two in the afternoon, we went out with Kiran to Riverside Park. We spread a blanket over the grass and lay down for a while. I fell asleep. New York's last summer Sunday. Everyone's gone to their holiday homes on Long Island, and tomorrow's a public holiday. The streets are empty. I napped for a while. Then I wandered around the park; watched people playing football. I'm somewhere between the start and the middle of the central chapter. I'm writing about Tolstoy's epilogue to *War and Peace.* Rereading the text now, I notice that Tolstoy refers to Europe as *a small corner of the world.* On my desk, Montaigne, Dostoyevsky, Tolstoy, Borges, and Van Gogh's extraordinary letters . . . I like immersing myself in those worlds. In the evening we walked with Kiran all the way to 80th Street and sat outside at a restaurant on Broadway. We had *fish and chips* as the temperature cooled . . .

Morning: Rain pelting down outside. I'm working on the book about novels. As I'm having lunch with Rüya at the Japanese-Chinese restaurant on 116th Street, the rain outside reminds me of old Japanese lithographs. Rain in COLUMBIA. Some time with Rüya. Museum worries... Thinking of Istanbul.

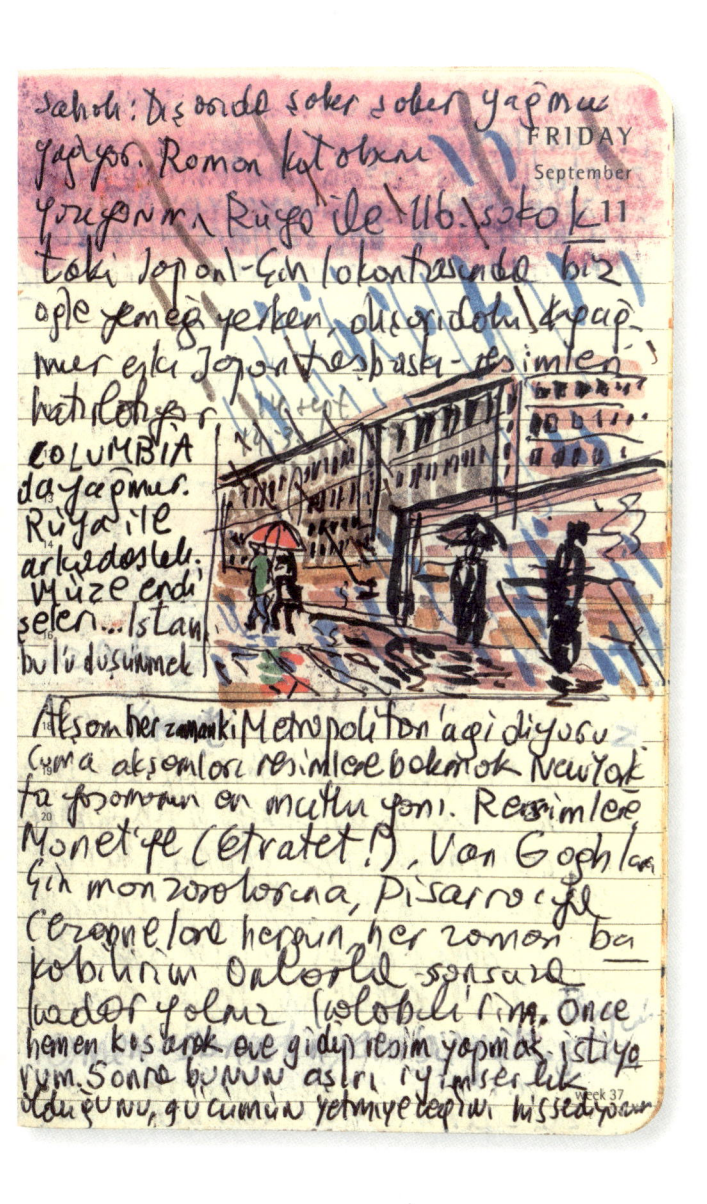

In the evening, the usual trip to the Metropolitan. The best part of living in New York is looking at paintings on Friday evenings. I could stare at these paintings, at the Monets (Étretat!), the Van Goghs, the Chinese landscapes, the Pissarros, the Cézannes, every single day, and be left alone with them until the end of time. Afterward, all I want to do is hurry back home and start painting. But then I realize that my optimism is misplaced, and I don't really have the strength for it.

2009

I forget sometimes that I spend my life staring at an empty page, that I am always forcing myself to stare at one. If, after all that effort, my imagination should awaken, the empty page suddenly springs to life . . . Thoughts on the novel around the world over the past twenty years. Spent the day writing today. I wrote about the idea of novels and their centers, etc., from Cortázar to Julian Barnes: but putting a great deal of meticulous thought into it, and grueling effort . . . I didn't leave the house all day.

NEW YORK

In the afternoons, I go to the Avery Library to write my novel. I sit at more or less the same desk every day. One of the long tables in the basement, close to the shelves. When I get stuck, I sometimes—often—start pacing about among the shelves. The Avery is the world's biggest art and architecture library. I'll be writing my novel, then get up all of a sudden and start wandering around like a sleepwalker: I'll pick up a volume from the shelves at random: Renaissance Architecture, Klee, Perspective, William Blake, Goya, or an old issue of *Parkett* magazine. And of course there's nothing quite like an old black-and-white exhibition catalog.

New York days . . . I wake up at 8 in the morning and work until 12. I'm working on the book about novels. Then I go to the office, or meet up with Rüya . . . In the office, I deal with emails, endless emails, and museum-related issues. When I grow weary of these tangled matters, I spend some time browsing the internet, looking at the news, trying to figure out what's going on in Turkey. Reading the news from Turkey is invariably a suffocating and demoralizing experience. Not only with reference to the future of the country . . . but also because the vulgarity, coarseness, ignorance, and belligerence that characterizes our journalistic discourse taints my mind and my imagination, and this nasty, ruthless political climate crushes my soul . . .

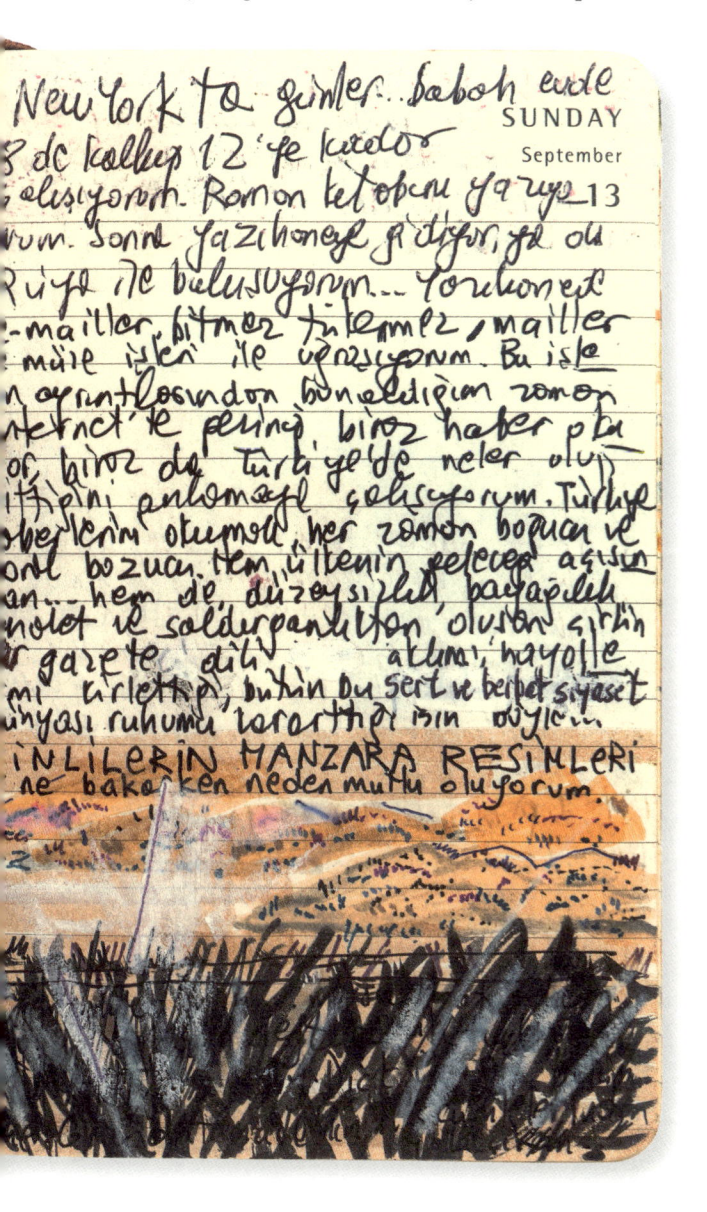

Why do I feel happy when I look at CHINESE LANDSCAPE PAINTINGS.

I sat at my desk after dinner and made two weird drawings in the other Moleskine notebook. Once again, a synthesis of Chinese painters and impressionists, ships, rocks, and the mountains and seas I like. I wrote . . . the first sentence from chapter 87 of *Moby Dick,* "The Grand Armada," into the image, and based my drawing on those words.

Went for a walk in the Cambridge morning, feeling despondent. I am struggling with the last few pages of the last chapter of the Norton book, and this fills me with a peculiar feeling of dejection and gloom.

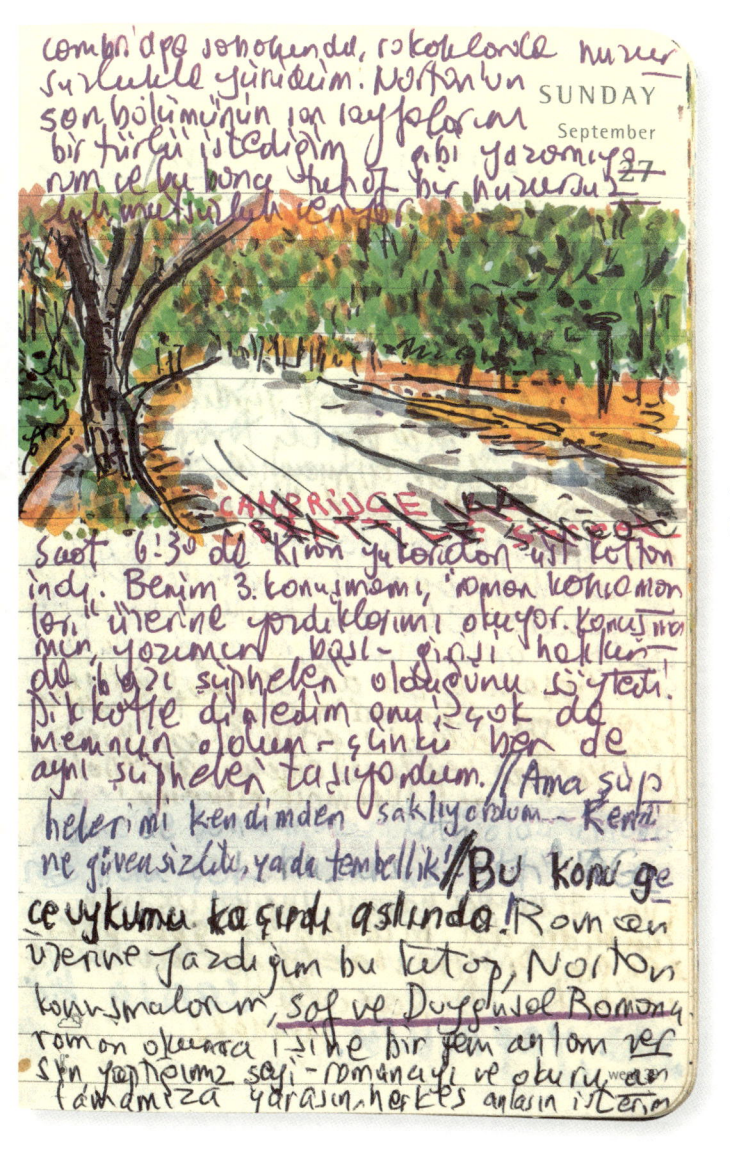

CAMBRIDGE 144
BRATTLE Street

Kiran came downstairs at 6:30. She's reading my 3rd lecture, my discussion of "novel characters." She told me she had some doubts about the beginning, the opening of the lecture. I listened carefully; and I was quite glad—for I was harboring similar doubts myself.

But I'd hidden my own doubts from myself. A lack of confidence, or perhaps out of laziness.

I actually lost some sleep over this last night. I want this book about novels, these Norton Lectures, *The Naïve and the Sentimental Novelist,* to bring new meaning to the act of reading a novel, to help people understand writers and readers, and what it is that we do.

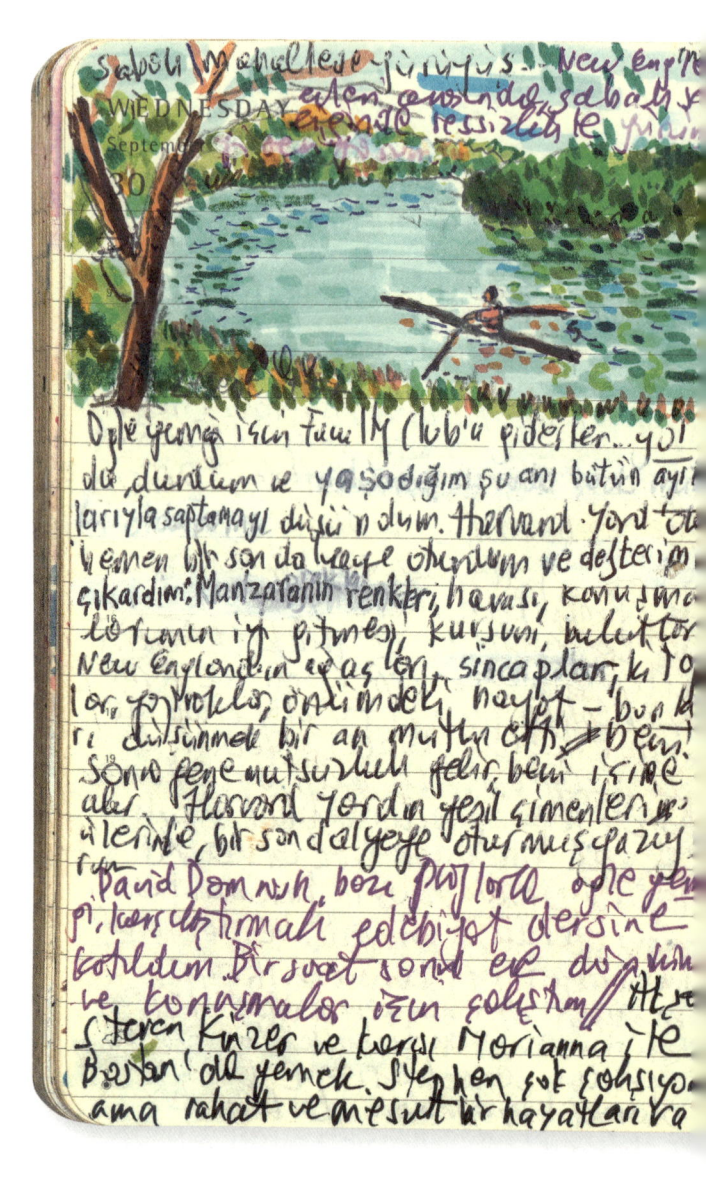

A morning stroll around the neighborhood... Walking among New England homes in the cool, silent morning.

Heading to the Faculty Club for lunch... I stopped along the way and decided to immortalize this moment in all its details. I immediately sat on a chair in Harvard Yard and brought my notebook out: the hues, the mood of the landscape, the fact that my lectures were going well, the leaden clouds, the New England trees, the squirrels, books, leaves, the rest of my life—thinking of these things cheered me up for a moment. But soon the melancholy returns and draws me in. I'm sitting in a chair on the green grass of Harvard Square, writing. Lunch with David Damrosch and some profs. I joined the comparative literature class. After an hour, I went back home to work on the lectures.

Dinner in Boston with Stephen Kinzer and his wife Marianna. Stephen works a lot but they have a comfortable and contented life.

I had to run . . . RAIN in Harvard Square
In the evening, the Ig Nobel Prize ceremony! An event organized by Harvard's nerdy scientists and satirical magazine, gently mocking the Nobel Prizes . . . Real Nobel winners sit on the stage and hand out these half-playful, half-earnest alternative Nobels. I was shy at first, but when I was called onto the stage I went up and embraced the fun . . . I'm glad to be at Harvard, I like the people here, the feel of its libraries . . . and the Norton Lectures are going well. But I can also sense that I don't fully belong here, and I pause for a moment to look at my watch.

Listening to Mozart on the train to Lyon, thinking and daydreaming. I must write more novels. I must be more distinctive. I must boldly tackle all the topics in my mind... But drowsiness and fatigue slowly lure me in until I fall asleep on the fast train. I'm tired.

In the morning, two interviews at the Gallimard offices. At the hotel, we discussed translation issues with Jean Mattern. I went to the Gare de Lyon. At the station, I ate a salad while watching the trains. Off to Lyon on the fast train! In Lyon I took a 45-minute walk from the hotel to a hill. They organized a ceremony and presented me with the city's medal of honor. Then a walk through a lovely park toward a literary evening. Lots of people! A large, jam-packed hall! I spoke for an hour and a half with the editor of *Le Monde*'s books supplement. In the audience I spotted my German translator Gerhard and his wife. I invited them to dinner too. I was feeling half dead by the time I went back to the hotel.

The loneliness of being... talented, bright, educated, confident in your success, and yet still a Turk...

LYON → MILAN: I woke up at 5:30. Washed, got dressed. Will five hours of sleep a night be enough for me? I don't know, but I am trying to make do, and we will see what happens in the end. Last few morning hours in Lyon . . .

I'm sitting in Lyon airport, waiting for the plane's departure time. I have an interview with Claudio Magris in Milan.
I got on the plane and replied to most of the questions in writing. In the meantime I also took photographs of the Alps from the airplane window, their sharp, high, dark peaks piercing through the fog.

LYON

I've settled into a nice room at the Grand Hotel Milan at Malpensa Airport. Interview with Claudio Magris. He is 10 years older than me. A professor of German literature. Intelligent, gracious, kindhearted, and cultured, a true intellectual. This year he was awarded the Peace Prize of the German Book Trade. As we were eating, I mentioned that the Nobel is about to be announced, and teased him that he might win it this time. He said no, they're announcing it next week. Clearly he's interested and hoping for a Nobel himself. But when the Nobel was eventually announced, Herta Müller won it. I'm glad. I met her once in Germany. A considerate, sensitive, thoughtful woman.
In the evening an event on *The Museum of Innocence* at a theater. Then we went to the Stendhal restaurant with Marco, Yasemin, Andrea, Carlo, the usual crowd. I can understand Stendhal's affection for Italy. I love Italy.

213

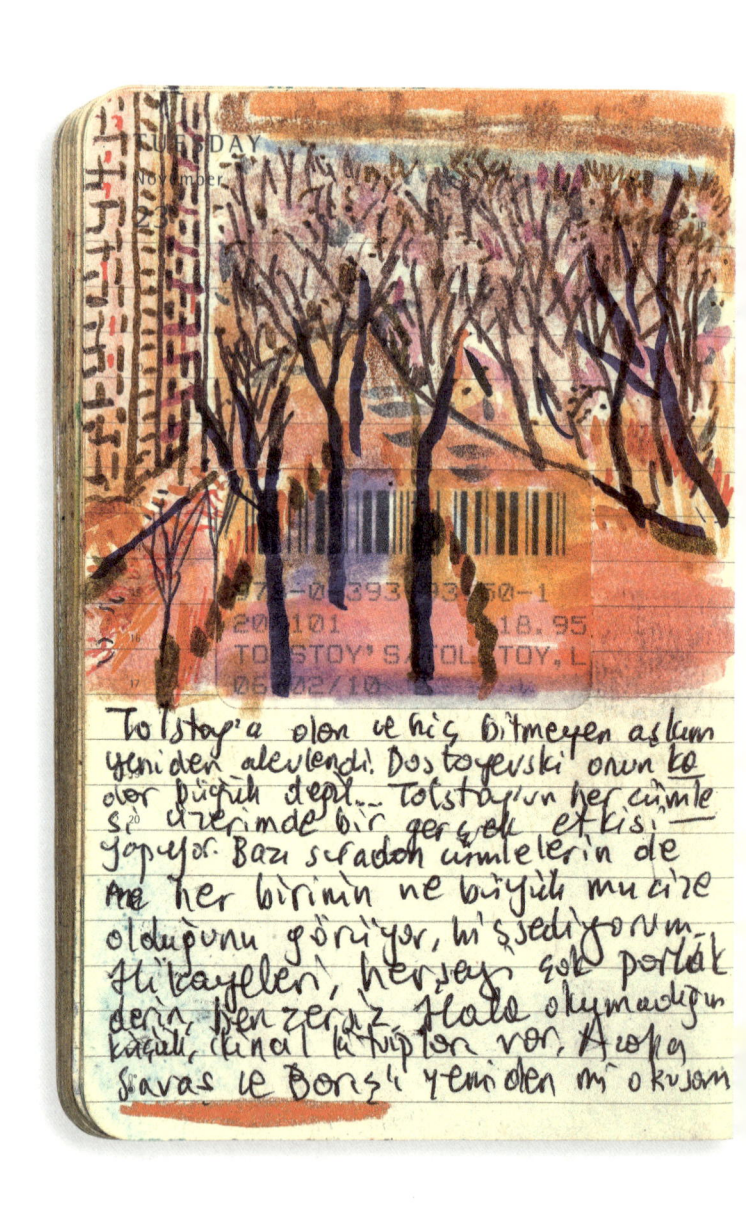

My enduring love for Tolstoy has been rekindled. Dostoyevsky doesn't quite measure up... Tolstoy's every sentence rings true to me. I can see, I can feel, the presence of something miraculous even in his more ordinary sentences. His stories, everything he does, is brilliant, profound, and unique. There are some shorter, peripheral books of his that I haven't read yet. Perhaps I should read *War and Peace* again.

SANTA MONICA
BOSTON → LOS ANGELES

I get to Boston airport early. I sent some emails from the business lounge. I also asked Emre to help me find a museum director. Then I went to the gate. I showed them my ticket and went inside: there was a very long queue on the jet bridge. I gave my ticket to someone working at the gate and called Istanbul to discuss museum business with Murat. Suddenly I sensed that the hostess might have forgotten about me. As soon as she saw me: she started screaming to stop the plane. We started running. The airplane door had closed. She banged against the door and began to shout at the people inside. The airplane door opened, and I was declared a *1st-class passenger.* As it wasn't my fault, I was only moderately embarrassed... I *almost* missed my flight. I really wouldn't have wanted to miss it.

SANTA MONICA Beach

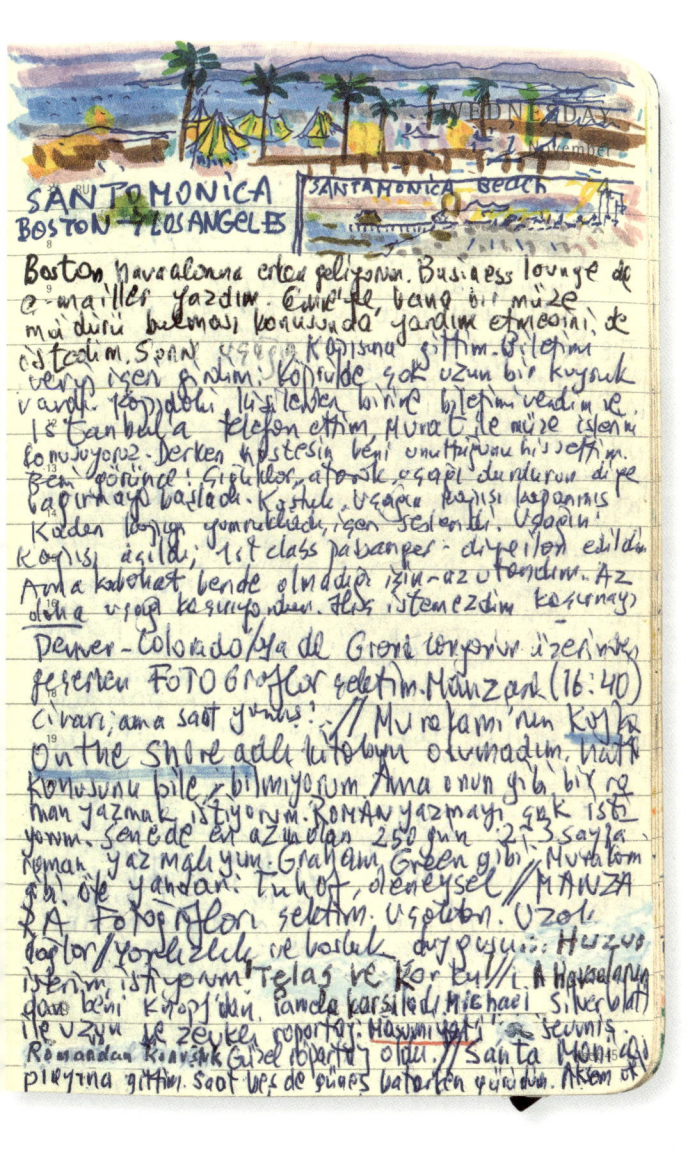

I took PHOTOGRAPHS as we flew over Denver-Colorado / or the Grand Canyon. That was the view at around (16:40), but the time stamp on the photos is wrong! I've never read Murakami's *Kafka on the Shore,* I don't even know what it's about. But I would like to write a novel like that. I want so much to write a NOVEL. I should write 2–3 pages of a novel on at least 250 days of the year. Like Graham Greene, like Murakami. But also: strange, experimental.
I took some LANDSCAPE photographs. From the plane. Distant mountains.
A feeling of solitude and emptiness. I would like, I would want, some peace. Anxiety and Fear.
Pamela from Knopf came to greet me at LA airport. A long and pleasant interview with Michael Silverblatt: he liked *Innocence.* We talked about the novel. A good interview.
I went to Santa Monica Beach. I took a walk at five as the sun began to set. Back to the hotel for the evening.

2009

Morning: Breakfast by the hotel pool—the Beverly Hilton. Interview with Nathan Gardels in the hotel lobby. Pamela from Knopf took me to downtown Los Angeles. A beat poet who is going to write a piece for the *LA Times* showed me around LA: Frank Gehry's Disney Concert Hall, the LA Times Building. The Bradbury Building where *Blade Runner* was shot. I was glad to walk around LA city center. Armenian jewelers, Hispanic crowds → (Note: this was happening at around 12–1, but the camera clock was 3 hours ahead on NY time.) Then on to a radio program in Pasadena. Just like my first American book tour 10–12 years ago. The host, who hadn't read the book, asked me questions which I answered with good grace. Afterward I went to the Getty Museum and research center on the hills overlooking LA. An overwhelming joy. Thomas, the museum director, gave me a three-hour tour. He had ordered a copy of the German edition of *Innocence,* and there was a copy of *Red* in his office.

LOS ANGELES

This place, so like a monastery, an eagle's nest, reminded me of Fatehpur Sikri in India. Armed with a Thomas Bernhard–esque fury, the museum director showed me around the world's largest art library. Underground archives and *stacks,* the glass-paneled room where you can study photographs and architectural blueprints, researchers' rooms. Rooms set aside for guest writers-researchers... And finally invited me to come and do my research and writing here. From the top of the mountain, you can see the haze of the Pacific Ocean in the distance beyond the rocky coast. This place is a romantic monastery where you can run away from life and live instead among history and documents. Afterward we toured the museum: I saw a Chardin and a Gauguin I had never seen before... Ah, to look at art, to daydream, to paint, and to feel that the painting I've made is beautiful and admired.

The view as I left the museum after dark was like a Caspar David Friedrich landscape. We descended toward downtown LA in the dark for an hour. I did a short reading from *Innocence* to an audience of 450 in a theater in Little Tokyo. Enjoyable. People chuckling. I feel at ease.

A weariness. I woke up well into the night, at 5 o'clock. But I managed to go back to sleep. In this second sleep after 5 o'clock, I had a weird dream: a pornographic cassette. A tiny spy cassette, breaking with a crackle like a porcelain vase, and filling me with a sudden terrible DREAD.

On the plane from Los Angeles to San Francisco, strange, empty, rocky islands in the distance—I photographed them. The time is 13—it must be 16 on the camera clock... I took some more photographs which reminded me of my own paintings of dark mountains... I wish I could write a book on landscape painting. A book of both essays and reproductions. And a novel. I can only truly feel the eternity of landscape, of the world, when I am on a plane and looking out at distant mountains, jagged rocks, and dark ridges. At around 13:20 (16:20), I took photographs of the rugged mountains, the sea, and the clouds all bleeding into one another. In truth I'm a hopeless romantic.

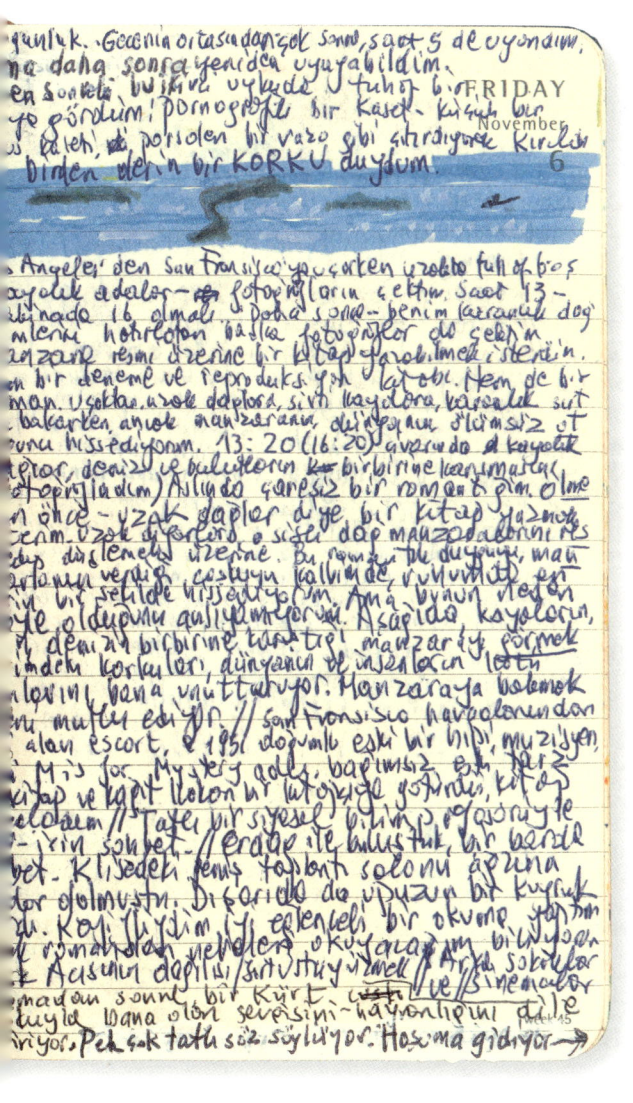

Before I die—I would like to write a book called *distant mountains*. A book about painting and imagining distant realms and misty mountain landscapes. I can feel this romantic longing, and the exhilaration of gazing at a landscape, penetrating the deepest recesses of my soul. But I don't understand why this is. Surveying the landscape below, where the rocks, the mist, and the sea merge into one, allows me to forget my fears and all that is wicked in people and in the world. Looking at landscapes makes me happy.

The guide who picks me up at San Francisco is a longtime hippie born in 1951, a musician, who takes me to sign books at M is for Mystery, an old-school independent bookshop infused with the smell of books and paper.

A TV interview with a kindly professor of political science.

I met up with Erdağ, we went to a bar to chat. The spacious assembly room in the church is full to the brim. A rather long queue outside, too. I felt buoyant. A fun, successful reading. I know which parts of the novel to read now. How Heartache spreads / swimming on your back.

Backstreets and

Film people

A calm, comfortable day in Miami or, rather, on the seafront of the Loews Hotel on Miami Beach. I am making a detailed plan for my new novel—THE COMMENTER. While sitting on the beach. In the meantime I'm also reading Leo Damrosch's book on Rousseau. How could someone like Rousseau even exist. His fascination with mountains, with Alpine landscapes . . . ! Lying on the chaise longue at the beach, I came up with much of the plot of THE COMMENTER, visualizing the backbone of the novel as I built it. Plotting the new novel, imagining this novel, is great fun: thinking about its assortment of wrathful fictional citizens. The meeting between K and X. The enraged, demonic female COMMENTER, etc. etc. I am making quick work of planning the novel, but I also want to start writing it straightaway.

THE LOEWS HOTEL
IN MIAMI BEACH

Dinner with old friends from Knopf, Sheila and Ben Moser. They're here for a book fair in Miami. Ben has written a biography of Clarice Lispector. I gave a blurb for his book. Sheila is sweet, kind, charming.
After the reading, a Kurdish man fervently declares his fondness and admiration for me. He makes many lovely comments. I feel gratified.
The bookshop that organized the event and everyone involved in it were so lovely, and so good. I spent a lot of time happily signing hundreds of books. Spanish translations.
I went back to the hotel to pick Kiran up, then fish and wine at the Seafood Grill.

In the hotel room this morning, I lie in bed as if I were reading the newspaper, but reading Leo Damrosch's life of Rousseau instead. Admiringly. As I reflect on the fact that his father was branded a "traitor" despite telling his son he must love his country, his home first destroyed and later seized → (page 19) . . . I realize that behind my interest in building a museum—setting up a charitable trust, etc.—there is a wish to maintain a foothold in Turkey, to resist the destruction of my home, to weather time, and to feel like I genuinely belong in Turkey.

After breakfast, walking around Miami's art deco streets with Kiran . . . I stepped into the art deco tourist center and gift shop. And I saw that the kind of bonnet my mother used to wear was being sold as an old nostalgic item. *As featured in Vogue 1950s, retro, bathing cap* it said on my mother's bonnet. (See photo 12:27.)

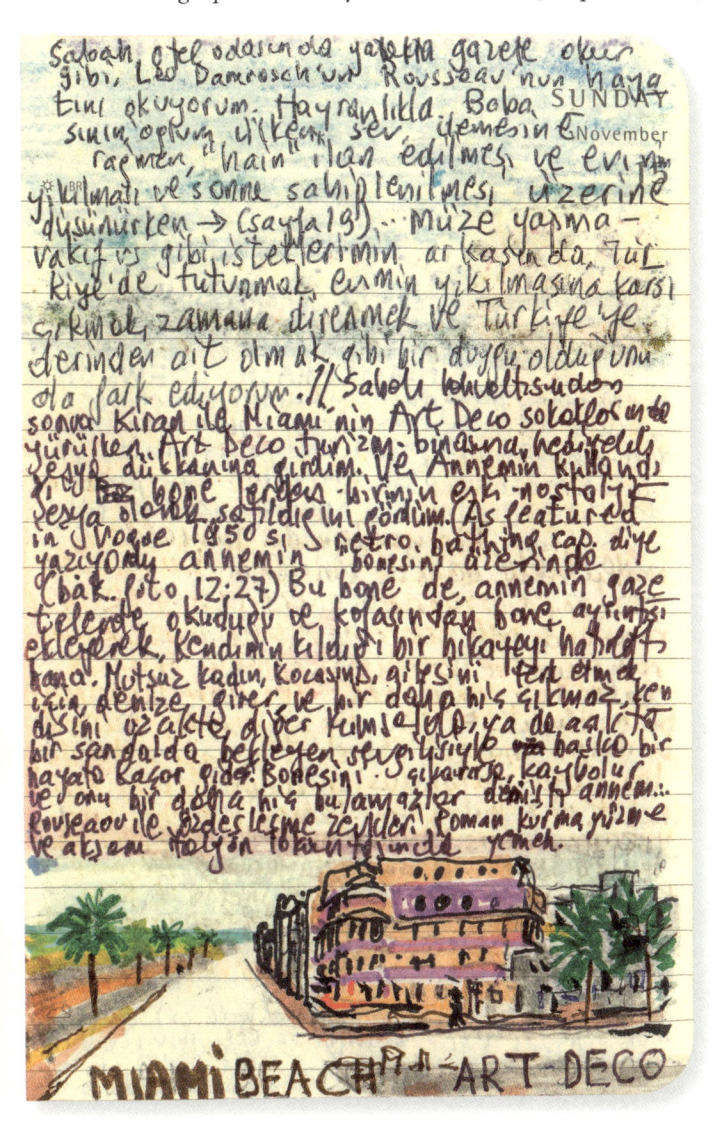

MIAMI BEACH—ART DECO

This bonnet reminded me of a story my mother had read in the papers and made her own by adding a bonnet-related detail. A miserable woman, wanting to leave her husband and her family behind, slips into the sea and never comes back, escaping toward a new life with her lover waiting for her far away on another beach or on a rowboat floating in the open water. My mother said that if the woman had taken her bonnet off, she would have been lost and they would never have been able to find her again . . . The joys of identifying with Rousseau. Plotting the novel, swimming, and dinner at an Italian restaurant.

219

LINCOLN MEMORIAL—WASHINGTON DC

In the breakfast hall of the Hotel Palomar in Washington: Gregor is unhappy that I've postponed the museum meeting we were supposed to have on 10 December. So am I. This morning I was a guest on Diane Rehm's radio program. With her tiny figure and her slow solemn way of speaking, she is quite a "character." She had me on her program in 2004 for *Snow;* I remember now.

From there, I came straight to Washington's Reagan airport. I've picked up a grilled chicken salad, etc., and sat in a corner of the food court to write.

Confession: there's something about American airports, about traveling, about going from one city to the next, that I love.

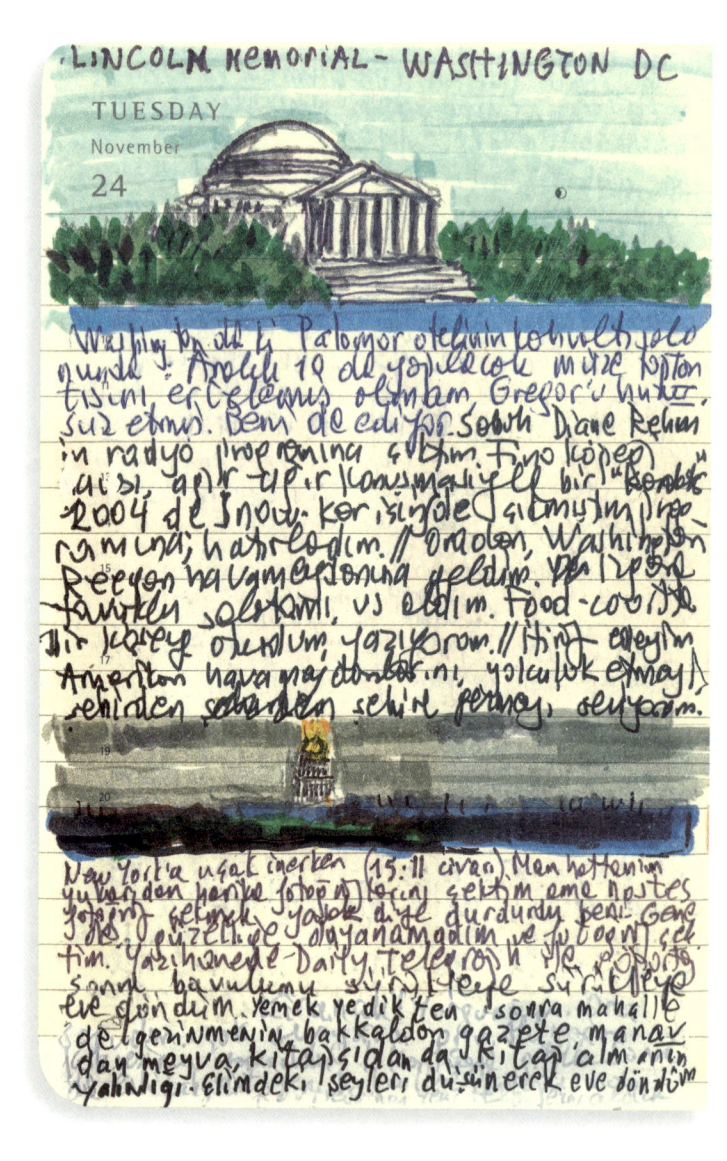

As the plane approached New York (at around 15:11) I took some spectacular photos of Manhattan from the air, until the hostess told me photography wasn't allowed. But in the end the view was too beautiful to resist, so I kept going. At the office, interview with *The Daily Telegraph,* after which I went home, dragging my suitcase behind me. Some food, followed by the simple pleasure of wandering around the neighborhood, picking up the newspaper from the convenience store, fruit from the greengrocer, books from the bookshop. I went back home, thinking along the way about all the stuff I was carrying.

Thanksgiving Day. I spend most of the morning sitting at home, ruminating. Kiran has gone to her mother's. A feeling of emptiness. I phoned Asuman: we grumbled about how slowly the museum is progressing, how the construction work hasn't even started yet. I spoke to Murat. I have this feeling of emptiness. It's probably because I haven't worked on a novel-story-essay in a while. I must make a start on the new novel, or on a story. The Norton book needs one final read-through before it's delivered, and the Everyman foreword to *Red* needs writing.

my flat with the lights on

I've enjoyed Daniyal Mueenuddin's stories. "Nawabdin Electrician." Very good. Reading a good story was a real tonic. Afterward I was able to think and dream about my new novel for a little while. Rüya arrived downstairs at 5 o'clock. I took a photo of our building as the sky began to darken. My apartment was the only one with its lights on. (17:01) Walking and talking with Rüya along Riverside Park all the way to 72nd Street. We bought tickets at the Loews cinema near 68th Street. We went to a restaurant and had a lovely father-daughter dinner. Then we cuddled up, father and daughter, to watch the film adaptation of Cormac McCarthy's *The Road* (in the movie it's a father and son). It was a happy, merry evening. I'm so glad Rüya is here.

In Berlin! In a hurry!

from the photos dated
15-1 at 9:45, 9:46

Sammlung Scharf-Gerstenberg Museum, Schloßstraße 70. Met Gregor and Brigitta at 11 o'clock. We did a very thorough tour of this museum of surrealist art which Gregor has renovated and designed a new entrance for. Andreas and Anna Leube also came by in the morning. Goya, Piranesi, Max Ernst, etc., Rousseau's painting of the donkey and the woman having sex, strangeness. Lunch at an Italian restaurant, then on to the Gropius museum. An exhibition of Islamic miniatures entitled *Taswir*... They've put an excerpt from my essay on Meaning on the wall. It's fun to be looking at miniatures again so many years after *My Name Is Red*.

White

a person

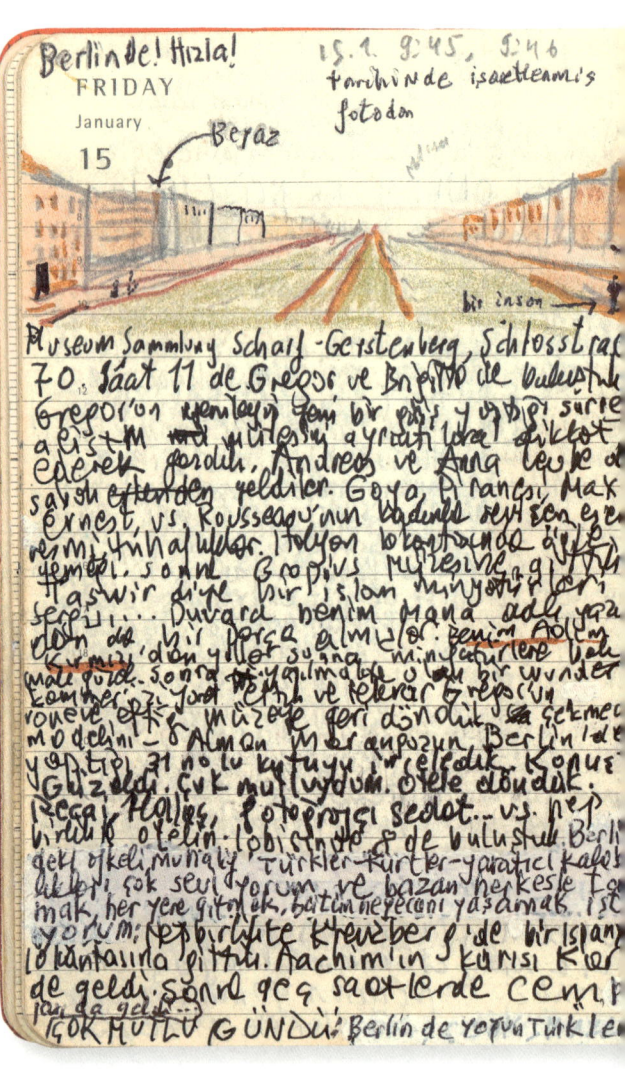

Afterward we visited a *Wunderkammer* in construction, then returned to the museum Gregor renovated. We studied the design of the drawers—cabinet number 31, made by a German carpenter in Berlin. We talked throughout. It was lovely. I was very happy. We returned to the hotel. Met up with Recai Hallaç, Sedat the photographer, ... etc. in the hotel lobby at 8 o'clock. I love Berlin's angry, dissenting Turkish-Kurdish-creative multitudes, and sometimes I feel the urge to meet everyone, go everywhere, experience all the excitement firsthand: we went to a Spanish restaurant in Kreuzberg. Aachim's wife Karin also came. Later in the night, Cem and others joined us too...

SUCH A HAPPY DAY: so many Turks in Berlin! The companionship, the affection, everything made me happy.

BERLIN → BARCELONA

A cold Berlin morning. I hardly slept all night. Yet a strange happiness. The streets of Berlin, the airport, everywhere looks empty. On my way to Barcelona via Munich, I doze on the plane and make calls from Munich airport to Rüya, Kiran, and Murat the museum assistant.

The lobby of Barcelona's Hotel Majestic is full of Turkish Airlines personnel, hostesses, managers. Momentary puzzlement.

Dinner with Bashkim Shehu. His father used to share power with Enver Hoxha in Albania back in the day, but was later executed due to Enver Hoxha's suspicions and paranoias. His son was jailed. Then he found asylum in Barcelona. He consults for the CCCB. He smokes, he seems bad tempered and also like a very good person. I drew him a plan for the ideal exhibition. We got along straightaway, like two people who come from the same corner of the world and share the same culture.

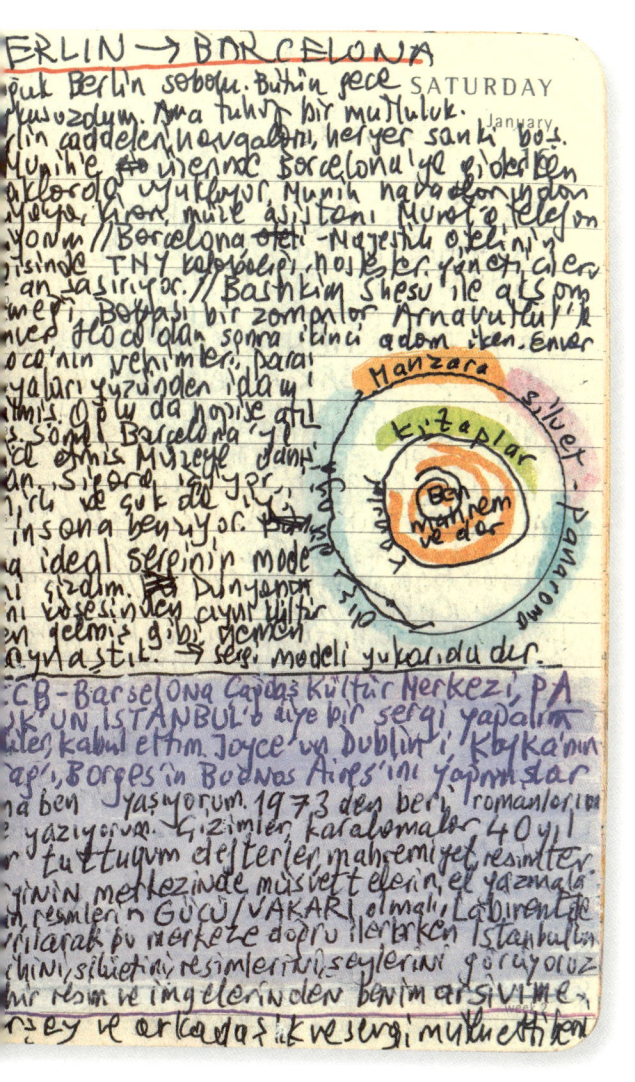

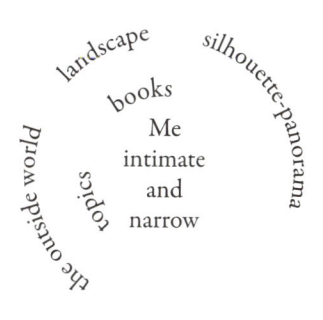

the outside world · topics · landscape · books · silhouette-panorama · Me intimate and narrow

→ See above for the exhibition plan.

The CCCB—Center for Contemporary Culture of Barcelona—has suggested putting together an exhibition on PAMUK'S ISTANBUL, and I've agreed. They've already done Joyce's Dublin, Kafka's Prague, Borges's Buenos Aires. I'm still alive, though. I've been writing my novels by hand since 1973. Drawings, scribbles, notebooks I've been keeping for 40 years, private life, my paintings. The POWER/GRAVITAS of draft manuscripts, handwritten pages, and drawings should form the heart of the exhibition. As we wind our way through the labyrinth toward its center, we see the history, the silhouette, the pictures, the objects of Istanbul, from images and symbols of the city to my own archives.

2010

I met Gregor at the museum building at 3 o'clock. The construction work is moving forward, though, as always, at a slower pace than we had planned. Evening with Gregor, the girls, Cem... We go to the Savoy seafood restaurant in Cihangir. A tradition of taking everyone who is working on the museum out for dinner. The restaurant is busy, packed. When people at the other tables start taking pictures of me from a distance... feelings of fame, loneliness, insecurity, rise up in quick succession. There is always a point when I grow tired of people and crowds. Some hurtful thing is bound to happen, some ordinary hurtful thing: that's how I end up feeling.

entrance to the
flat next door

cobblestones

The Museum of Innocence.
View of the ground floor from the
street as construction work proceeds

I am trying to finish the museum one object at a time, just as I would write a novel one word at a time. The hardest part is bringing out the poetry of ordinary objects. My imagination slows down, and the banality of daily life makes everything harder. I'm wearing myself out. In the mornings, I paint. I'm trying to finish the *Red* foreword, going through it one last time. A sense of futility, of pointlessness . . . I would rather be inside Mevlut's story. The mood, the newspapers, etc. in Turkey are another source of despair. These past five years have been a relatively calm period for me, with the press giving me much less trouble than before, but the constant attrition, the intolerance between the secularists gunning for a military coup and the political Islamists, have obviously worn me down. I need to spend more time on my own, like I did when I was writing *The Black Book*. Most importantly, I mustn't read the newspapers . . .

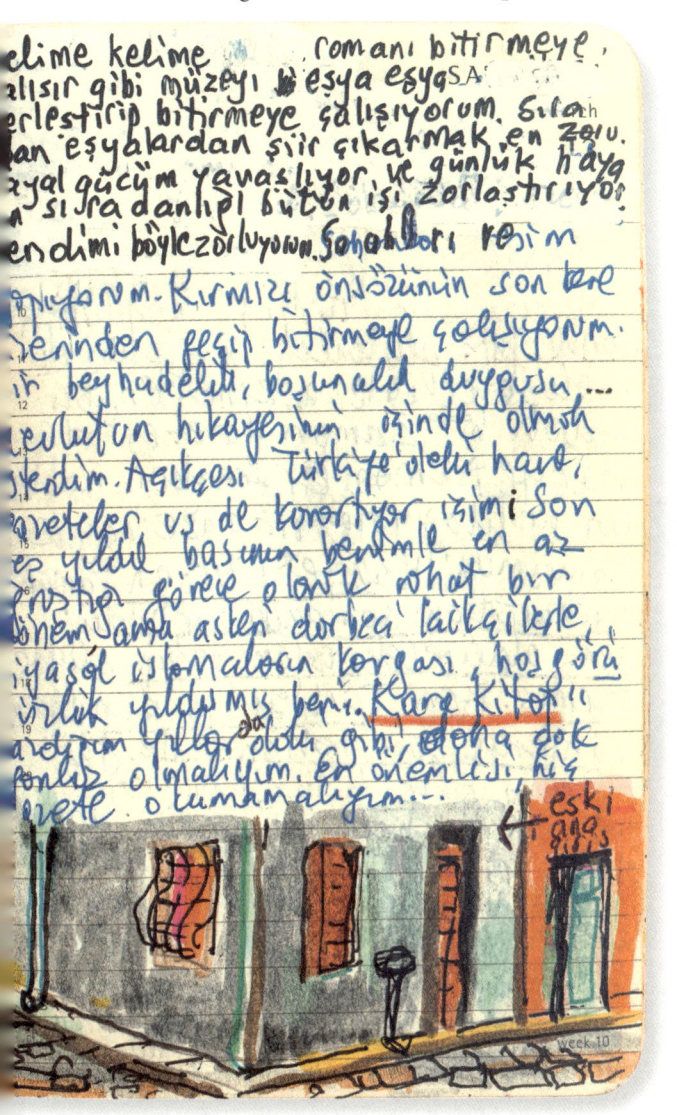

← the old main entrance

En route to Egypt-Cairo, at the airport—I've come to the spot where I had my very last cigarette who knows how many years ago. I got myself a *lahmacun,* I couldn't resist. I take photographs as the plane flies south over the Princes' Islands and Bursa.

I decide on the plane that I will write 6–7 pages every day in the big notebook I've brought with me. What do I want in life... To write... This obsession with writing... On the subjects of happiness and desire... The gentleman sitting next to me on the plane is a conservative printer. Kiran came to greet me at Cairo airport. We took a car to the train station. Tired. Old... Poor. The Cairo crowds. In the tea shop, I write in my blue notebook. We get on the train. As we travel from Cairo—to Alexandria, night begins to fall. There is such melancholy in this landscape... Light... Poor neighborhoods... In Alexandria, they dissolve into a purple light: the Windsor Palace Hotel, with an aura of the past about it. But our room is freezing. The Fish Market restaurant is good. Dinner.

The Bay of Alexandria!

Alexandria. In the hotel room at night, I slept with my trousers on. I was cold. The room was freezing. Alexandria is cold, windy! I wake up in the middle of the night and complain to Kiran! Morning. The streets. We visited some bookshops. Friday crowds. I'm writing everything down in a big blue notebook. Cavafy's house. Empty. Sorrowful. They've turned it into a museum. The director has been updating the exhibition. We introduced ourselves! Walked around the streets for a long time. Every now and then we ducked into a tea shop and made notes in our notebooks. Alexandria: writing about a city, exploring it on foot and through the tea shops where you stop to write . . . Kiran and I are in this tea shop across from the hotel. I've got a sore throat from walking around all day and drinking cold mango juice. I have one and a half cups of tea to warm me right through. The teahouse is full of men. They are playing Rummikub and other similar games. Smoke from water pipes and cigarettes . . . The television which is always on, the smell of cigarettes, etc., remind me of the tea shops on Heybeli Island . . . We went to the Cecil Hotel. The one from Durrell's novels. I must write about this world. An ordinary place. We've come here to the Fish Market restaurant again.

In the morning we sit in the breakfast room on the top floor of the hotel and write for an hour. After a month without success, I finally come up with a good beginning for the "afterword" I need to write for one of the translated editions of *Cevdet Bey*. Rather than *Buddenbrooks,* I will write about the development and downfall of Nişantaşı...

A walk to the old Ottoman neighborhood and the castle built from the ruins of the famous Lighthouse of Alexandria. An outing on a horse cart... Going through the poorer neighborhoods is dispiriting. The Library of Alexandria. Not bad, from an architectural point of view! But the book selection is sorely lacking. Inside, it's full of students. There are books on display, donated from all over the world. The informal homeyness of the place, the work desks, the computers... If there had been a library like this one in the Istanbul of my youth, respectful of the readers who frequent it, and equipped with a small selection of books, I would have spent all my time there! Later, poor neighborhoods all along the Mahmoudiyah Canal...

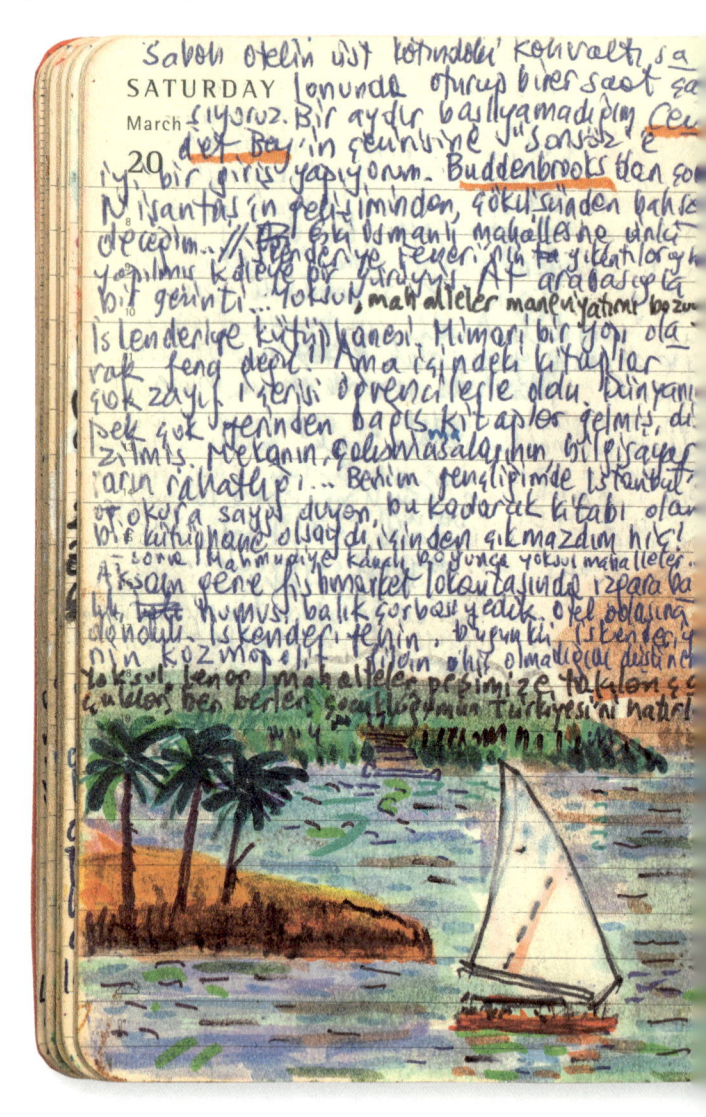

In the evening, back to the Fish Market restaurant again for a dinner of grilled fish, hummus, fish soup. We went back to the hotel room. Thinking all the while that there is nothing cosmopolitan about Alexandria, the Alexandria we see today. The poor outer neighborhoods, the kids trailing behind us, the barbers, reminded me of the Turkey of my childhood.

I woke up at six in the morning. We had breakfast upstairs on the top floor of the hotel, then went to Alexandria train station (I took some photos). For two hours and fifteen minutes, I patiently observed the Nile delta, the villagers riding on the backs of their donkeys, and everything else around me. Green fields, poor villages, irrigation canals, dirt roads, trucks, coffee shops, wheat fields, cattle, palm trees, tiny villages, children … Utility poles, canals, stretches of green, village roads, villages … I saw so much. And I looked at everything with such eagerness, wanting to understand and to feel it all. Then the train stopped at the edge of a field. I took some photographs of a farmer loading greens onto a horse cart (9:34). I took some good photographs of Alexandria station too at 7:50.

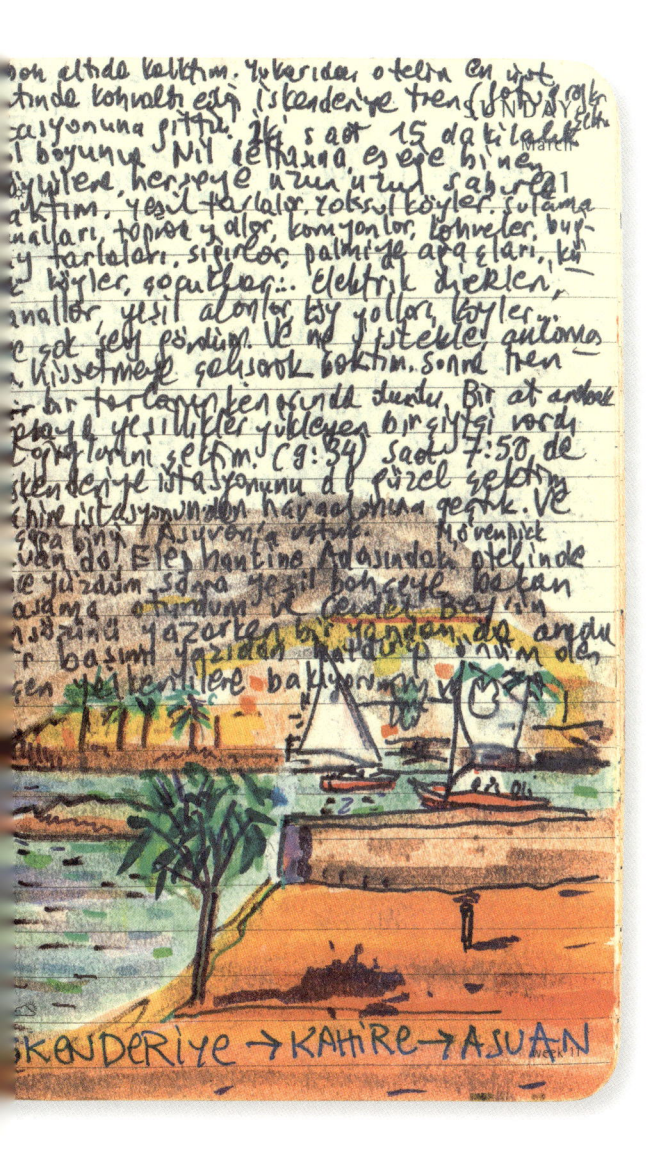

ALEXANDRIA → CAIRO → ASWAN

We went from Cairo station to the airport. Then got on a plane and flew to Aswan. I went for a swim first, at the Mövenpick Aswan, their hotel on Elephantine Island. Afterward I sat at my desk overlooking the leafy gardens, lifting my head up every now and then from the afterword to *Cevdet Bey* to watch the sailboats floating past me.

Early this morning I listened to an interview Cem Bico recorded and sent to me. It's not very good; there's too much repetition. It's the story of someone who has found success in Bodrum running restaurants and nightclubs. For some reason I found the man infuriating. I did not enjoy hearing his success story, and at the same time I felt bad for seeking out this kind of detail.

Kiran and I packed our bags. We are going on holiday to GREECE. Working on the museum has been exhausting and exasperating. I want to step back into the world of my novel, and leave my Turkish museum exertions behind.

At the airport in Yeşilköy, I ate some *lahmacun*.

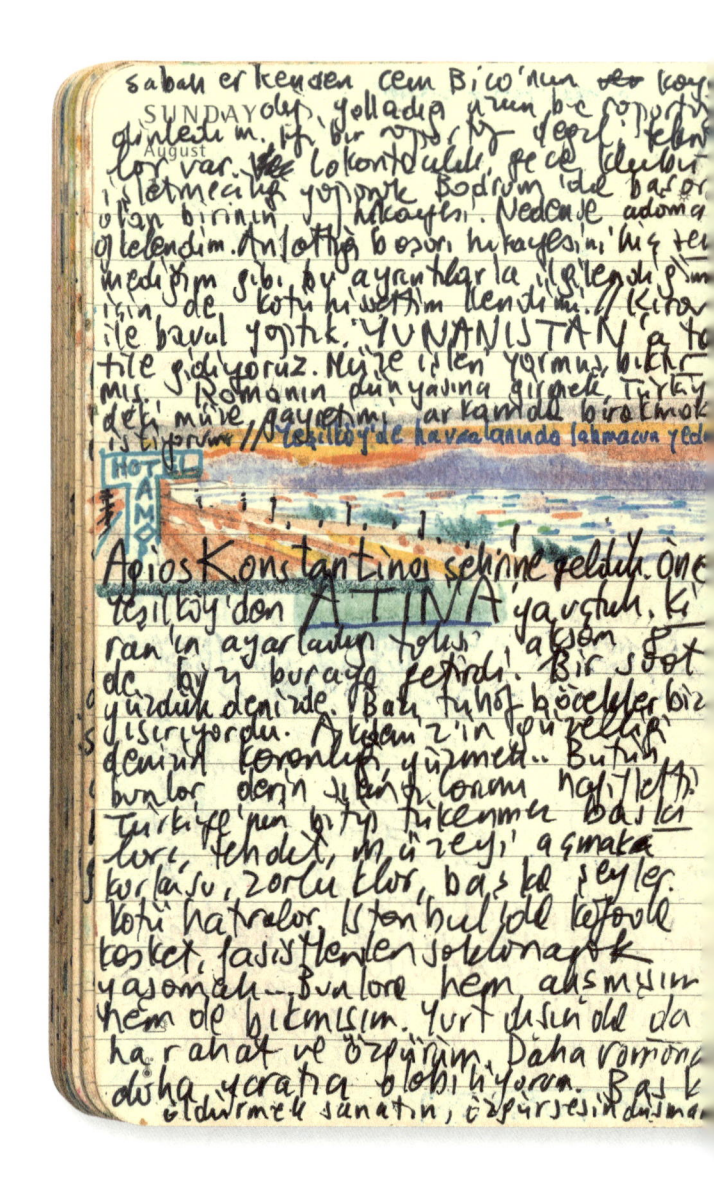

We've arrived at the town of Agios Konstantinos. First we flew from Yeşilköy to ATHENS. The taxi Kiran booked brought us here at 8 in the evening. We swam in the sea for an hour. There were some weird bugs biting us. The beauty of the Mediterranean, the darkness of the sea, going for a swim... These things all served to alleviate my anguish. The endless pressures of life in Turkey, the threats, my misgivings around opening the museum, the obstacles we face, and all sorts of other things. Bad memories. Living in Istanbul with a cap on your head to hide from the fascists... I am both used to all this now, and fed up with it. Abroad, I am freer and more comfortable. I can be more creative, more of a novelist. Intimidation and death are the greatest enemies of art and of free expression.

Morning in the small town of Agios Konstantinos. A cool breeze from the Aegean. All of these things produce a sudden clarity, a sense of elation in my mind. I must finish the museum without exhausting myself... But what I'm really excited about is the new novel: A STRANGENESS IN MY MIND. The interviews my young colleagues collect and send me and everything else around this project feel exhilarating. But I know that in the end, the true power of this book will stem from my own imagination. I don't want to read any other novels either: I must push myself until I've discovered something new to do in this novel. In the cool morning air, I can feel the power of this discovery, and of my own freedom.

VIEW FROM THE WINDOW ON THE WAY TO ALONISSOS

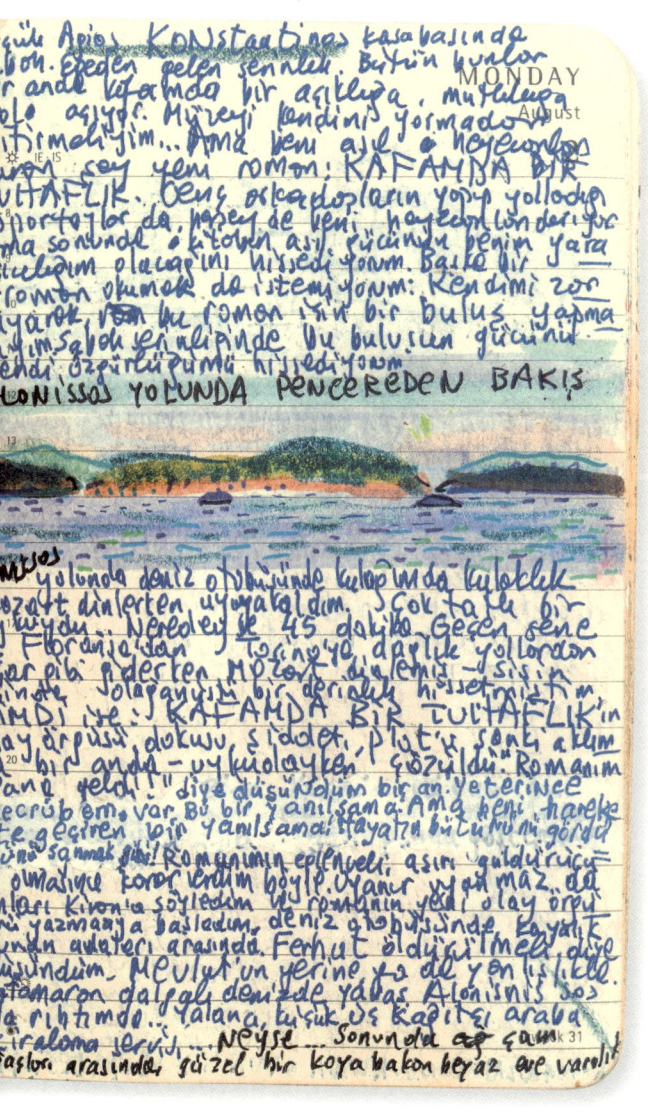

I fell asleep on the ferry to Alonissos while listening to Mozart from my headphones. A delightful nap... Nearly 45 minutes long. I was listening to Mozart last year too, gliding along mountain tracks on the way from Florence to Turin—surrounded by fog and feeling an extraordinary sense of profundity. And NOW: it's as if the chain of events, the texture, the violence, the plot of A STRANGENESS IN MY MIND, have suddenly fallen into place—all while I was asleep. "My novel has come to me!" I thought for a moment. I am experienced enough. I know this is an illusion. But it is an illusion that spurs me into action: it's like thinking you can see the whole of life! I decided that my novel should be entertaining, extremely funny, etc. As soon as I woke up, I told Kiran everything, and started jotting down the new plot for the novel, right there on the ferry, surrounded by rugged Greek islands. I decided that Ferhat must be killed. Either in Mevlut's place, or by mistake. The catamaran moves slowly through the wavy water. At the Alonissos docks... A lying, small-time crook of a rental car dealer... Never mind... In the end we made it to our destination, a white house in a grove of pine trees, overlooking a beautiful bay.

231

At about 10 o'clock this morning, after all the uncertainty and torment, I suddenly shift—from a depressive mood to a manic state. At the same moment or perhaps half an hour before, I made the following decision: FINISH THE MUSEUM BUT DON'T OPEN IT. LOCK THE DOOR AND HIDE IT. Don't DESTROY yourself with the MUSEUM.

Write your new NOVEL, write about MEVLUT's adventures! Forget forget forget about everything else.

The novel is picaresque in nature, and operates by uniting the humor etc. of Don Quixote–Sancho Panza–Dickens with metaphysical concerns. A nice afternoon and evening with Thomas and co.

How wonderful it is to go for a swim in the sea in the evening, then sit at your desk with renewed energy and vigor to write and invent novels.

Continued from Thursday. I like my novel. After dinner with T and Margareta (on a hill in the old town) we went for a walk. Then I drove them to the interior of Alonissos Island,

I wake up at 9 and try to write. At 11 we picked Thomas and Margareta up and went to one of the beaches in the north. Agios Dimitrios. A magnificent beach that reminds me of Ölüdeniz. Small pebbles. The translucence, the incredible blueness of the sea, were almost unbelievably beautiful. I swim like a little boy, diving into the sea, doing flips in the water, and thinking of my novel.

Then a delicious lunch at a taverna… The sun, the blue of the Mediterranean Sea, the green of the olive trees. We went back home. A nap. The novel. Daydreams. Thomas and Margareta came around in the evening. I made them grilled peppers and aubergines, tzatziki, etc. Wine, conversation. Thomas is talking about Handke. Night. Mozart. Between 5 and 7 I worked on Mevlut and Ferhat's electricity inspection story, privatization, etc. I've already written this chapter once before. Too didactic. Lacks poetry. I'm trying to write the whole chapter again from scratch. But it's hard. It reminds me of how difficult it is to write novels.

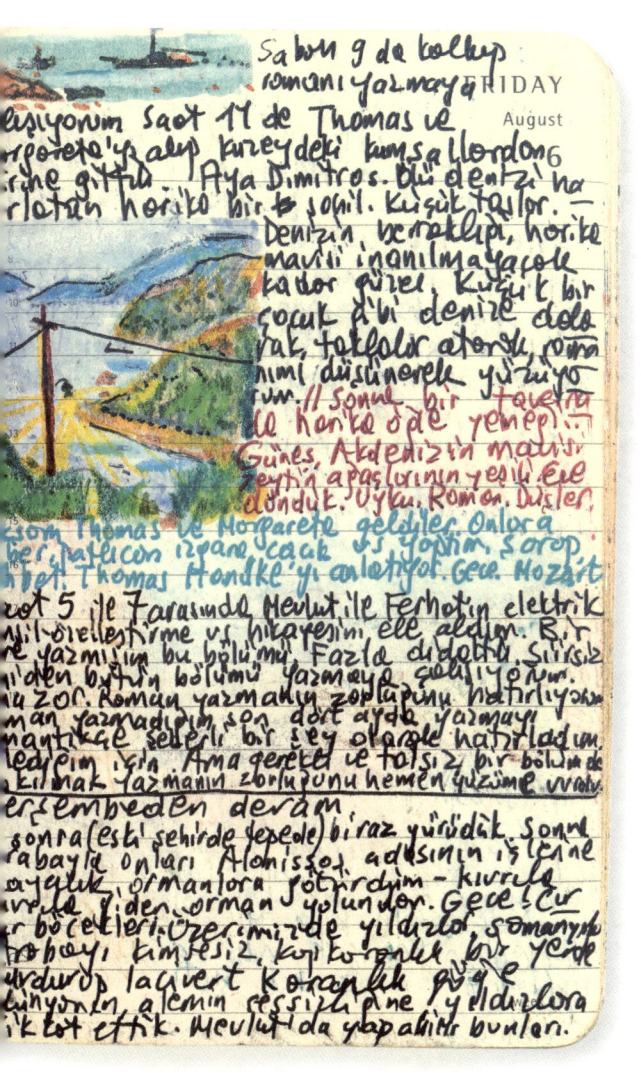

These past four months when I haven't been writing my novel, I've thought of writing as some romantic, sugarcoated thing. Because I missed it. But getting stuck on a necessary yet troublesome chapter has served as an immediate and brusque reminder of how difficult writing can be.

among the rocks and forests—along the winding forest road. Nighttime! Crickets. Above us, the stars, the Milky Way. We stopped the car in a deserted, pitch-black spot and turned our attention to the deep dark blue sky, the stars, the silence of the world, and the whole of creation. Mevlut could do this kind of thing too.

In the morning, a cozy light filtered onto our bed. I got up soon after and worked for three hours, from nine to twelve, tunneling right into the novel. Mevlut and Ferhat are at a restaurant in Kurtuluş. Ferhat is teaching Mevlut how to inspect meters, drawing on examples from the restaurant's attempts at electricity fraud. It's a subject I know well. After a swim at Agios Dimitrios and lunch in Steni Vala, I continued working on the novel at home. Its simplicity and lightness both amuse and distress me... But this chapter I'm writing—rewriting is good preparation for the chapters to come—patience, Orhan.

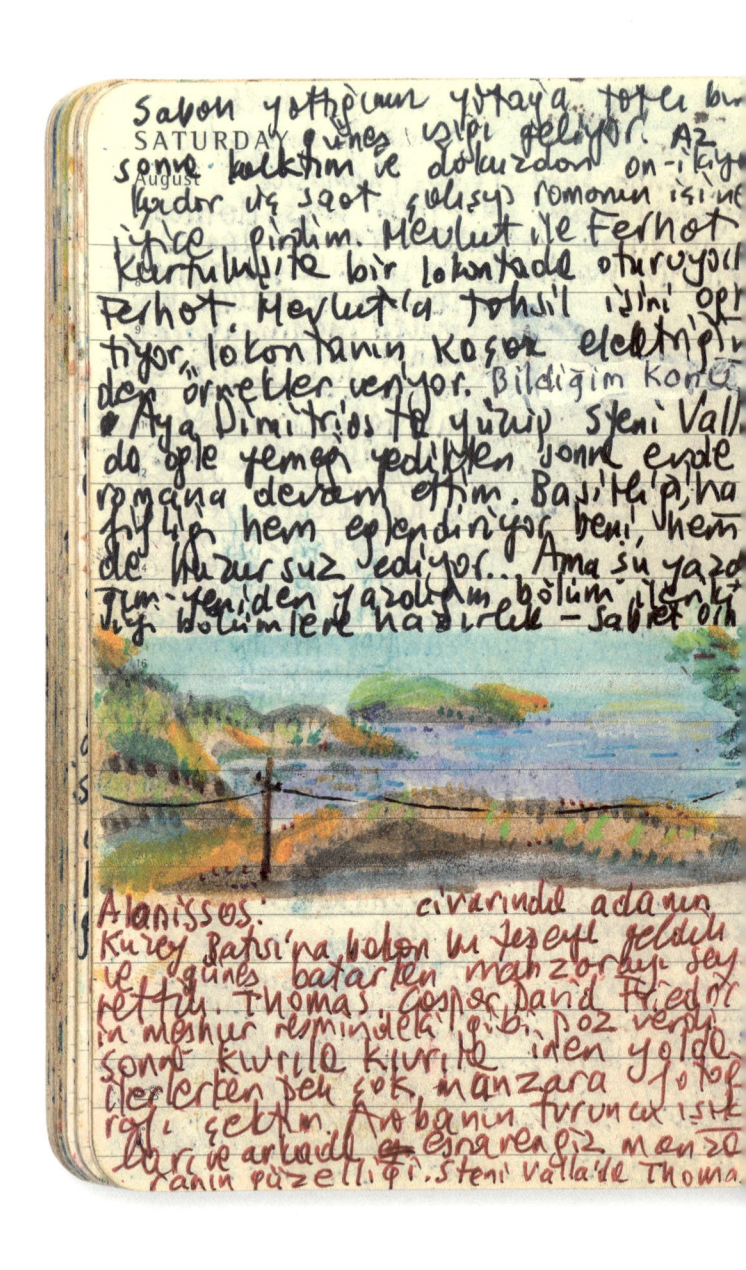

We've come to this hill near Alonissos overlooking the northwest of the island, to admire the sunset. Thomas posed like the man in Caspar David Friedrich's famous painting. Later, as we went down the twisting road, I took several photographs of the view. The car's orange headlights and the beauty of the mysterious landscape behind us. Last dinner with Thomas and co. in Steni Vala. True friends. Good people.

This morning, as I am writing some of the novel's simplest, most ordinary pages ... I am listening obsessively to the 2nd part—movement—of Mozart's Piano Concerto no. 21. The power of the music seems to bring Mevlut and Ferhat's conversation about electricity inspection to life, elevating it beyond the realm of the ordinary. But the music will not mislead me. I can feel that this too will be in my novel, a divine love, something profound and belonging to the afterworld. This profundity will be uncovered by Mevlut's wanderings in Istanbul and by his imagination.

I drew this picture here of the view we saw yesterday so that as long as I am carrying my notebook with me, I can open the page it's on and look at it whenever I want. So that I can carry with me wherever I go this LANDSCAPE and the loveliness of these days spent doing nothing but writing, swimming, and listening to Mozart.

It's wrong to look at a landscape as if it were a painting. We should look at paintings as if they were landscapes.

In the evening I made some grilled peppers and zucchini, tzatziki, etc. Thinking about my novel in the meantime. I'd forgotten how difficult it is to write a novel, how hopeless the author feels.

Waking up at 7:30 every morning, making tea-coffee, and cutting fruit while dreaming of my novel. I've been living like this for fifteen years. Before, I used to go to bed at four in the morning. For the past fifteen years, I've been going to bed at eleven. Every morning, the terror of not liking what I wrote the day before! The world of the novel is so delicate! It needs the author's unalloyed confidence... You have to believe in it even if you don't believe in it. It is essential for the writer to believe in their own world if their imagination is to work. Nine-thirty sees the start of a tinkling summer shower. Went for a swim in the sea with Kiran. The turquoise sea, the lead-gray sky, the green of the pine trees reflecting on the water. The novel on my mind. Swim out, Orhan, swim farther, out into your characters' lives as you would into the water. As I swim in the sea, it isn't raindrops that I can feel falling on me, but the lives and words of others. The bedsheets, our books, and even the notebook in which I've been writing my novel have all got wet.

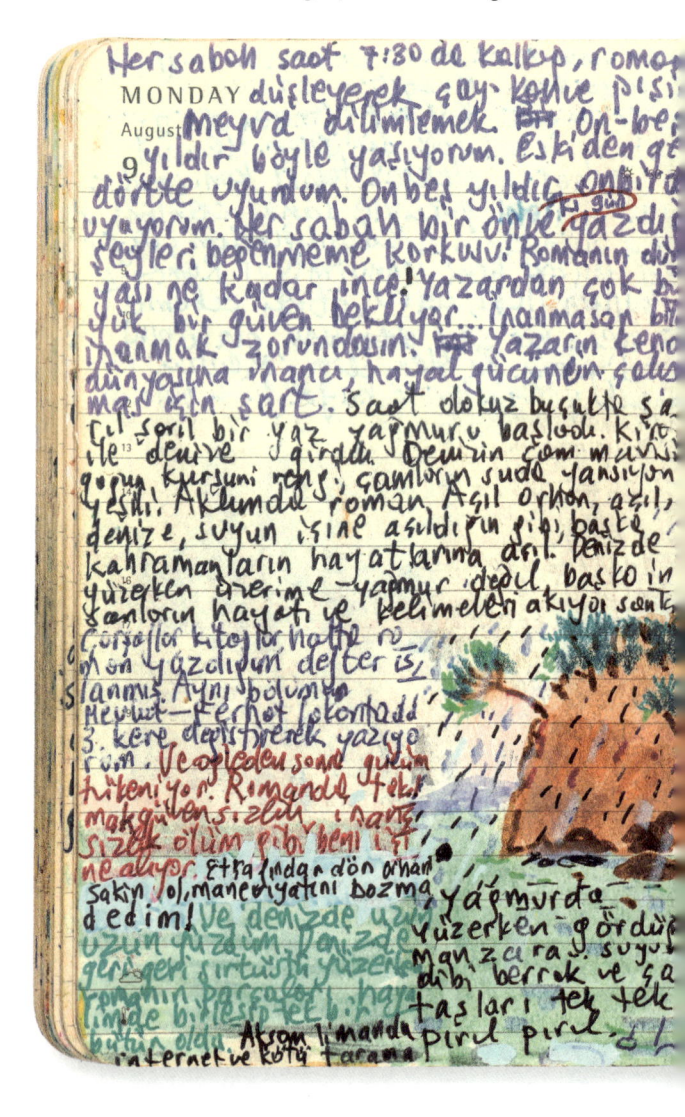

I am revising and rewriting the same chapter, Mevlut-Ferhat in the restaurant, for the 3rd time. In the afternoon, my strength runs out. Getting stuck while writing a novel, losing confidence and belief, can be overwhelming, like death. Swim around it, Orhan, keep calm, don't let your head drop, I told myself. And I swam and swam. As I was swimming on my back, backward into the sea, the pieces of the novel came together in my imagination to form a whole. In the evening, internet at the port and a bad *taramasalata*. the view as I swam in the rain. the water is clear right through to the bottom, every pebble perfectly visible.

Morning. The fear before starting a new chapter: Where is this novel going? Does it work? I keep telling myself, Don't be afraid, Orhan. This is how I've written all my novels. A strange, unknown country. When you were writing about the Kars of *Snow* or the miniaturists of *Red,* or Enishte's soul's journey to paradise in *Red,* were you feeling confident then? The fear was always present. And yes, there was a sense of excitement-euphoria too. Because I knew how original my creation was going to be.

We drove around these hills

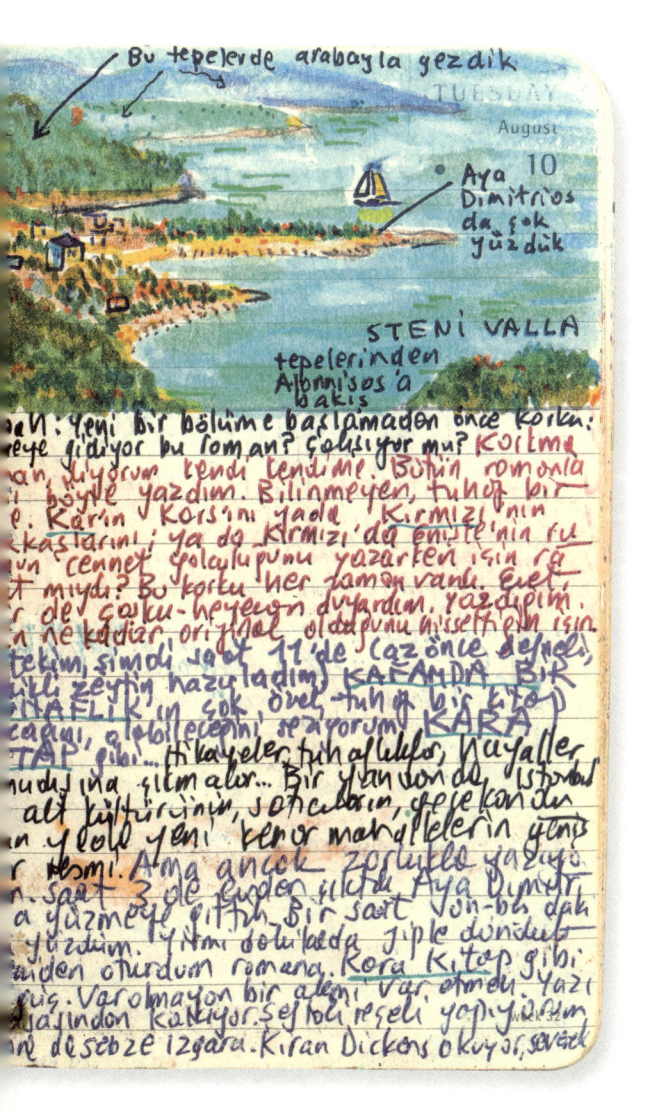

We swam for ages in Agios Dimitrios

View of Alonissos from the hills of STENI VALA

So it is that right now, at 11 o'clock (I have just been preparing olives garnished with bay leaf and thyme), I am beginning to feel what a strange and special book *A STRANGENESS IN MY MIND* can and will be. Just like *THE BLACK BOOK* . . . Stories, eccentricities, day-dreams, digressions . . . And at the same time a broad portrait of Istanbul's subcultures and street vendors, its *gecekondu* homes and its newest far-flung neighborhoods. But I am struggling to write. At 3 o'clock, we left the house. We went for a swim in Agios Dimitrios. I swam for an hour and fifteen minutes. A 20-minute drive back in the jeep. I returned to my novel. It's a demanding task, like *The Black Book*. Bringing a nonexistent realm into being. I get up from my writing desk and make peach jam. Then some grilled vegetables. Kiran is reading and enjoying some Dickens.

I took a sleeping pill last night, so I still haven't woken up properly or got my mind and body to work fast enough. I swam for an hour in the magnificent bay below. Without pushing myself too hard. With a feeling of despair about the novel.

But now that I've sat at my desk... I've suddenly shifted into a "manic" state: I must keep an inventory of Mevlut's financial difficulties. My mind speeds up optimistically, enjoying the novel again. Afterward I called my mother up to wish her a happy birthday. "I feel bad that I spend my life doing nothing...," she told me. "WHEN YOU DON'T DO ANYTHING, TIME GOES BY VERY QUICKLY, BUT THE CLOCK'S HANDS NEVER SEEM TO move. LUNCHTIME never comes. I'VE WATCHED THE *FORBIDDEN LOVE* TV SERIES THREE TIMES ALREADY..." I immediately think of the loneliness that envelops Mevlut, and a character in a novel discussing the meaning of life and time... Being a novelist means... liking the novel you're writing, and being able to put everything you experience into that novel...

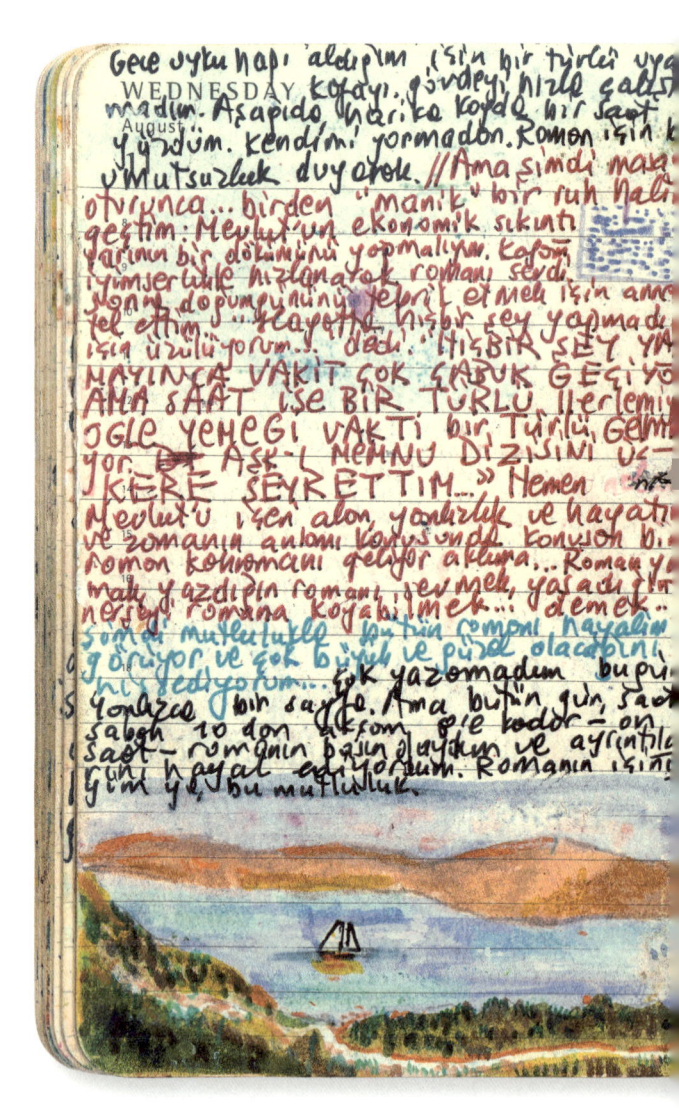

Soon I can joyfully see the whole novel laid out in my mind, and I can tell that it is going to be a vast and beautiful thing... I haven't written very much today. Just a page. But I've spent all day, from 10 in the morning to 8 in the evening—ten hours—sitting with the novel and picturing its details. As long as I'm inside the novel, I'm happy.

Last night, we went for some grilled mullet–white wine in Steni Vala, then came back home. Shortly thereafter, there was a power cut. I went straight to sleep. It seems our macho neighbors next door were arguing with each other. In the morning, no electricity, no water, etc. My phone was dead too, so we had no choice but to go down to the docks for coffee, pastries, internet, telephones, etc. The power didn't come back until 12 o'clock. *Once again, a powerful sense of how difficult this novel is going to be, and that it might take me years to write.* Once a novel is finished, you tend to think you made it all up in one sitting. But that's not the case. I've imagined this world, dug this well, one spoonful of dirt at a time, scooping the earth out with my bare hands, constantly making changes as I go along.

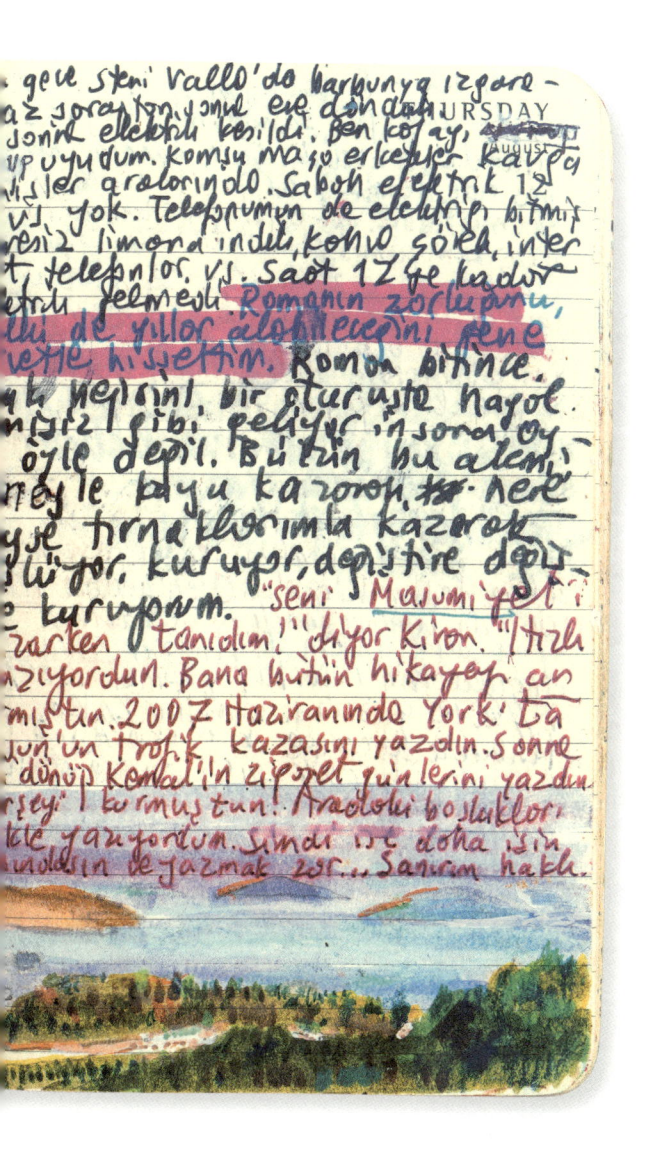

"I met you when you were writing *Innocence*!" says Kiran. "You were writing so quickly. You told me the whole plot. You wrote about Füsun's road accident in York in June 2007. Then you went back and wrote about Kemal's visits. You'd already planned the whole thing! You were having fun filling in the gaps. Now you're at the start of the road, and writing is more difficult . . ." I think she may be right.

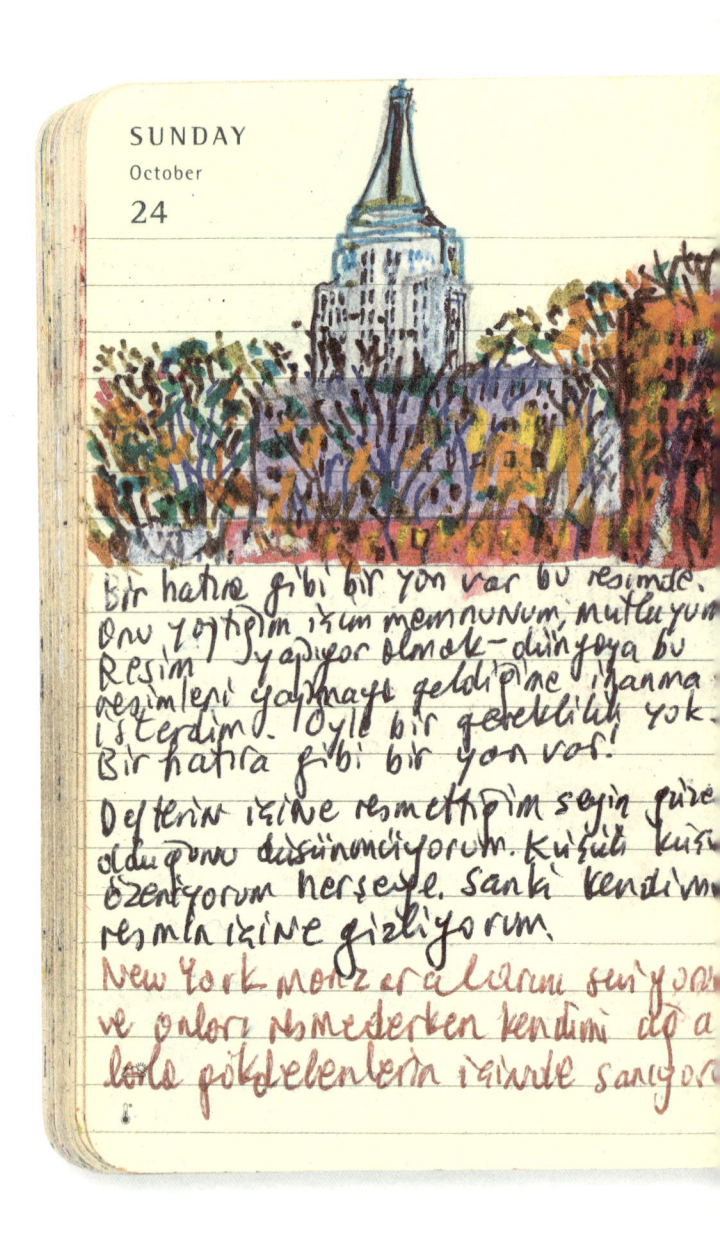

Something about this drawing is like a memory. I'm pleased and glad that I've made it. I would like to spend time painting—to believe that I was born to make these drawings. There's no such need. Something about it is like a memory!

I don't think that the things I draw in my notebook are particularly beautiful. I take painstaking care over every detail. It's as if I were hiding myself in the image.

I like New York cityscapes, and when I'm drawing them, I have the illusion of being among the skyscrapers and the trees.

I use this notebook to make little notes about everything. It's as if I were hiding the world in here. As if I were trying to live on these pages the life I cannot live. The life I want to live = a painter's life. I just haven't been able to transition into that life! Can using writing to emulate that other life offer sufficient consolation? I must keep doing what I'm doing without dwelling too much on these kinds of questions . . . A journey to a faraway mountainous land. Eventually this dream reveals every secret, or how GOD sees the matter—and the whole of creation. But I wake up, afraid, before I can find out what happens at the end. And I remember the vestiges of the dream in the form of a landscape painting.

the brick
skyscraper
across the road

In the morning, I went for a half-hour walk on Riverside Drive, as I've been doing every morning these days. A chilly November cold. New Yorkers walking their dogs. I bought some fruit from the convenience store.
The novel: a feeling of futility. The truth is that I haven't been working well. Spent the afternoon in the office dealing with emails and other bits and pieces.

Morning. I had a look at the hotel on 94th Street. I took the train to 72nd. I rummaged around the Barnes and Noble on 66th. It's cold. Time to put on a coat. But I'm content walking down Broadway in the cold New York morning with a bag in my hand. It turns out I'm early. 42nd Street. I roamed around Times Square and Broadway for a while. I savored the morning, that most ordinary time of the New York day. Work, books, reading and writing, wandering around the streets of New York . . . I'm happy with it all! I'm sitting at a café as I write this, watching people coming and going on Broadway. Lunch with George Andreou . . . Time goes by so fast. I would have liked to have more of it to spend with George.

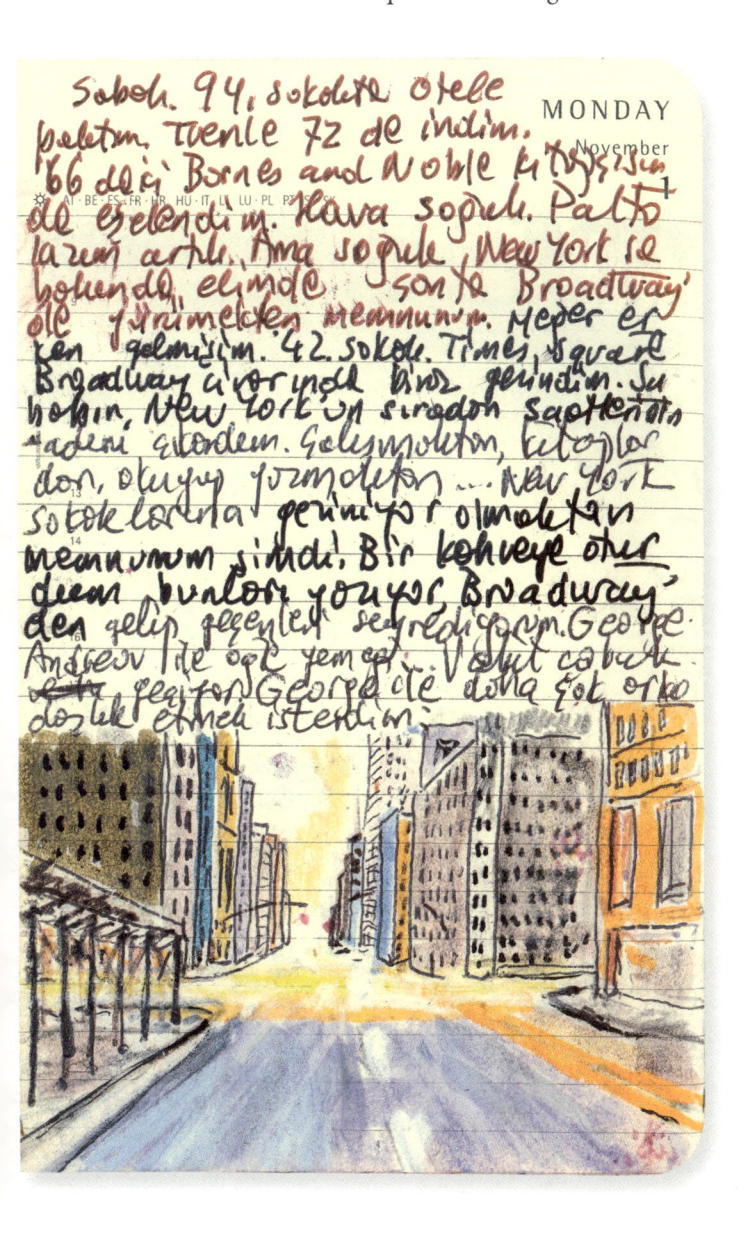

Snow-wind. Leadlike. Carefree Orhan is having lunch on the way home, a salmon sandwich and a coffee at the Café Pizza on the corner between 104th Street and Broadway, and reading a copy of *The New York Times* left behind by the customer before me. Sunday morning streets. The diners are teeming with people. I checked my email at the Butler Library, then came to the Avery: the joy of writing novels in the library... On the one hand I'm reading *Anna Karenina,* which I plan to teach in class; on the other, I am trying to write about boza seller Mevlut's adventures...
Being alone with my novel, reading Tolstoy, and thinking about my own book at the same time: these really are unparalleled pleasures. In the evening Kiran and I went to see Woody Allen's latest film. *You Will Meet a Tall Dark Stranger.* Light, easy, but equipped, as usual, with a strong narrative drive. An absorbing watch.

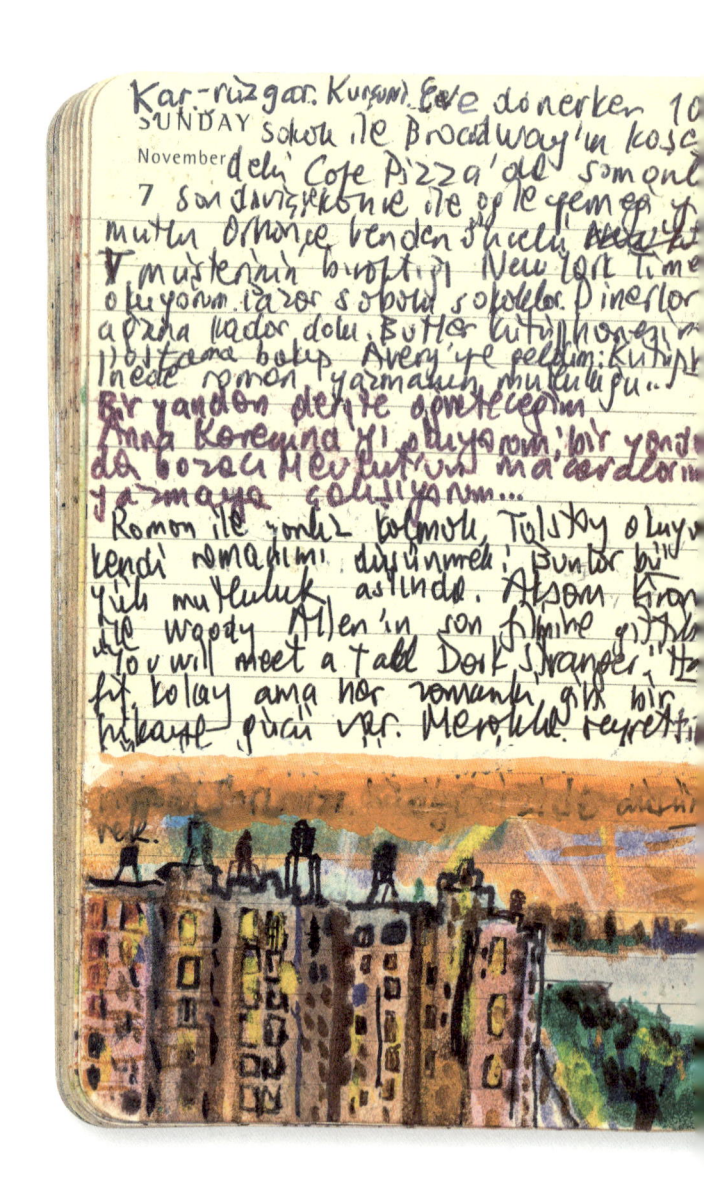

At home this morning, I spend three hours wrestling with the novel. Good. Mevlut carrying yogurt with his father . . . His lunch . . . etc. It's very windy. Dark, rainy, overcast skies, a perfect day for working!

But after a while I suddenly find myself at the Avery Library, checking emails from Istanbul. I lose my temper. All the craftsmanship, which I assumed would be fairly simple, has turned out to be complicated. I'm sick and tired of this never-ending series of museum troubles.

In this state of irritation, all the great scenes I've pictured for the novel start to lose their color, and my mind is poisoned: my frustration with the museum weighs heavily on the novel and on my writing. I had lunch sitting on the ground in front of the Amsterdam hospital. Wind, rain like snow, cold. Write, Orhan, write. Here in the basement of the library, I am pouring all the strength I have into trying to write Mevlut's story.

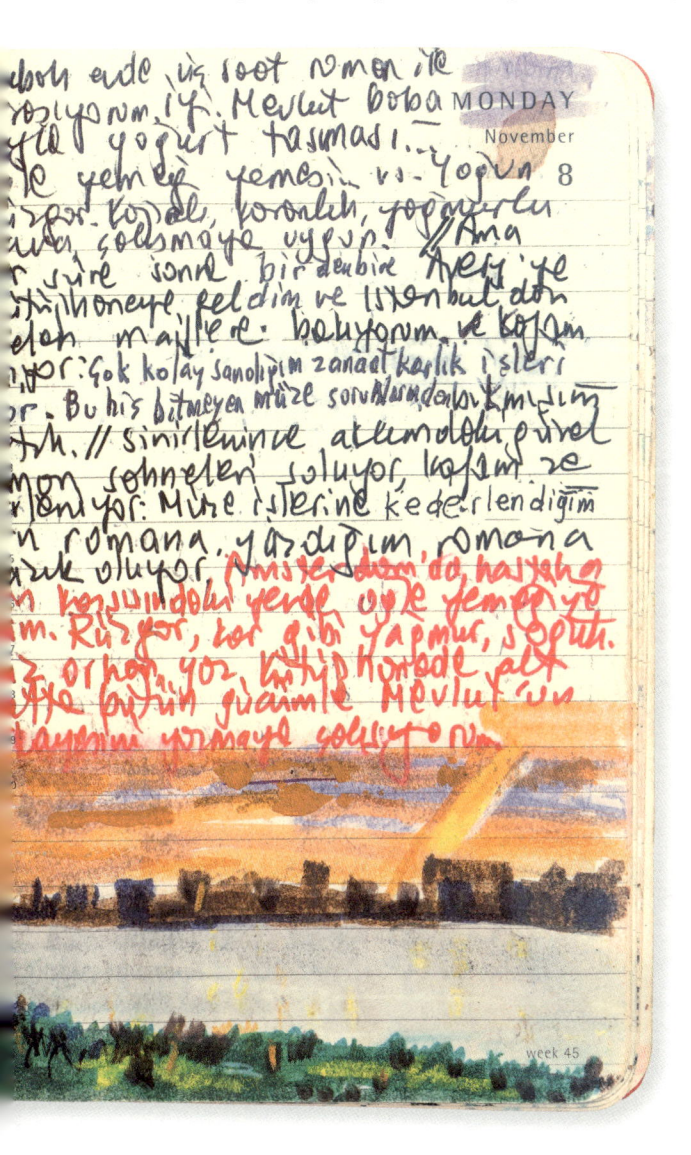

Like a shadow I woke up unprompted before the dark night had ended. Like shadows we passed through the cold and silent streets of Edmonton. While waiting at the airport, I turned to the last few chapters of *Anna Karenina:* reading them again; for the class on Tuesday: when suddenly I found the perfect solution to the plot, the story, of *A STRANGENESS IN MY MIND.* MEVLUT is all too familiar with the tale of the dog that fed on Europeans, with the story of the island of Hayırsızada... And he tries to break this spell and its force (which is the reason the dogs attack him). I have therefore returned to the story I had come up with in 2007, when I had first started imagining this novel.

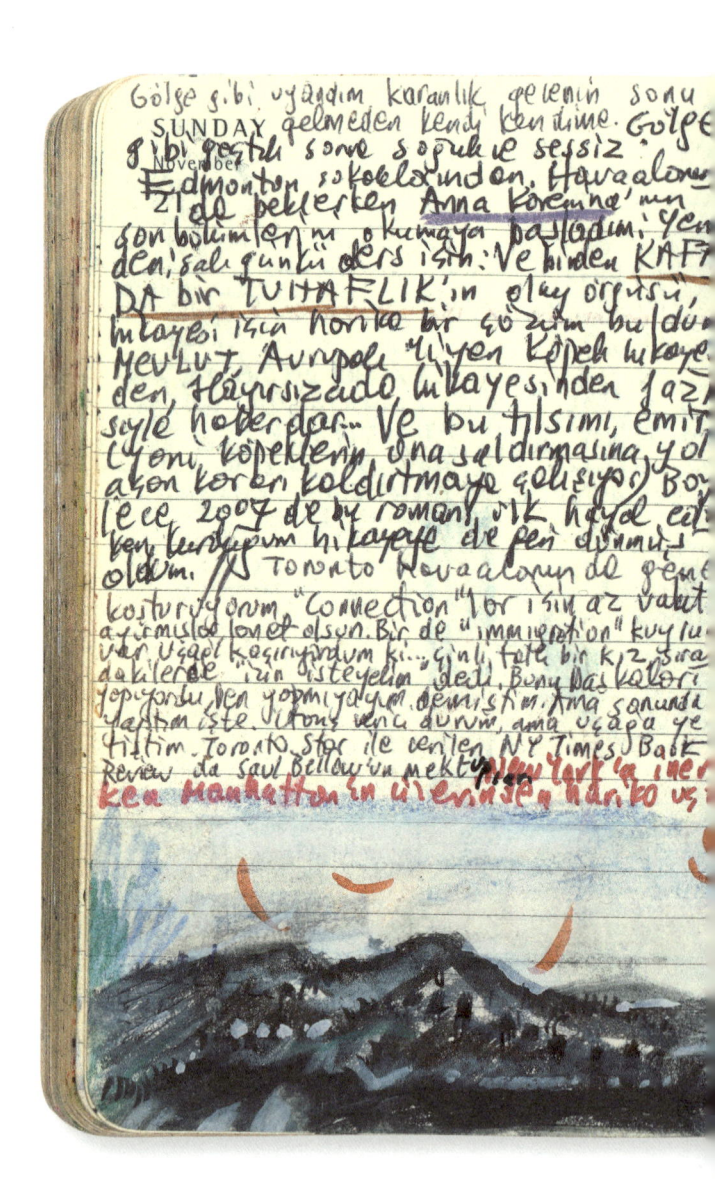

At Toronto airport, in a rush again. They haven't left enough damned time for the "connection." There's also the "immigration" queue. I was going to miss my flight, when...a sweet Chinese girl suggested we should "ask for permission" from the people ahead. Other people had already been doing this, though I'd decided not to. But in the end I did. It was mortifying, but I did make my flight. Saul Bellow's letters in the *NY Times Book Review* that comes with the *Toronto Star*. A glorious glide over Manhattan as we descended toward New York.

Last night in New York I opened my notebook and eagerly jotted down what I saw and experienced in strange, melancholy Edmonton. Several times I told myself, Oh, I should put this in my notebook. For example: At lunchtime on Saturday I walked along the bridges that traverse the skyscrapers and connect them to one another until I reached a "food court." Poor people, homeless people. They're sitting around, killing time, near the cheap fast-food hamburger shop vj's. I got talking to an Arab man selling döner kebab and salad. "Where are you from?" When I told him Turkey and New York, he said he used to sell döner kebab in the Bronx, but business was slow there. So I came here. There's plenty of money, plenty of work, here. I told Kiran about the audience who came to my book signing. I have no idea when this happened, I said, but it seems I've become the Third World, non-Western reader's writer.

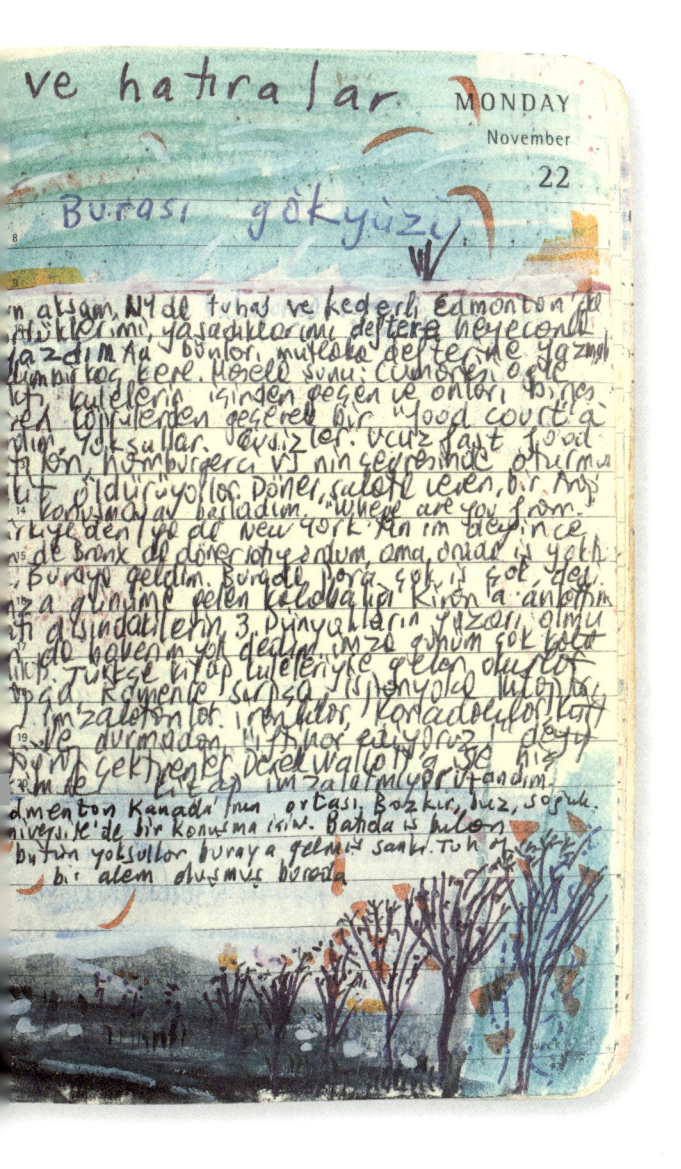

and memories

This is the sky

There was a large crowd at the book signing. Readers coming with piles of Turkish editions, people asking me to sign Arabic, Romanian, Serbian, Spanish editions. Iranians, Canadians, Kurds, and a constant stream of people taking photographs and telling me how proud they are of me. No one's asking Derek Walcott to sign any books. I felt embarrassed. Edmonton is right in the middle of Canada. Steppes, ice, cold. I've come for a talk at the university. It feels like every destitute soul who has managed to find a job in the West has come here. This has created its own peculiar world.

passing by 108th Street and Hudson...

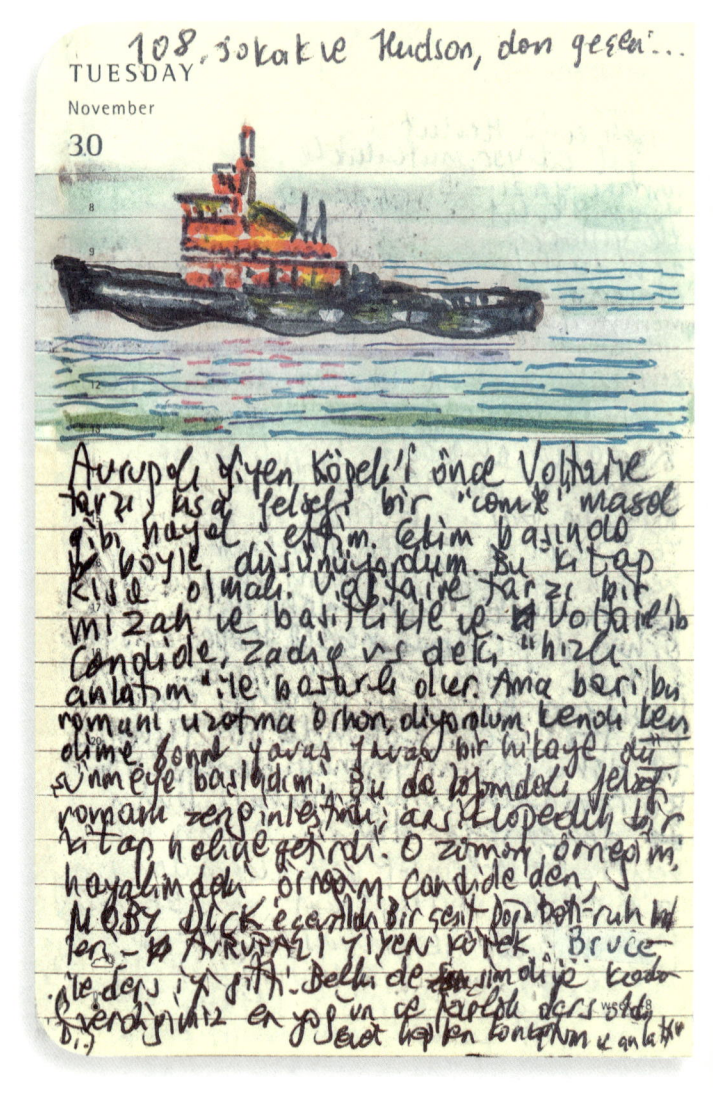

Initially I envisaged The Dog That Fed on Europeans as a short philosophical "conte," a fable, in the style of Voltaire. That's what I was thinking at the start of October. This book ought to be short. For it to succeed, it must have the humor and simplicity of Voltaire's work, and the "quick narration" we find in Voltaire's *Candide, Zadig,* etc. At least try to keep this novel short, Orhan, I tell myself. Then I gradually began to think of a story. This enriched the philosophical novel I had in mind; turning it into a more encyclopedic book. Soon the template I was working from, the template for my imagination, went from *Candide* to MOBY DICK. An East-West kind of thing—states of mind—THE DOG THAT FED ON EUROPEANS. The class with Bruce went well. It may be the most intense and cleverest of our classes yet. I did most of the talking and teaching.

Last night I dreamt of yogurt-sellers. They were selling yogurt from buckets hanging off a pole across their backs. Ah, so this is how the yogurt buckets looked, I thought during the dream. As I work on the novel this morning, I'm wondering "Where did I first see those yogurt buckets, what photograph were they in?" Kiran and I worked at home until later in the day. At 4 in the afternoon we took the train from 125th Street to Cold Spring to visit Anita. There's a problem with the meniscus in her knee. We went to the supermarket to do her shopping. At home I made her some fish with tomatoes and peppers. I have so much respect for Anita. I wish I could express it more. I was glad we visited.

THE HUDSON ON THE WAY TO COLD SPRING

2010

This is exactly what the George Washington Bridge looks like from our bedroom.

At home this morning I think of Mevlut and merrily work on my novel. I am excited about the prospect of several more years of friendship with Mevlut. The pleasure of working, of writing. Kiran is still in Cold Spring with Anita. Lunch with Rüya.

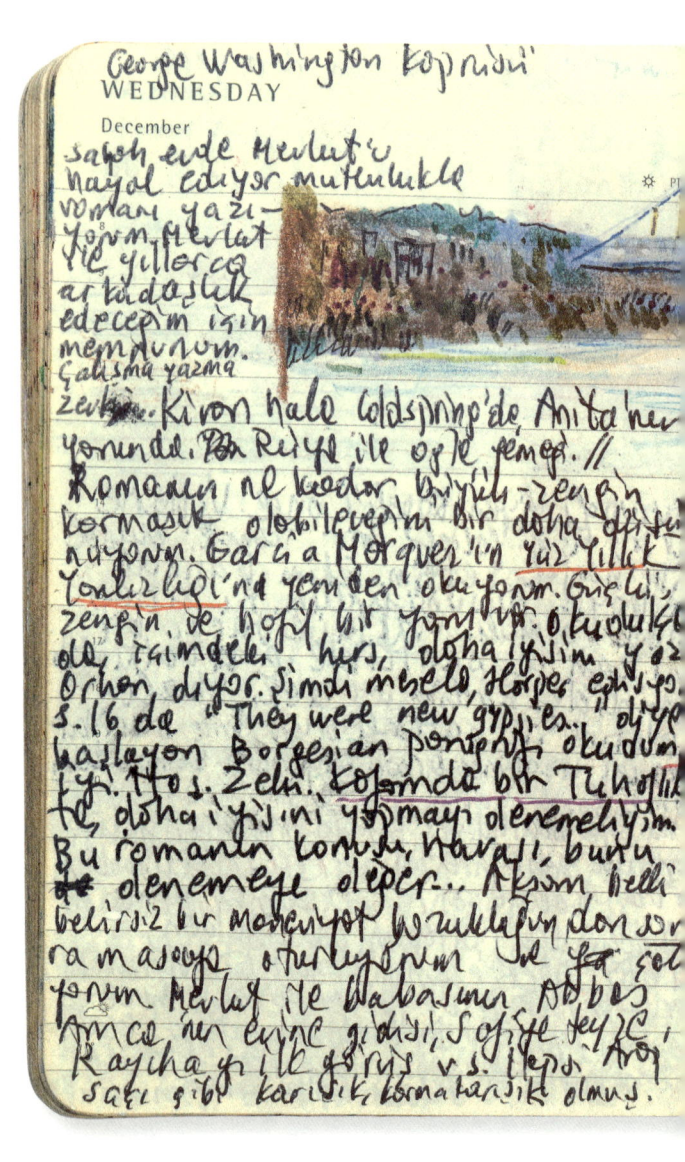

Once again I'm thinking about how vast-rich-complex I can make this novel. I am rereading Garcia Marquez's *One Hundred Years of Solitude*. It is at once rich, powerful, and light. As I read, the ambitious side of me says, Write something even better, Orhan. Right now, for example, on p. 16 of the Harper edition, I have just read the Borgesian paragraph that starts with "They were new gypsies..." Skillful. Charming. Clever. I must try to do even better in *A Strangeness in My Mind*. The subject, the atmosphere, of this novel are worth the effort... In the evening, after a spell of faint dejection, I sit at my desk to work. Mevlut's visit to his father and his uncle Abbas's house, Safiye Teyze, the first time he sees Rayiha, etc. They're all a chaotic, tangled mess.

Lunch at Le Monde with the writer Elizabeth Kostova. She is the author of a bestselling historical novel called *The Historian*. We'd first met at book fairs in London and Washington. Her husband is Bulgarian; he runs a literary charity in Bulgaria. She invites me to it. She is intelligent, and interested in art. Friendly, kind.

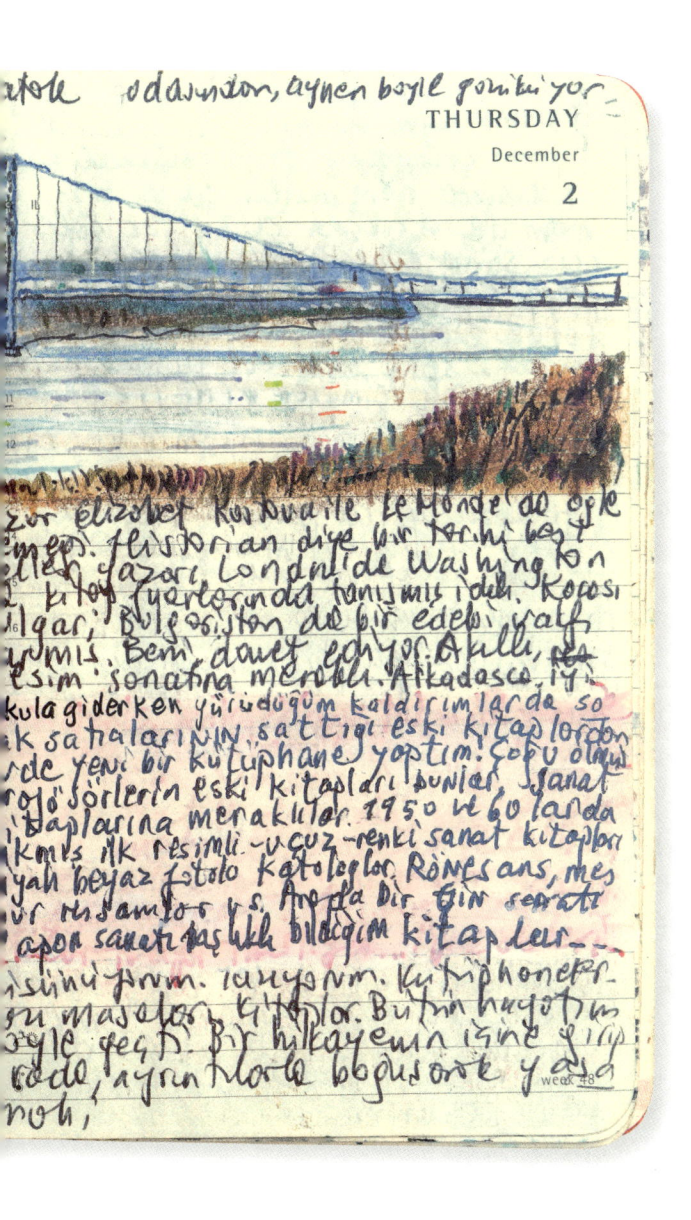

On the way to the university, I browsed the secondhand bookstalls along the pavement and filled up a whole new library at home! Mostly old books by dead professors. Some of the earliest cheap-illustrated-color-printed art volumes, published in the 1950s and '60s, and black-and-white exhibition catalogs, all perfect for collectors of art books. The Renaissance, famous painters, etc. Here and there, a volume I recognize on Chinese or Japanese art . . . I'm thinking. I'm writing. Libraries. Writing desks, books. This is how I've spent my whole life. To step inside a story and live there, grappling with all its nuances.

2010

Kiran and I went to the garage sale between 25th Street and 6–7th Avenues. I've bought many period-specific items for the Museum of Innocence here, and many gifts for Füsun... It was actually Kiran who suggested we go. I left the house with some reluctance, exhausted as I am by museum matters, and by how slow everyone is, the carpenters, the architects, the decorators, the artists.

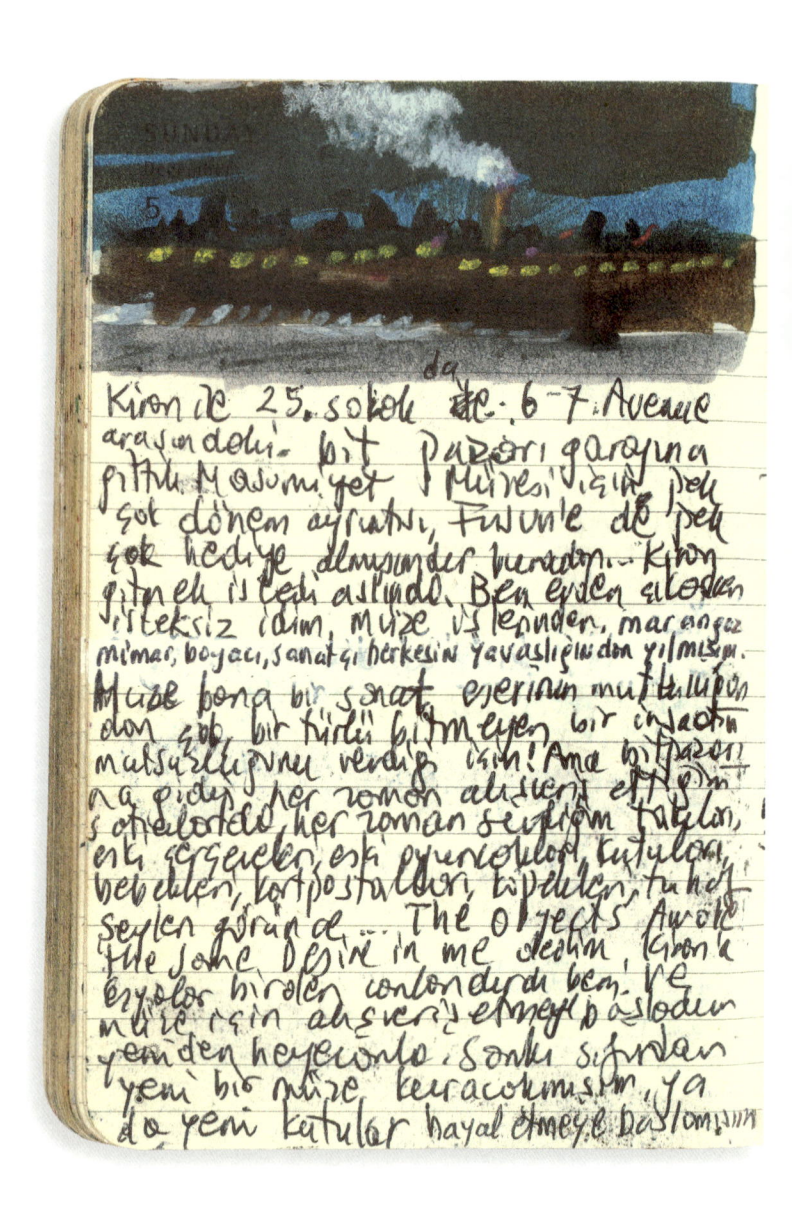

The fact is that the museum is not really bringing me the joy of a work of art, so much as the misery of an eternal construction site! But when I went to the flea market and saw the vendors I always buy from, displaying the jewelry, the old picture frames, the old toys, boxes, dolls, postcards, dog figurines, and all the other strange objects I always enjoy... The Objects Awoke the Same Desire in me, I told Kiran. They revived me. And I merrily started shopping for the museum again. As if I were creating a new museum from scratch, or have been thinking of a whole new set of boxes.

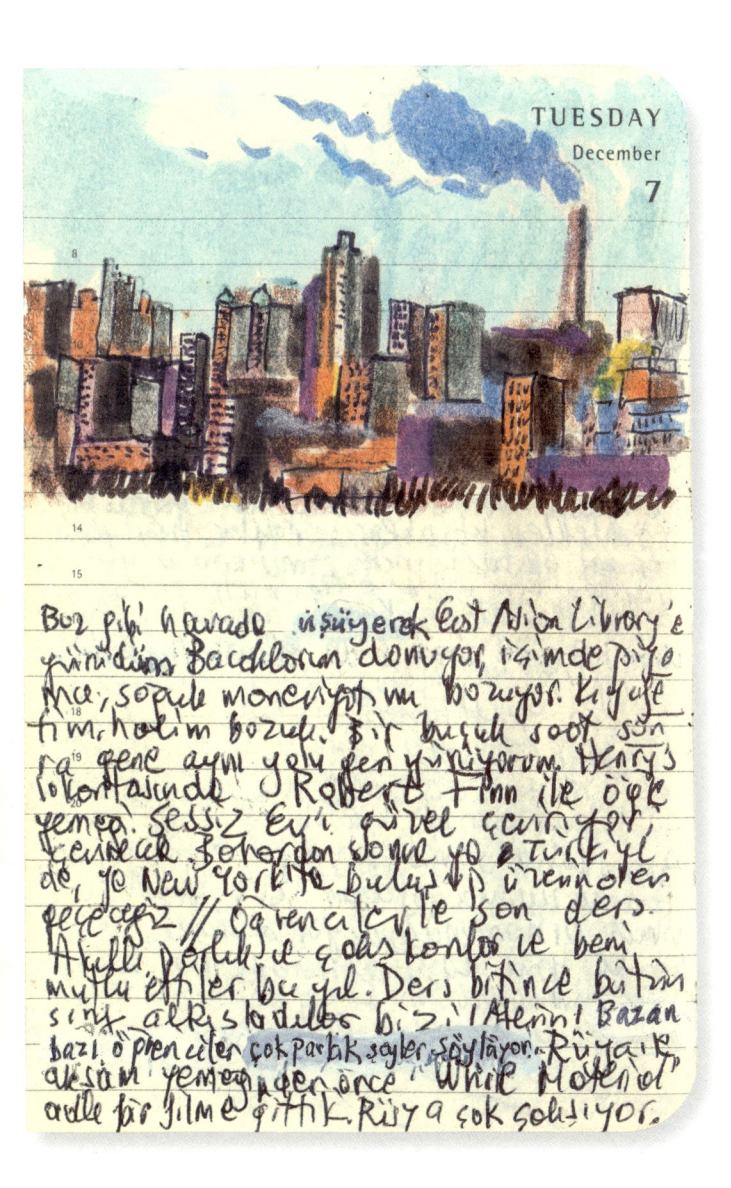

I walked in the bitter cold to the East Asian Library. My legs are freezing, I've still got my pajamas on, the cold is weighing me down. My outfit, my mood, are all awry. One and a half hours later, I'm walking back along the same route. Lunch at Henry's restaurant with Robert Finn. He is doing a good job, he will do a good job of translating *The Silent House.* We're going to meet after the spring, either in Turkey or in New York, to go over it together.

Our last lecture today. These clever, bright, hardworking students have made me proud this year. At the end of the lecture, the whole class started applauding us. Well done! Every now and then a student will share a rather brilliant insight. Before dinner, Rüya and I went to see a film called *White Material.* Rüya is working very hard.

I have placed this double-spread inspired by CHINESE LANDscapes precisely at this point of MEMORIES of DISTANT MOUNTAINS—on purpose.

ÇİN MANZara resimlerinin etkisiyle yaptığım bu çift sayfayı UZAK DAĞLAR ve HATIRALAR'ın tam bu Noktasına - özellikle yerleştirdim.

In autumn 2011, during a trip to Latin America, Kiran and I broke up and did not see each other again. It was a very difficult time for me. Until I met Aslı again.

I woke up in the middle of the night, at 2:30, and finished the novel—*A Strangeness in My Mind*. When I told Aslı the next morning, both her and my first reaction was to exclaim, "That's unbelievable!" It was an emotional moment for us both. If it hadn't been for Aslı, *A Strangeness in My Mind* would not have taken the shape it has, nor would I have been able to finish the novel.

It was Aslı who suggested out of the blue that I should move the scene where Mevlut elopes with Rayiha from the middle of the novel to the beginning. I didn't even ask her why. I just did it, and rewrote the novel accordingly. I also accepted many of the cuts Aslı suggested. Especially those she mentioned last summer. As I went through her notes on what might be cut, I would agree with her, feel a little downcast, and start smoking again, only to give it up the next morning. I also liked how clever, beautiful Aslı was able to empathize with not-so-beautiful Rayiha. I wrote the book by reading it aloud to Aslı and discussing it with her every day. Perhaps I'm lucky, but then so is Mevlut . . .

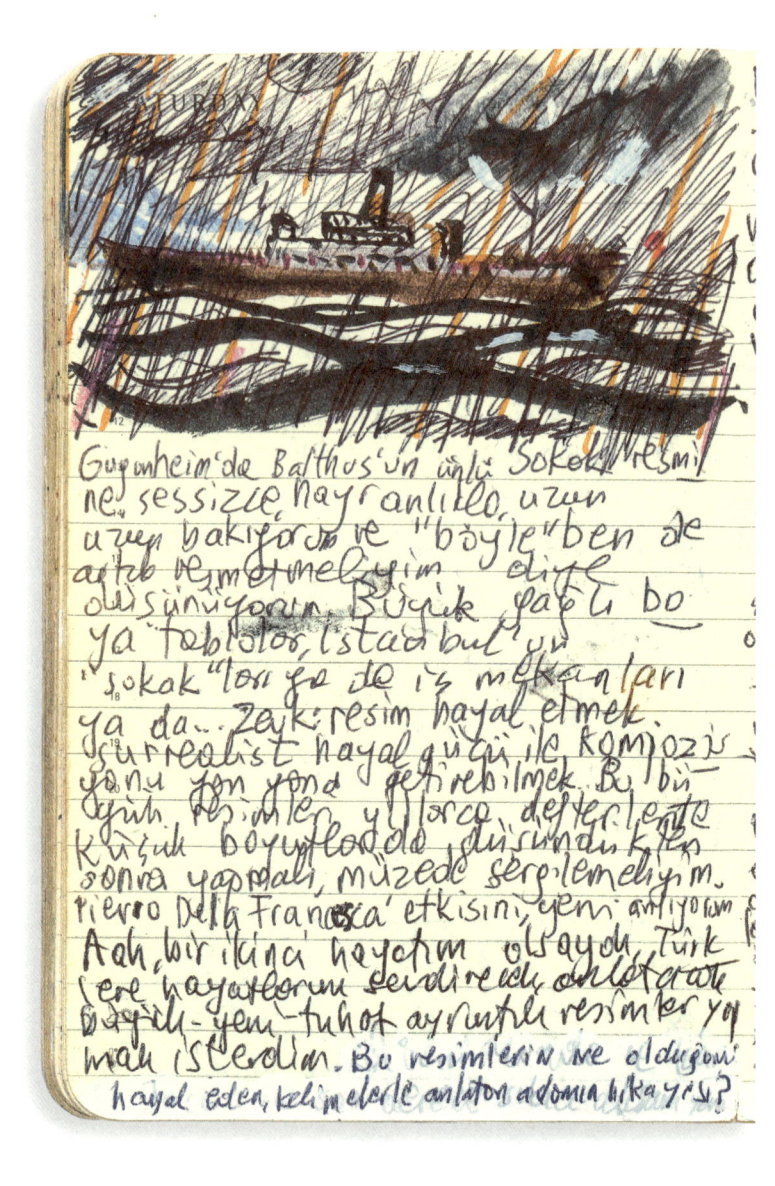

At the Guggenheim, I stare long and hard in silent admiration at Balthus's famous painting *The Street,* and think to myself that I should start painting "like this" as well. Big oil paintings, the "streets" of Istanbul, or its interiors, or... Pleasure is: Imagining a painting for the first time. Managing to bring together surrealist imagination and composition... After many years spent thinking these big paintings into smaller versions for my notebook, I should really paint them properly and display them in the museum. I have only now started to realize the influence Piero della Francesca has had on me. Oh, if I could have had a second life, I would have liked to make big—new—paintings filled with all sorts of strange details, paintings that would make Turkish people love and understand their lives.

The story of a man picturing what these paintings might look like, and describing them in words?

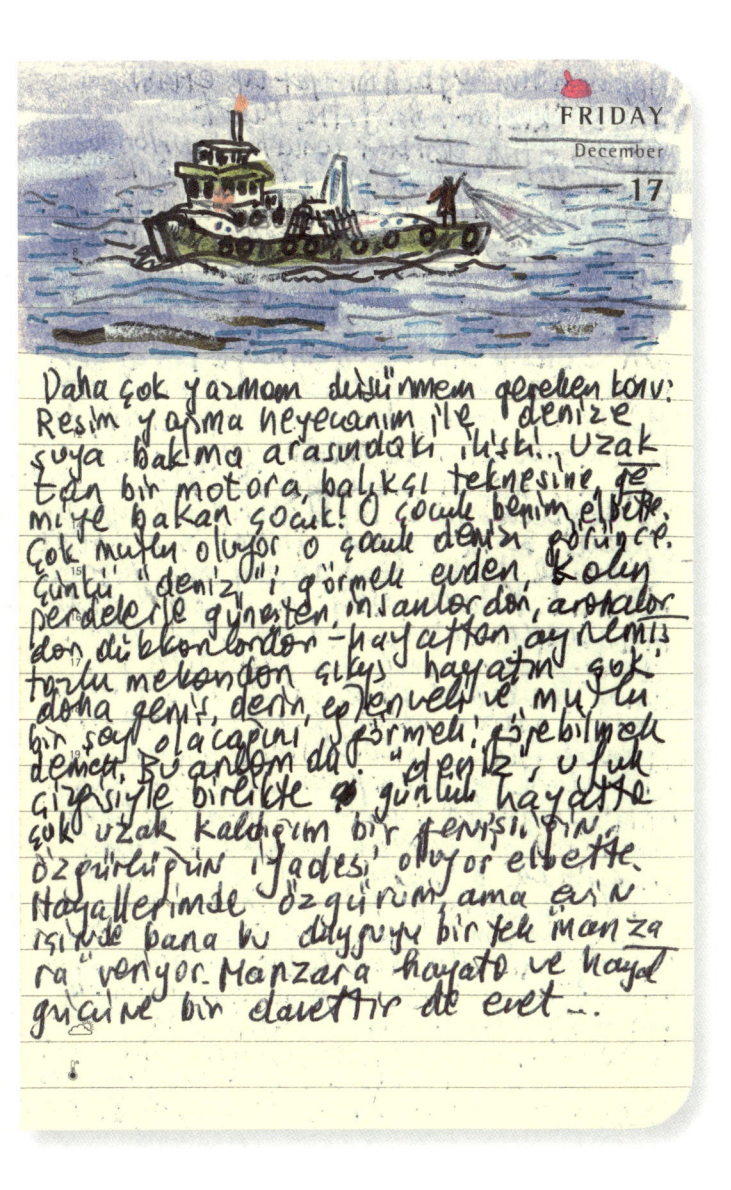

Something I must write and think about more: the connection between my urge to paint, and the act of looking at the sea, at water … A child observing a motorboat, a fishing vessel sailing in the distance! Of course that child is me. He is so happy when he looks at the sea. Because looking at the "sea" means discovering that past the house, past its heavy sun-soaked curtains, beyond all the people, the cars, the shops—outside of these dusty rooms separated from life, there is another life, so much broader, deeper, happier, and more enjoyable than this one. In this context, the "sea," together with the horizon, are of course expressions of a freedom and a breadth of experience that are well beyond my reach in my everyday life. In my daydreams I may already be free, but inside the house, the only thing that can give me that feeling is to look at the "view." Among other things, landscapes are doubtless also an invitation to live and to exercise your imagination …

HAYDARPAŞA

Afternoon. Ferry from Karaköy to Kadıköy. It's hot. On the upper deck of the Kadıköy ferry. Istanbul is quiet in the still, lethal summer heat. Almost like a provincial town. Koşuyolu Street. Antiques stores. Flea markets. By 5 o'clock, though, the city is teeming with crowds. Everyone's out in the streets. The smell of pan-fried potatoes and mussels. People out for a Saturday stroll. This time the heat and the light give Istanbul a completely different complexion.

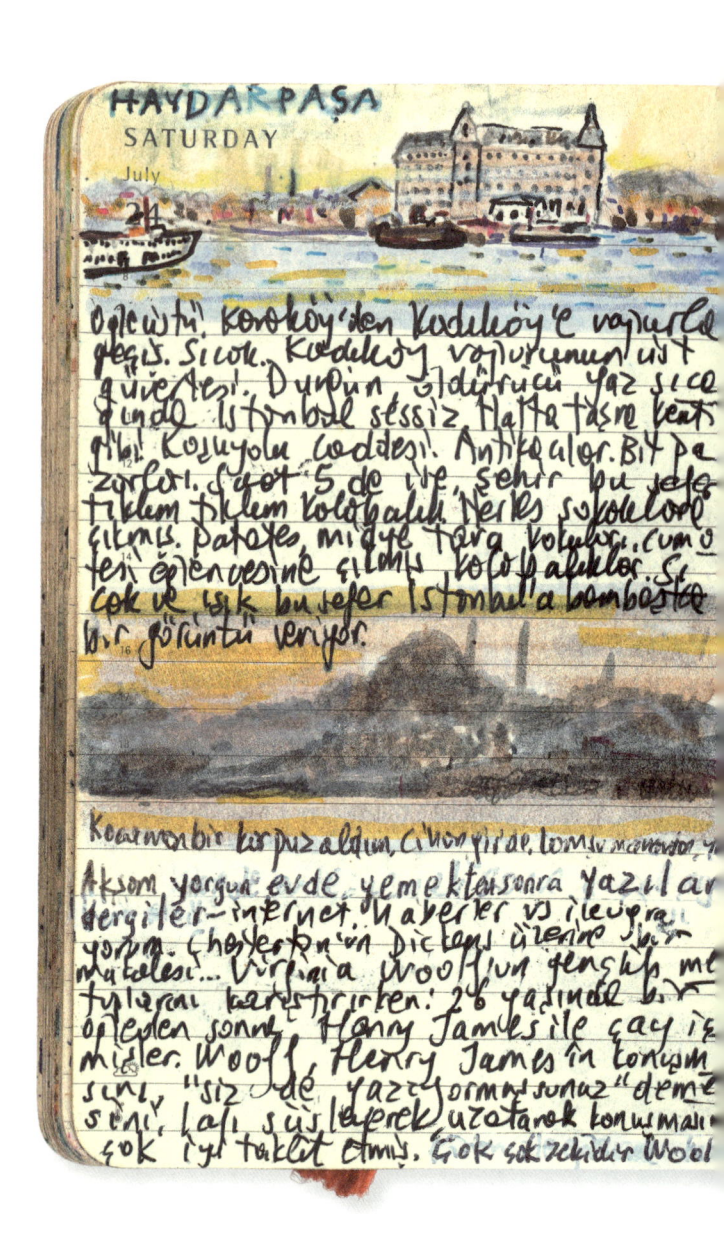

I bought and ate an enormous watermelon from the nearby greengrocer in Cihangir. At home in the evening, I wearily look through articles, magazines—the internet, the news, etc. An essay on Dickens by Chesterton... Leafing through Virginia Woolf's letters from her youth: one afternoon when she was 26 years old, she had tea with Henry James. Woolf does an excellent imitation of James's way of speaking, his "do you write too," his florid verbosity. She is exceptionally clever, Woolf.

IT RAINED

A well-attended party at Zeynep Çelik's Umur Apartments on Hüsrev Gerede Street. Perry's birthday. A gathering of people I've known for 40 years. Friends from high school and university, professors, etc. Many familiar faces. I have a cheering drink, eat two plates of savory pastry, and chitchat with the other guests. Feride Çiçekoğlu, Ayşe Yönder, Selim Deringil, Edhem Eldem. A merry crowd... Everyone knows and respects each other, they are fond of each other. They are as happy as any academic can be in Turkey. But everything is steeped in the atmosphere of an Ottoman-Turkish get-together... The feeling of being among your own is at once comforting, and an empty consolation... The writer must always be alone.

After working on the Everyman introduction to *Snow*, I opened the Google Map of Istanbul and picked out a route. Nuri arrived at 12:30. We took a taxi to Esentepe. 1 hour later, we had reached the center of Gültepe. I wrote this at a diner there. It seems I left my notes unfinished. Between 1 and 4 o'clock, I walked down from Esentepe along the perimeter wall of Zincirlikuyu Cemetery, on a road which the map told me was called DEREBOYU St. in the neighborhood of Telsizler, and up a steep, steep hill all the way to the top of Gültepe. Then back down again . . . I must make sure to include in the novel the extent to which this TERRAIN is dominated by SHARP hills. I kept walking. On to the outer edges of Gültepe! Suffocating. Narrow alleyways. All the apartment blocks bundled together. Namık Kemal neighborhood! I walked northward. The first *gecekondu* neighborhoods of Istanbul's "European shore" . . . Gültepe. It's part of the city, the modern city now. But there is still such a provincial feel to it. Of course there are no more illegal *gecekondu* buildings left (with one or two exceptions). Ugly, shabby high-rise blocks.

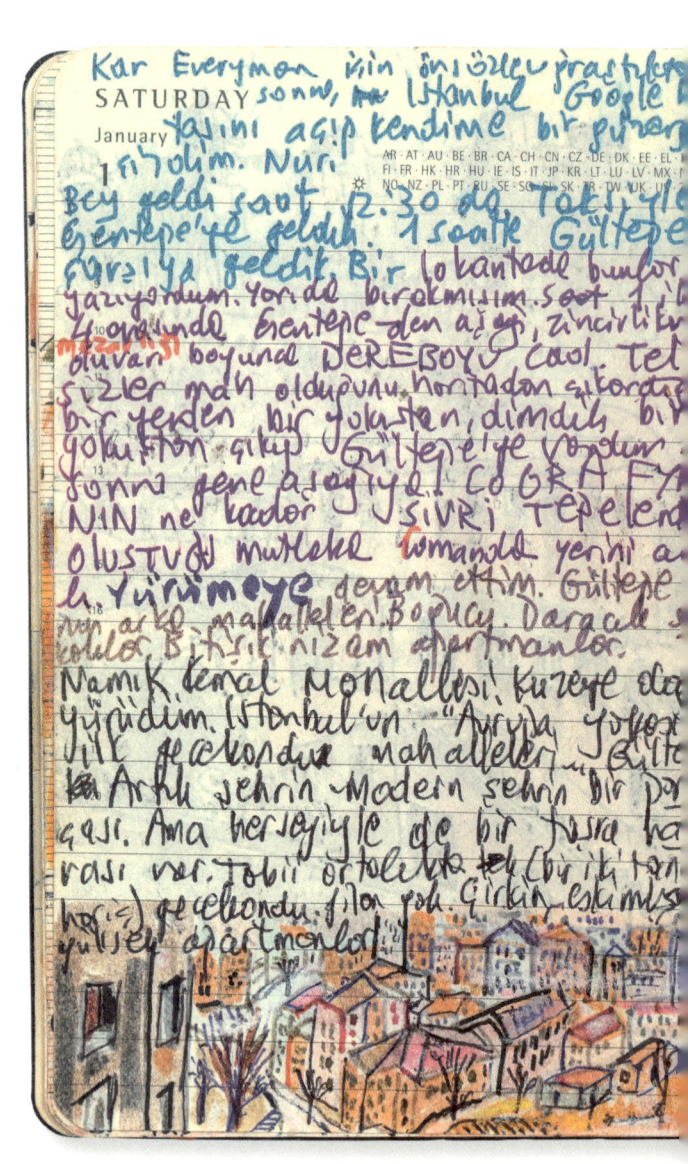

As I worked on the introduction to *Snow,* I took the manuscript of the novel out from its cupboard. The decade-old cardboard box fell apart. Sheets, notebooks, half-written pages, notes I'd made for the novel . . . They all spilled out. Back from those days when I was first writing the novel. I glanced at the last few notebooks and pages. There are very few corrections. I must have been writing very quickly, absorbed in the work . . . Novels should be written quickly; and corrected at leisure. I realized that unfortunately I am not going to be able to finish the introduction yet. This new year's holiday could have been a good time to work—but I didn't write enough; I didn't manage to, and I am annoyed at myself. The peace of a Sunday afternoon! The silence! The regret! I'm irritated that I haven't been able to do enough work in this nice, quiet three-day holiday. I did some painting, but not very well. A picture of Kemal looking up at Füsun's windows in the Nişantaşı night. It is developing into a standard "impressionist" painting. I must find a way out of this stalemate. How I would love to become Mevlut and forget about everything else. But on the other hand, I am pleased with how the museum is going now.

This morning, before sending them off to Hüsnü for typing, I went one more time through the first 60 pages of *Strangeness* which I wrote in New York. It's broadly fine. I have such a craving to write this novel. If only I didn't have to bother with this museum. On the subject of the museum: I MUST REMAIN CALM.

My eyesight: according to Doctor Davut, I last came in January 2005, so 6 years ago. My myopia has worsened; and this in turn has aggravated my farsightedness. The hereditary cataract that runs in my family is absent, though! Your eyes are in good health, he told me reassuringly. A winter's day; Valikonağı Avenue, Nişantaşı . . . These streets where I've spent my whole life . . . I wish I could like them more. Sadly Nişantaşı has become a dull, tiresome place.

I bought oil pastels and acrylic paints from the stationery shop on Akkavak Street.

I stopped by the bank, withdrew some cash to give to Cem and Feride.

While I write, or go downstairs to work on the museum, etc., I spend some time with Sermin. Sermin is very intelligent, very decent. She doesn't just keep the house tidy and cook my meals, we've become good friends now. She's the one who supervised Cem's renovations of the bathroom, kitchen, parquet, etc.

At 2 in the afternoon, meeting with Feride-Cem in flat 9 to discuss the charitable trust—museum—expenses—payments—money.

I should really pay attention, as it is my own money after all, but I find the subject so boring. Having to deal with these kinds of meetings when I could be sitting at my desk, writing my novel. But Feride and Cem are sweet. Now if only Cem would finish these renovations in time . . .

I take some money from my wallet and hand it over.

Afterward I went to the skin doctor in Nişantaşı. The moles on my neck and chest—apparently they're not moles but something else, and a very kind woman burned them all off. Good. These weird moles, these strange growths, would emerge in the gap between my undershirt and my skin, sometimes they would chafe and start to hurt. *These places I have been to see for A Strangeness in My Mind, I can't get them out of my mind . . . This mother, this older lady, these children, this light . . .*

In the morning, meeting with Gregor and Thomas at number 9 downstairs to look at the vitrines. Then we go on to the museum. Cem was there too. Despite all his assurances, Cem still hasn't finished the work. He hasn't managed to keep a single one of the promises he's made this year; a certain "strangeness." There's nothing Gregor and I can do but grumble. The various other details we discuss at the museum are not that important. But yes, all these details have turned out so well because of the care we have taken over them. In the evening we took a taxi with Thomas and Margareta to the back entrance of the Hagia Sophia. We walked around for two hours. Sultanahmet—the backstreets of Cankurtaran—Sultanhamam, Beyazıt, Süleymaniye Mosque, Mimar Sinan's tomb, Vezneciler, the Vefa boza shop... A long, pleasant walk. I took lots of photographs too; enjoying every shot; savoring the emptiness and beauty of Istanbul on a winter's night. The loveliness, the authenticity, the uniqueness of Istanbul, fill me with joy and a kind of pride... And others too, if they are able to appreciate it.

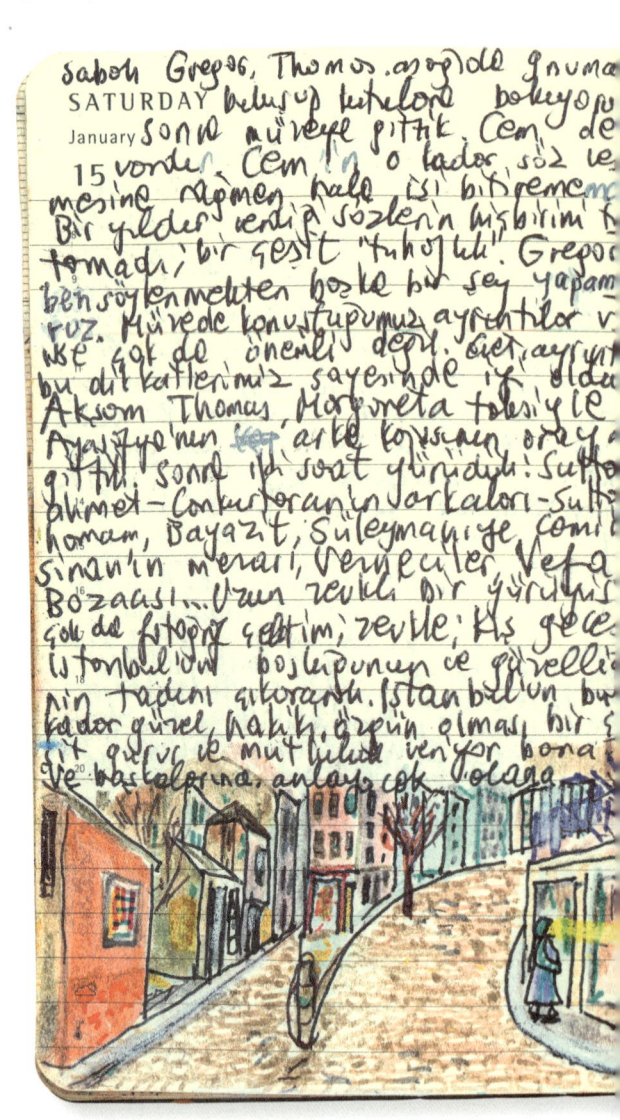

This morning I finally finished the text for the Everyman edition of *Snow*. We put on our coats, Thomas, Margareta, and I, and took 2 ferries to get from Kabataş to Büyükada. A rainy, cloudy winter's day. I took photographs, enjoying myself. From 3:30 to 6:30, we wandered around the empty streets of Büyükada... We tried to work out where it would make most sense to rent a house for the summer. Then we went to the Ali Baba restaurant. Friendly, rambling, amiable conversation. Büyükada's wintry melancholy. A strange hush. The streets growing even clearer after sunset... When the island empties out, its mystery fades, and it looks smaller to me than it actually is. I would love to spend this summer on Büyükada, writing and swimming... I found the remarkable silence and the intensely provincial feel of Büyükada immensely appealing.

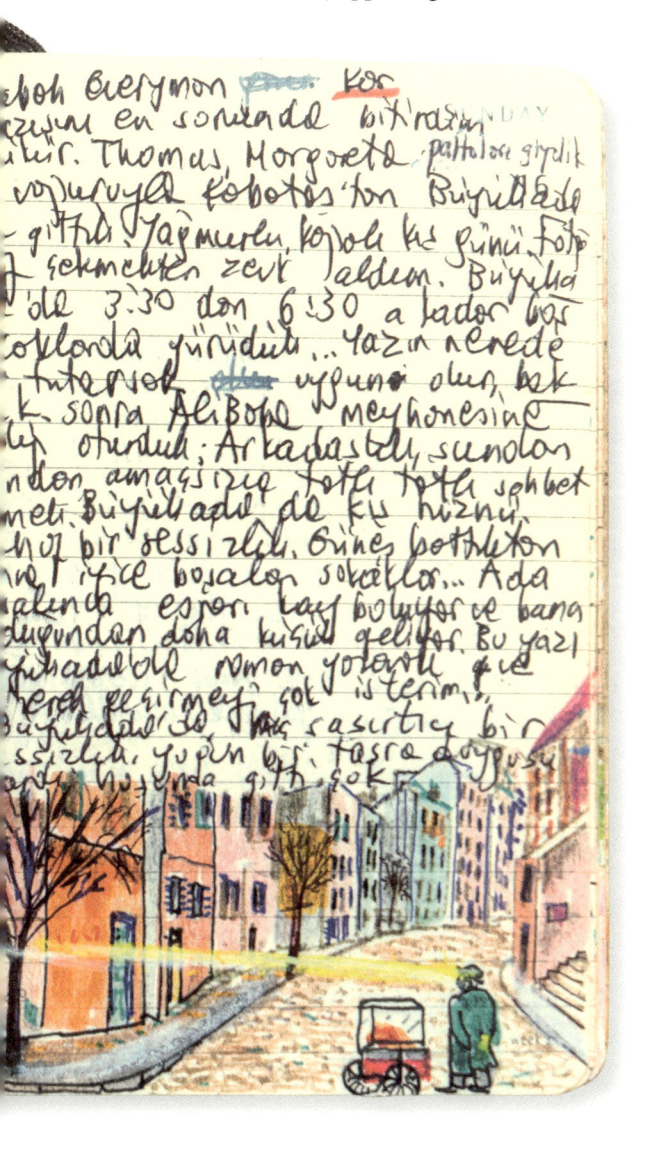

A happy day. I'm working on the novel. In the afternoon, with Nuri on our tail, Aslı and I walked all the way to Eminönü. The bustle, the vitality, of Istanbul. At 18:10 we got on a City Lines ferry full of tourists and Istanbul lovers... And set out on a Bosphorus cruise. Meanwhile I'm leaning off the side of the deck, taking videos of the Bosphorus views on my phone. Kabataş, Beşiktaş, Ortaköy, Bebek... What a lovely journey. After a while I surrender myself to the poetry of the landscape. Once we pass Kandilli, I have the impression that a Bosphorus like something out of Yahya Kemal is still there and still possible. I have such profound respect for this whole landscape, for the historic culture of waterside mansions and coffee shops along the shore.

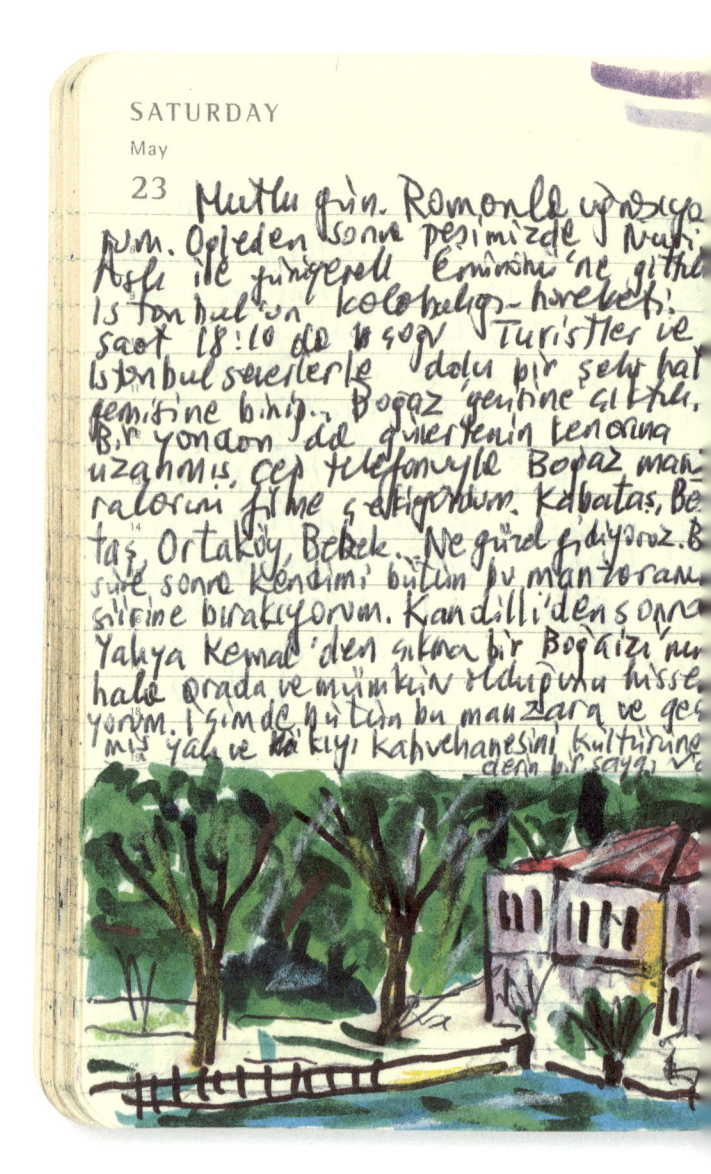

I spent my childhood around old wooden-timber houses with the paint peeling off their walls and pockmarked with rot-darkened spots. While we in Nişantaşı lived in modern concrete blocks, most of the city lived in teetering-ramshackle buildings made of brick and wood. 90% of wooden buildings were unplastered. Unplastered timber would soon turn a color somewhere between brown and ash. Like those mud-brown, mixed-breed, colorless street dogs! Some of the city's poorer neighborhoods looked that color from a distance, the color of mud-brown/ash-gray timber. The color of unpainted timber brings about a sense of History within me, of bygone times and poverty, and has always been an important element within my vision of Istanbul.

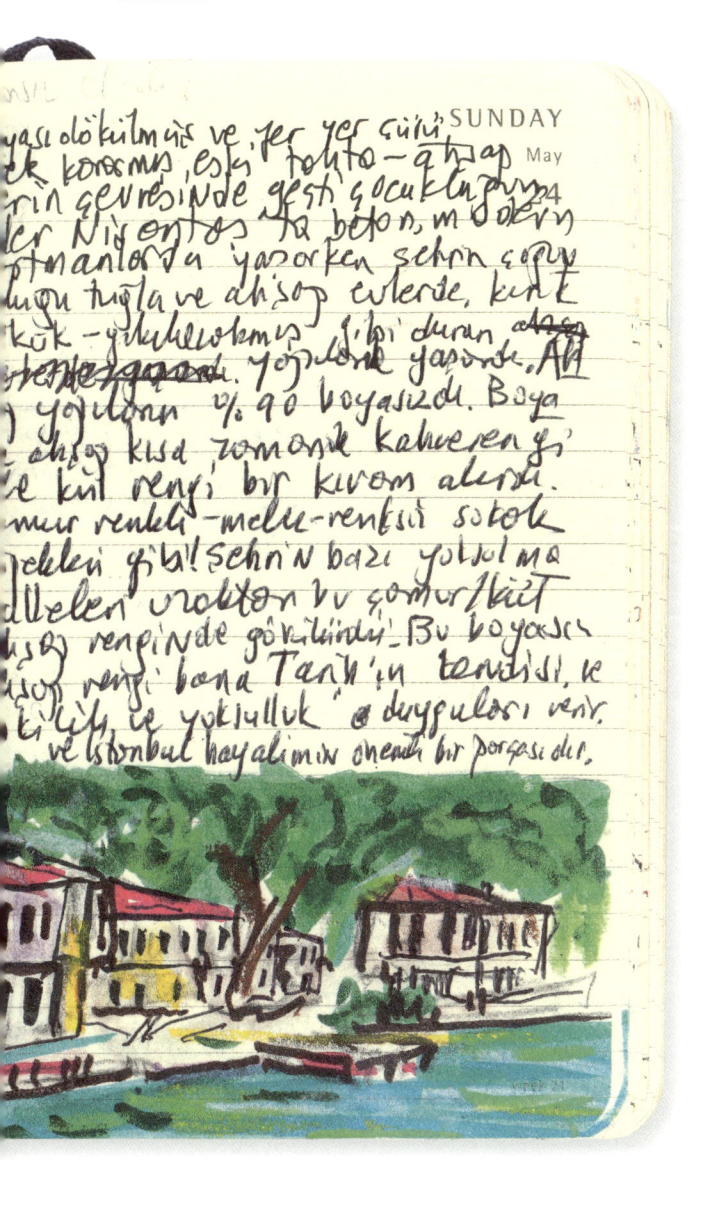

When I saw an old postcard of ŞIŞLI MOSQUE, I couldn't help myself. I drew this picture. The mosque, whose construction began at the end of the Second World War, may be made of concrete, but its flavor is Ottoman through and through.

Weight towers

1. My grandmother's house, the house where my mother grew up. My grandmother lived alone. When we went to visit her, she would throw the keys down at us on the pavement, so that she wouldn't have to come downstairs and open the door. Şevket and I would race each other to see who could "catch the keys" (she'd wrap them in tissue) first.

When Falih Rıfkı pointed out that supporting columns weren't necessary, given the building was made out of concrete—he was told, "It's the classical way!"

I should do this for all the other corners of Istanbul that bring back memories.

When I started learning how to read and write, I took to naming and calling out loud all that my eyes could see. At first everyone was charmed by how I kept reading every scrap of writing that I saw. I also loved reading out the billboards on the sides of apartment blocks, but eventually my mother and everyone else grew tired of this, so I started reading them silently to myself instead.

2. THERE ISN'T ACTUALLY A HOLLOW here. But whenever I got bored as we walked along this street (my legs aching) on our way to visit my grandmother, I would sometimes imagine that there was a hole in the ground just like this one. Just as my mother would imagine escaping on a hot-air balloon.

3. Here is the court where I stood trial in 2005 for talking about the Armenian genocide. People threw stones at us on the way out.

From 10 to sometime between 1 and 2 o'clock, with my bodyguard Nuri behind me, I went on a long brisk walk around the backstreets of Beyoğlu, Tünel, and Tophane. I went around the back of the Doğan Apartments, and when I eventually reached a spot I had never seen before somewhere behind Tophane, I stopped and quietly observed the street. There was nobody around. I spied a shy and inquisitive cat. This was Hacımemi Street. Small, two- or three-story houses with bay windows. These types of houses have always felt smothering to me. Then again, to have come for the first time to a place that feels so familiar, so recognizable. To have stumbled upon a street like this for the first time after having lived in this city for sixty-eight years . . . I have noticed on this walk that Beyoğlu is actually very lively; even on this coldest of winter days, there is plenty in the shop displays and behind restaurant windows to keep the passerby occupied.

you had come

back then back then

here before

I drew the bricks on this wall here one by one, and I'd like to think about that a little more. As I placed, drew, and colored each brick, I was as happy as a child. But it also felt like filling in a coloring book.
Istiklal Street, Yüksek Kaldırım Street, and the Galata Tower are just ahead.

In ISTANBUL, I think of Büyükada with longing. The crow that perched on the chimney would arrive at sunset or in the early hours of the morning. Crickets, cicadas, crows, furious seagulls ... many other birds whose names I don't know but whose songs I am fond of. A sardonic bird whose call sounded like a sigh, the crows' gruff squawks would fade away into the hills behind me. As I was writing the novel—*Nights of Plague*—I had these sounds in the back of my mind too. I transferred some of Büyükada's flowers, colors, and crows into Mingheria...

The Sedef Island boat returns from Kartal

The ship selling gas to the boats that travel between Sedef Island and Büyükada on Sundays

The July–August 2012 Sunday bustle between Büyükada and Sedef Island

The boat carrying passengers to nearby Naki Bey beach

The Sedef Island boat

sea taxi

THE MOTORBOAT THAT TAKES PEOPLE TO
THE AYA NIKOLA PUBLIC BEACH FOR FREE

FRIDAY
~~TUESDAY~~

There's something about driving around an EMPTY ISTANBUL that evokes metaphysical thoughts. At 2 in the afternoon, Cengiz the driver came to pick me up in Aslı's car... As it is a hospital vehicle, no one on the empty roads nor (the police) at the roadblock in Dolmabahçe asked us any questions. I took videos of the deserted streets on my mobile phone. Between 2:30 and 6:30, a meal with Edhem and Sedef Eldem, wine, good company. We started out in the attic. Then the sun went down. The number of infections and deaths worries us all. They've had their first vaccine shot too. We feel safer because we're vaccinated. Later we looked out from Moda to Fenerbahçe, Fenerburnu, and at the Princes' Islands in the background, marveling at the calmness of the sea.

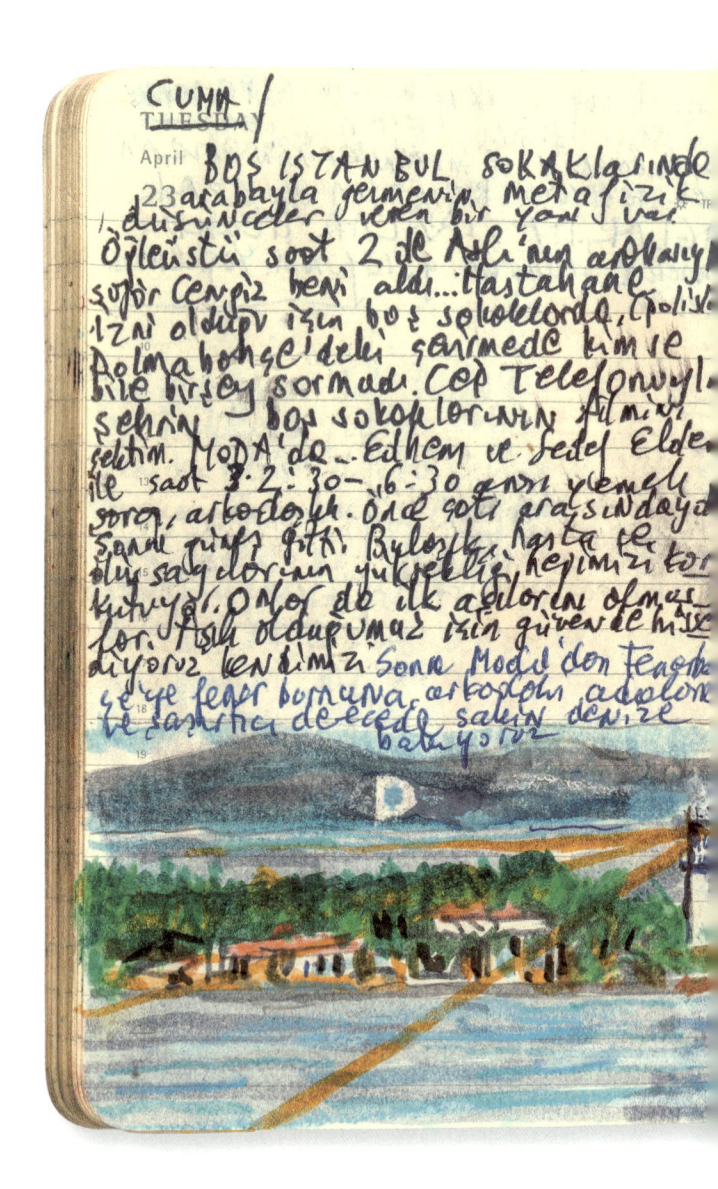

SATURDAY
~~WEDNESDAY~~

I have been working on *MEMORIES OF DISTANT MOUNTAINS*. Choosing the illustrations, selecting the pages... Deciding what order to put them in... By February 2021, I have made a lot of progress on the book... I have already selected the first 120 double-spreads... The task now: to spend this year reading and evaluating these 120 pages from a "literary" perspective, that is to say bearing their textual/narrative-storytelling qualities in mind. I think the book will be around 400 pages. As I go through it now, browsing the notes/pictures I've made in these diaries... I can see that the best pages are those dated 2010–2013... And that increasing the number of notebooks and drawing on bigger-sized pages... reduced the quality, the beauty, of the work.

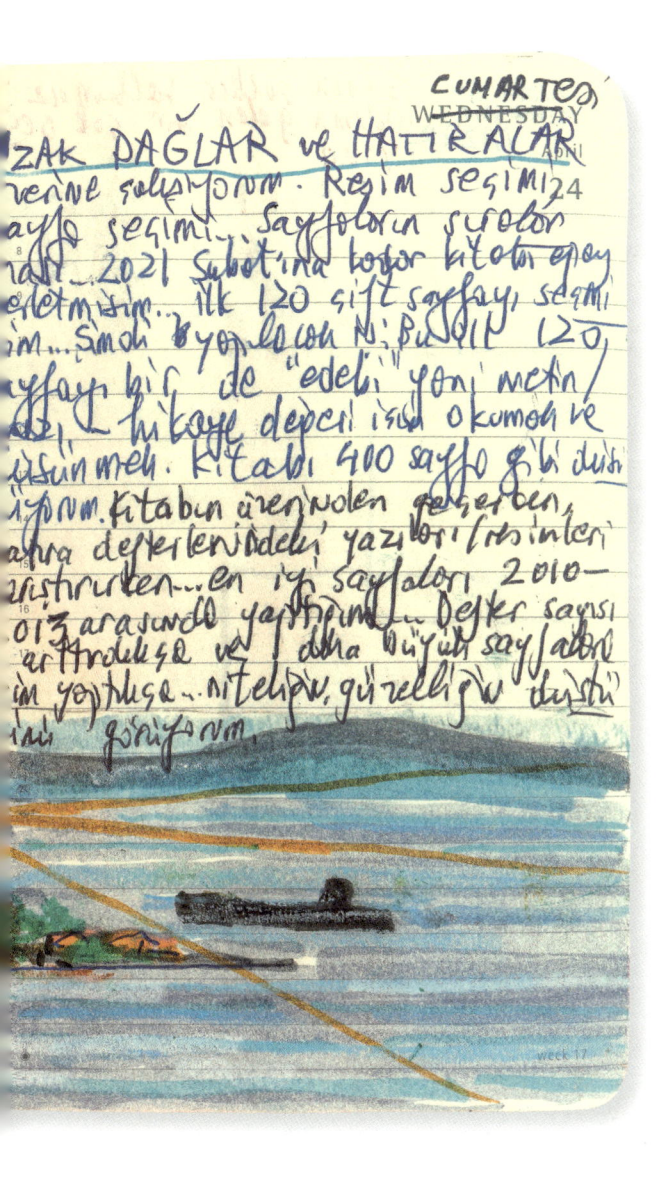

WALDEN-ISTANBUL

What I find most appealing in Thoreau's oeuvre is: his JOURNALS. He is always writing in his journals. One day he writes with great gusto and at tedious length about the nature that surrounds him. The next day he can happily write about the same corner of the same lake again. Or he'll go back to a day he'd already written about in his diary two years ago, and add something new, just like I do. Then he'll start daydreaming about all the books that will come out of his diaries. WALDEN is that kind of book.

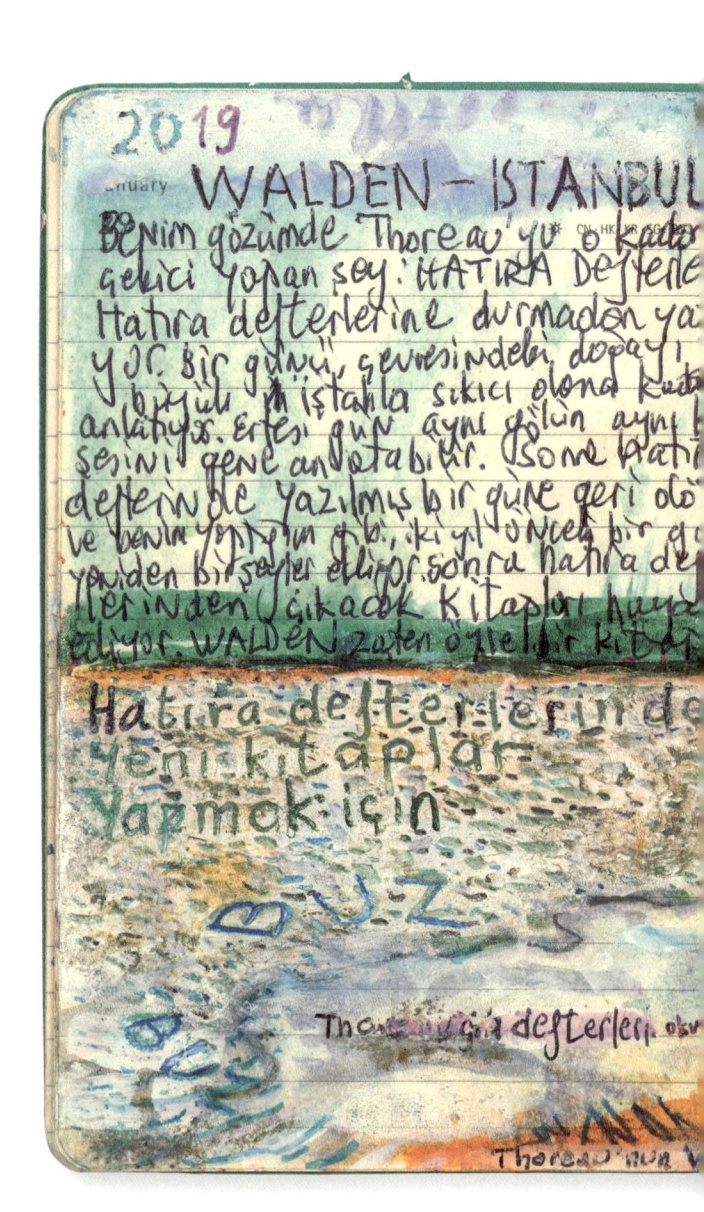

For making new books out of journals

ICE

ICE

"The scenery of Walden is on a humble scale, and, though very beautiful, does not approach to grandeur, nor can it much concern one who has not long frequented it...," Thoreau writes modestly in the chapter of *Walden* entitled "The Ponds." Then he spends all his time describing all he sees in this humble landscape.

For Thoreau, diaries are meant to be read, written over, cut up, and reassembled

What Thoreau did for Walden, I am doing for Istanbul.

TOLSTOY IS THE GREATEST OF ALL NOVELISTS. I TURNED TO A RANDOM PAGE IN HIS JOURNALS. 23 JANUARY 1855, HE WROTE: "AM GREATLY DISSATISFIED WITH MYSELF." ON 25 JANUARY 1855: "HAVE PLAYED SHTOSS FOR TWO

In *Anna Karenina*, Levin gives his diary to Kitty before they marry. Why? So that Kitty can see what a terrible person he is.

I stopped when I saw the great man's grave.

When *A Strangeness in My Mind* won the 2016 Yasnaya Polyana prize, I finally visited that place I had dreamt about for forty years. The first, larger house, lost to gambling, had been dismantled and taken away. It was no longer there. I examined the other, smaller house, the great master's photographs, his belongings, the writing desk I had seen in pictures, as if they were sacred relics. Then I walked to his grave.

DAYS AND TWO NIGHTS. THE RESULT IS EVIDENT—THE LOSS OF THE HOUSE AT YASNAYA POLYANA. IT SEEMS USELESS TO WRITE: AM SO DISGUSTED WITH MYSELF THAT I SHOULD EVEN LIKE TO FORGET THAT I EXIST."

Unfortunately Tolstoy stopped keeping journals while he wrote his greatest novels. Why?

The world was silent but everything felt so profound.

As we walked among the beech trees toward Tolstoy's grave, I had the exhilarating feeling that we might run into him at any moment. I was in awe. The whole world covered in pure white snow.

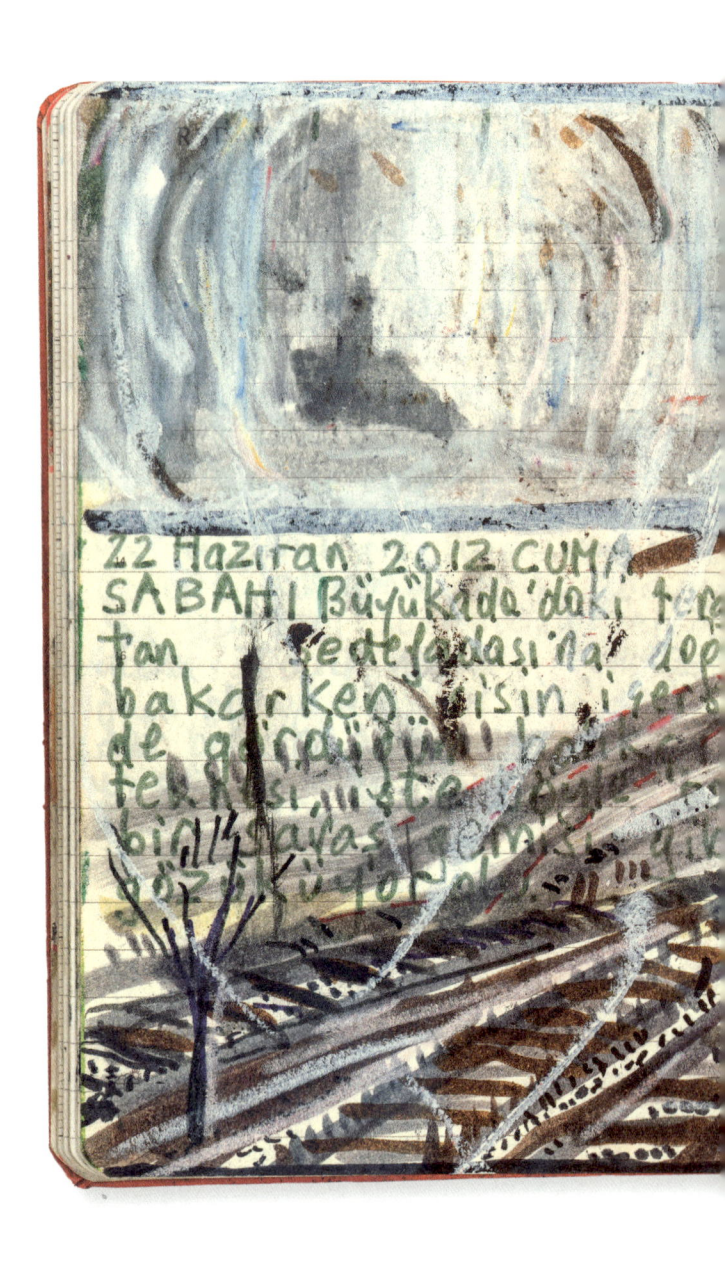

The MORNING of FRIDAY 22 June 2012, looking out toward Sedef Island from the terrace of the house on Büyükada... The fishing boat I see through the fog looks just like this, like a warship.

FRIDAY

In the end we must accept that we are but ourselves . . . If I could only live in a quiet corner, out of sight . . . Then I would be able to notice how much magic there is hidden in life's other minutiae. *The Black Book* is that kind of book. But I have lived all my life as if I were writing *The Black Book*. It is a doorway to another realm implied by objects. That is where Mevlut must return. That dark guilt, that tenebrous night, that is where the objects are and where I belong. I continue to write, my imagination carving the objects out one by one.

The color leaking onto here from the page behind is a little like light filtering into a room at night, like old memories surfacing throughout the day to distract you from the present you are living through. There is a now ... and there is something beyond the now ... The traces, the colors, of the past appear both on this page and on the other.

I realized I need to find this distant landscape

someone came by, asked me how I was doing

rayı bulmam
i anladım

sual eyledi

MONDAY
April
11

I SPENT TEN DAYS WRITING AT THE BAGA HOTEL IN AKYAKA

FADED old curtains

We went swimming in other, farther bays too, and to wicker cedar island
This is where I wrote about Mevlut's middle school days
I wrote a lot in the hotel room in Akyaka

We took a boat to this distant
bay and swam there too

GULF OF GÖKOVA

I DIVED INTO THE
SEA FROM HERE

I have started writing *Nights of Plague* in a state of remarkable, almost bizarre euphoria. It's thanks to Bozburun, this place where I can be cut off from everything else. I got out of bed at six in the morning, sat at my desk, and started writing. The whole world looked glorious. How happy I was, writing my novel with that splendid view, those cliffs and those dark blue mountains before me! I am simultaneously here, facing the purple mountains and indigo sea; and on MINGHERIA, whose shape my imagination is seeking to carve out one building at a time. As the *Minerva* slowly sails toward the city and castle of Mingheria, those aboard, its passengers bound for China, admire the beautiful view. The sea is cold. But I still went in twice. The morning looked like the painting below.

THE SMUDGES ARE REMINISCENT OF DÜRER'S WATERCOLOR LANDSCAPES

There is no greater pleasure than to sit at the desk I've set up by the window, look out at the view, and think about my novel as everything else beyond the view and the novel falls away. . . . The crisp air, the cool sea; the endless silence . . . the insects . . . the birds . . . The world is ready to enter the novel.

Between 5 and 6 in the afternoon I read about the 1st–3rd Crusades on the internet. The Crusades, Sidon, the fortress of Acre, the kingdoms the Crusaders established in these lands . . . These are all of course crucial when thinking about Mingheria and the castle of Mingher.

The temperature in Bozburun was already quite low. Now it's getting even windier. I'm happy sitting at my desk all day. We go on long companionable walks with Aslı. "Don't I always tell you this is just the life I want, Aslı?" I say.

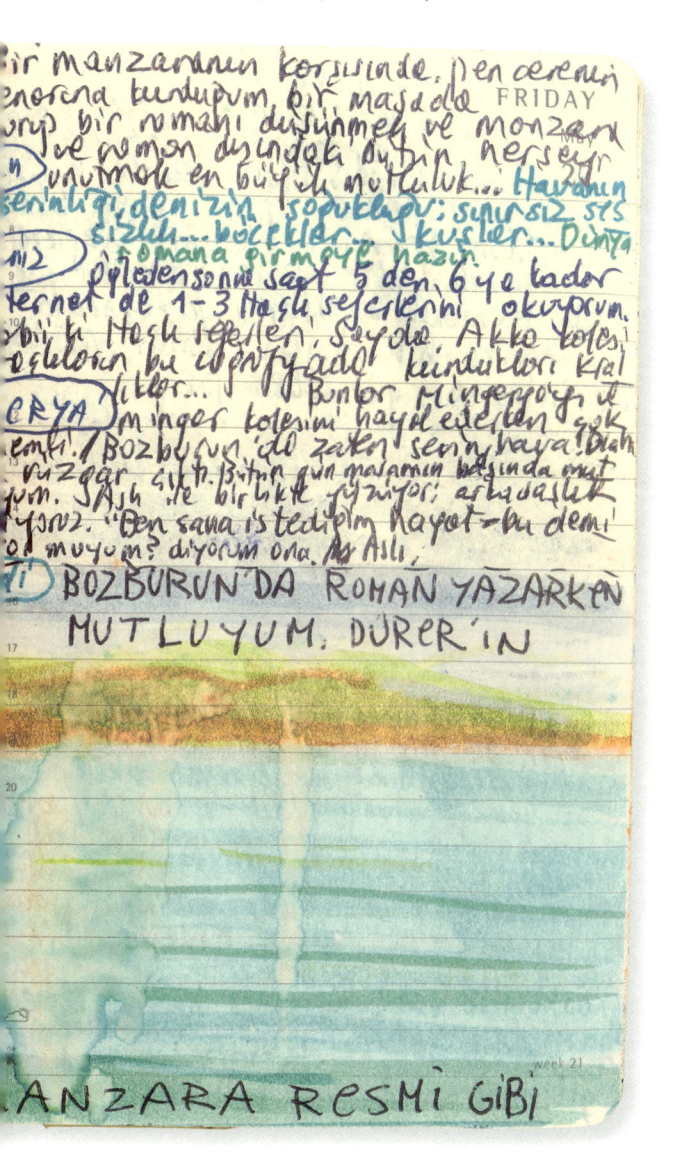

I AM HAPPY IN BOZBURUN, WRITING MY NOVEL.

The wooden eagle that sits
on the bookshelves.

shutters

New Jersey

The empty notebooks
where I write my novels

Ugly lamp

The notebook where I
am writing this now

The chair I've been sitting
in for 15 years

On 10 December 2019, in New York, I have given my last lecture of the term at Columbia University, packed my bags, and am about to return to Istanbul, when I find out that Erdoğan, furious at the Nobel being awarded to Peter Handke, has said, "They gave one to a terrorist here, too!" Journalists and all the rest of the world are asking me: "What are you going to do?" I'm wondering whether I will be able to return to Turkey, thinking of all the people on the streets and the government officials who will start giving me the "terrorist" treatment, when the president's spokesperson announces that it wasn't me they were referring to. So it is that the view before me etches itself forever into my memory. Many pages from *The Museum of Innocence*, *A Strangeness in My Mind*, *The Red-Haired Woman*, and *Nights of Plague* were written upon this desk. For 15 years I have been writing novels in New York, right here and at the Avery Library and other libraries too.

NY city liner
Hudson River

the old radiator that makes weird noises

my suitcase packed and shut

When I returned to Turkey, nobody even mentioned this: they just asked "How was America?," as if nothing had happened.

I was going to write

TUESDAY
October
22

YAMAG oblon

about the sense of fear
and foreboding I feel around mountain slopes,
but I didn't . . .

FEARS AND DREAMS OF MOUNTAIN SLOPES in Ankara in 1960

In ANKARA we lived for a year in a house on the corner between Adakale Street and Yüksel Street. (That's where I was during the military coup of 27 May.) This is where I first discovered what I would call a sense of neighborhood, something I had not experienced in Istanbul. Things like children living in the same houses and apartment blocks meeting up on the street or on adjoining back gardens to play football, hide-and-seek, and nine men's morris, picking teams, inventing enemies, and starting fights... We would go to war with the kids from the neighborhood on the hill. That hilltop neighborhood is now home to one of Turkey's largest mosques, the Kocatepe Mosque. In 1960, the site where the mosque stands today was an empty stretch of flat ground.

I had this dream so many times afterward that I am not sure whether it actually happened.

On the edge of the plateau overlooking Incesu creek, there was a very steep slope where the soil was soft. Some kids would take any planks of wood they managed to get hold of and use them like sleds to slide down on. One day, I tried this too. As I hurtled down the slope, I saw our rival children's gang at the bottom. They were screaming and shouting, swearing at me, waiting with rocks in their hands. I tried to stop, but I couldn't. It was as if the slope were slipping along with me, as if we were sliding together toward the enemy. I kept trying to grab hold of the earth, but I couldn't.

KIDS from the neighborhood below

ME

This landscape reminds me of something else I share with the poet Ka. A propensity for MISTAKING the view before me for a memory! Or the opposite: mistaking memories for DREAMS!

Memory and Dream are each a moment—each an image. I was once there, but whether it was in a dream or in the past, I do not know. I experience the present as if it were the past . . .

BOSNIAN LANDSCAPES

I remember how EXCITED I was by the film *BRAZIL*. I did not know that it was inspired by a collage of a series of photocopies. Collage and Dada are behind everything. Behind the mountains

Max Ernst

Because combining images and text in a certain way produces MEANING.
Forget Max Ernst . . .

Please be quiet

Then and now

on your own
cross quietly

toward the valley

downward

in this valley

over there time will stop

rocky banks

If you follow the river you will reach the valley where words and images are one

THIS PAINTING I'VE MADE OF "A SERIES OF DISTANT MOUNTAINS," INFLUENCED BY THE CHINESE MASTERS AND BY OLD LANDSCAPE PAINTERS, SHOWS THAT MEMORIES (and MEMORY ITSELF) ARE LOCATED SOMEWHERE BEYOND THE DISTANT MOUNTAINS

be patient and you will remember

BÜYÜKADA

there used to be a town
here, back in the day

A LADDER THAT LEADS DOWN
TO THE WATER

the religious lodge overlooking the world

HEYBELI ISLAND

THE MIRROR OF
THE SEA

THE PEAK OF MEMORIES

A view upon death

MONDAY
October
14

TUESDAY
October
15

week 42

K's apprehensions are also behind these mountain landscapes I have drawn from memory and from remembered dreams
Placing this house upon this stretch of land in the distance is a first for me . . .

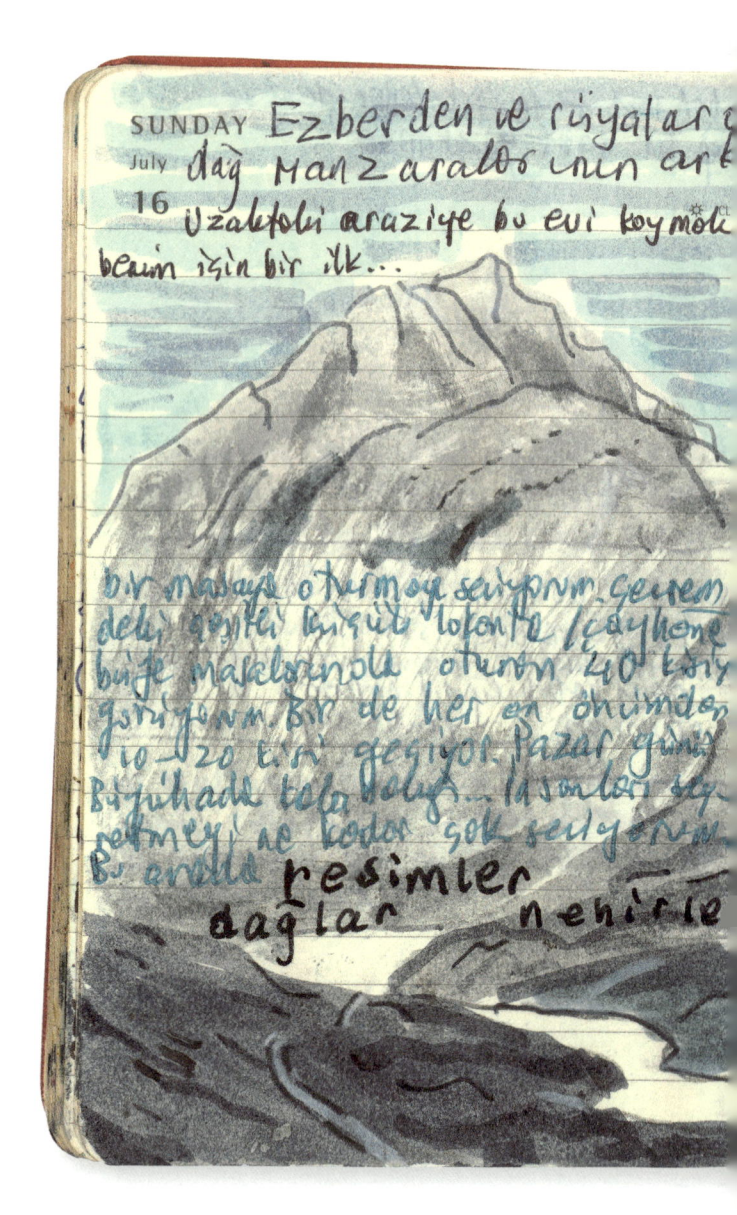

Meanwhile
   I dream
      of paintings

I like sitting at a table. I can see 40 people sitting around me at tables in various small restaurants/teahouses/cafés. And there are 10–20 people walking past me at any given moment. Sunday crowds on Büyükada . . . How I love people watching.

With Aslı before work in the morning. There is a magnificent light on the terrace and I am fervently taking photographs. I hand the camera over to Aslı! Then I spend the whole day working on my novel.

mountains
and rivers

I am going to describe that dream shortly. The eagle's nest ... It is the scariest dream of my life ... But ...

Walking in the backstreets of Beyoğlu-Cihangir, between two and three o'clock, taking endless photographs. Old bookshops, chilly alleyways, deserted, melancholy spots, shivery cats: this is my country, these streets and these people. I am INSIDE my novel. I'm pleased with my novel. But other commitments are slowing me down. To be a writer, to do nothing but write—my books should include my drawings too

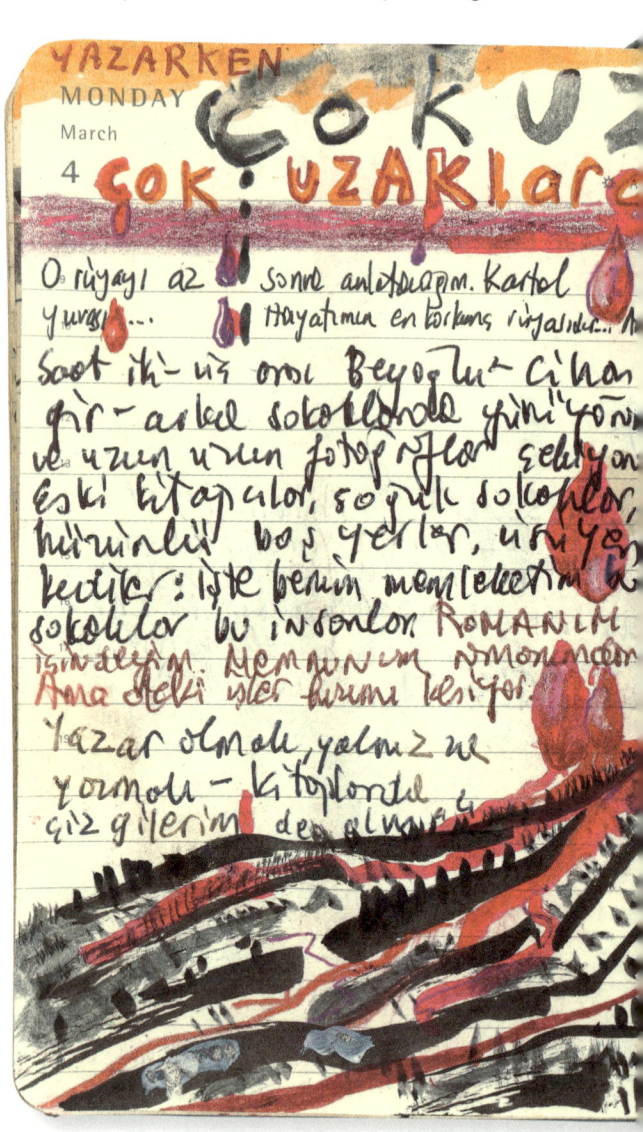

Everything was so far away

I don't know
not all the
time
I really
don't know.

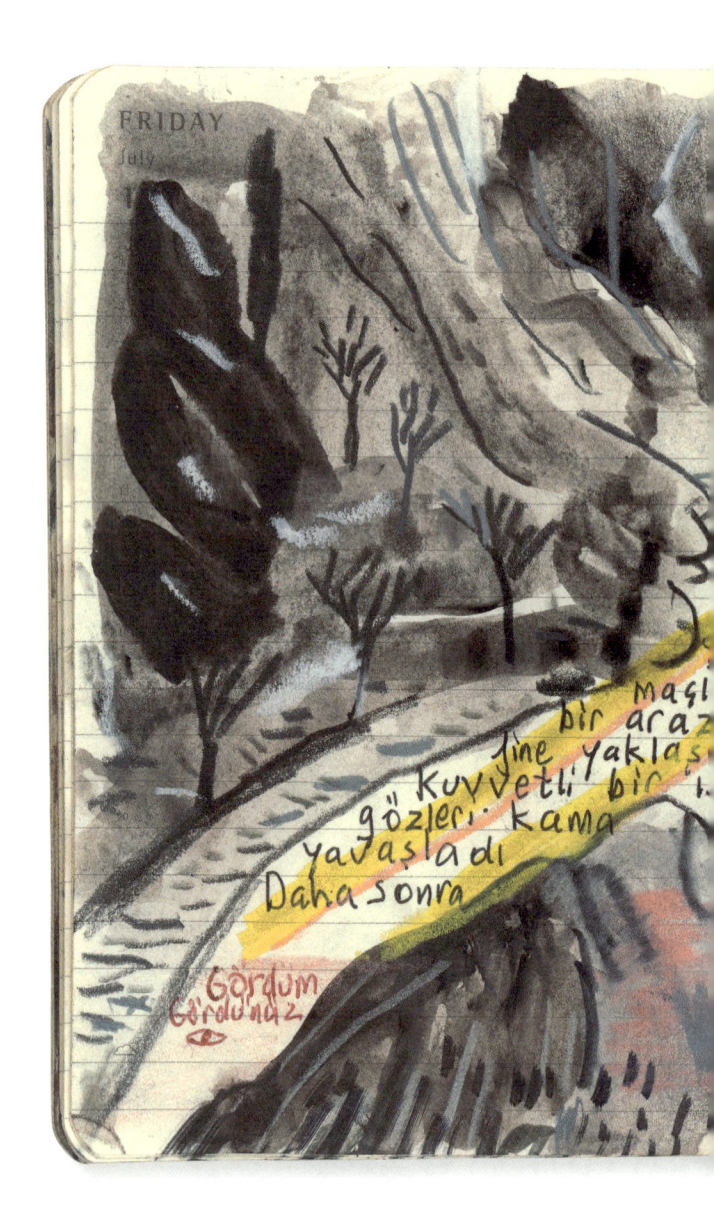

I saw it
You saw it

In this familiar dream, Ka is walking on rocky ground flanked by steep slopes toward his target when a powerful light dazzles him, and he slows to a stop. When he realizes that there is an eye 👁 where the light is coming from, he will be gripped by fear ... For I have had the same dream too.

When he realized there was an eye watching him from somewhere, at first Galip was not afraid. But soon the all-seeing eye stopped hiding and revealed itself.

THE EYE KNEW HIM
AND HE KNEW THE EYE

He had created this eye himself. So that it would see him and watch him. He did not want to venture beyond its line of sight. Under that gaze, under that eye, he felt AT PEACE.

mysterious things

It was as if he EXISTED because of that constant gaze and his own clear awareness of it. This fact had become part of his MIND. Sometimes he could sense, to his distress, that one day the eye might forget about him.

always　　　　　　　　　　　　　　　　　　　this is somewhere too

　　　　　　　　　　　　　　　　　　　　　　　　　　in the beginning
　　　　　　　　　　　　　　　we asked for a team
the crowds on the balcony　　　　　　　　　　read this
　I looked and forgot　　　　　　　　　　　　carefully
　　　　　　　you　　　　they are fooling themselves
　　　　　　　you are in　　toward me
　　　　　　　inside that picture
　　　　　　　　　　　　　　　　　　　memory is often a color
there's no room　　　　　　　　　　　　on paper the universe is infinite

this morning　　this is
　　　　　an enchanted
　　　　　　　word

　　　don't go farther

　　　　　　on this shore
touching for
the sake of touching
gazing without thinking

　　　　　　　　　　　　　　　　　　　　　　it's not far
　　　　　　　　　　　　　　　　　　　　　　　not here
the way under the water is through here
what's left behind　　　　　　　　　　　　　somewhere

then once more
you will always look

not this picture
nobody will accept it
always there
without thinking
you're somewhere here 👁 behind
long since

sometimes to be happy it is
enough to write

windy and cool
    paintings don't talk they see
where you write on a painting there is no color

Nothing is as it seems
When you find a new window
You must prepare for the view

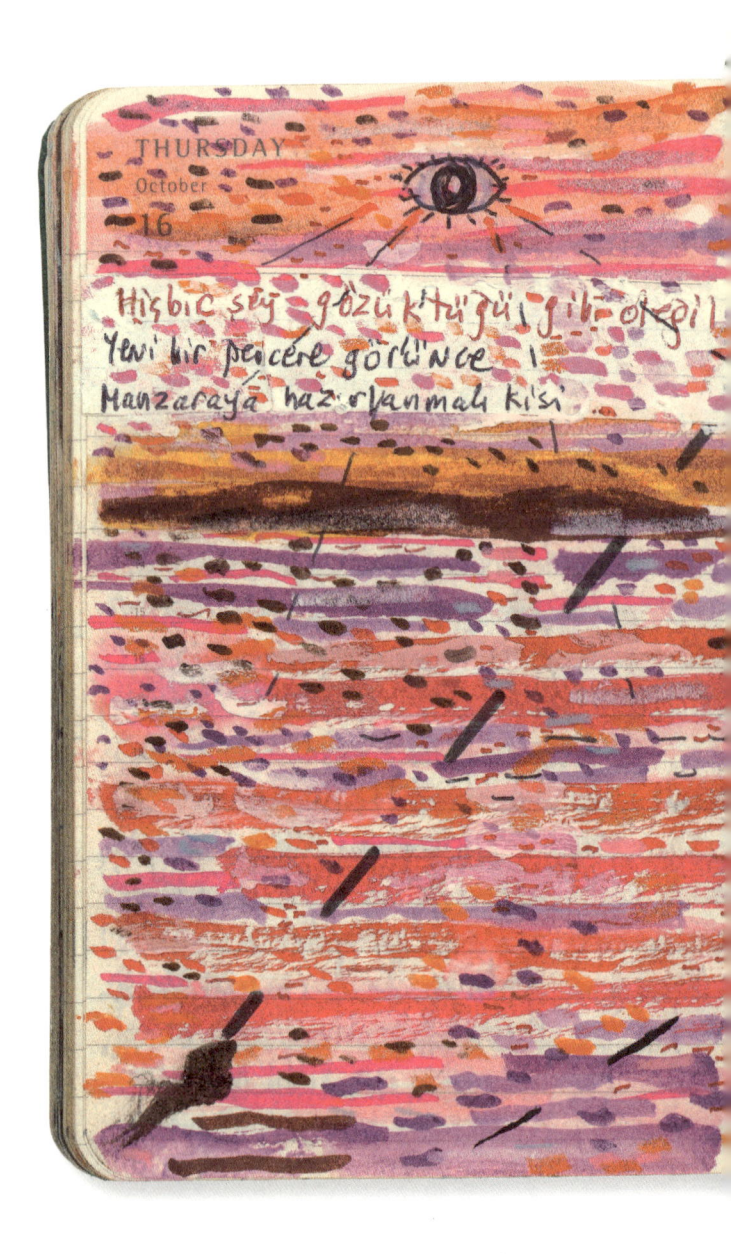

The island across from ours
As it appears to our eyes
has always occupied our thoughts.

In this novel I just can't seem to write, writer and painter K and O, after much fighting and arguing, finally reach the place beyond the distant mountains, at which point they realize that WORDS and Images are one and the same. That is the secret beyond the DISTANT mountains. In fact they already knew this from their memories . . .

But they had set out on this journey anyway, because knowing is not remembering, but seeing what you remember.
THE IDEA OF DISAPPEARING BEHIND THE FARTHEST OF ALL MOUNTAINS IS A FANTASY OF REUNION WITH OUR ANCESTORS—OF A RETURN to heaven . . . I was there! the person must say

reasons I identify with the romantic painter poet WILLIAM BLAKE

he likes flames and fires
he writes, and he paints
words and images mingle on the page
he sees the page as a whole
he uses the branches of a tree to split up the page

he envisions everything on the page
he sees words and images together
he likes watercolors
he likes to inscribe words onto paintings

He likes drawing the rays of the sun as if they were arrows
He uses Tree Branches to divide the page

he draws his own house from the outside → saying this is where I lived
he drew a spider's web

he uses dark colors
to paint distant
mountains

Once upon a time words
and images were one

back then, words were images and images were words

I will write down all my worries and fears about NIGHTS OF PLAGUE

I am right there as I describe the bustle of the city

the drawing up of quarantine regulations is described in excessive detail
on exposure to the microbe, gradual onset of fever and wrathful ravings
without anybody writing about it
nights of plague
the cemeteries are filling up
do not forget us

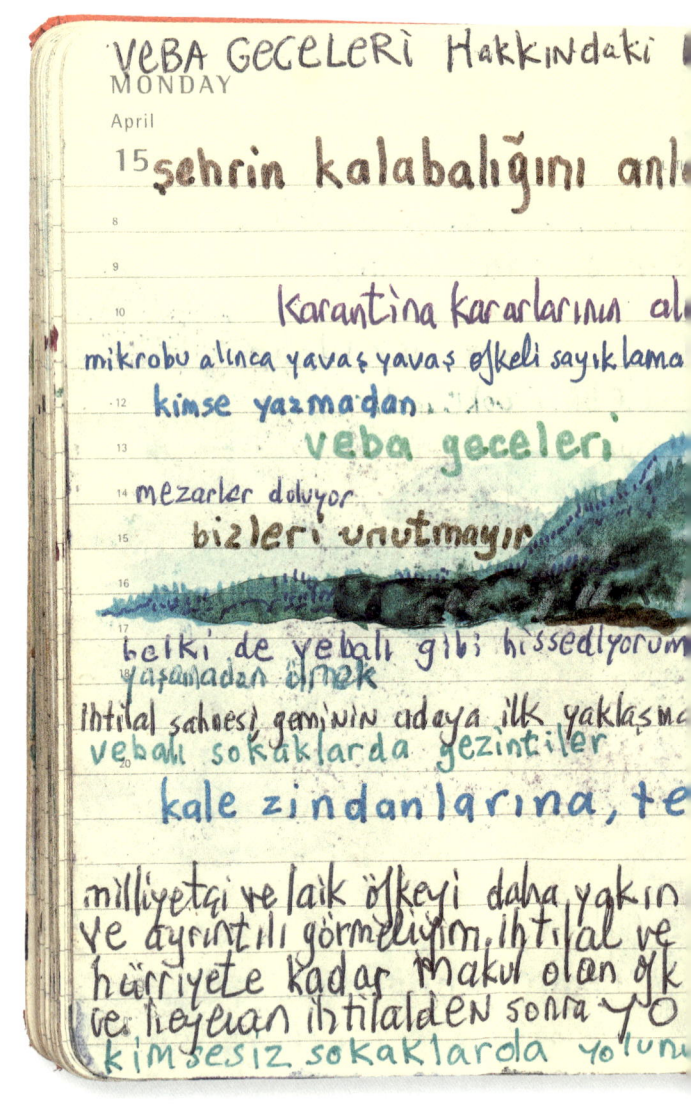

perhaps I am feeling
like a plague patient
to die without having lived
The revolution scene, the ship's first approach to the island, the Pasha's excursions in his
armored carriage, the outings on the beautiful plague-ridden streets
we will enter the castle dungeons, the houses, the isolation facilities

I must take a closer, more detailed look at the nationalist and secularist rage. The anger
and fervor which seemed reasonable when leading up to revolution and independence
turn INTENSE AND IRRATIONAL once the revolution is achieved
the plague victim getting lost and going mad as he wanders through the deserted streets

the Mingherian coast

with every word I write, the novel becomes memory

maybe I could catch the plague and take antibiotics

I need to see more of the plague in day-to-day life
only the sick can understand sickness

Knowing that he was being observed at all times, he became aware of his own existence as he gazed at the landscape. Sometimes the meaning of the world would rise like a black sun from behind the distant mountains.

So it was time for him to read the landscape

even so, you don't have to reveal everything, says ASLI

Ka was relieved when he realized that the eye could see the SECRET behind the distant mountains. The secret of the whole universe would now be revealed through the meaning of this landscape.

So many things remained unexplained and unspoken. I could grasp them not through logic, but through my emotions. Dangerous slopes, cliff edges, turns, intersecting roads . . .

Those
who went
before me
never returned

I was scared to look down but I would look anyway. In the end I would not be able to write that book, and I would guiltily forget about this journey.

THURSDAY
December
13

Çin'li şair alim
Uzak Dağlor'a
Ka'da coşkuyla y
üzerine．．．
istiyordu. Çoğu d
iktidar değişimle
siyasal sürgüne
bir parçası olo

The LANDSCAPE paintings of Chinese master poets (the literati) kept the painter Ka company on his journey to the Distant Mountains. Like the Chinese painter-scholars, Ka too wished to inscribe poems onto the travel and landscape scenes he had so enthusiastically painted. He never forgot that the learned poet-painters, most of whom were government employees and clerks, were sent into exile every time a new government took power. Their exile was of course somewhere among those DISTANT MOUNTAINS which are such an indispensable part of landscape painting.

Inspired by these landscape paintings, I have been contemplating a book entitled THE CHINESE HAD ALREADY THOUGHT OF THIS.

SATURDAY
December
8

A WIDE VIEW
LANDSCAPE
PINGYUAN LEVEL
IS ONE OF THE

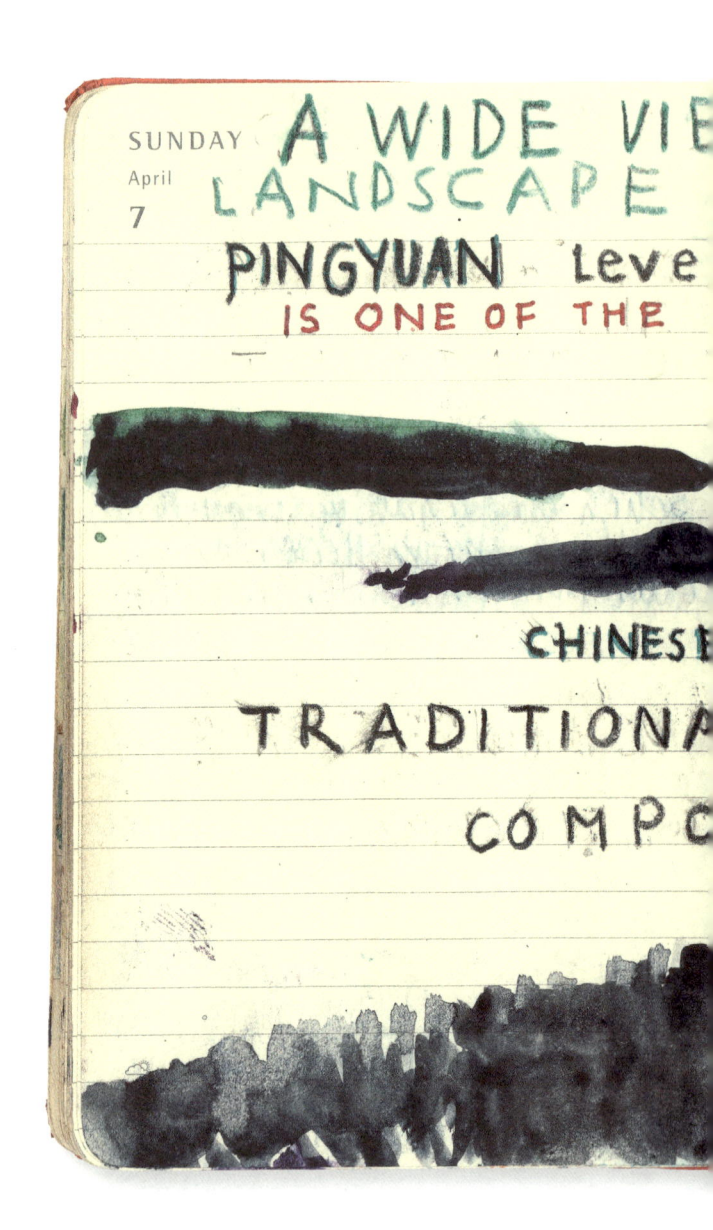

CHINESE
TRADITIONAL

OF BROAD
OF LOW LANDS
DISTANCE
THREE WAYS OF

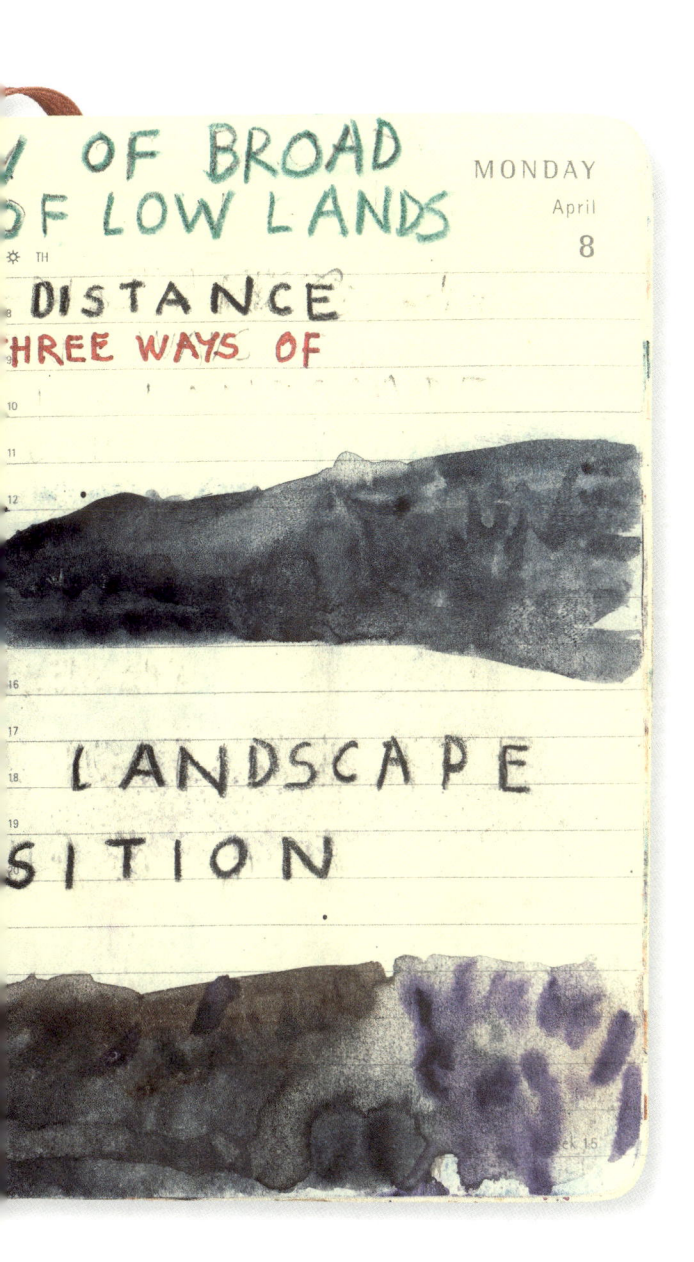

LANDSCAPE
COMPOSITION

TUNG YUAN DOES
CHISEL OUT LOFTY
EXTRAORDINARY
BUT RATHER
TOGETHER DOTS
KIND OF POINTILLIST
scenery of his paintings
focus when one

**NOT CAREFULLY
PEAKS OF
APPEARANCE
STRINGS
AND DASHES IN A**
technique so that the
only comes into
steps back from them.

The view from the eagle's or hawk's nest looked something like this. I can't say it was exactly like this, though. This book depicts memories, not truth.

But in the end I was happy to have got there.
Everything was in its right place, and I was observing it all.

the dream I should
have described
through images is
painted in words in
the page that follows.

I crossed valleys and passed rocky cliffs and finally found the Hawk's nest I thought was an Eagle's. As I carefully made my way down the cliff, I saw that instead of an eagle, the nest contained a freshly dug grave. When I got closer, I realized with horror that it was my own grave.

My grave was covered in hot wax. If the wax was hot ... it must mean I had only just died, and my grave had been stamped with a seal judging-evaluating my life. The seal had of course been affixed by GOD. If I looked up I would see Him soaring away from the eagle's nest and into the distance. As I was straining with all my strength to lift my head toward the heavens, I woke up in fear.

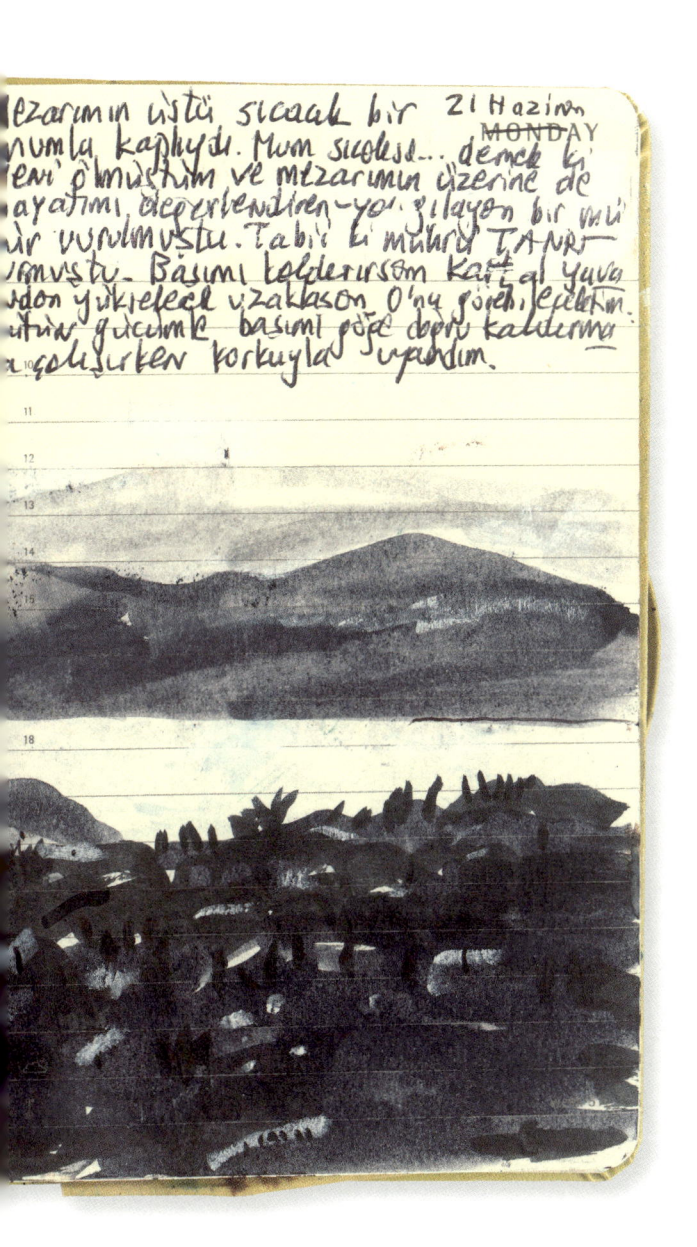

21 JUNE

I have had other nightmares similar to this one. On one occasion, I traced and marked out the route I took, the valleys and ravines between the distant mountains, the eagle's nest, and the location of the cliff.

345

After this dream, I BEGAN TO SENSE that, contrary to William Blake's illustrations, the sun rises from WITHIN the landscape, not without

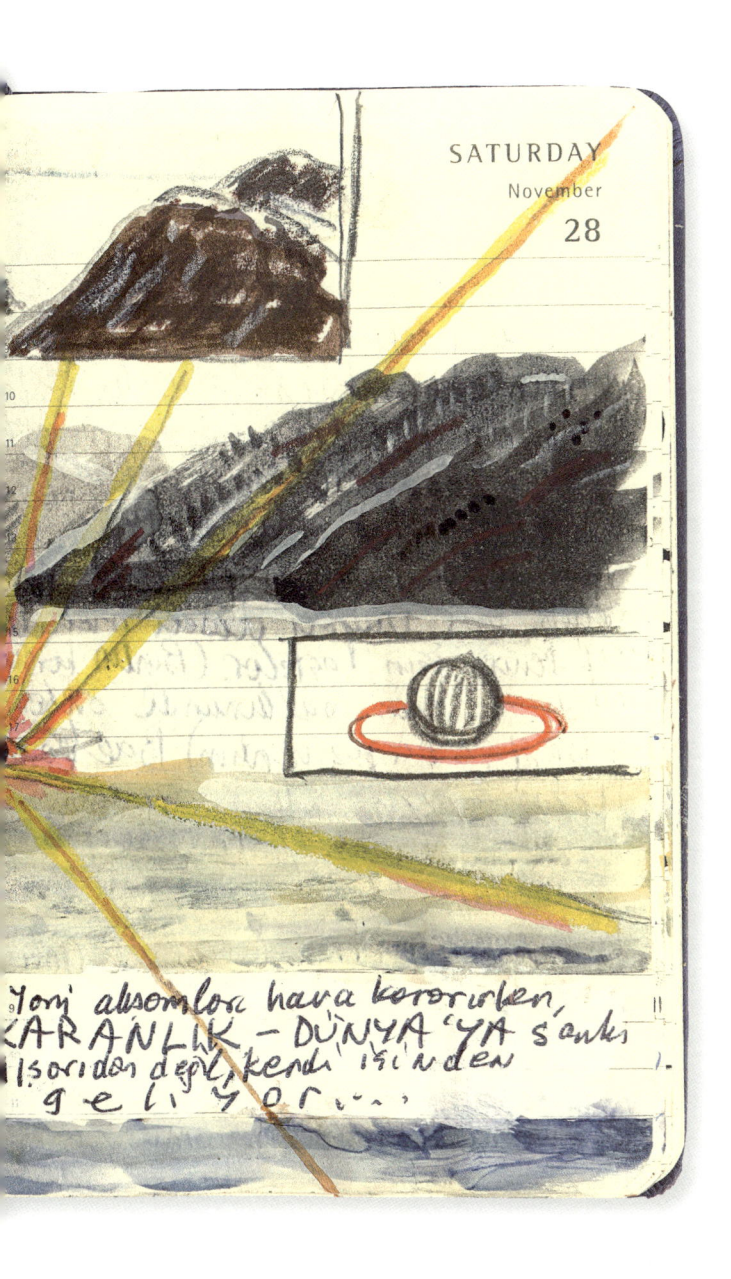

So when the sky darkens at night, it's as if that DARKNESS were issuing from the EARTH itself, rather than from the outside . . .

I HAVE OFTEN IMAGINED A COUNTRY WHERE
BUT FROM WITHIN THE EARTH ITSELF

THE SUN RISES NOT FROM THE HORIZON,
OVER THERE, NIGHT AND DAY are one

In the late afternoon, a bout of loneliness sent me to the Avery Library—where at least there would be other people around. I spent two hours trying to write. The skirmish, the gunfight, is over; Ramiz and the other insurgents have fallen, hit by bullets. The Major is among the dead and wounded . . . Tomorrow he will grab a flag / something I will describe as a flag from inside the cupboard/trunk and wave it before the people assembled in the square. It will be one of the most memorable scenes from this novel I've been writing for three years.

While working at the Avery . . . I saw on the magazine shelves a copy of the November–December issue of *Magazine Antiques* announcing an exhibition of Hopper's paintings on hotels—hotel lobbies—hotel magazines . . . I want one of the protagonists of my PLAYING CARDS novel to paint in the style of HOPPER. Paintings of hotels from the first 40 years of the 20th century . . . At the same time, my hero will be like İhap Hulusi: lottery tickets, the labels on *rakı* bottles, scenes of bourgeois satisfaction, etc. etc. As I work my way through *Nights of Plague* . . . I keep thinking and dreaming of other novels. I need to hurry up and finish this book. I mustn't let anything else get in the way.

THE MET   I am about to write some of the novel's most surprising pages. Or perhaps I should say I am writing them right now... The Mingherian revolution is about to begin... I have been concentrating on the novel when I lift my head up to look out of the window and suddenly realize that I have a guest.

It is a hawk. It has come down from its nest on the mountain slope.

It is perched on my windowsill, observing me: it watches me fixedly, and I watch just as fixedly back, taking photographs and videos—and sitting perfectly still.

For Nights of PLAGUE

A person who is too scared of DARKNESS-SOLITUDE to sit at home alone, and so goes out looking for other people . . . finds them . . . and catches the disease from them.

ON 4 APRIL ON THE TRAIN FROM BARCELONA TO MADRID—TALKING it over with ASLI, we decide that sending the beginning—a few sections of the NOVEL off to EKIN OKLAP this summer for her to translate . . . would be an unnecessary rush . . . ASLI also says—just like that, quite spontaneously . . . that this novel needs another year and a half . . . Thus giving voice to thoughts I had been hiding even from myself . . . It took me some time TO ACCEPT THIS TRUTH, and it was a painful one to acknowledge.

—And

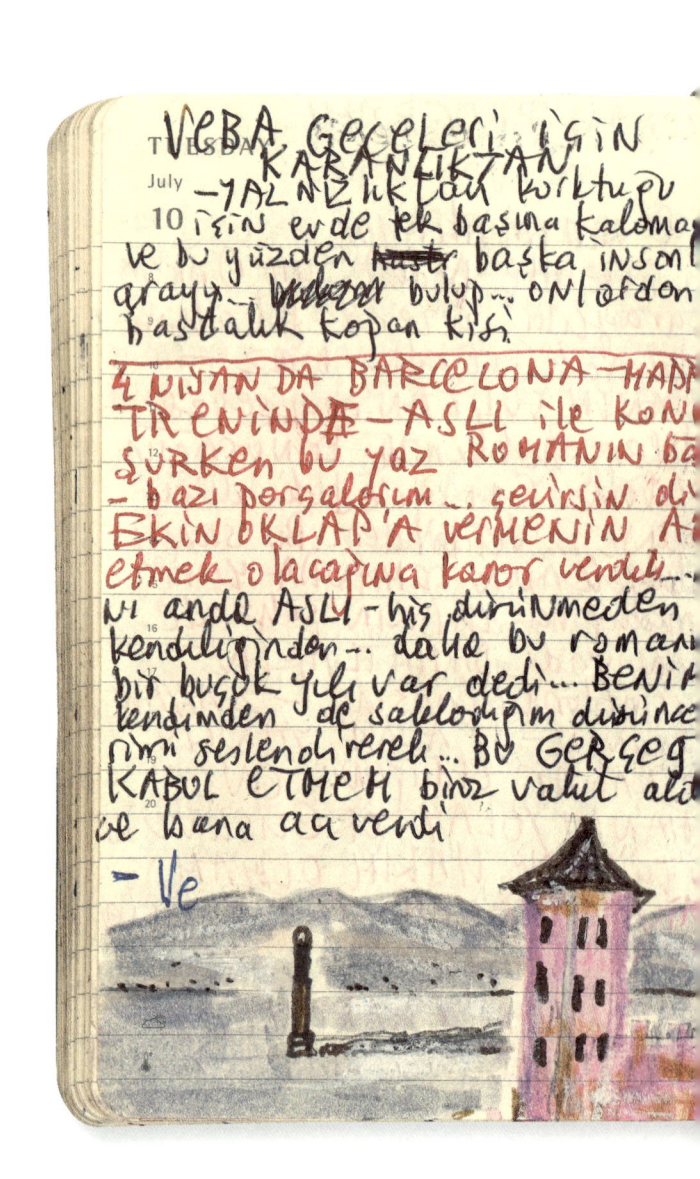

→ Nights of PLAGUE

The passages in the NOVEL discussing and debating NATIONALISM, NATIONHOOD, AND DISAPPEARING nations ... are veeery IMPORTANT / and Entertaining —on the way to Tehran just now ... I learn from reading Wikipedia pages about Iran that at the start of the 20th century, more than 50% of the population of modern-day Iran spoke Turkish at home ... Over the course of one hundred years, this proportion has fallen to 15–17%. Through repression, ethnic discrimination, etc., the IRANIAN state managed in one hundred years to make their people forget Turkish ... Major Kamil and his entourage ... could be debating these very questions ... But what they are doing while protecting the Mingherian language ... is putting pressure on other languages and schools. As soon as they take power, they will, of course, immediately start persecuting the Rumelian Greeks.

Don't forget the houses' windows
every dot is a window
back neighborhoods

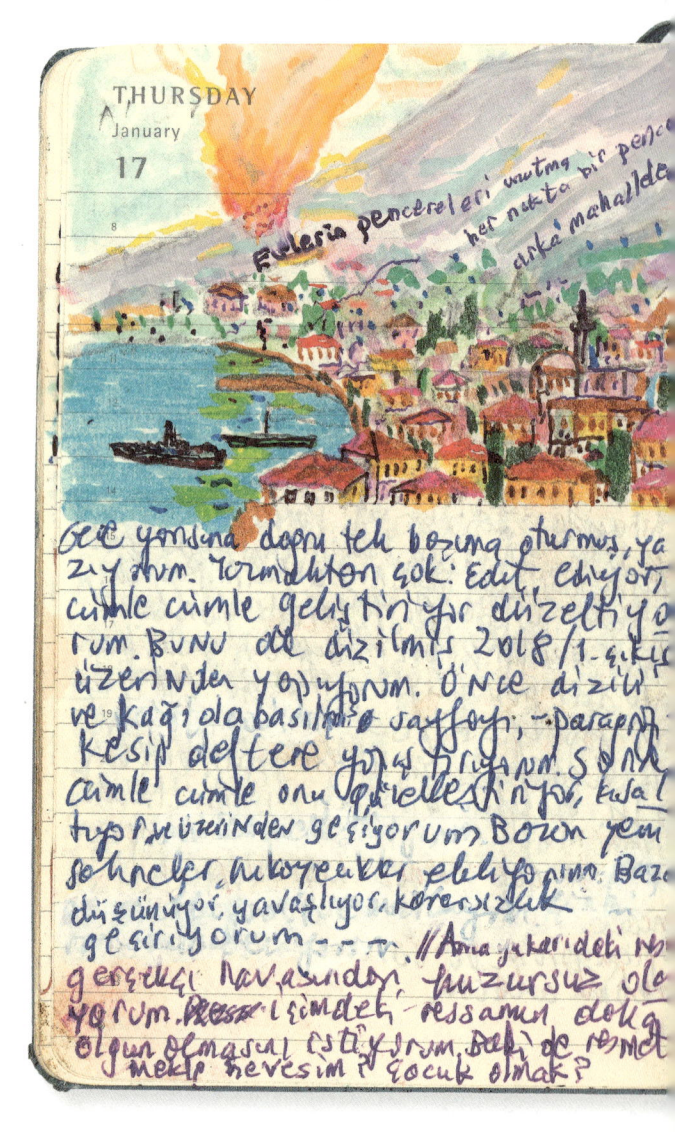

It's nearly midnight and I'm sitting on my own, writing. Not so much writing, as: editing the text, developing and revising it sentence by sentence. I'm working from the typed-up 2018 / 1st draft. First I cut out the typed-up, printed-out page-paragraph and stick it into my notebook. Then I go through the whole thing one sentence at a time, making improvements and cuts. Sometimes I add new scenes, new subplots. Sometimes I mull things over, slow down, hesitate . . .
But I am displeased with the realism of the drawing above. I would prefer my inner painter to be more mature. Could it be that my urge to paint? is a longing for childhood?

The novel should broach the subjects of panoramas and landscapes, and national identity, by gazing upon a mountain view. The child painter inside of me is well aware of all these questions, and yet still comes out with this picture.

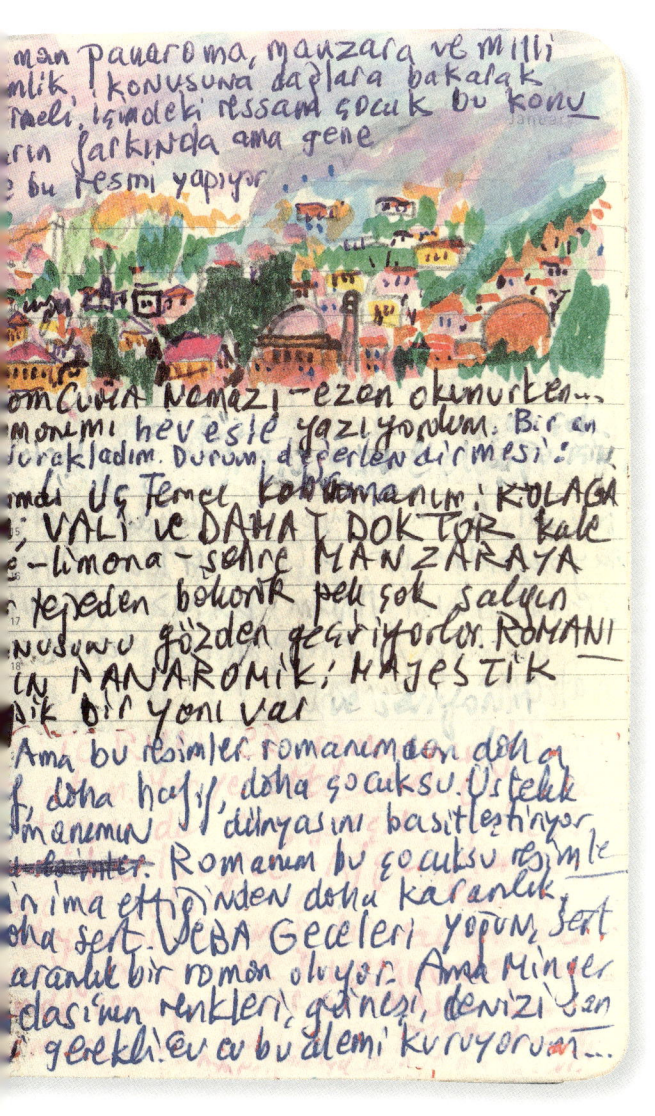

I was engrossed in writing my novel when... the call to prayer went out—for Friday prayers. I paused for a moment. The latest situation is as follows: right now my Three Main Characters: THE MAJOR, THE GOVERNOR, AND THE DOCTOR AND PRINCE CONSORT, are looking down from a hill toward the castle—the docks—the city—the VIEW while discussing a broad range of issues concerning the epidemic. There is a PANORAMIC; A MAJESTIC, epic side to MY NOVEL.

But these drawings are lighter, more naïve, more childish than my novel. They also oversimplify the world of my novel. The book is darker, harsher than what these childish drawings suggest. NIGHTS OF PLAGUE is turning into an intense, dark, brutal novel. But it seems to me that the colors, the sea, the sunshine of the island of Mingheria might be necessary too. So I am constructing this world, one house at a time...

I am going through the English translation of Nights of PLAGUE. A momentous feeling. As I read some of the chapters-sections that many (most) readers have deemed boring, excessively detailed, etc. . . . On Ottoman princes . . . on the fear of poisoning, etc. . . . I think to myself, I'm glad I wrote them . . . (I may have gone on a little too long when describing the departure of the last ship, and the mood at the docks.) As I read the English version of the novel, I genuinely think this is a fascinating subject, and I don't understand why anyone would get bored with it. I've simply written the novel I would have liked to read. Some ill-informed types have said . . . there shouldn't be this much historical detail in a novel! Yes, some people find facts and details to be boring. Perhaps I shouldn't react at all! And some readers may well be right. It is part of my job to try to understand readers who don't understand me and get angry for no reason . . .

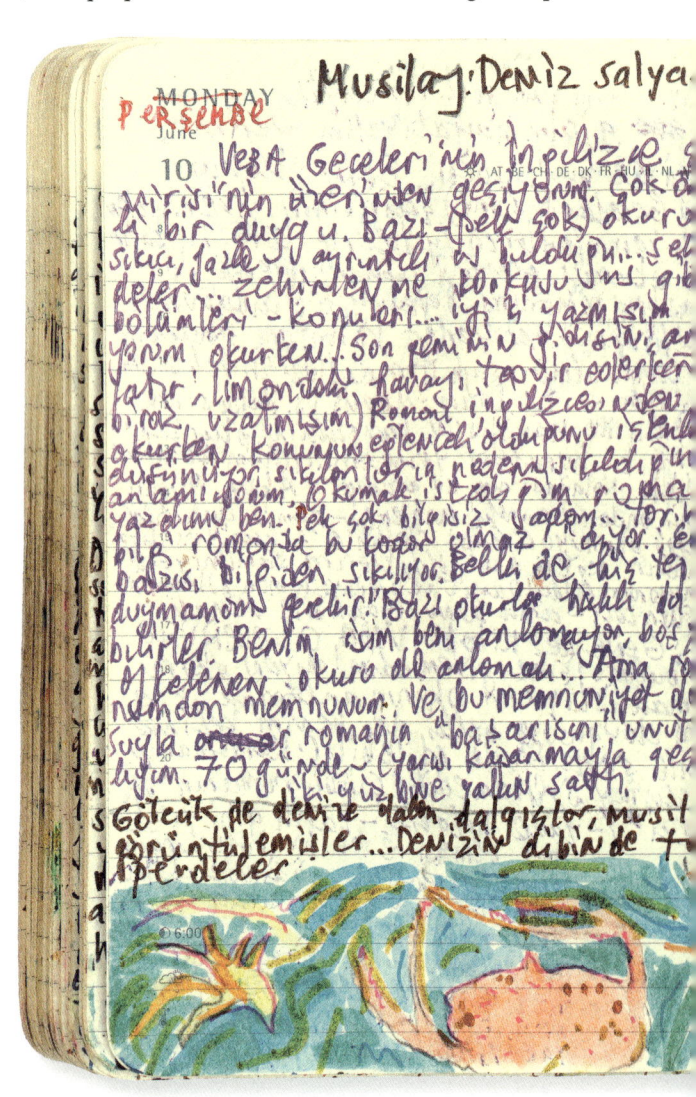

But I'm satisfied with my novel. And I must take care not to dismiss this satisfaction, nor the "success" the novel has enjoyed. It has sold nearly two hundred thousand copies in 70 days—(half of those in lockdown).

Divers in the sea in Gölcük have recorded images of the mucilage . . . Tulle curtains floating on the seabed.

The man who was swallowed by a whale: mucilage — FRIDAY

Rüya came by in the afternoon. We talked for two hours. Clever, sensible, charming, pretty. She'd been to see Aunt Gönül, and my mother. One is 92—the other 99 years old. I'm glad to hear her talk about them in such a sweet, loving way... Writerly, literary observations. I can see that she lives life with much more serenity than I do. It seems there are renovations going on—a new kitchen being fitted in the lower floor of the house on Sedef Island. She's been going to the island, and described with sorrow and revulsion the "mucilage" she has seen up close.

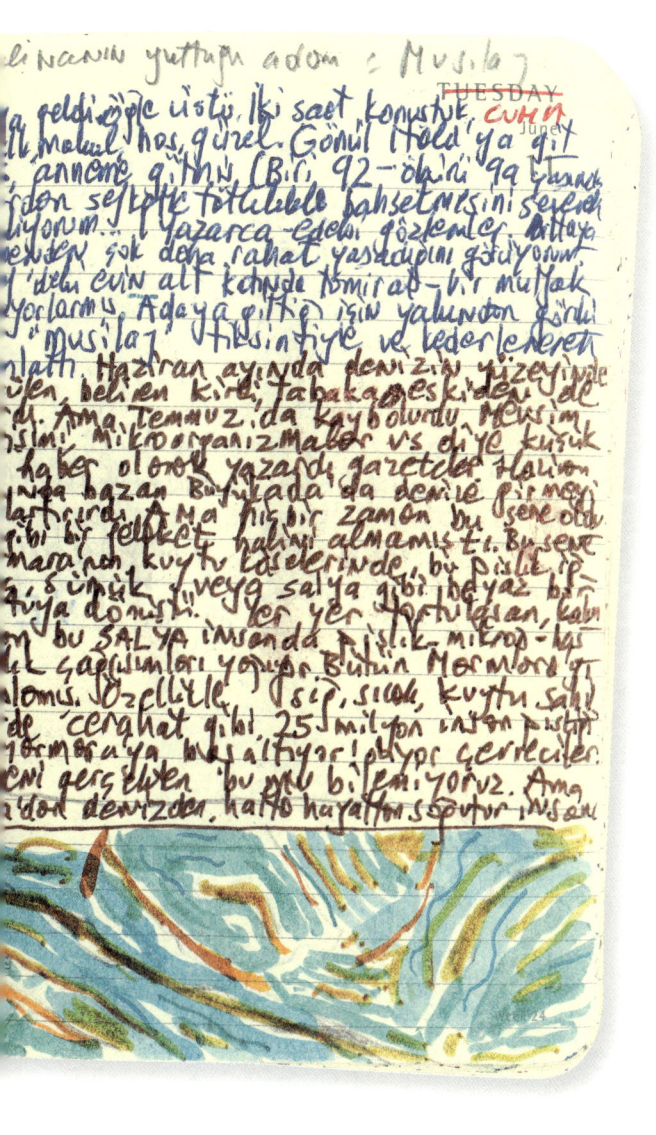

The coating of filth that we began to see when it appeared in June upon the surface of the sea has always been there. But it is usually gone by July. There will be brief mentions in the newspapers of changing seasons, microorganisms, etc. Sometimes it makes swimming in Büyükada in late June less appealing. But it has never reached the disastrous proportions we have seen this year. This year, even the farthest corners of the Marmara Sea are covered in this filth, which has turned into a disgusting white sediment similar to mucus or slime. This SLIME, which can in places be seen thickening and crusting over, evokes thoughts of filth-microbes-illness. The whole of the Marmara Sea is covered in it. On more remote beaches, and where the water is warmer and shallower, it looks like pus. 25 million people are emptying their filth into the Marmara Sea! say the environmentalists. We don't know if that's really the reason this is happening. But it does make you feel weary of Büyükada, of the sea, and even of life itself.

Büyükada
15 July
Why. There used to be a mosquito net here. When I wake up in the morning I see these trees before me, and glimpses of the sea from between the branches of the pine tree. The world seems beautiful to me.
Büyükada

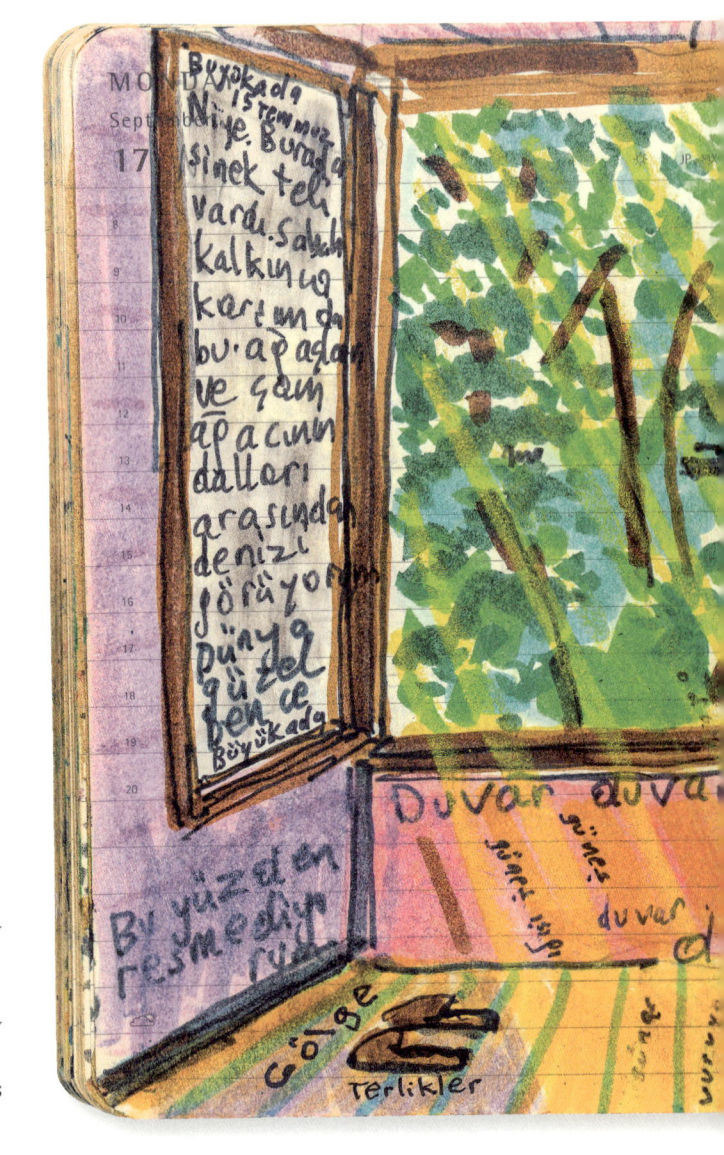

This is why I draw

Shadow

Slippers

    Wall   wall

sunlight—sun
sunlight hits

wall
wall

curtain

curtain   drawing isn't easy

the opposite wall

the opposite wall

the bed

the bed

the bed

I will see it all and   this notebook
write it all down

sunlight sun

A happy busy day. Woke up early this morning but still managed to write 3 more pages. Then I went back to reading NOSTROMO for the class at Columbia. Conrad was a talented, skillful novelist... Intense, clever, sophisticated. But I did not reveal my true thoughts on NOSTROMO to the students. The author spent very little time in Latin America. Nevertheless he decided to write a political novel about LATIN America. At the time the population of Latin America was 30 MILLION. The same as France. But today the population of Latin America has increased tenfold. For CONRAD to attempt a Latin American novel despite having spent very little time in Latin America... There is a literary and a human problem here. How innocent really is our desire to represent others, to describe others to those who do not know?

When this room's bird-patterned floor tiles caused some kind of rheumatism in my legs, I returned to the city.

Walking around the streets of Büyükada at 6:30, in the dark, to "get some exercise"... I come across "old codgers" around my age, ambling slowly by: "Good morning, *ustad*!" they call out... I walk almost at a trot, sweating as I go... They stutter along... struggling.

In this cloudy weather... seeing an occasional glimpse of the sun cheers me up. Then I sit alone, writing, writing, writing. I should be happy with my lot. Garden, sun, pine, fig, and palm trees. I've spent the whole summer in this room, writing *Nights of Plague*. Though the curtain was actually a different color.

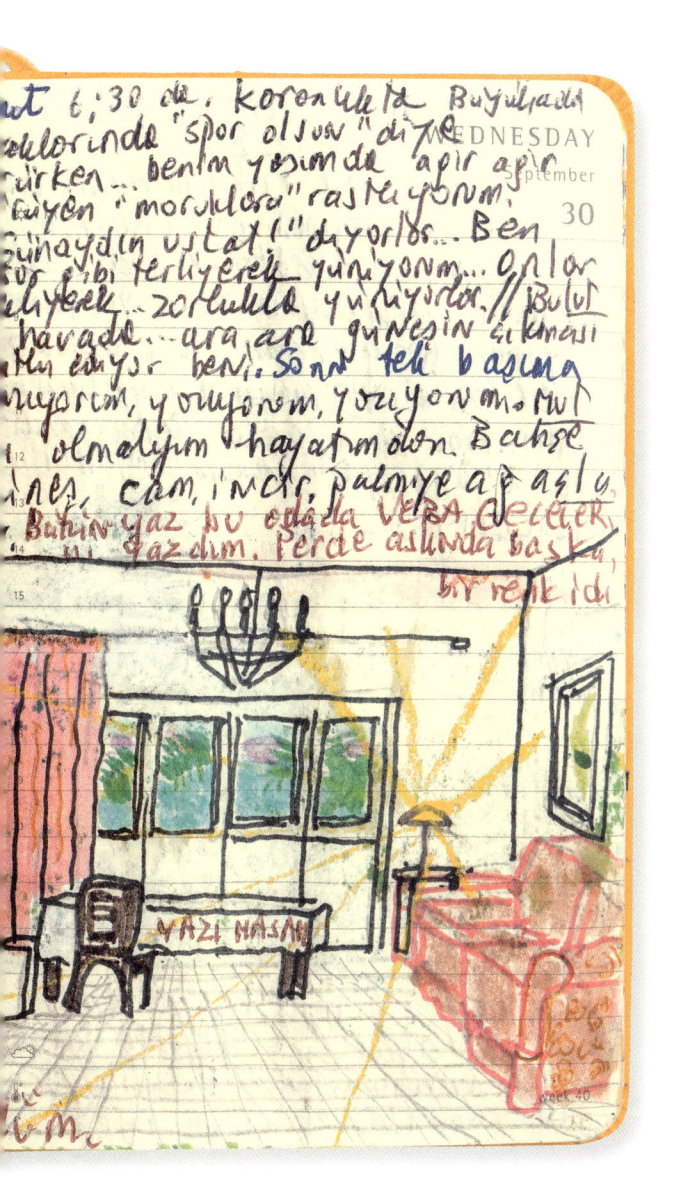

MY WRITING DESK

I'm reading *CONRAD: NOSTROMO*.
I am relishing the depth and breadth of imagination exercised by our teasing, sarcastic, gifted writer. Aslı's absence continues to provoke a state of overwhelming misery. My writing pace has slowed again. I have never worked so hard in my life. But even so I won't finish the novel as fast as I would like to. Oh God, there is still so much I have to write about before I complete this novel. It is exciting to read NOSTROMO. I would be pleased if a critic were to say that NIGHTS OF PLAGUE is influenced by CONRAD'S NOSTROMO. But how many people will have read that novel? Nostromo is set in the imaginary country of COSTAGUANA, but the reader can immediately tell that this is PANAMA. At the very start of the book, CONRAD describes the country / the LANDSCAPE where the events of the novel will unfold. In class tomorrow I will ask my students what the significance may be of including in the novel extended descriptions of the LANDSCAPES of an imaginary country.

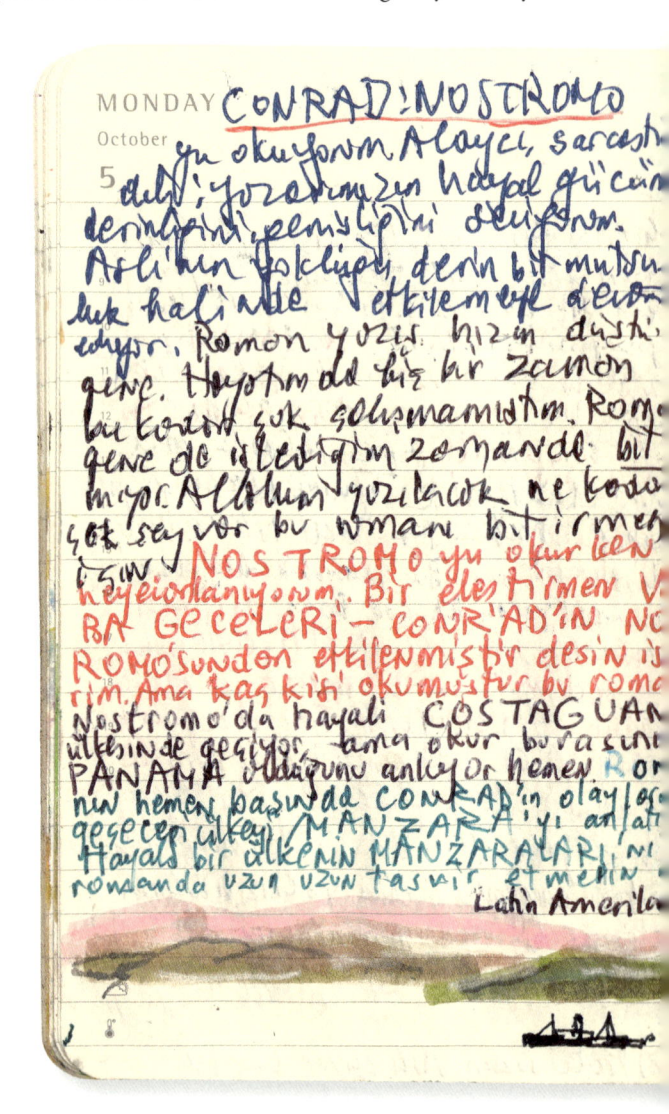

Trump has been discharged from hospital and has returned to the White House... He has a combative, provocative air about him... The polling companies say he is going to lose the election. A president who trivializes the outbreak of coronavirus, who doesn't believe in masks or quarantine measures... Just like IN MY NOVEL! It is late afternoon... I am reading CONRAD's NOSTROMO for the class at 5. And I enjoy the discussion with my students. The weather is warming again. I went to the beach and swam for 20 minutes. The sea isn't cold. But it feels oddly eerie. The link between landscape painting and Nationalism: the LANDSCAPE portrays the nation. Nathalie from Gallimard has written to say that it will not be possible to publish MEMORIES OF DISTANT MOUNTAINS this year. Yes. It is sadly so. I'm glad we won't be rushing the book out. But there is a lot of work to do.

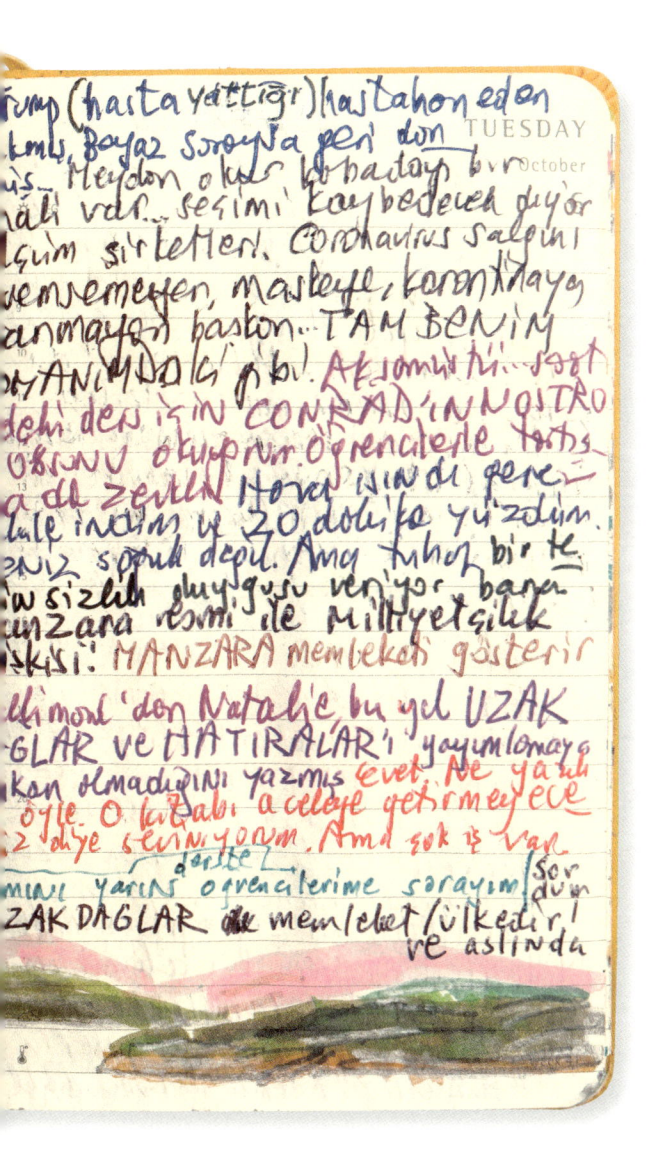

I've asked
Latin America and DISTANT MOUNTAINS are in fact a nation and a country!

I've been here all summer, dreaming of the island of Mingheria. The colors of the world beyond the balcony window are similar to those that Governor Sami Pasha sees from his office.

I'VE WRITTEN NIGHTS OF PLAGUE

There's a pleasing quality to this view that's reminiscent of the paintings MATISSE made in southern France depicting balconies and shutters opening onto the Mediterranean Sea. As I crafted my sentences and sent my protagonists running up and down the hills of Mingheria, some corner of my mind was always reminding itself that I had been observing, "seeing" the light in this room, this pretty view, the massive pine and fig trees every day, so that eventually, the view and the world I created in my imagination blended into each other.

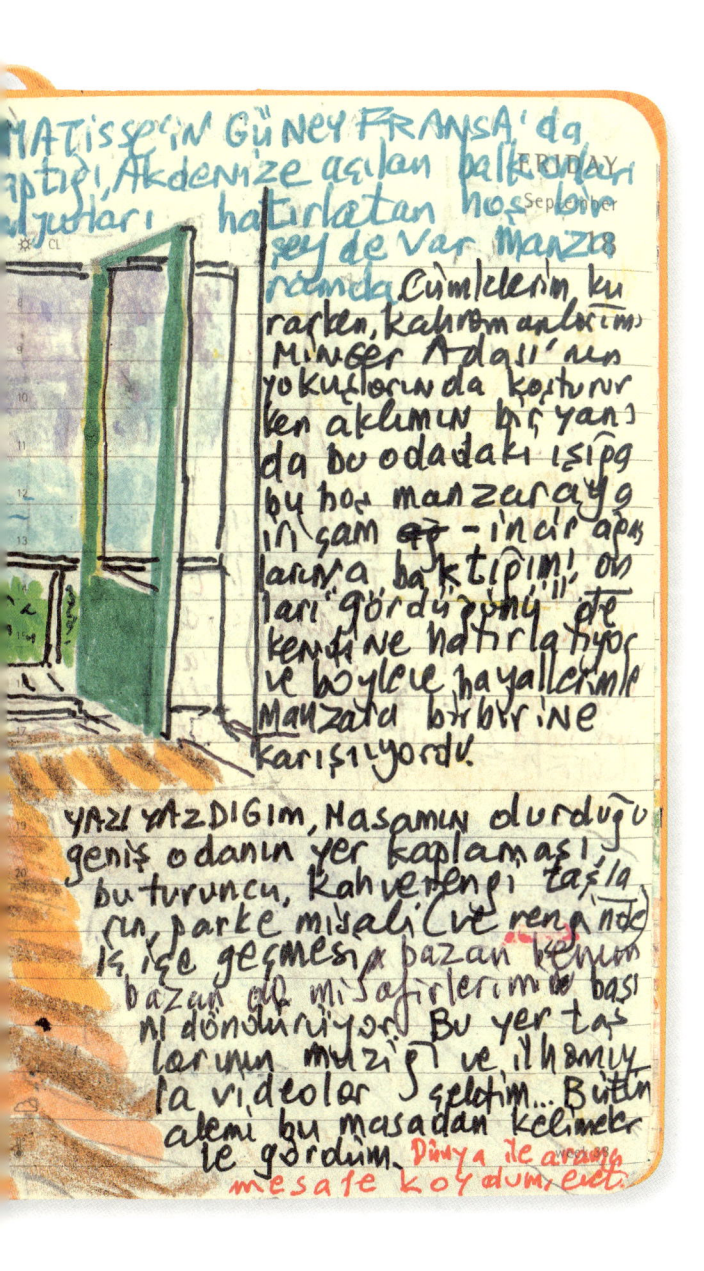

The way the orange and brown tiles on this floor interlock, like the tiles of a parquet floor (and the same color too), here in this room where I WRITE MY BOOKS and where my desk is located, can sometimes make my head spin, and my visitors' heads too. I've made videos inspired by the music and the influence of these floor tiles... Sitting at this desk, I have seen the whole of creation put into words. And yes, I have put some distance between myself and the world.

view from the swing in the house on BÜYÜKADA

THIS IS THE LAST TIME I LOOK OUT AT THIS GARDEN UNFORTUNATELY THE TIME HAS COME TO LEAVE THE ISLAND AND THIS HOUSE

door

Unkempt garden, unkempt country

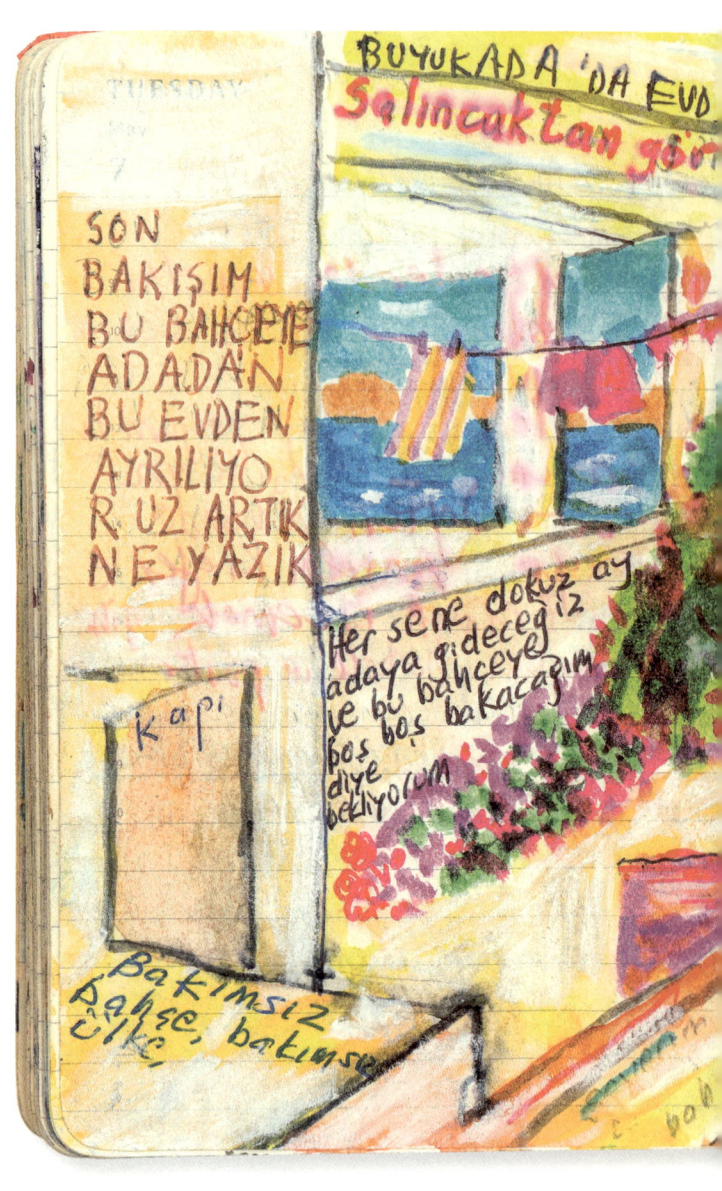

I spend nine months of the year waiting to return to the island, so that I can come and stare aimlessly at this garden.

the garden

pear tree

(Sometime between 1:40 and 4:10) I woke up and began to picture the final scenes of my Novel. (As I described in *Snow*, as in Coleridge's dream) I wrote down some dialogue and some of my ideas in my notebook. That is when I decided to have our writer Mîna Mingher meet Princess Pakize in 1959. As I myself was in Geneva the summer of that year, I came up with all sorts of ideas, and felt confident in my ability to evoke the city. I took copious notes, galvanized by all the colors and details I was dreaming up, and exhilarated by the thought of how fitting an epilogue these would make to Nights of PLAGUE.

THE BOOK'S FINAL SCENES: should I come up with more of these kinds of ideas, I will carefully write them all down. I will write and rewrite again and again, reveling in every detail, painstakingly balancing everything. I will go right back to the start of the novel if need be, to make additions and revisions. I will make sure to prepare the reader for this new ending and for these themes.

View of the State Hall—from the State Hall Square. To the left, the road leading up to Hagia Triada. The roof of the post office and other buildings.

Of course the state of agitation I'm currently in is partly due to the feeling of being unable to keep promises I have made to myself and to others. I'd told Tülay I would be done by December. I may have told Özgür November. I might have told myself September, if not the middle of summer. I've been writing nonstop for nine months, I can hardly find the time to reply to letters and emails, or even to write in this notebook properly.

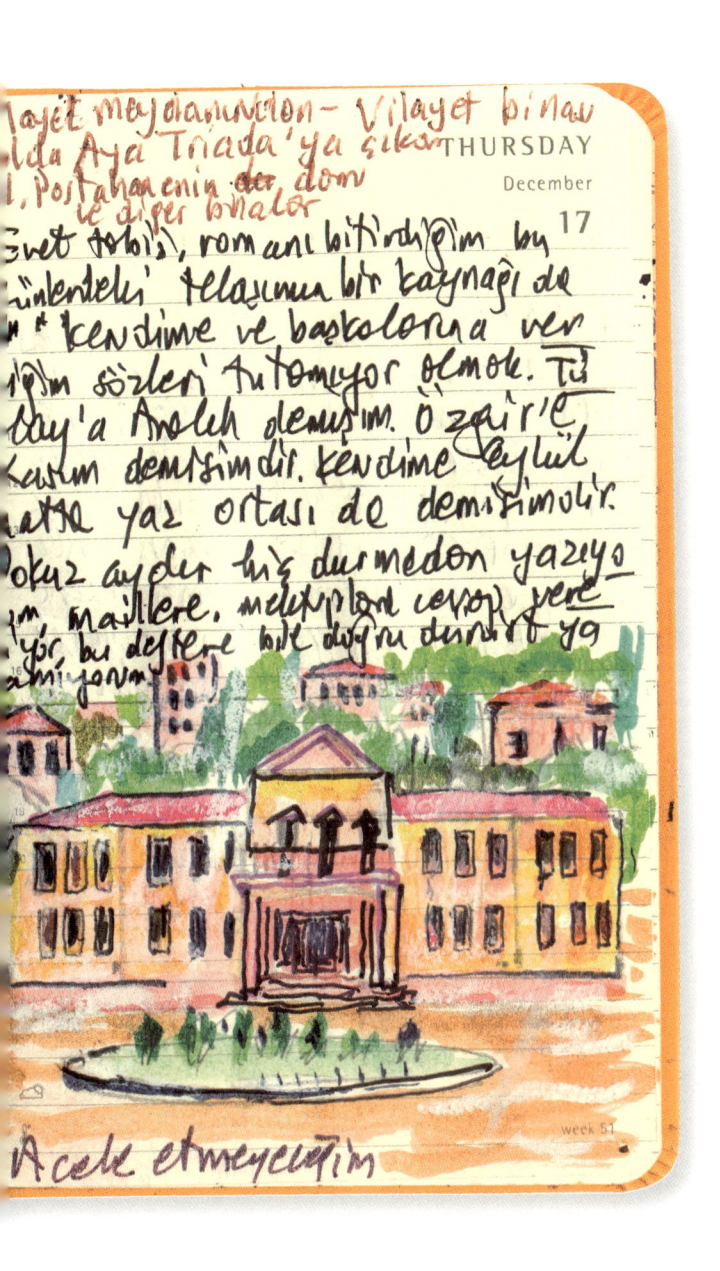

In other words: I won't rush this.

The typeset novel

As I've been too busy these past few days to write in here . . .
I've drawn this picture instead.

the desk where I
wrote the novel

my jacket hanging over
the back of the chair

I finished NIGHTS OF PLAGUE in this room in Cihangir, writing for 12 hours every day. At night I would sleep for three hours, then write for an hour, then go back to sleep for another hour.

Aslı took a photo of me while I was sleeping. I often fall asleep like this in Cihangir, between 11 and 12 in the evening.

around my forehead, an eye mask I got from a plane

The sound of the television Aslı is watching reaches through the distant mountains, the islands, the cliffs, the landscapes I see in my dreams, and the characters, the places,

Having spent the whole day working on my novel, I sometimes—often—fall asleep on the living room couch after dinner.

the objects I spend my whole day trying to put into words.

Chronology
2009 to 2022

2009

In January, Pamuk began working on the Museum of Innocence with the German architect Gregor Sunder-Plassmann. In February he traveled to Goa, India, with his girlfriend Kiran Desai, where he started to write *A Strangeness in My Mind*. In March he was awarded an honorary doctorate in Rouen, the city of Gustave Flaubert, and wrote a piece on Flaubert. In April he contributed a foreword to Ara Güler's book *Ara Güler's Istanbul: 40 Years of Photographs*. In May he visited Spain and the Alhambra and later taught a class on comparative literature at the Ca' Foscari University of Venice. Between June and September, he worked on the displays for the Museum of Innocence. In October, he went to Harvard to deliver the Norton Lectures, which were later published as a book under the title *The Naïve and the Sentimental Novelist*.

2010

In January he gave a speech on the future of museums and novels in Berlin and delivered the same lecture at the Center for Contemporary Culture in Barcelona. In February he swam in the sea in Goa and continued to work on *A Strangeness in My Mind*. March: traveled to Egypt—Cairo, Alexandria. May: a trip to Albania. Aside from a brief holiday in Greece, his summer was spent working on the Museum of Innocence and writing *A Strangeness in My Mind*. In autumn he taught for another term at Columbia University.

2011

In February and March, he was in Goa, where in the morning he worked on *A Strangeness in My Mind,* and in the evening he followed the events of the Arab Spring on TV. The uprisings led him to think about *Nights of Plague*. In April he purchased his first-ever touch-screen mobile phone. In spring he traveled to Bulgaria and Italy to give some talks. He spent the summer putting together the displays for the Museum of Innocence and writing *A Strangeness in My Mind*. Returning in September to teach comparative literature at Columbia where he held a professorship, he revisited his novel *The Silent House*. The

Museum of Innocence was completed that summer but hadn't opened yet, and Pamuk reached an agreement with the American art books publisher Abrams for the publication of its catalog, which was to be entitled *The Innocence of Objects*. He went to Brazil, Argentina, and Chile for a book tour. In December, near the end of this trip, he broke up with his girlfriend Kiran Desai.

2012

In March he attended his sister Hümeyra Pamuk's wedding in Dubai. In April the Museum of Innocence finally opened to the public. Sixteen years had passed from the moment he first conceived the project to its opening. Around this time Pamuk also published his "Modest Manifesto for Museums," which came to be widely taught in museum studies classes. He spent the rest of the year writing *A Strangeness in My Mind* and teaching at Columbia University in autumn. In the summer he began a relationship with Aslı Akyavaş, whom he married ten years later.

2013

Working to complete *A Strangeness in My Mind,* he continued interviewing street vendors and roaming around Istanbul's remotest neighborhoods. He was at the Venice Biennale when the Gezi Park protests erupted and wrote a piece criticizing the government's authoritarian and draconian response, and in September he traveled to the town of Imrenler—where the yogurt-selling protagonist of *A Strangeness in My Mind* grew up—near Lake Beyşehir in Konya Province and visited the local coffeehouses to hear the reminiscences of retired Istanbul yogurt sellers who had returned to this town and their ancestral villages. Later in autumn he gave a talk in New York to mark the 150th birthday of Constantine Cavafy.

2014

Pamuk wrote a piece on small museums for *The New York Times*. He traveled to Georgia, the UK, and Spain to give talks and promote his books. In April he taught at the University of Bologna with Umberto Eco for a week. In May he traveled to Tallinn, Estonia, to receive the prize that the European Museum Forum had awarded to the Museum of Innocence. Afterward he visited Anselm Kiefer's large studio on the outskirts of Paris and wrote a piece about it for *The Guardian* a year later. He also collaborated with the documentary film director Grant Gee on a film entitled *The Innocence of Memories*. He traveled to Lisbon with Aslı Akyavaş, where he received the Helena Vaz da Silva Prize for the dissemination of cultural heritage. In September he finished *A Strangeness in My Mind* while at Columbia, and the novel was published in Turkey in December.

2015

He began writing his new novel *The Red-Haired Woman.* Trip to Bursa in February. Death of Yaşar Kemal. The Museum of Innocence hosted an exhibition for the Istanbul Biennale, curated by Carolyn Christov-Bakargiev. Some notebooks containing paintings by Pamuk were displayed for the first time. He attended the Venice Film Festival to help promote Grant Gee's film on Istanbul and the Museum of Innocence, *The Innocence of Memories.* He embarked on a book tour of the United States for the launch of the English-language edition of *A Strangeness in My Mind.*

2016

At the start of January, Pamuk traveled to London to set up replicas of thirteen displays from the Museum of Innocence at the Courtauld Gallery in Somerset House. At the end of the month, he published his tenth novel, *The Red-Haired Woman.* He visited Paris for the screening of Grant Gee's *Innocence of Memories* at the Centre Pompidou. Trip to Toledo, Spain. He was on the island of Büyükada, writing *Nights of Plague,* during the attempted coup of 15 July and followed the developments on TV with Aslı Akyavaş.

2017

Blandine Savatier's stage adaptation of *Snow* was performed in Strasbourg. In February, Pamuk received an honorary doctorate from the University of St. Petersburg, and afterward he visited Tolstoy's house and grave in Yasnaya Polyana. The Museum of Innocence's display cabinets were exhibited in the Historical Museum in Oslo, and Pamuk attended the opening of the exhibition in May. Throughout the summer he continued to write *Nights of Plague.* He traveled to Sicily with Aslı to receive the prize named after the celebrated writer Giuseppe Tomasi di Lampedusa. After teaching at Columbia in autumn, he delivered a speech in Istanbul at the inauguration of the Tanpınar Center.

2018

January saw the opening of an exhibition consisting of displays from the Museum of Innocence in the Bagatti Valsecchi Museum in Milan. At the start of May, Pamuk was awarded an honorary doctorate by the University of Crete. This trip to Crete played a part in the shaping of *Nights of Plague* and the island of Mingheria. Toward the end of May, he traveled to Warsaw. He visited Auschwitz and felt ashamed of his own humanity. In early June he went to Kaş, where he continued writing *Nights of Plague* while looking out at a view of Kastellorizo, the island that inspired Mingheria. Autumn saw the publication of *Balkon,* his first book of photographs. While he was in New York, teaching at Columbia, he made a trip to Helsinki to promote *The Red-Haired Woman.*

2019

Pamuk took long nighttime walks in Istanbul to prepare his second book of photographs, *Orange*. In June he went to Sarajevo to watch the stage adaptation of *Snow*. He continued to write *Nights of Plague* in Istanbul and New York. In November, he set off with Aslı on a trip to Peru. Once a week, on Thursdays, he went to paint at his friend Inci Eviner's studio.

2020

In February he attended the Lahore Literary Festival in Pakistan. At the outbreak of the coronavirus pandemic, he was in New York with Aslı, and they promptly made their way back to Istanbul. In April he wrote a long article entitled "What the Great Pandemic Novels Teach Us," which was published all over the world. He stayed at home throughout the pandemic, writing *Nights of Plague* and never leaving Istanbul. He taught his autumn classes at Columbia on Zoom, from Büyükada. In November he published *Orange*, his second book of photographs.

2021

Nights of Plague was published near the end of March. In April he began to think about *Memories of Distant Mountains*. He also started work on the "Illustrated *My Name Is Red*," consulting nearly six thousand low-resolution reproductions he had obtained from the Topkapı Palace Library. In autumn he returned to New York to teach at Columbia as usual. He began to think about the possibility of an exhibition featuring his illustrated notebooks and his manuscripts.

2022

For the time being he set his new novel *The Tale of the Painter* aside and began instead to think about and write a novel entitled *The Card Players*. In April, after ten years together, he married Aslı Akyavaş. He made various trips to promote the translated editions of *Nights of Plague*—Germany in February, France and Spain in March. In May he went to Sardinia, Italy, to receive the Costa Smeralda Prize.

martılar pembe çünkü batan güneş
çok sinirli oldum çünkü mutsuz oldum vuruyor
mateşli yumurta yapar
n Aygaz bitti ama gene
domateslerin
asına yumurtayı
rdım...
ahçeden domates topluyoruz - hırsız
lar motor gürültüsü yüzmek gibi
tüm gün güzel geçti
n Nizam'a geçen sene kiraladığım eve yürüdüm
yüzerken derin biri Arada
bir çaresiz sedyle
k var bu geçen
rekli yazma
t eğinde dalgalar lot op
sam Anselm Kiefert'in
u boya resimlerine
aktım. dalgalar
Büyükada hayatın
derinliği!...